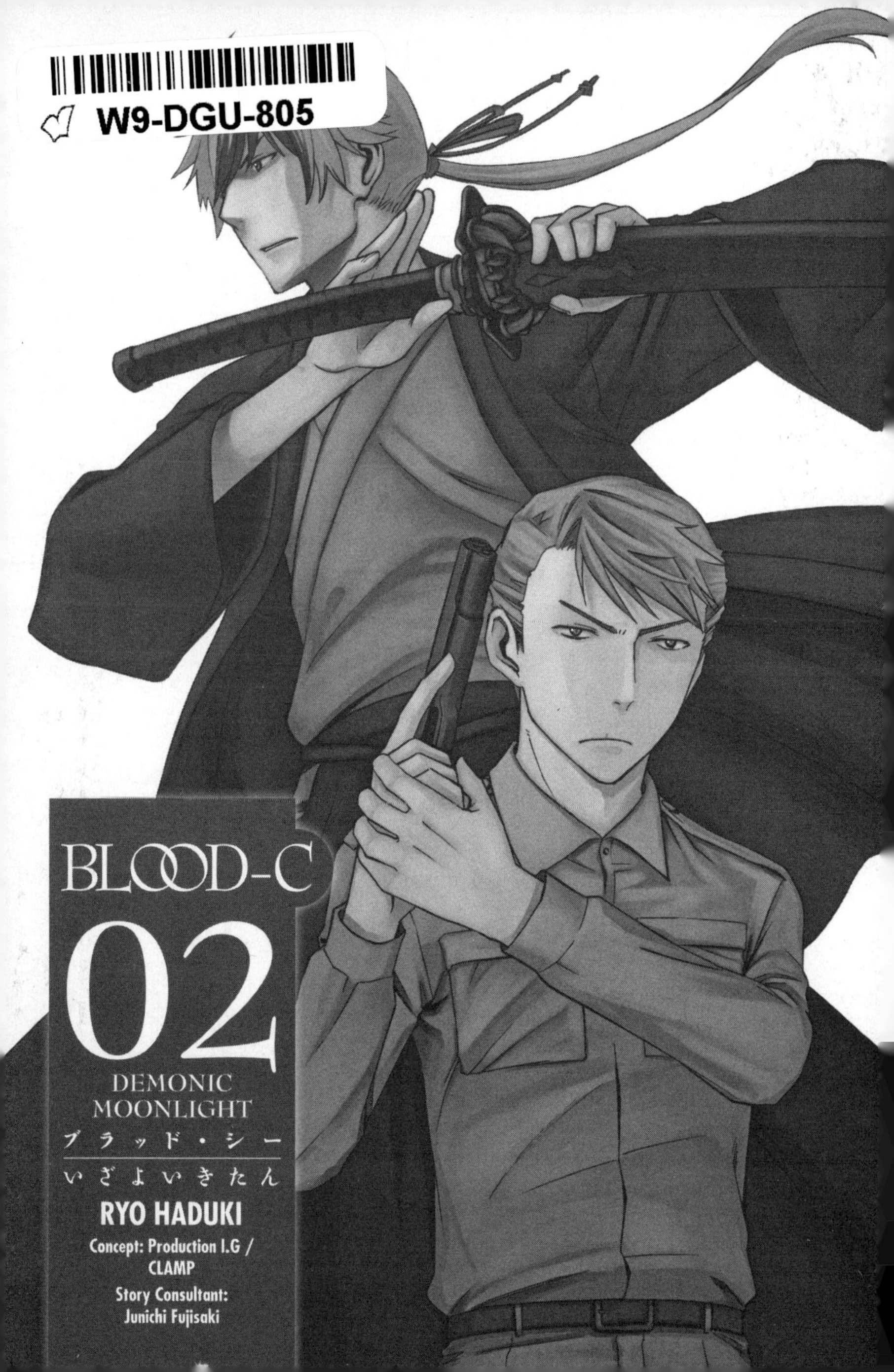

BLOOD-C
02
DEMONIC MOONLIGHT
ブラッド・シー
いざよいきたん
RYO HADUKI
Concept: Production I.G / CLAMP
Story Consultant: Junichi Fujisaki

CONTENTS

BLOOD-C
DEMONIC MOONLIGHT

02
RYO HADUKI

translated by
CAMELLIA NIEH

English adaptation by
PHILIP R. SIMON

lettered by
STEVE DUTRO

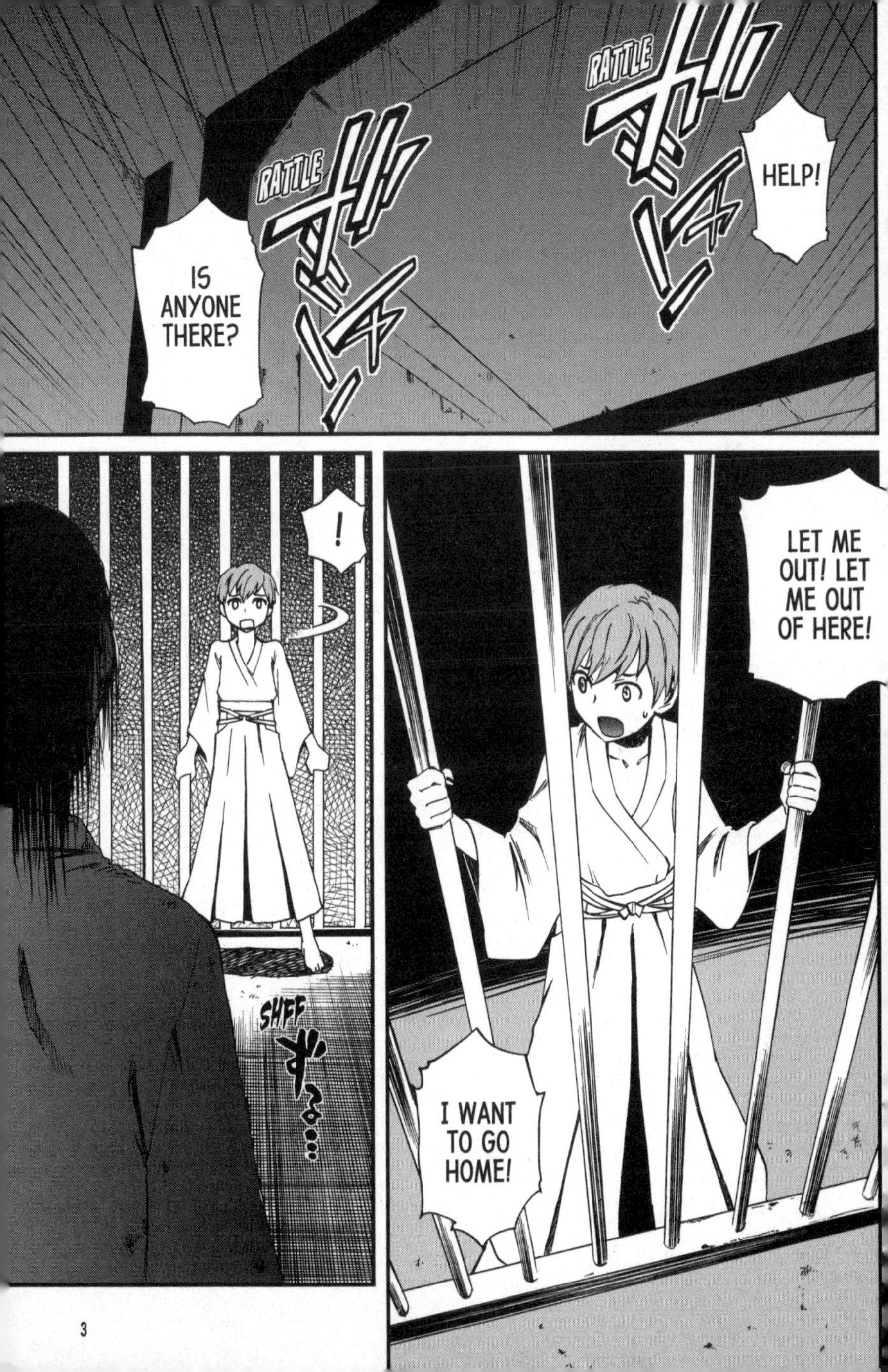
RATTLE
HELP!
RATTLE
IS ANYONE THERE?
LET ME OUT! LET ME OUT OF HERE!
I WANT TO GO HOME!
!
SHFF

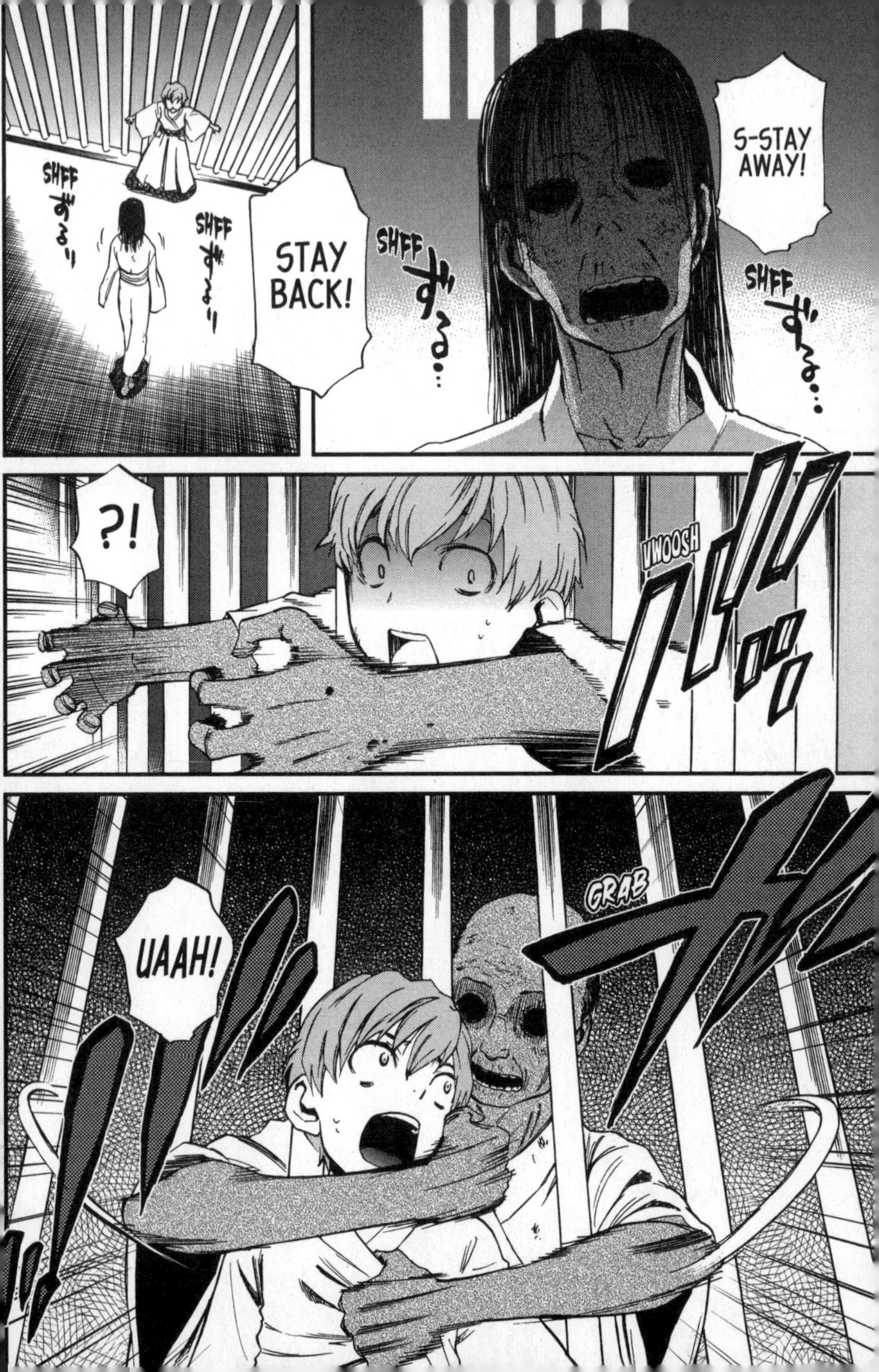
S-STAY AWAY!
SHFF ずる…
SHFF ずる…
STAY BACK!
SHFF ずるり
SHFF ずるり
VWOOSH
?!
GRAB
UAAH!

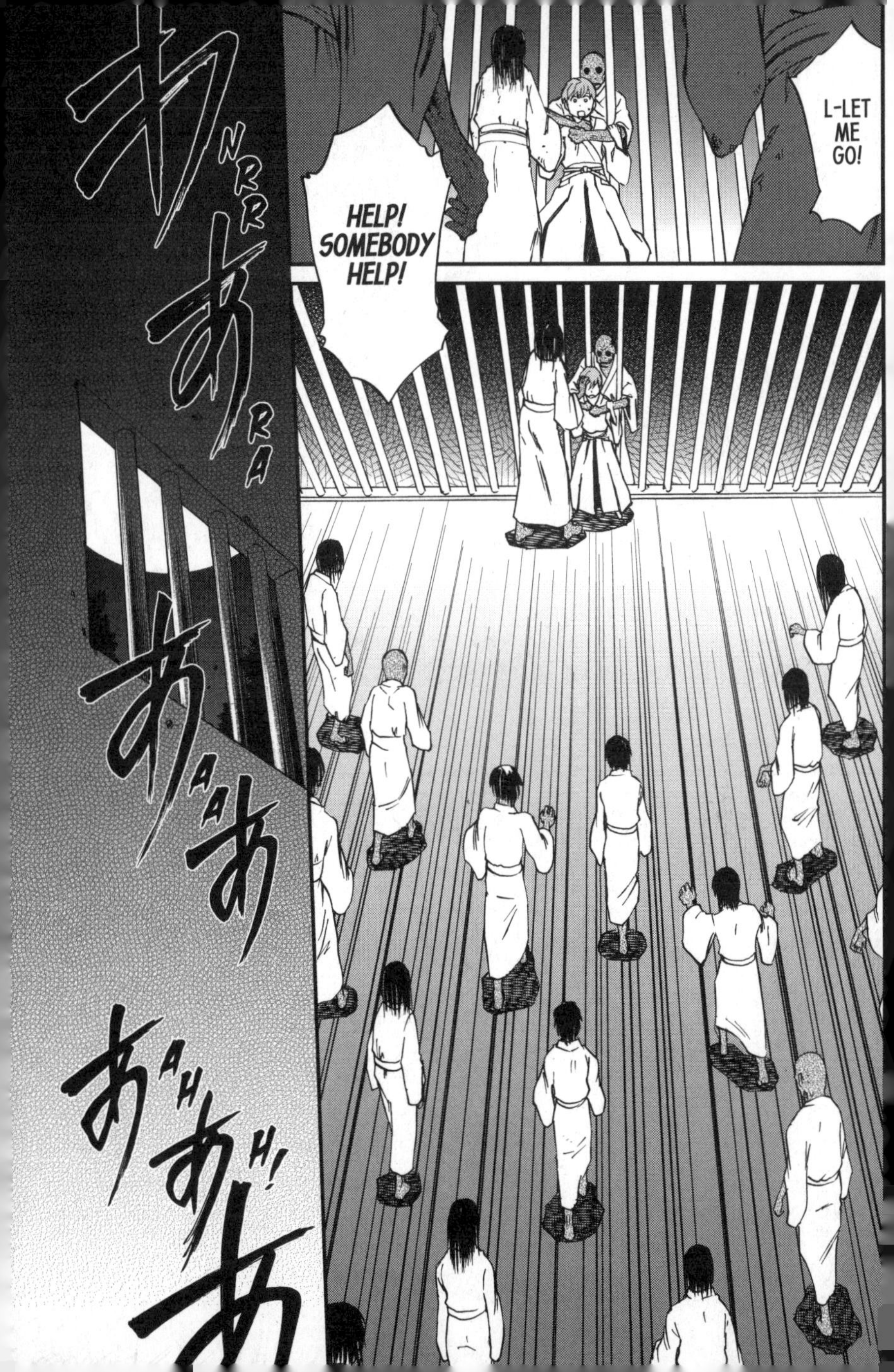
L-LET ME GO!
HELP! SOMEBODY HELP!
NRRRA
AA
AHH!

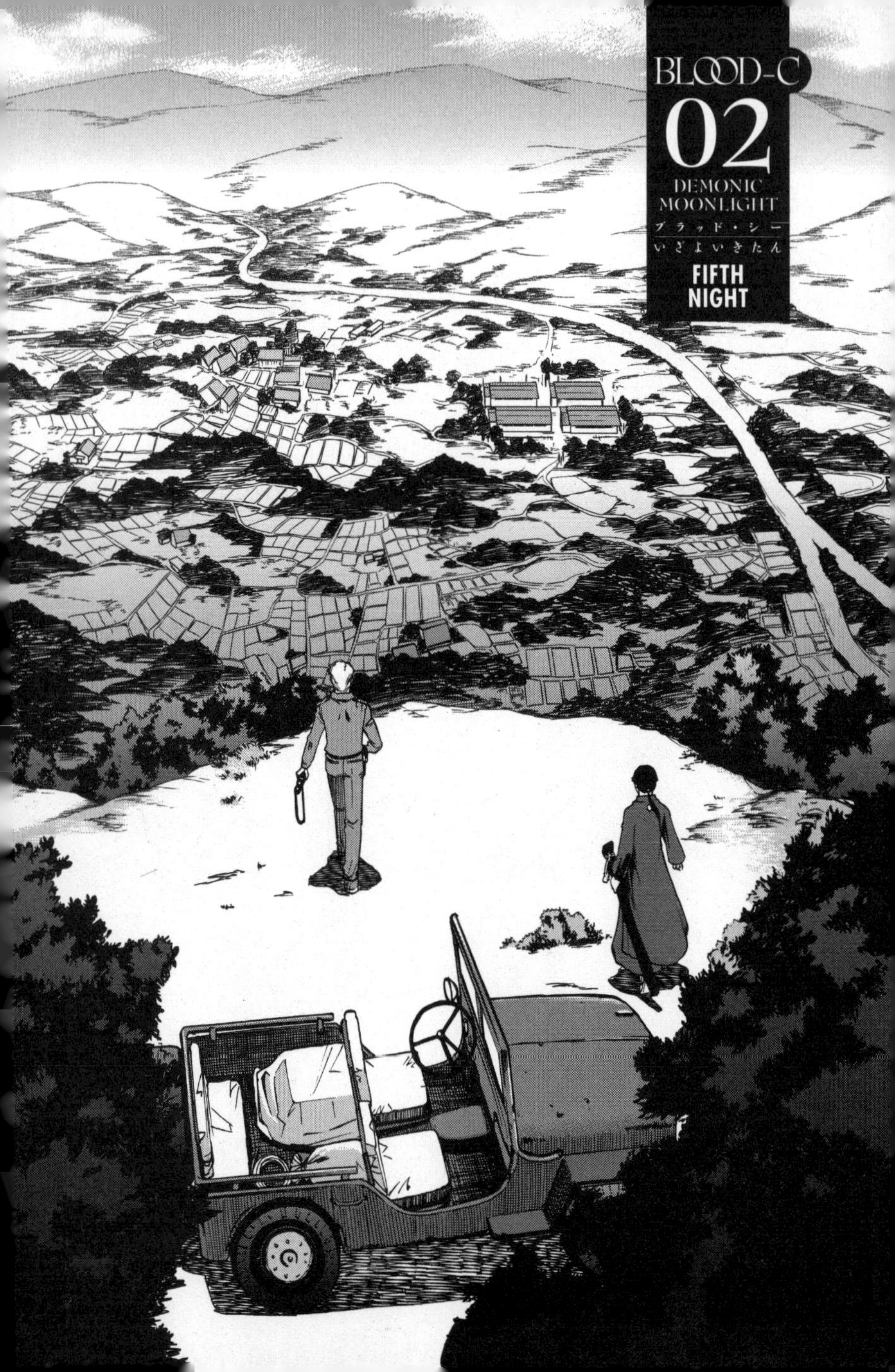
BLOOD-C
02
DEMONIC MOONLIGHT
ブラッド・シー
いざよいきたん
FIFTH NIGHT

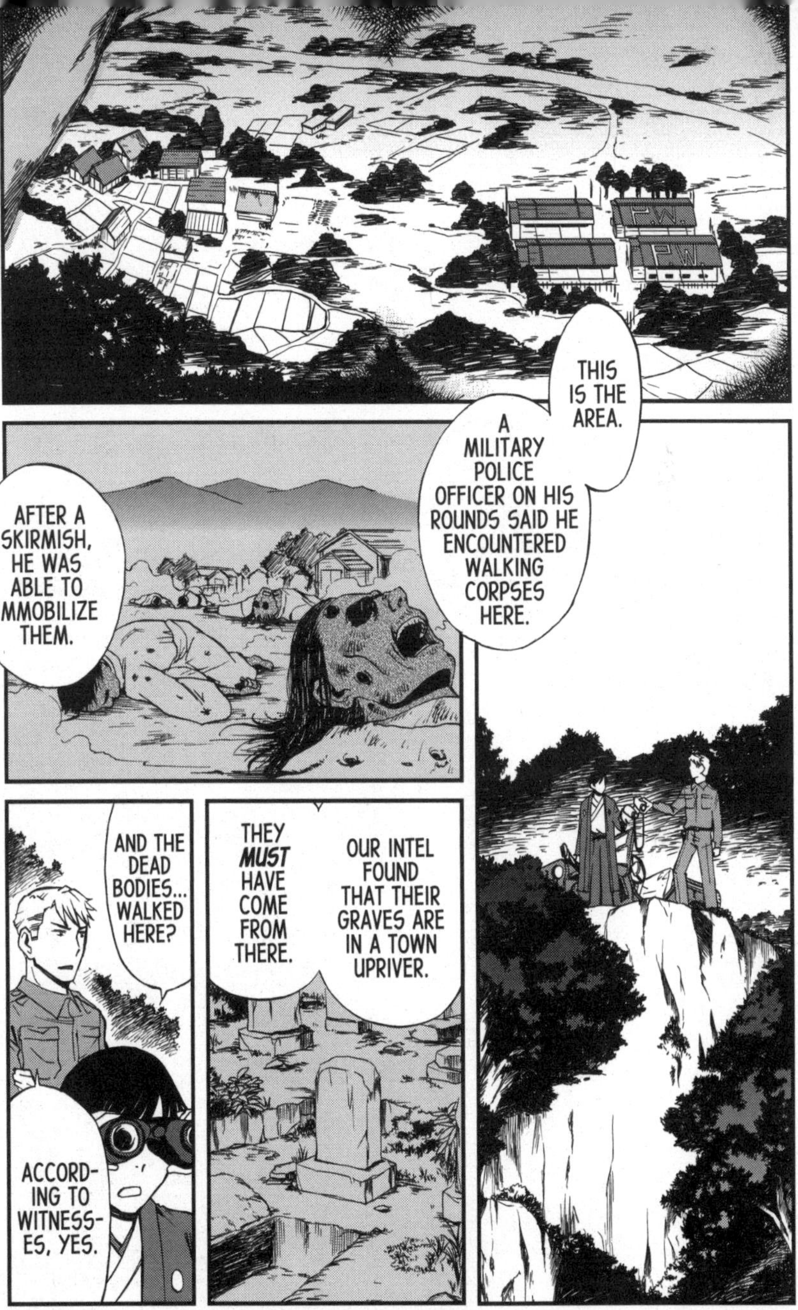
THIS IS THE AREA.
A MILITARY POLICE OFFICER ON HIS ROUNDS SAID HE ENCOUNTERED WALKING CORPSES HERE.
AFTER A SKIRMISH, HE WAS ABLE TO IMMOBILIZE THEM.
OUR INTEL FOUND THAT THEIR GRAVES ARE IN A TOWN UPRIVER.
THEY *MUST* HAVE COME FROM THERE.
AND THE DEAD BODIES... WALKED HERE?
ACCORD-ING TO WITNESS-ES, YES.

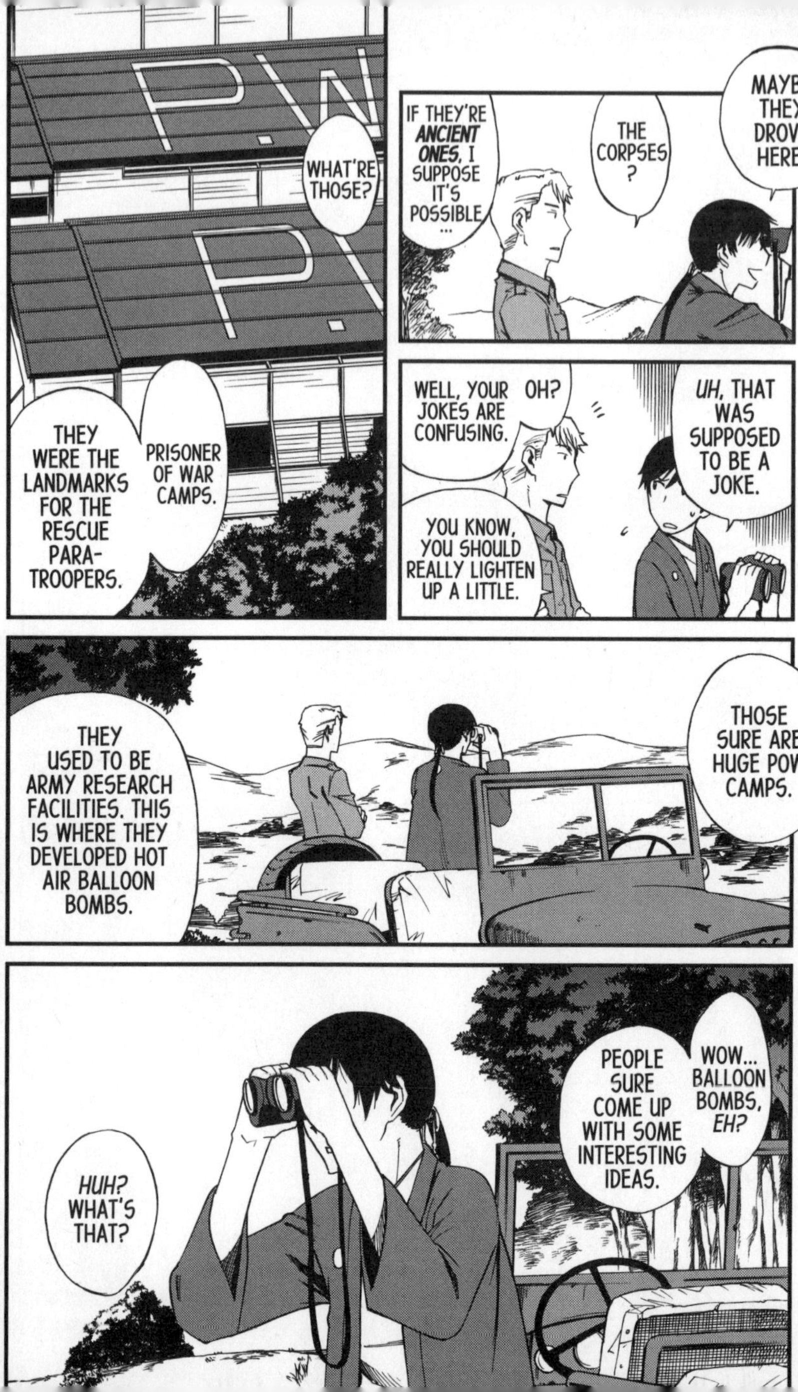

MAYBE THEY DROVE HERE.
THE CORPSES?
IF THEY'RE *ANCIENT ONES*, I SUPPOSE IT'S POSSIBLE...
UH, THAT WAS SUPPOSED TO BE A JOKE.
OH?
WELL, YOUR JOKES ARE CONFUSING.
YOU KNOW, YOU SHOULD REALLY LIGHTEN UP A LITTLE.
WHAT'RE THOSE?
PRISONER OF WAR CAMPS.
THEY WERE THE LANDMARKS FOR THE RESCUE PARA-TROOPERS.
THOSE SURE ARE HUGE POW CAMPS.
THEY USED TO BE ARMY RESEARCH FACILITIES. THIS IS WHERE THEY DEVELOPED HOT AIR BALLOON BOMBS.
WOW... BALLOON BOMBS, *EH?*
PEOPLE SURE COME UP WITH SOME INTERESTING IDEAS.
HUH? WHAT'S THAT?

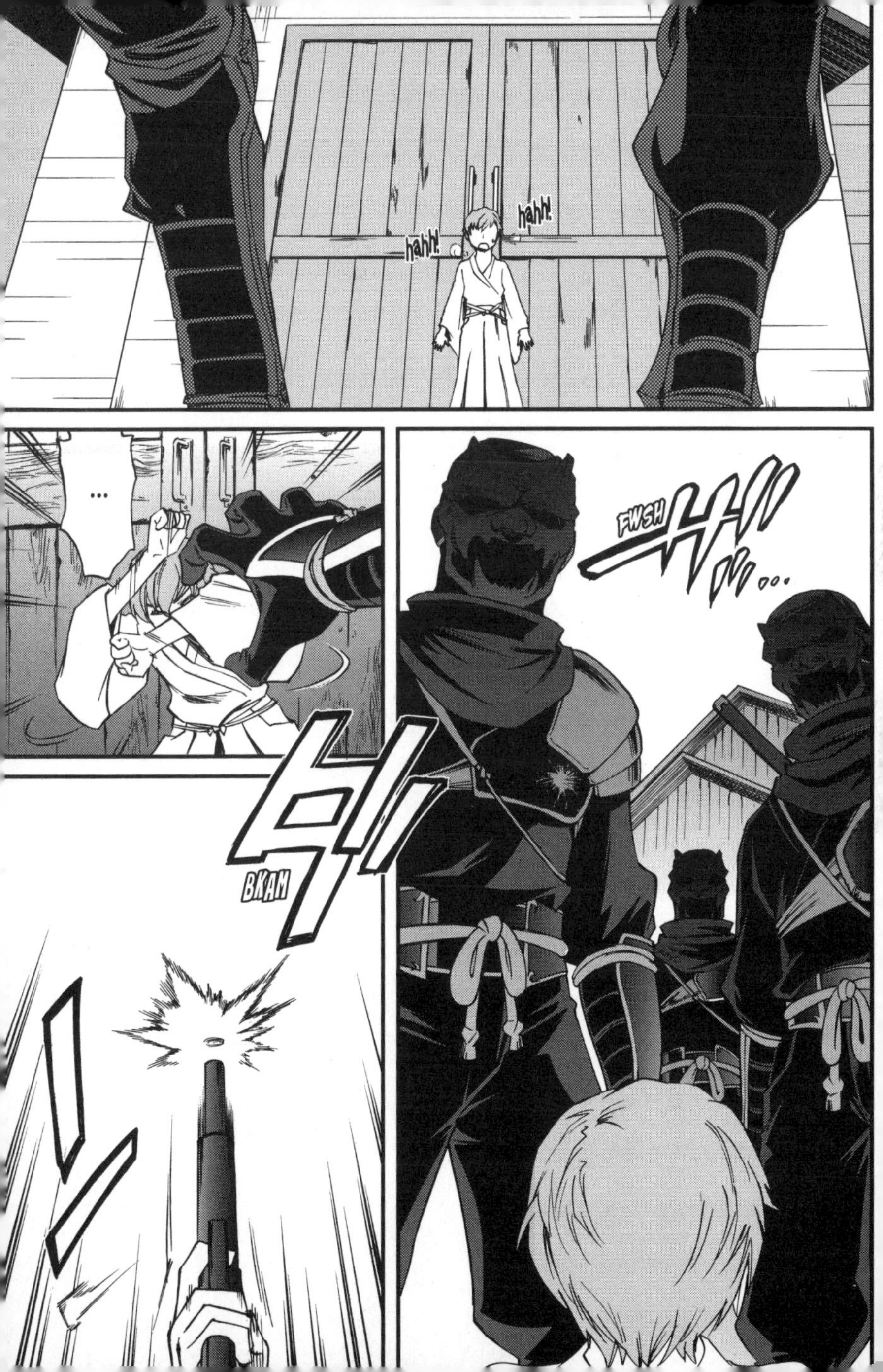
hahh!
hahh!
FWSH
...
...
BKAM

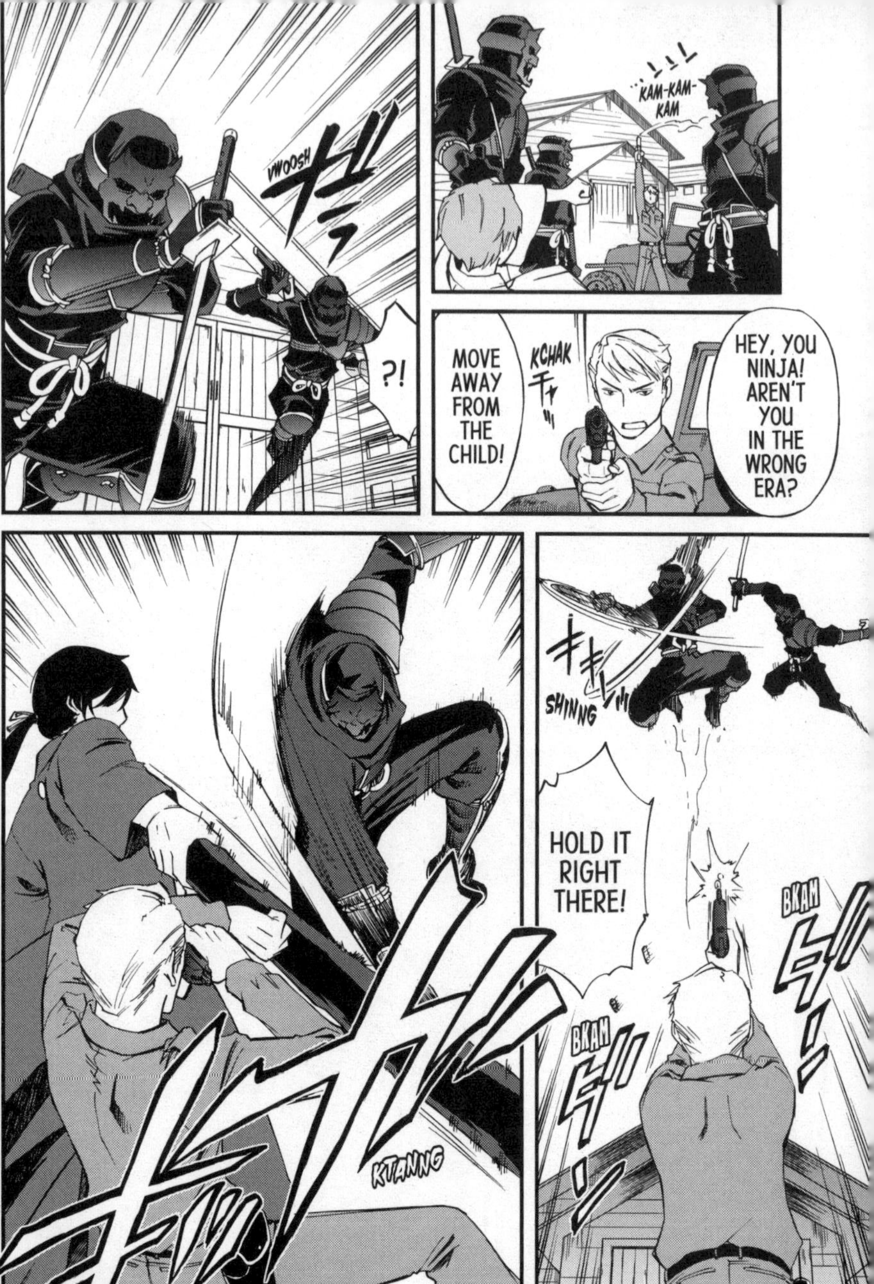
...KAM-KAM-KAM
HEY, YOU NINJA! AREN'T YOU IN THE WRONG ERA?
KCHAK
MOVE AWAY FROM THE CHILD!
VWOOSH
?!
SHINNG
HOLD IT RIGHT THERE!
BKAM
BKAM
KTANNG

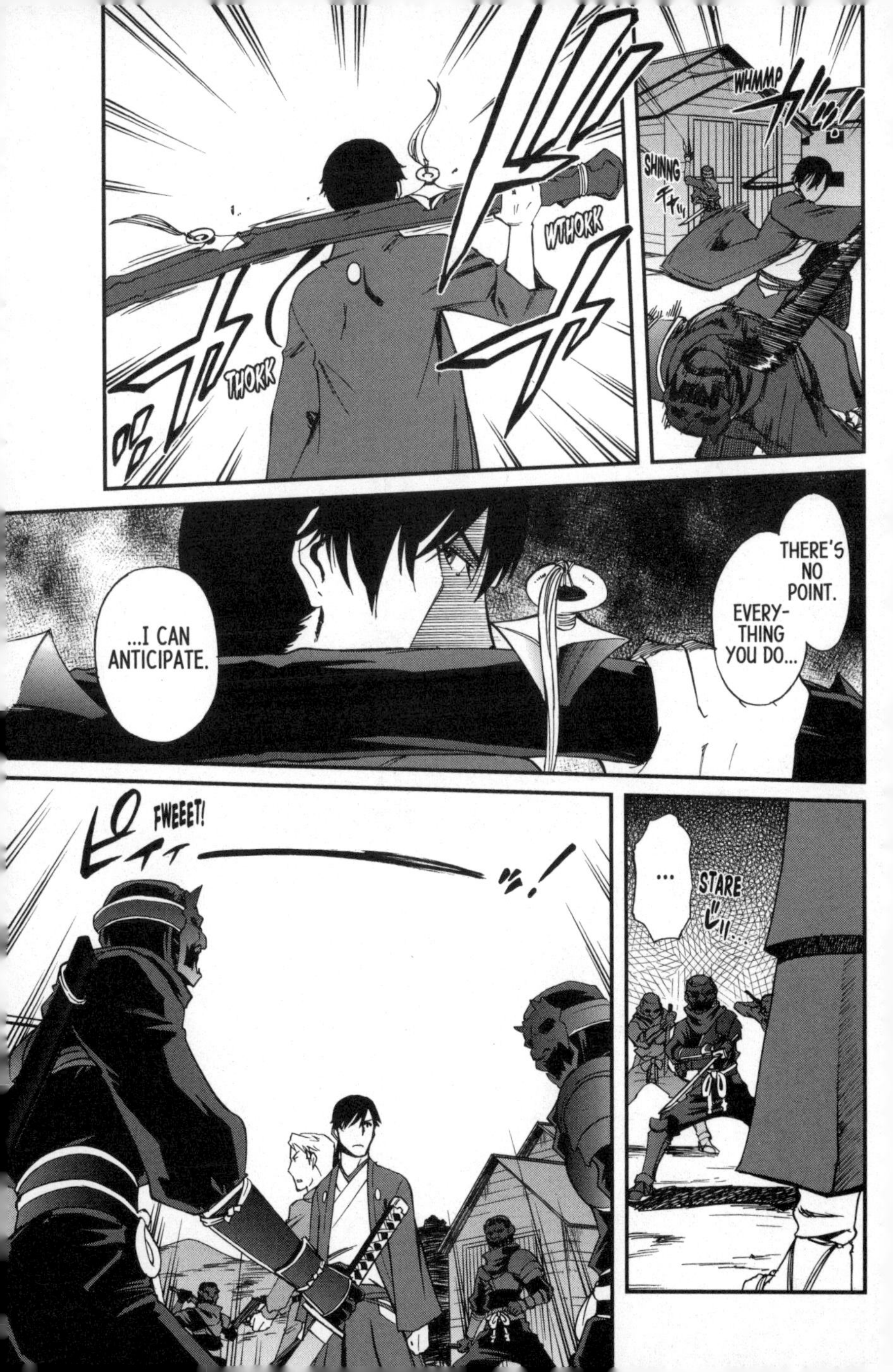
WHMMP
SHINNG
WTHOKK
THOKK
THERE'S NO POINT. EVERY-THING YOU DO...
...I CAN ANTICIPATE.
...
STARE
FWEEET!

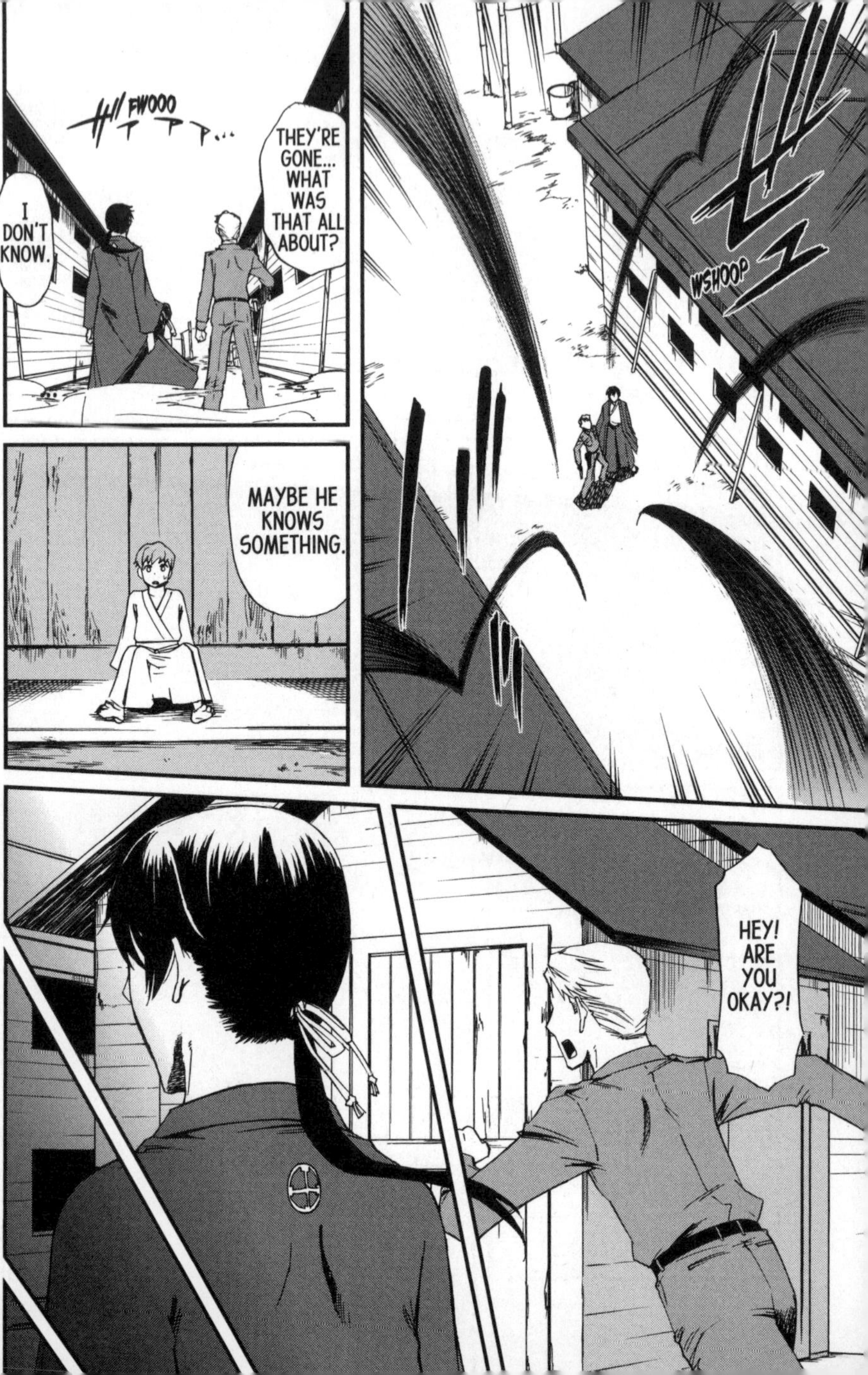
WSHOOP
THEY'RE GONE... WHAT WAS THAT ALL ABOUT?
FWOOO
I DON'T KNOW.
MAYBE HE KNOWS SOMETHING.
HEY! ARE YOU OKAY?!

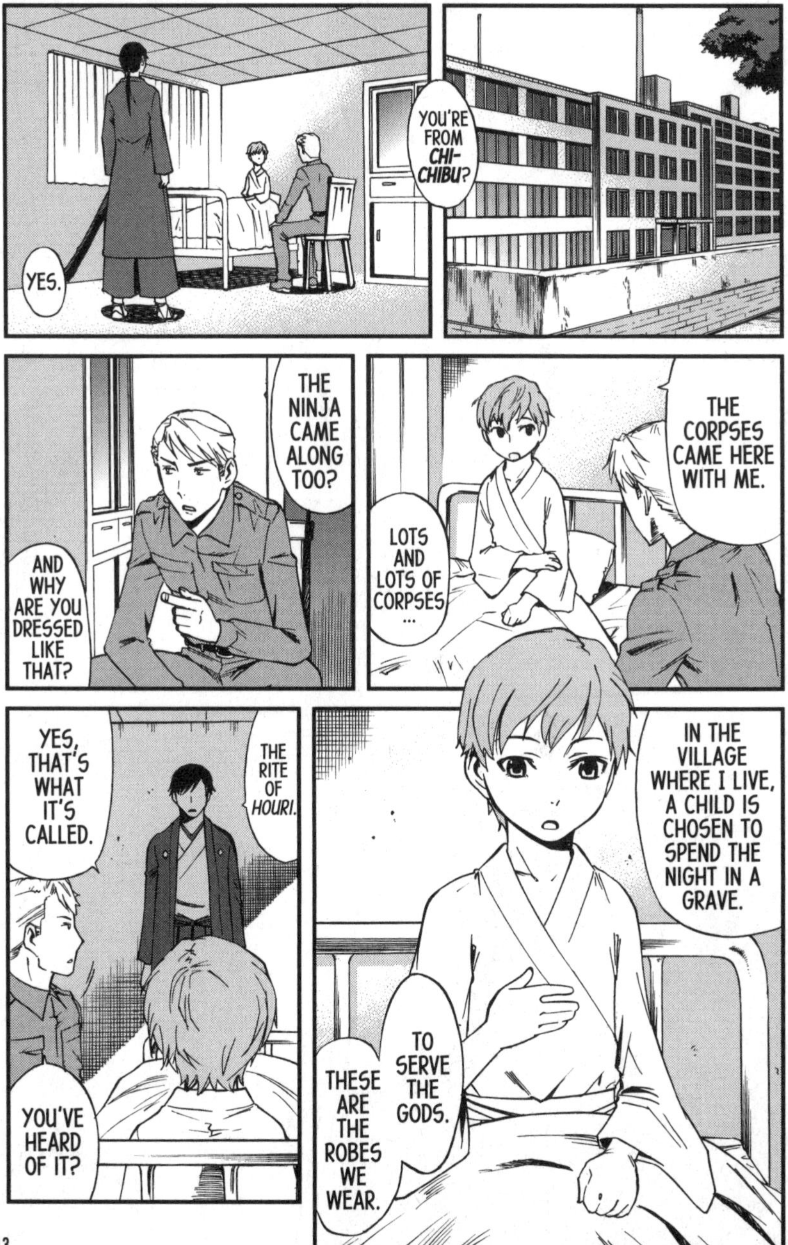
YOU'RE FROM CHI-CHIBU?
YES.
THE CORPSES CAME HERE WITH ME.
LOTS AND LOTS OF CORPSES ...
THE NINJA CAME ALONG TOO?
AND WHY ARE YOU DRESSED LIKE THAT?
IN THE VILLAGE WHERE I LIVE, A CHILD IS CHOSEN TO SPEND THE NIGHT IN A GRAVE.
TO SERVE THE GODS.
THESE ARE THE ROBES WE WEAR.
THE RITE OF *HOURI*.
YES, THAT'S WHAT IT'S CALLED.
YOU'VE HEARD OF IT?

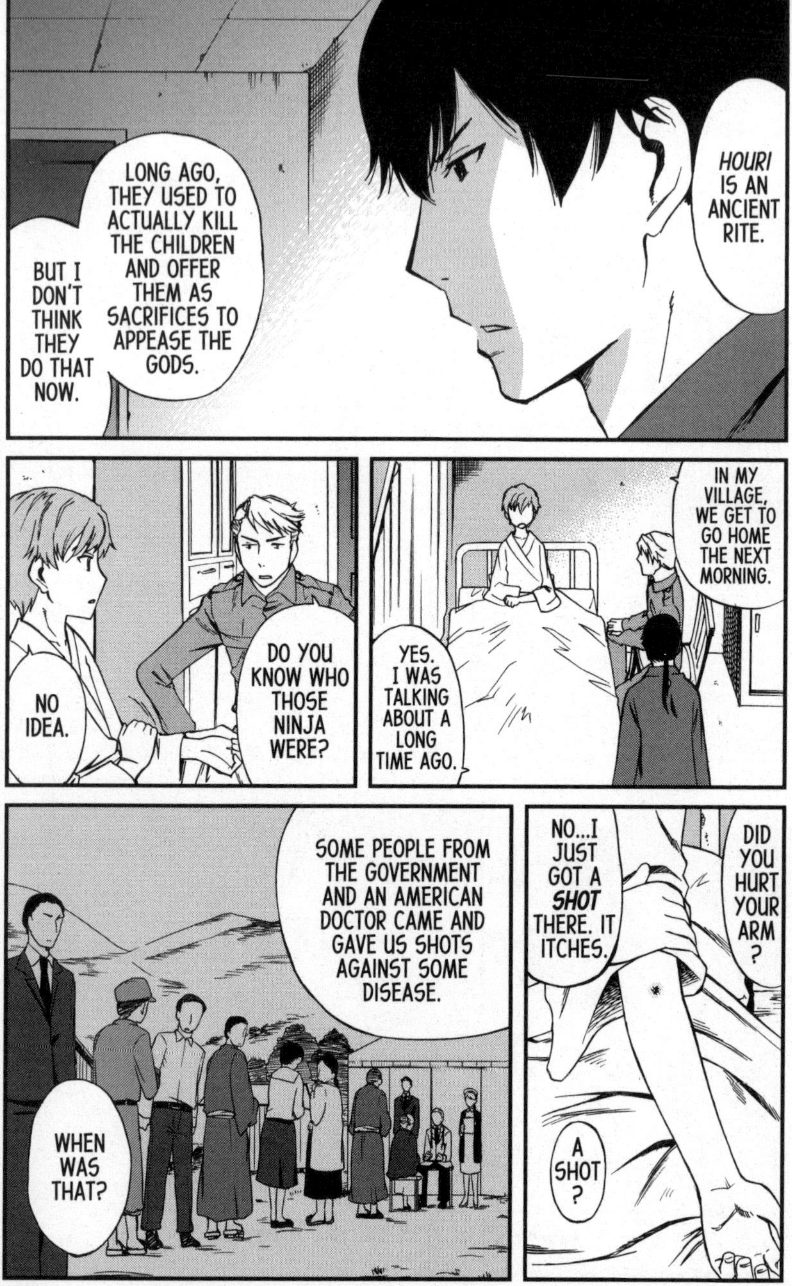
HOURI IS AN ANCIENT RITE.
LONG AGO, THEY USED TO ACTUALLY KILL THE CHILDREN AND OFFER THEM AS SACRIFICES TO APPEASE THE GODS.
BUT I DON'T THINK THEY DO THAT NOW.
IN MY VILLAGE, WE GET TO GO HOME THE NEXT MORNING.
YES. I WAS TALKING ABOUT A LONG TIME AGO.
DO YOU KNOW WHO THOSE NINJA WERE?
NO IDEA.
DID YOU HURT YOUR ARM?
NO...I JUST GOT A SHOT THERE. IT ITCHES.
A SHOT?
SOME PEOPLE FROM THE GOVERNMENT AND AN AMERICAN DOCTOR CAME AND GAVE US SHOTS AGAINST SOME DISEASE.
WHEN WAS THAT?

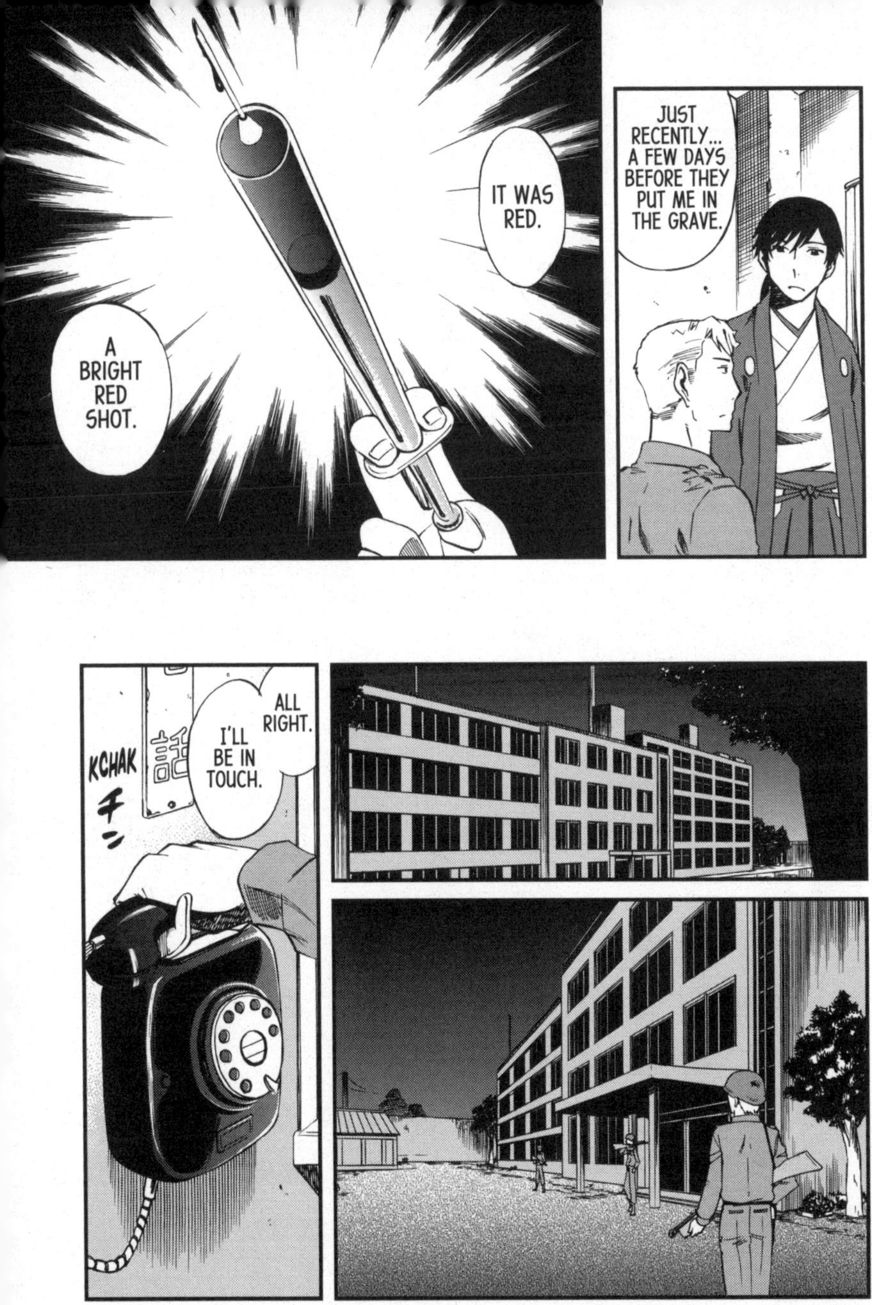
JUST RECENTLY... A FEW DAYS BEFORE THEY PUT ME IN THE GRAVE.
IT WAS RED.
A BRIGHT RED SHOT.
ALL RIGHT.
I'LL BE IN TOUCH.
話
KCHAK
チン

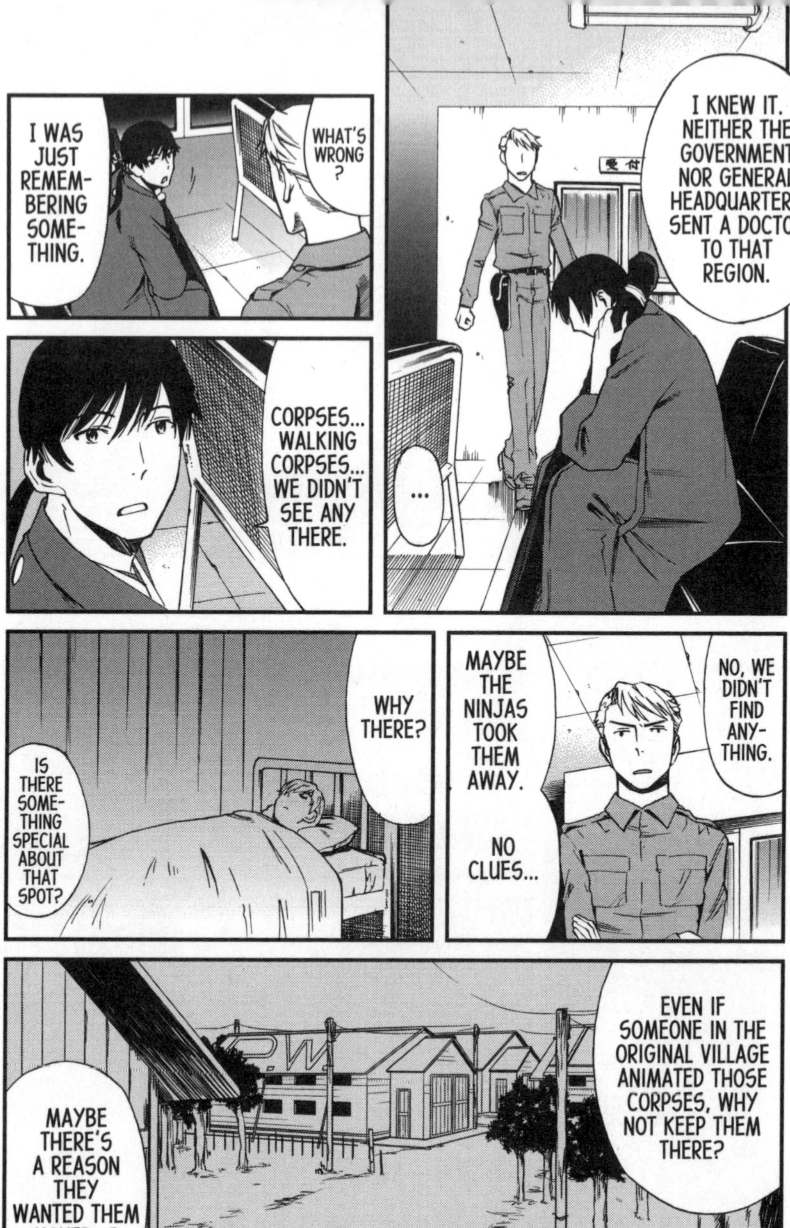
I KNEW IT. NEITHER THE GOVERNMENT NOR GENERAL HEADQUARTERS SENT A DOCTOR TO THAT REGION.
受付
...
WHAT'S WRONG?
I WAS JUST REMEMBERING SOMETHING.
CORPSES... WALKING CORPSES... WE DIDN'T SEE ANY THERE.
NO, WE DIDN'T FIND ANYTHING.
MAYBE THE NINJAS TOOK THEM AWAY.
NO CLUES...
WHY THERE?
IS THERE SOMETHING SPECIAL ABOUT THAT SPOT?
EVEN IF SOMEONE IN THE ORIGINAL VILLAGE ANIMATED THOSE CORPSES, WHY NOT KEEP THEM THERE?
MAYBE THERE'S A REASON THEY WANTED THEM MOVED...?

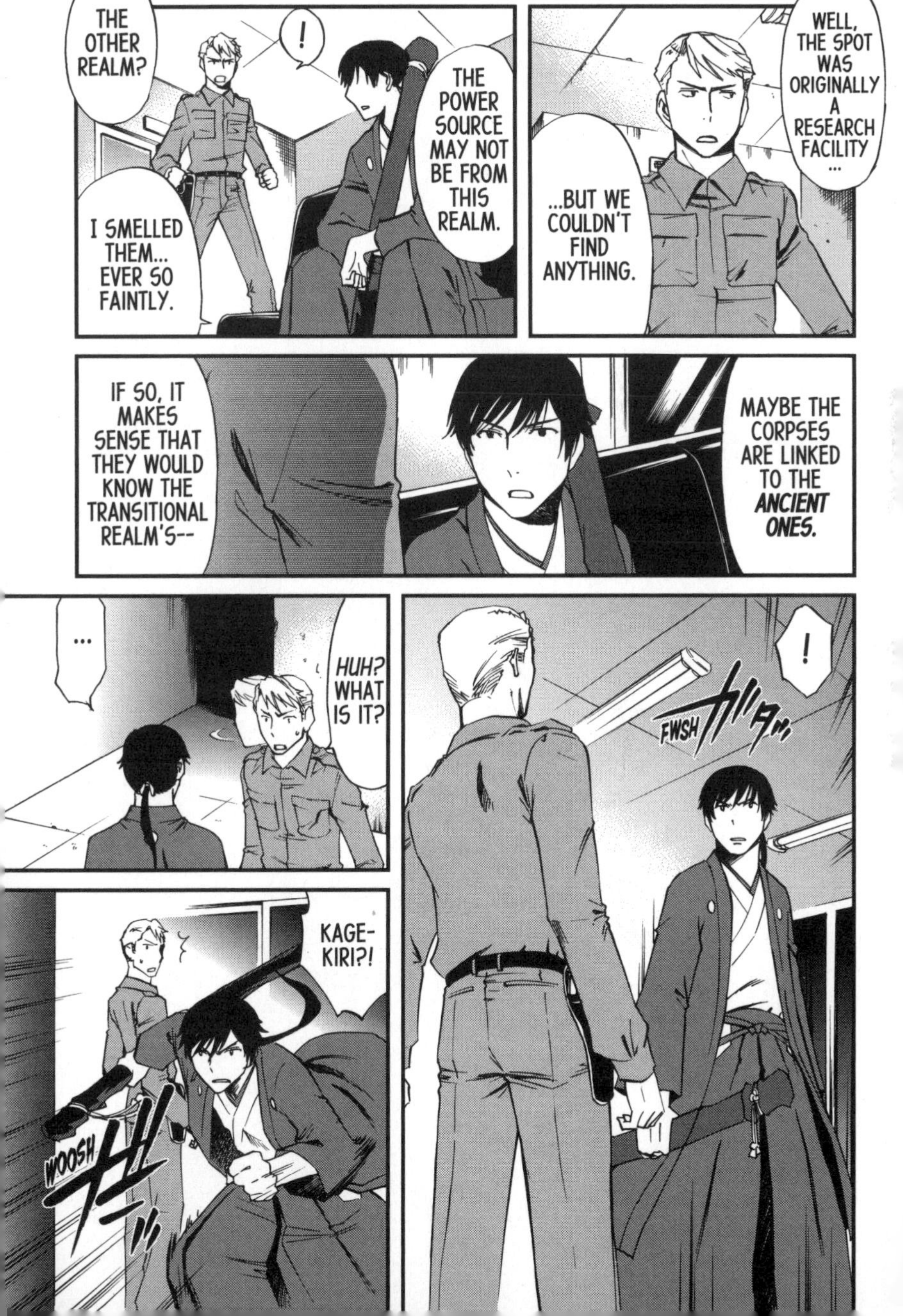

WELL, THE SPOT WAS ORIGINALLY A RESEARCH FACILITY ...
...BUT WE COULDN'T FIND ANYTHING.
THE POWER SOURCE MAY NOT BE FROM THIS REALM.
!
THE OTHER REALM?
I SMELLED THEM... EVER SO FAINTLY.
MAYBE THE CORPSES ARE LINKED TO THE *ANCIENT ONES.*
IF SO, IT MAKES SENSE THAT THEY WOULD KNOW THE TRANSITIONAL REALM'S--
!
FWSH
HUH? WHAT IS IT?
...
KAGE-KIRI?!
WOOSH

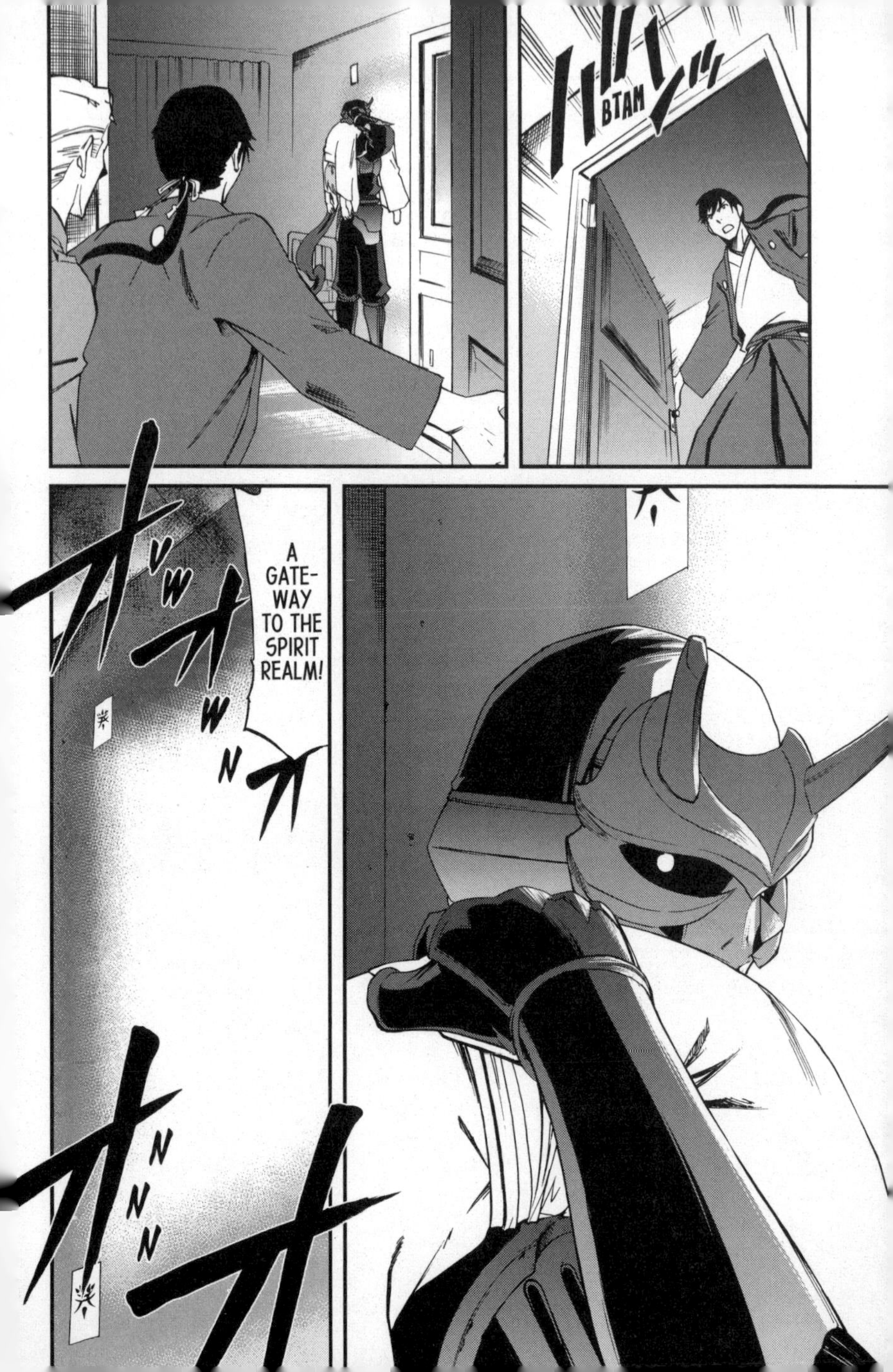
BTAM
A GATE-WAY TO THE SPIRIT REALM!
VWWWN
NNNN

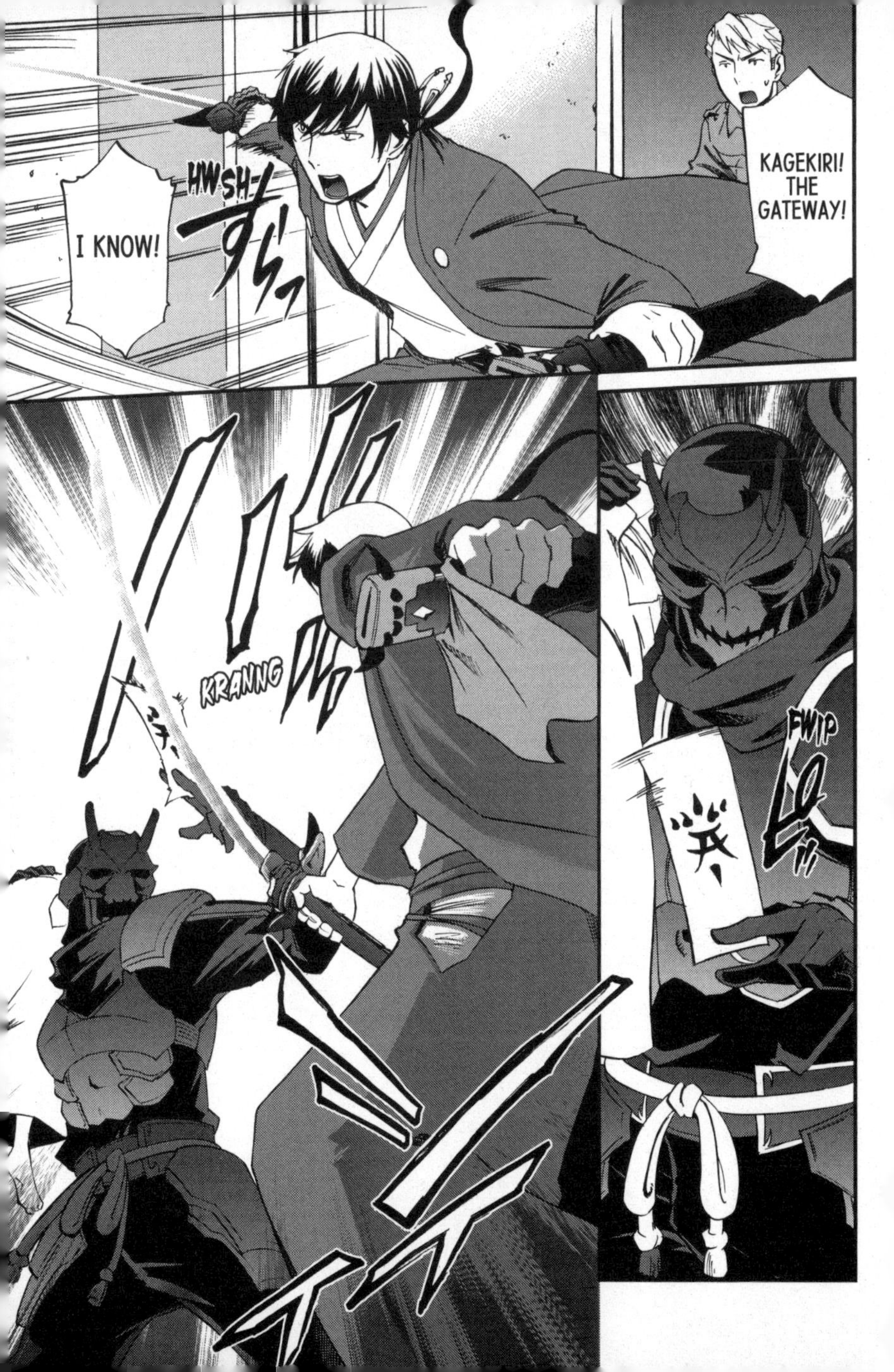
KAGEKIRI! THE GATEWAY!
HWSH
I KNOW!
FWIP
KRANNG

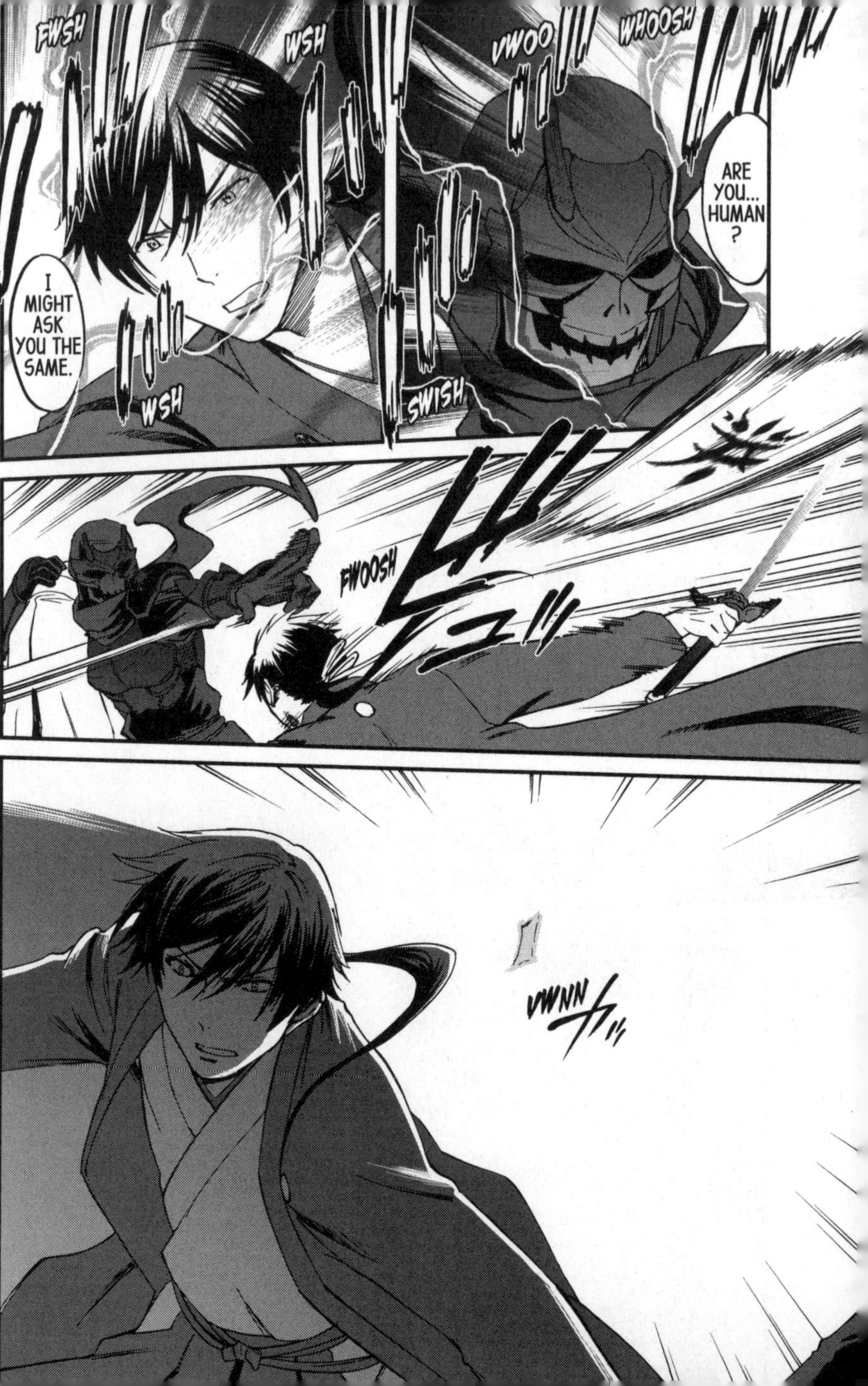
WHOOSH
VWOO
ARE YOU... HUMAN?
WSH
FWSH
SWISH
I MIGHT ASK YOU THE SAME.
WSH
FWOOSH
VWNN

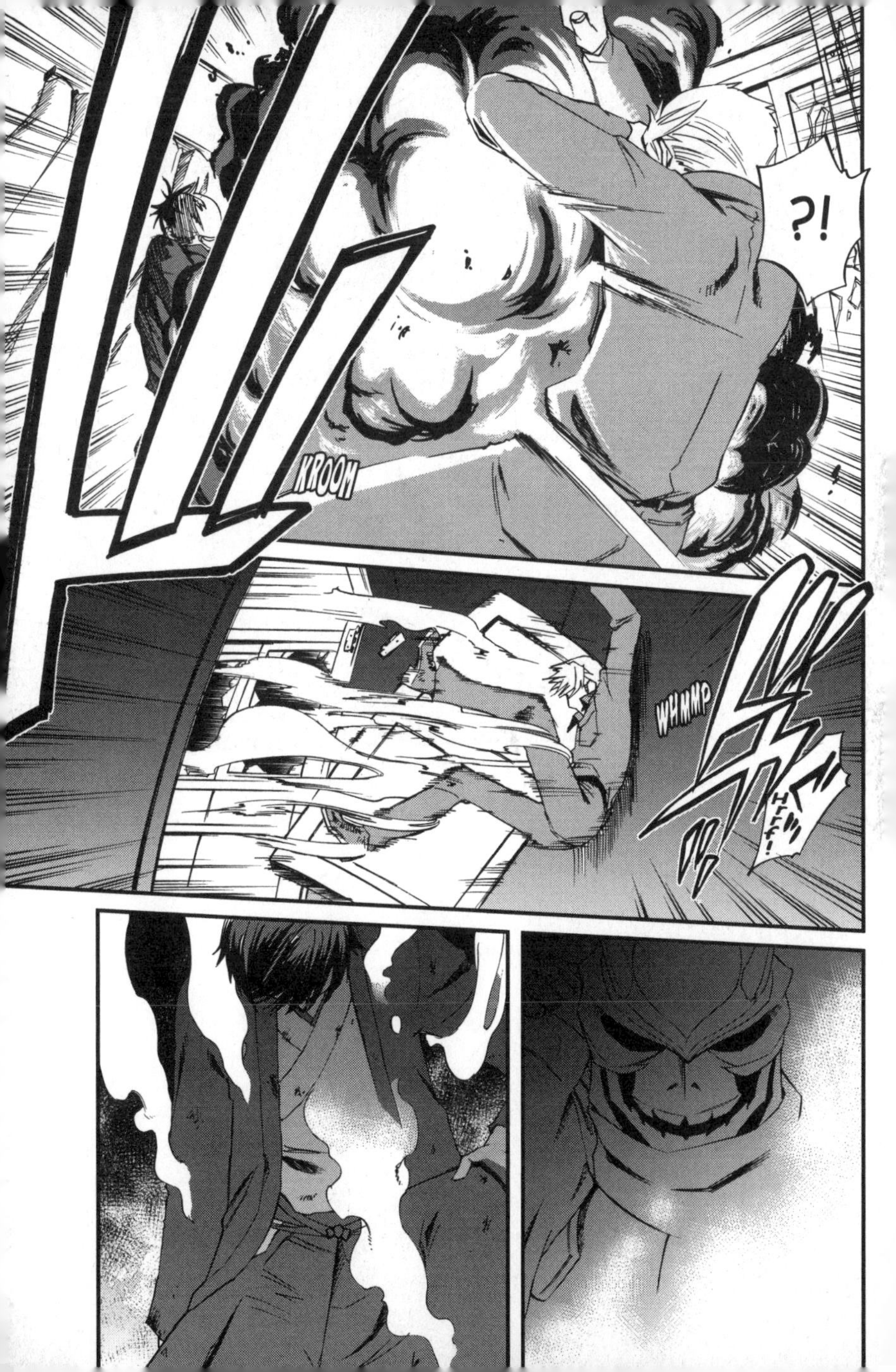
?!
KROOM
Hrrff!
WHMMP

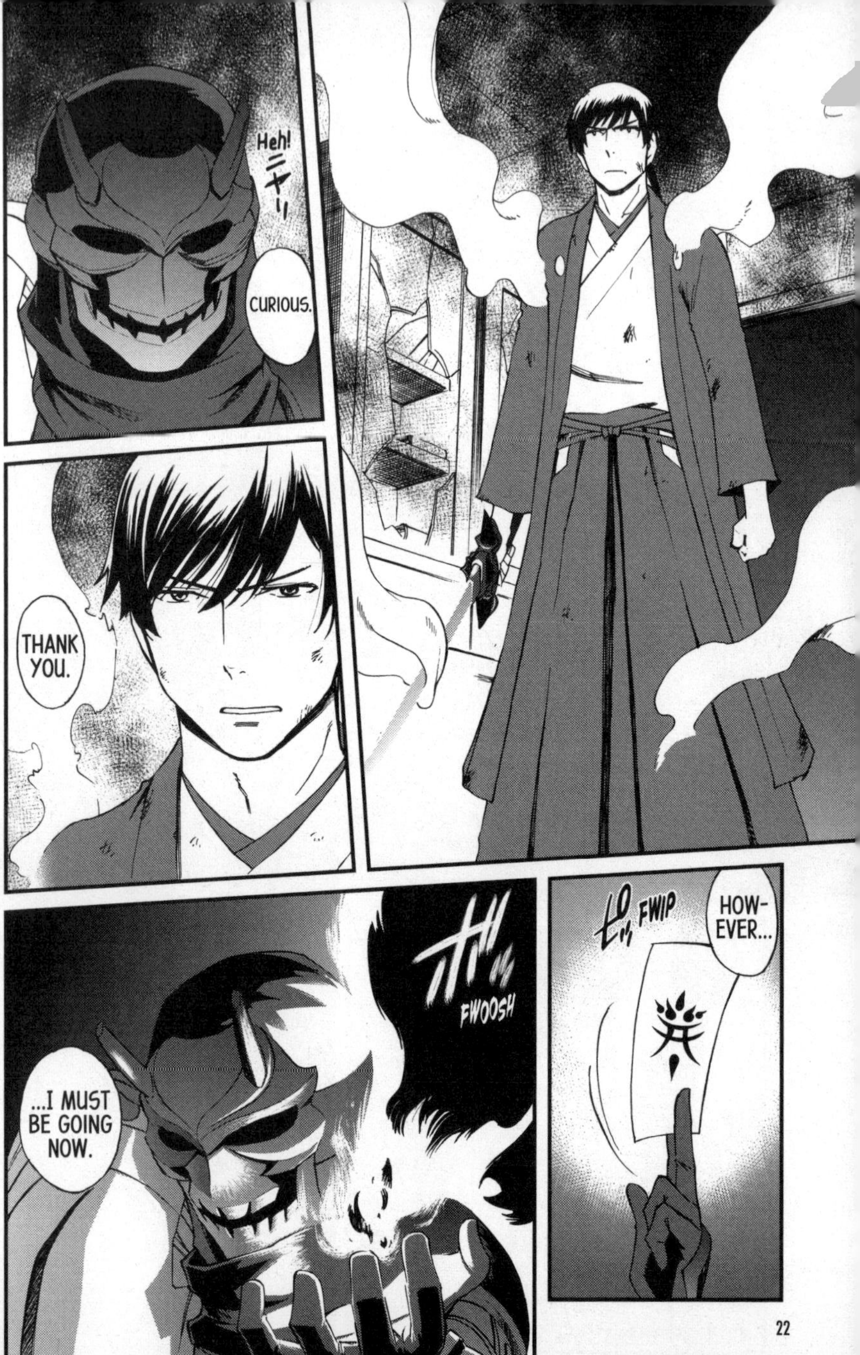
Heh!
ニヤリ
CURIOUS.
THANK YOU.
HOW-EVER...
FWIP
...I MUST BE GOING NOW.
FWOOSH

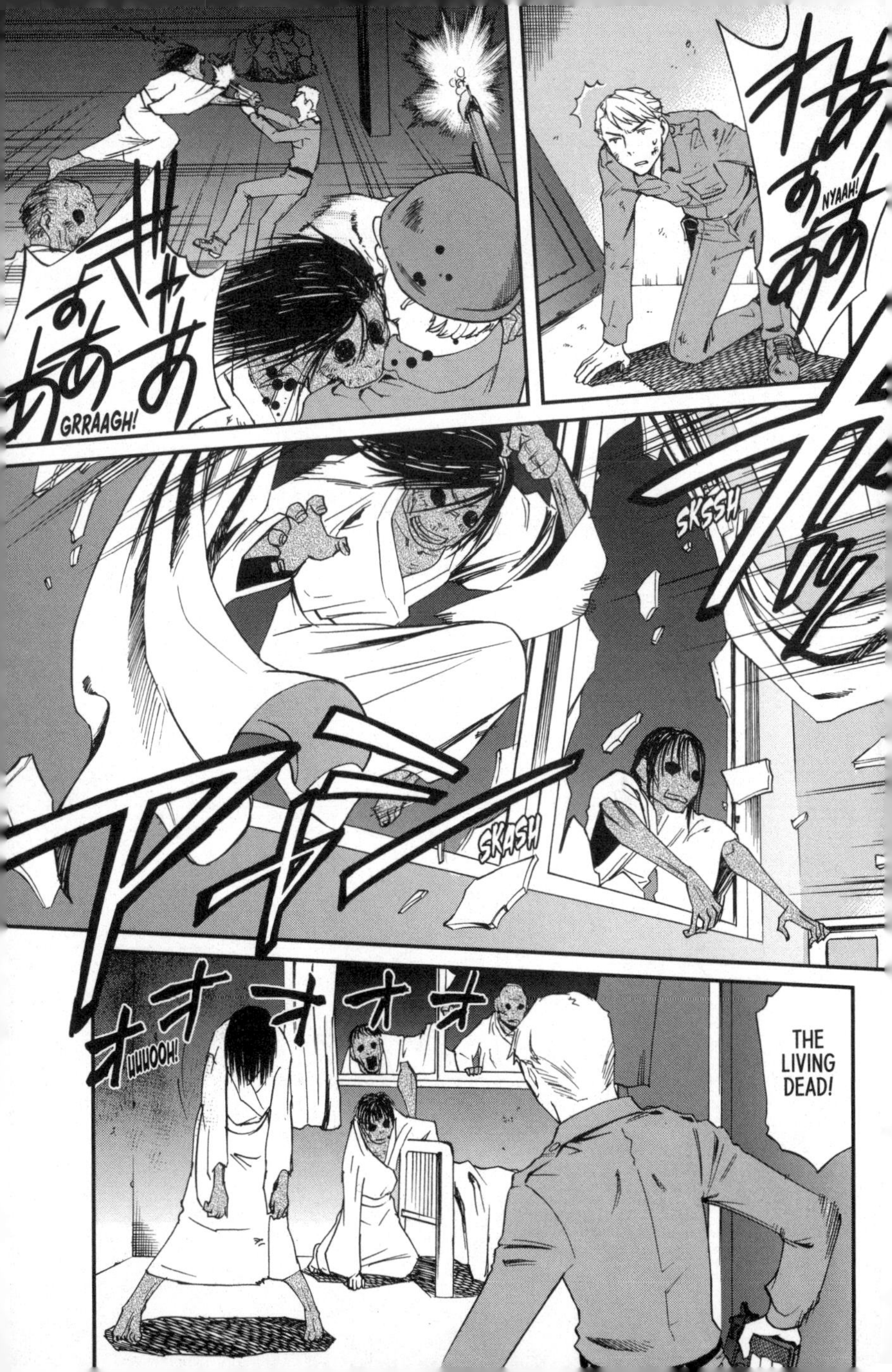
NYAAH!
GRRAAGH!
SKSSH
SKASH
THE LIVING DEAD!
UUUOOH!

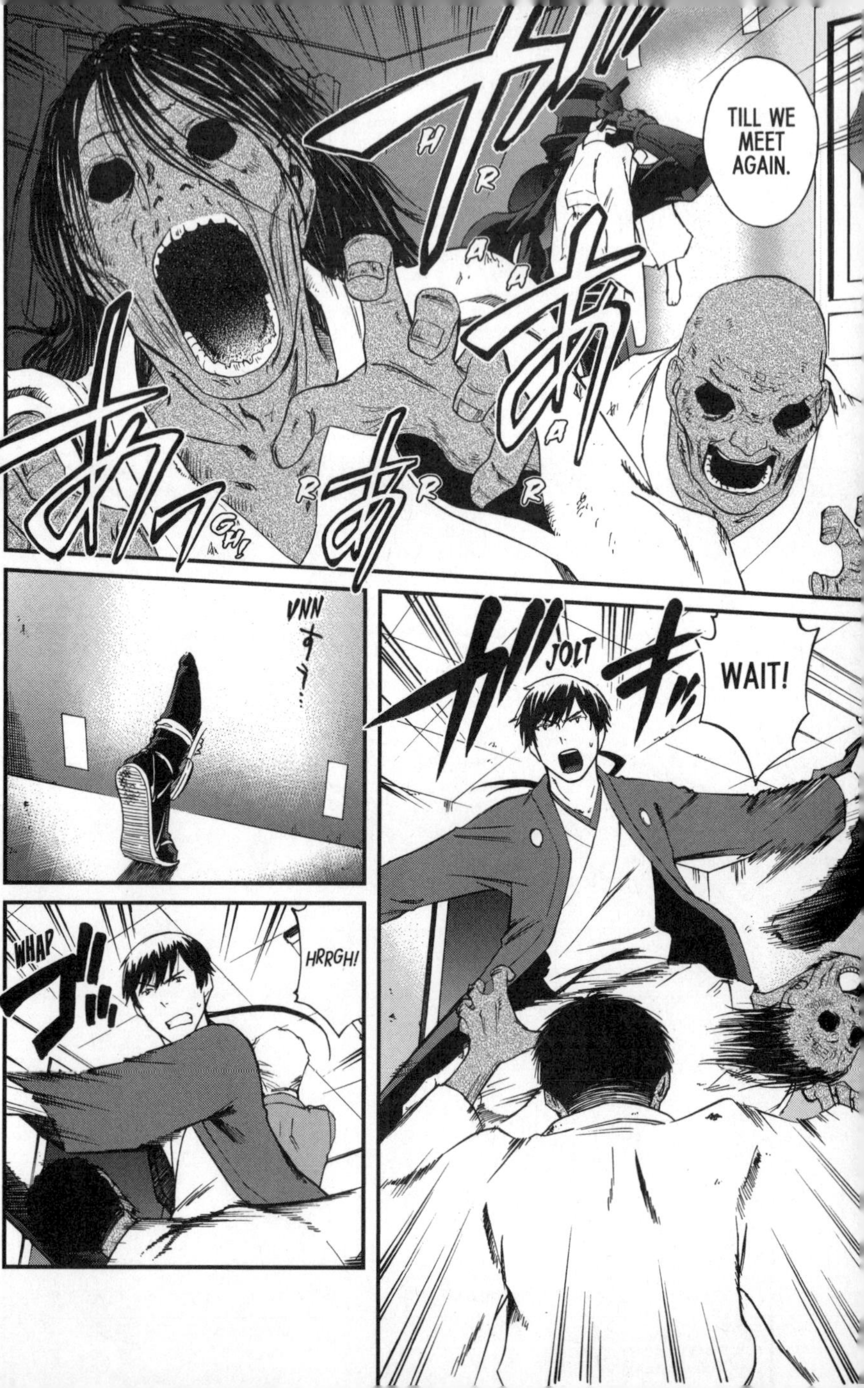
TILL WE MEET AGAIN.
HRAAARRRGH!
JOLT
WAIT!
VNN
WHAP
HRRGH!

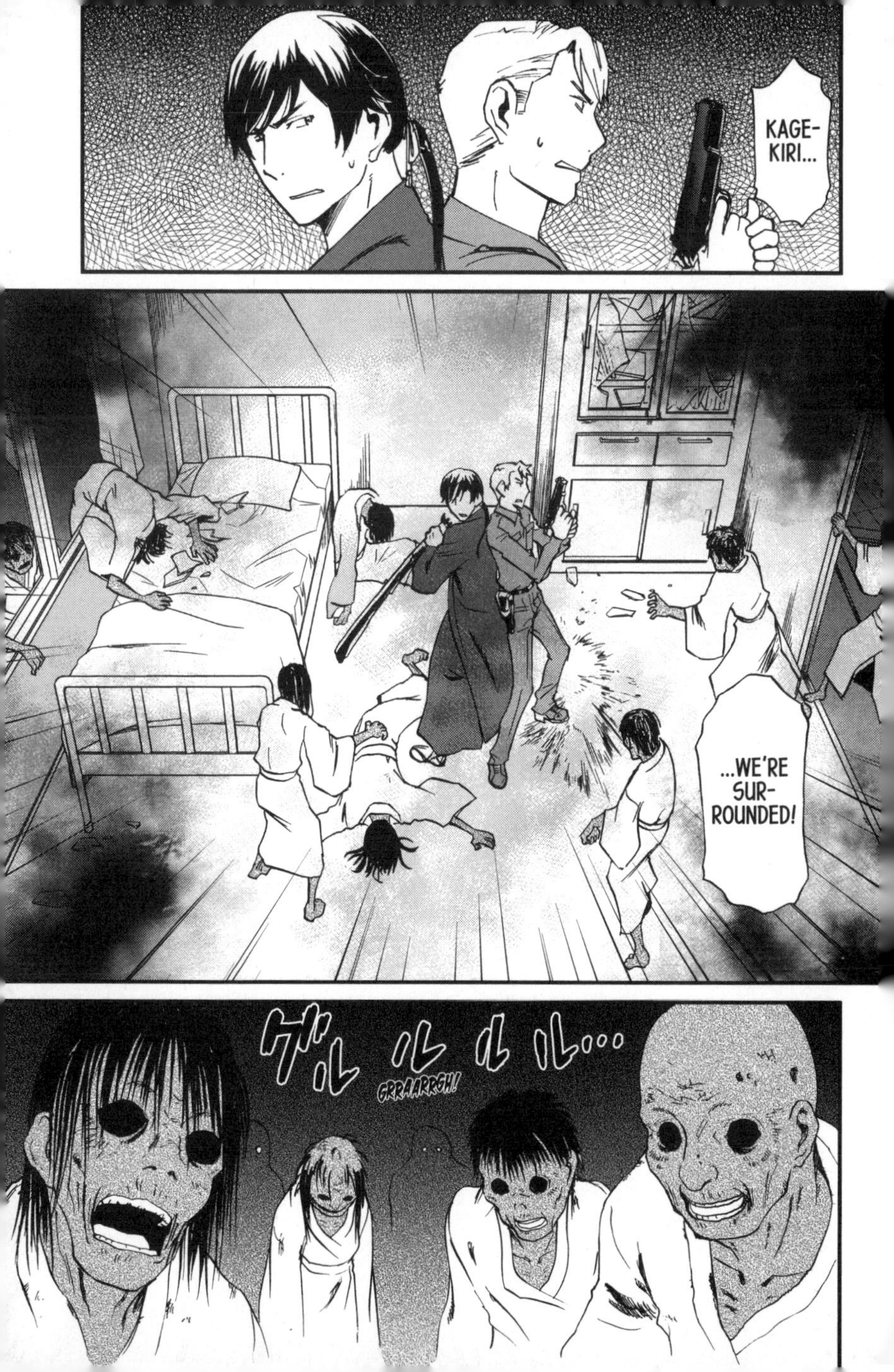
KAGE-KIRI...
...WE'RE SUR-ROUNDED!
GRRAARRGH!

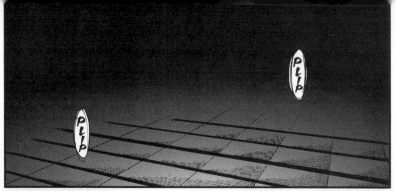

IF WE JOIN FORCES...

...WE'LL BE THAT MUCH CLOSER...

...TO THE REALM OF THE GODS.

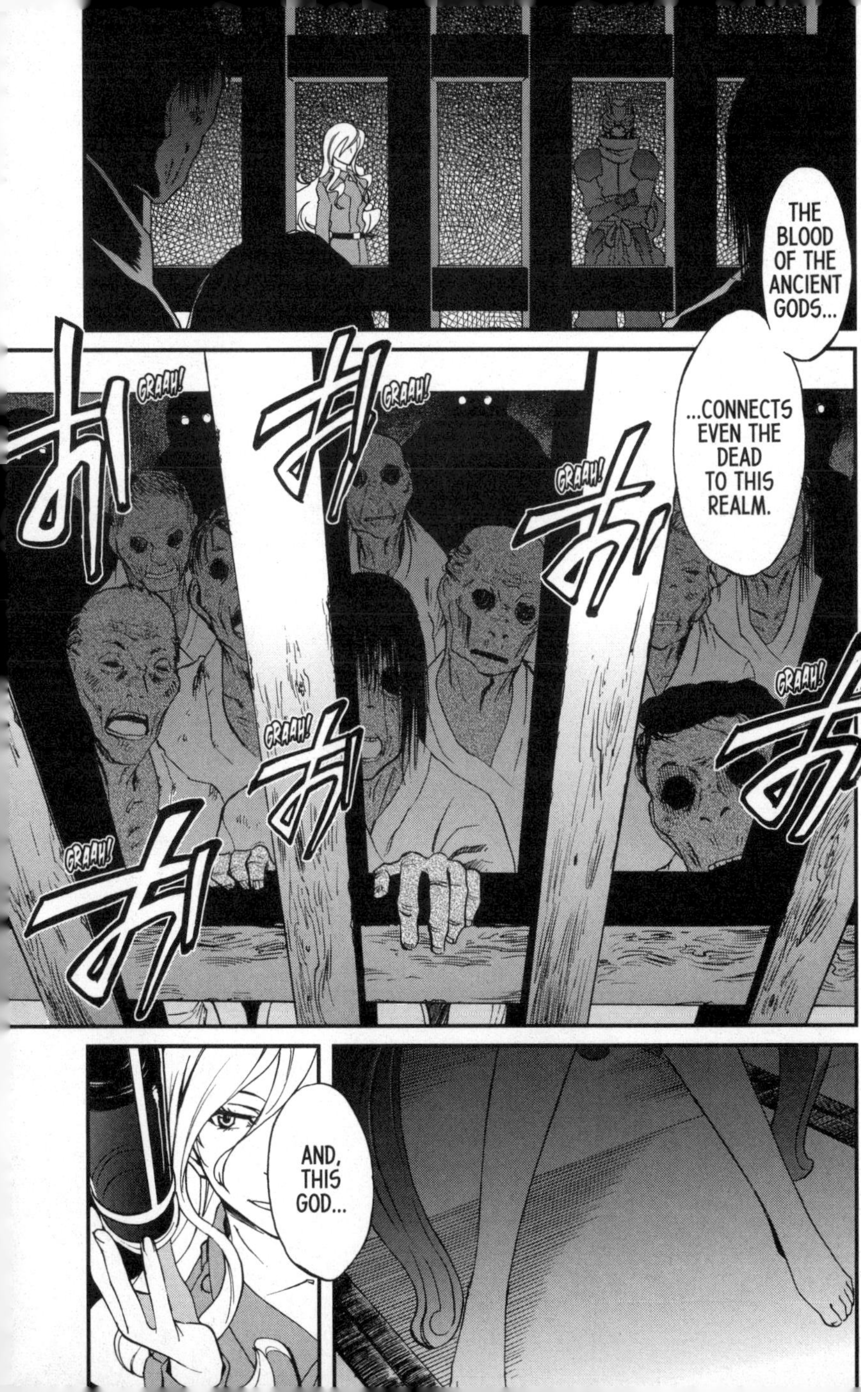
THE BLOOD OF THE ANCIENT GODS...
...CONNECTS EVEN THE DEAD TO THIS REALM.
GRAAH!
GRAAH!
GRAAH!
GRAAH!
GRAAH!
GRAAH!
AND, THIS GOD...

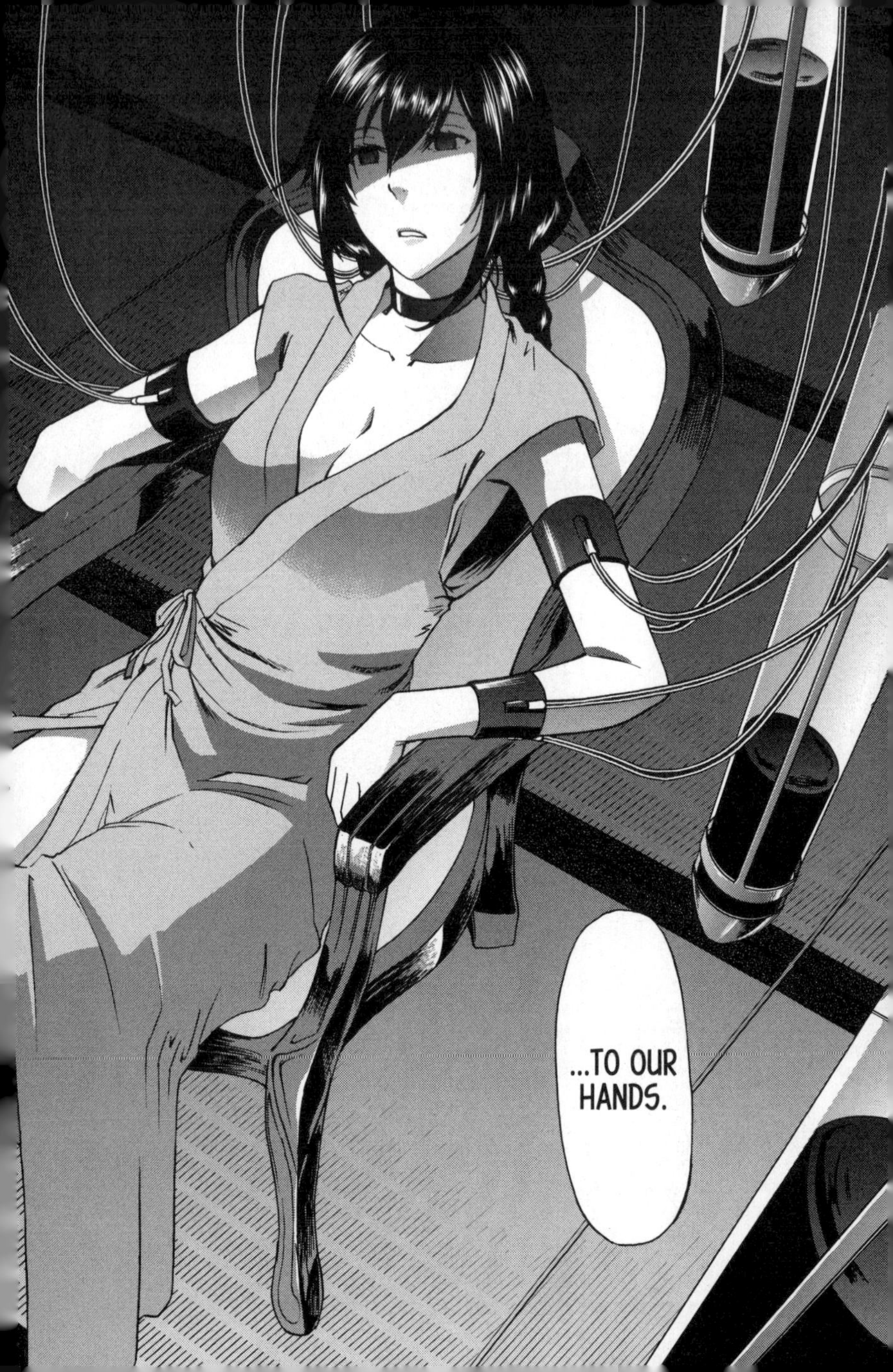
...TO OUR HANDS.

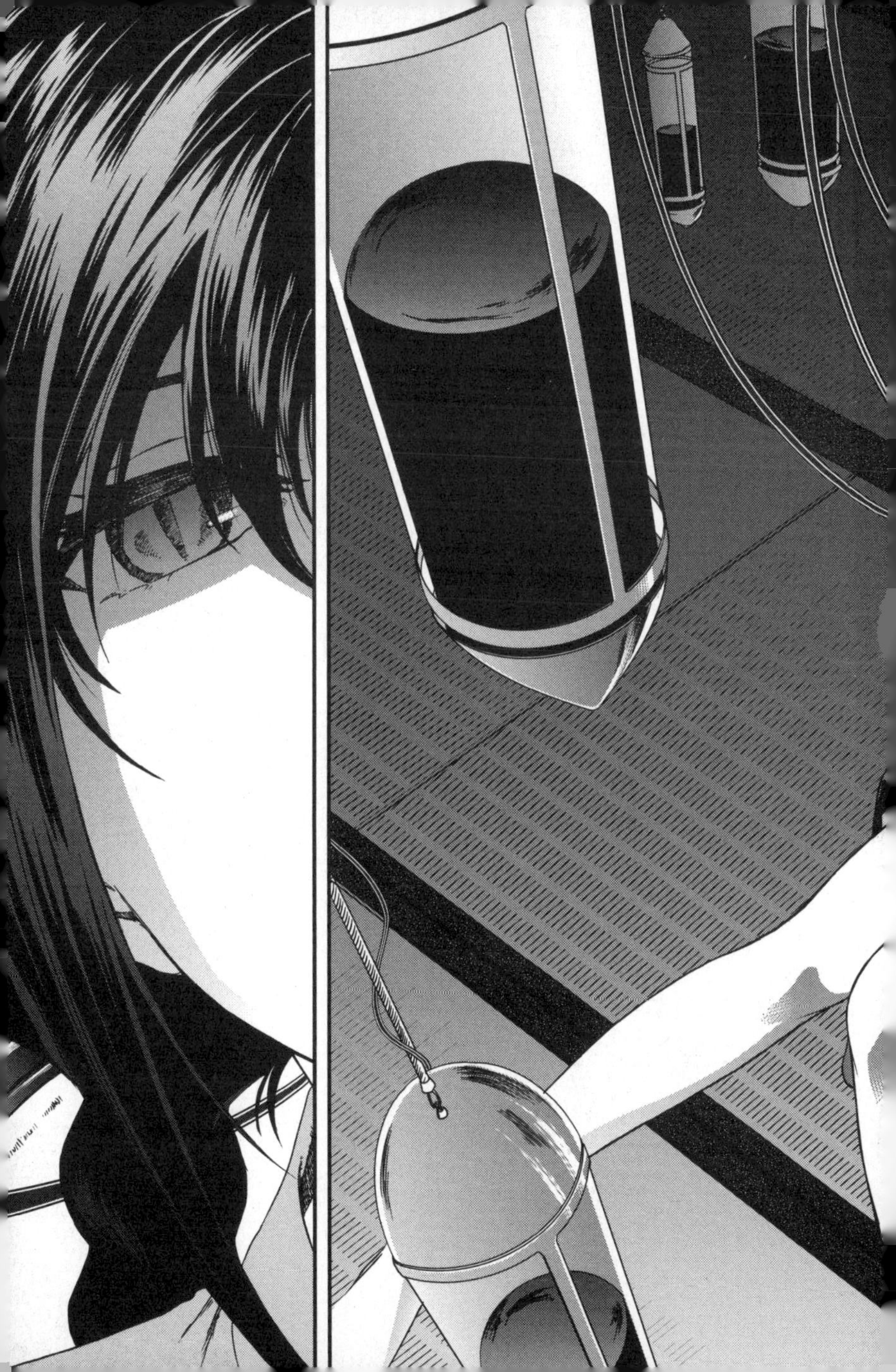

BLOODC

DEMONIC
MOONLIGHT

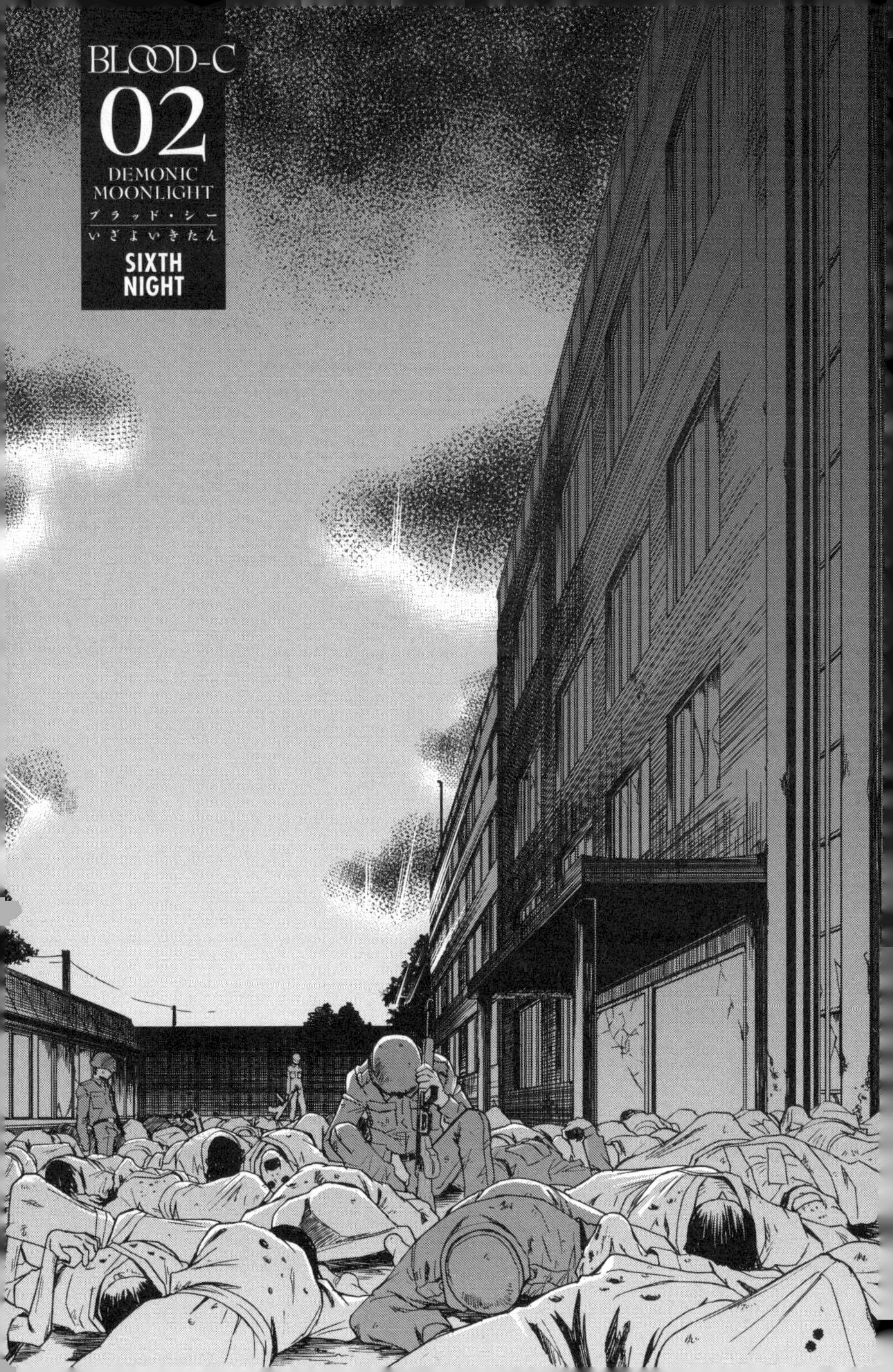
BLOOD-C
02
DEMONIC
MOONLIGHT
ブラッド・シー
いざよいきたん
SIXTH
NIGHT

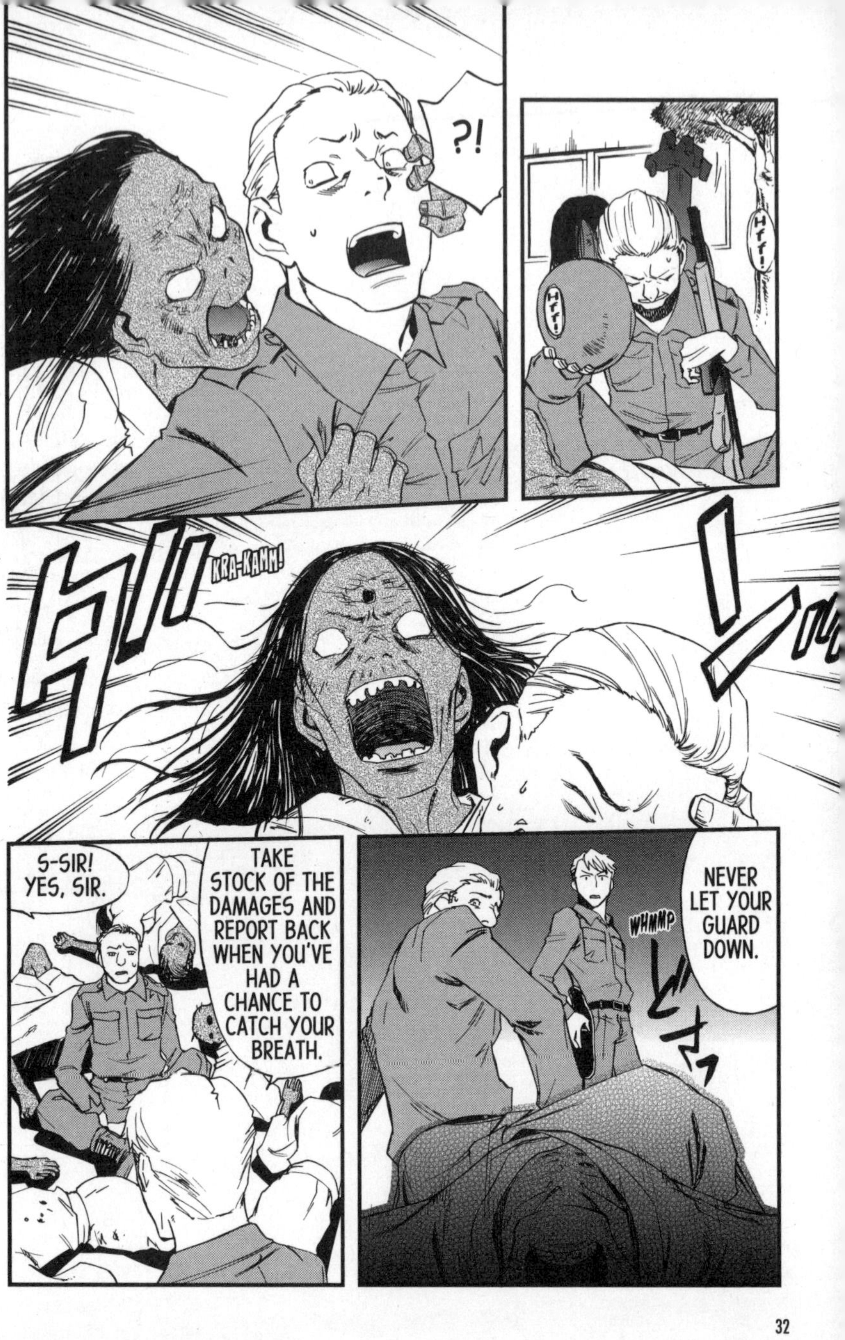
Hff!
Hff!
?!
KRA-KAMM!
NEVER LET YOUR GUARD DOWN.
WHMMP
TAKE STOCK OF THE DAMAGES AND REPORT BACK WHEN YOU'VE HAD A CHANCE TO CATCH YOUR BREATH.
S-SIR! YES, SIR.

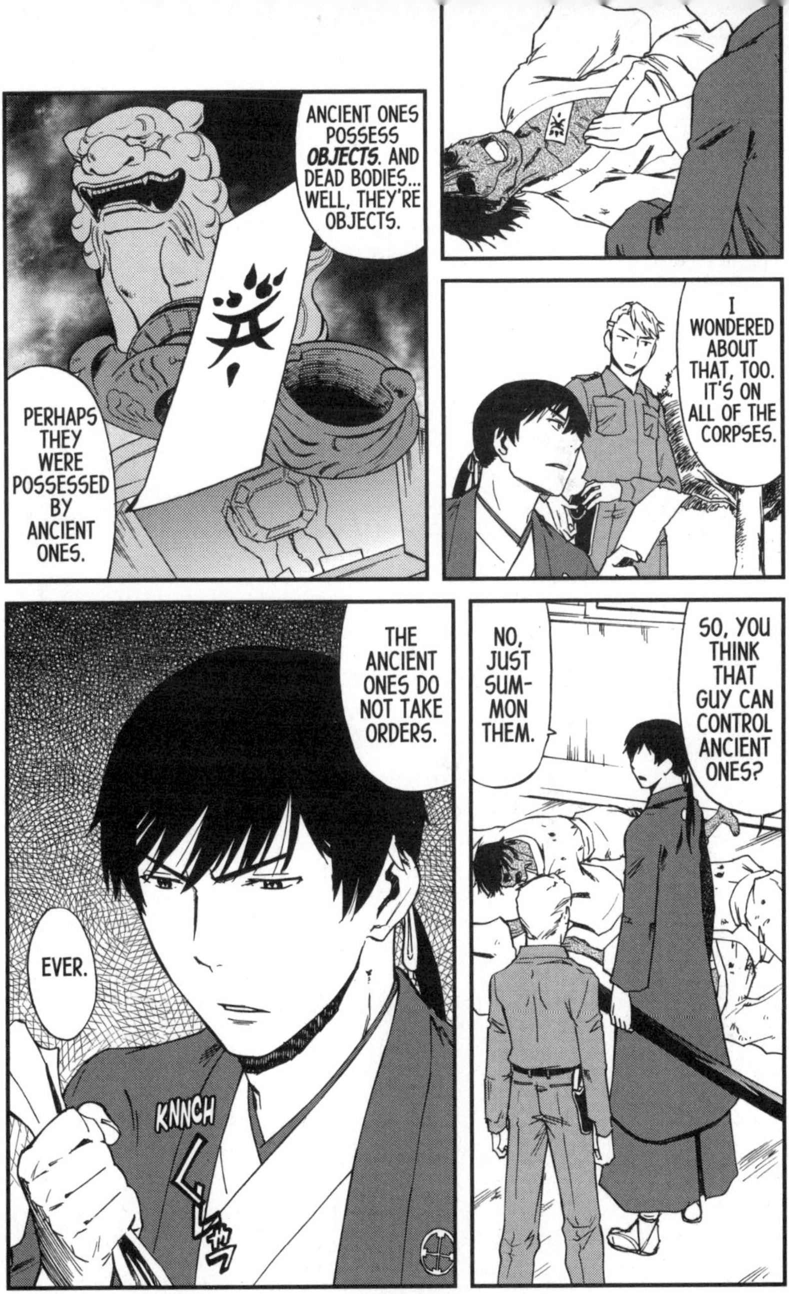
I WONDERED ABOUT THAT, TOO. IT'S ON ALL OF THE CORPSES.
ANCIENT ONES POSSESS *OBJECTS*. AND DEAD BODIES... WELL, THEY'RE OBJECTS.
PERHAPS THEY WERE POSSESSED BY ANCIENT ONES.
SO, YOU THINK THAT GUY CAN CONTROL ANCIENT ONES?
NO, JUST SUM-MON THEM.
THE ANCIENT ONES DO NOT TAKE ORDERS.
EVER.
KNNCH

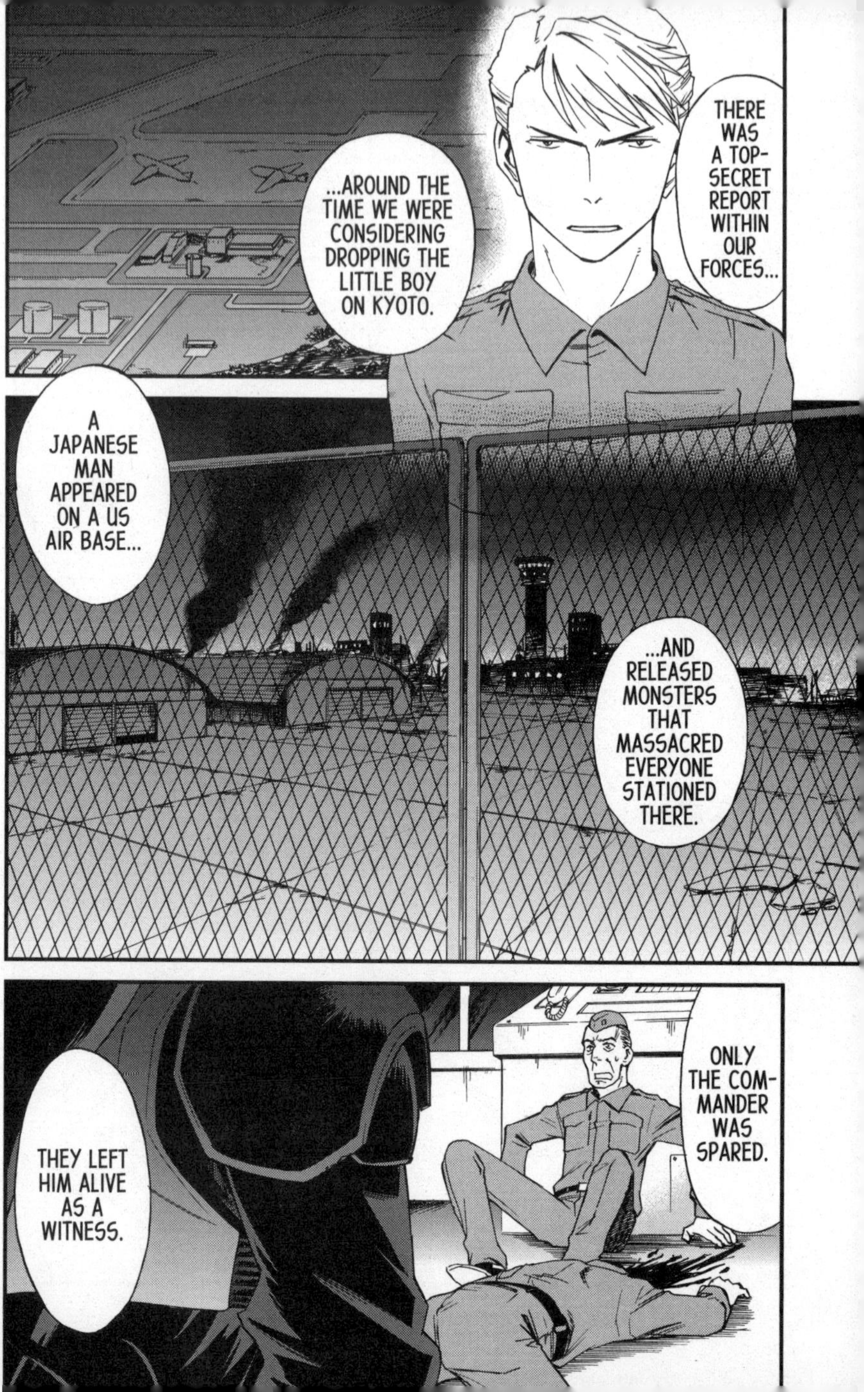
THERE WAS A TOP-SECRET REPORT WITHIN OUR FORCES...
...AROUND THE TIME WE WERE CONSIDERING DROPPING THE LITTLE BOY ON KYOTO.
A JAPANESE MAN APPEARED ON A US AIR BASE...
...AND RELEASED MONSTERS THAT MASSACRED EVERYONE STATIONED THERE.
ONLY THE COMMANDER WAS SPARED.
THEY LEFT HIM ALIVE AS A WITNESS.

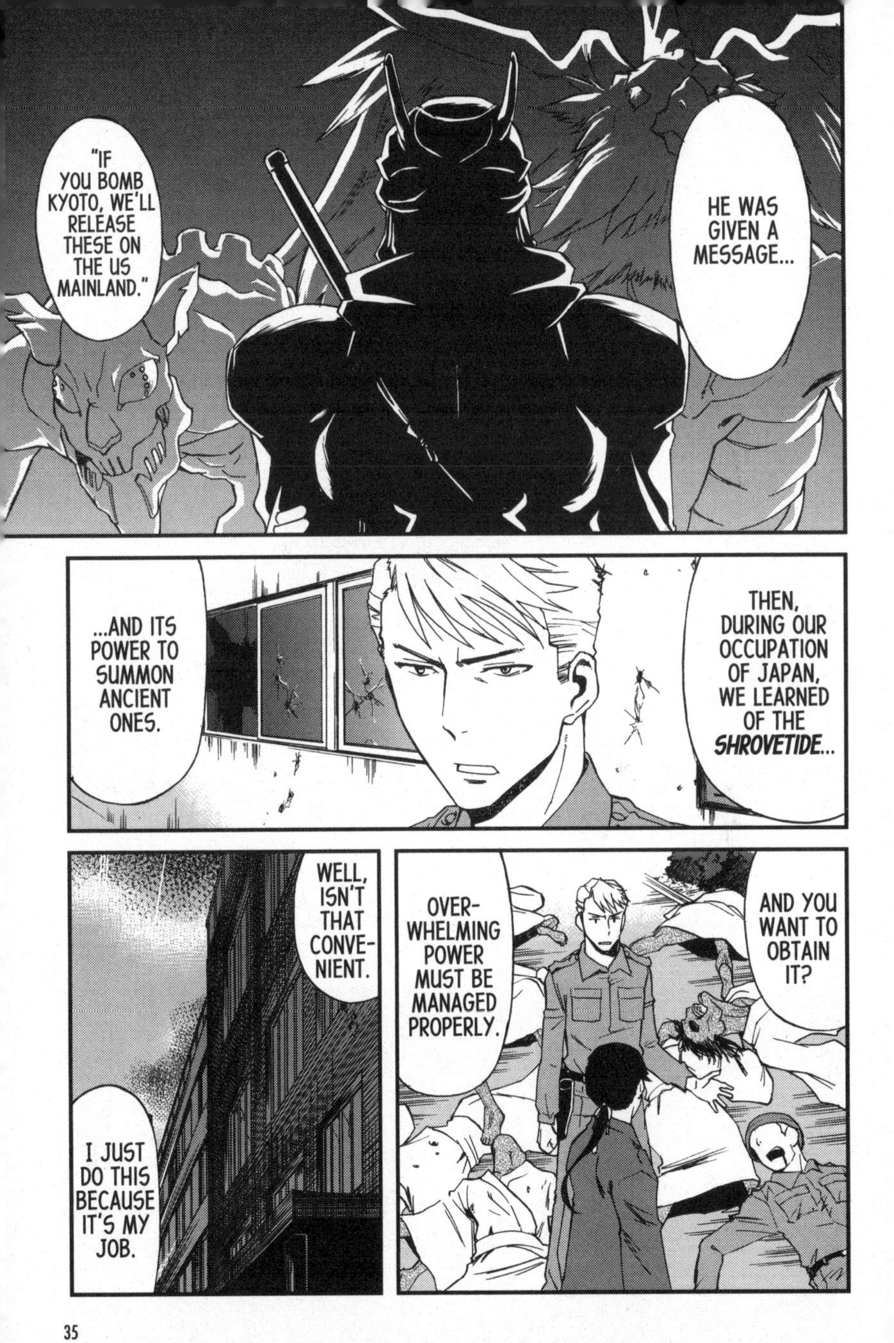
HE WAS GIVEN A MESSAGE...
"IF YOU BOMB KYOTO, WE'LL RELEASE THESE ON THE US MAINLAND."
THEN, DURING OUR OCCUPATION OF JAPAN, WE LEARNED OF THE ***SHROVETIDE***...
...AND ITS POWER TO SUMMON ANCIENT ONES.
AND YOU WANT TO OBTAIN IT?
OVER-WHELMING POWER MUST BE MANAGED PROPERLY.
WELL, ISN'T THAT CONVE-NIENT.
I JUST DO THIS BECAUSE IT'S MY JOB.

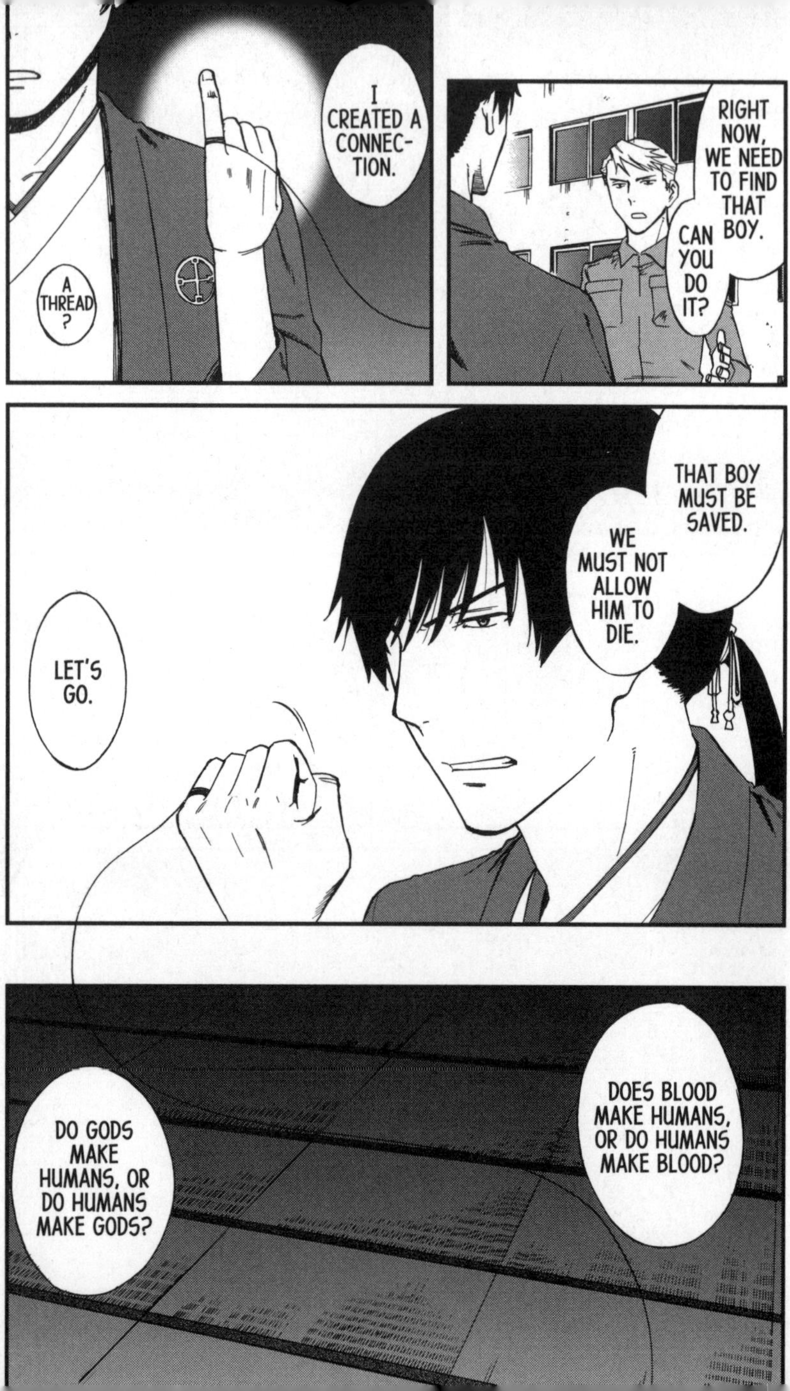
RIGHT NOW, WE NEED TO FIND THAT BOY.
CAN YOU DO IT?
I CREATED A CONNECTION.
A THREAD?
THAT BOY MUST BE SAVED.
WE MUST NOT ALLOW HIM TO DIE.
LET'S GO.
DOES BLOOD MAKE HUMANS, OR DO HUMANS MAKE BLOOD?
DO GODS MAKE HUMANS, OR DO HUMANS MAKE GODS?

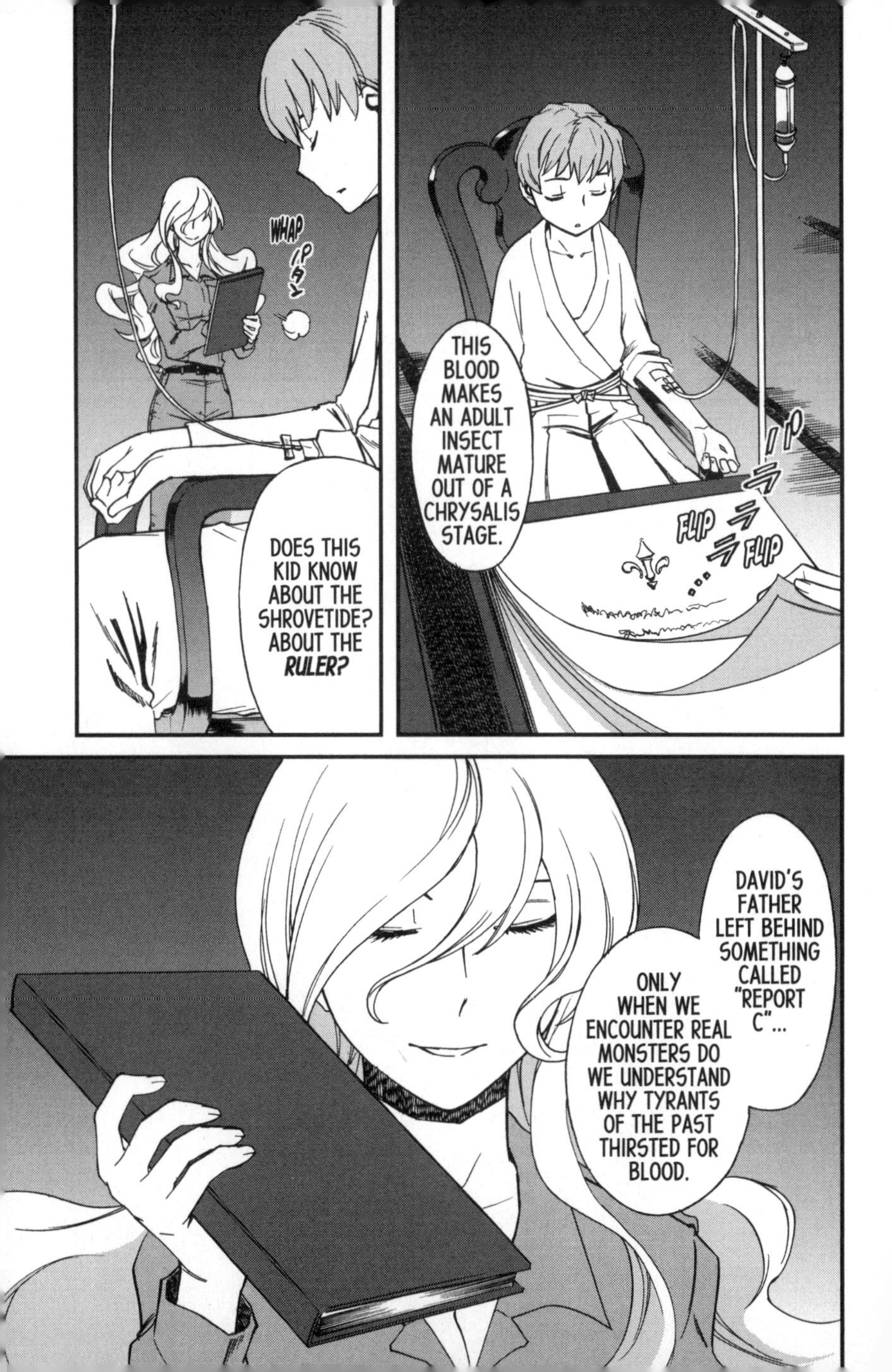
THIS BLOOD MAKES AN ADULT INSECT MATURE OUT OF A CHRYSALIS STAGE.
FLIP FLIP
WHAP
DOES THIS KID KNOW ABOUT THE SHROVETIDE? ABOUT THE *RULER?*
DAVID'S FATHER LEFT BEHIND SOMETHING CALLED "REPORT C"...
ONLY WHEN WE ENCOUNTER REAL MONSTERS DO WE UNDERSTAND WHY TYRANTS OF THE PAST THIRSTED FOR BLOOD.

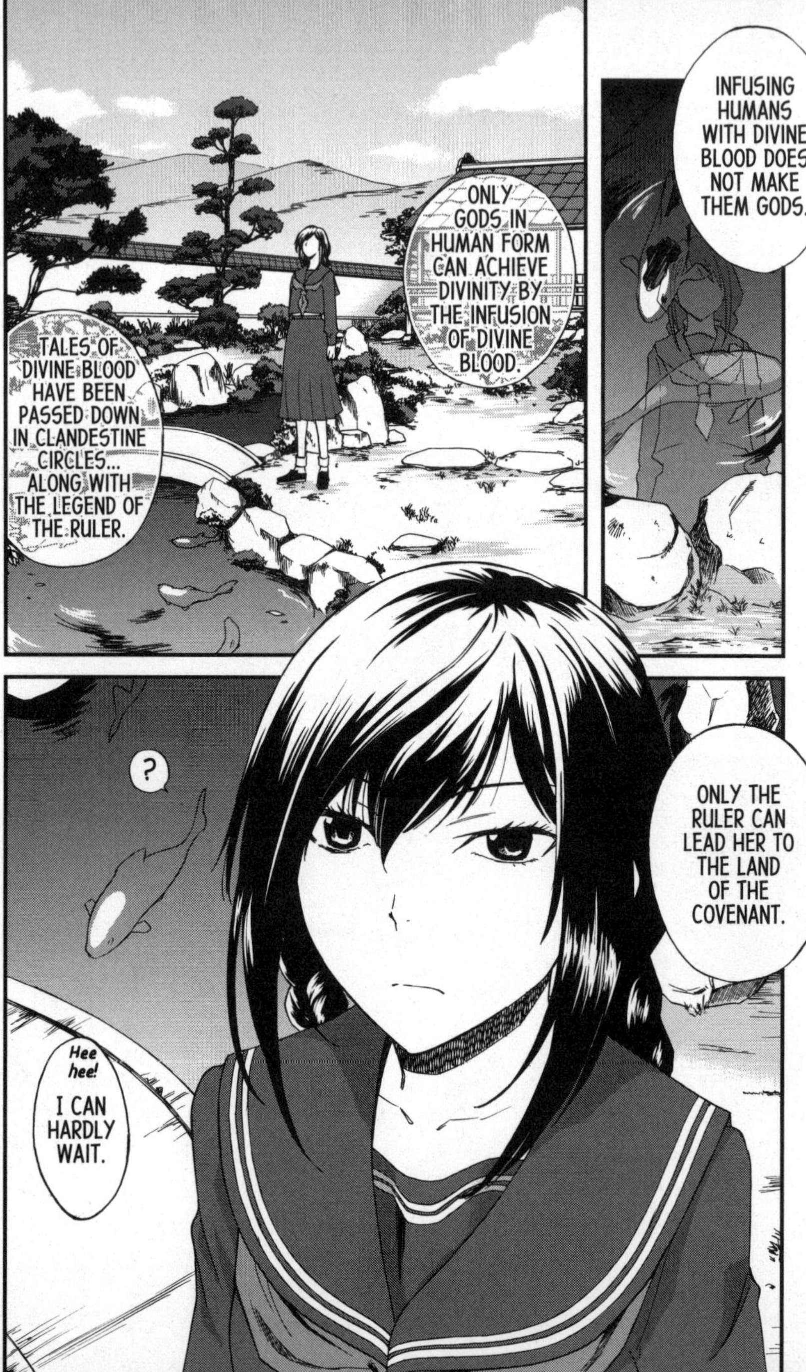
INFUSING HUMANS WITH DIVINE BLOOD DOES NOT MAKE THEM GODS.
ONLY GODS IN HUMAN FORM CAN ACHIEVE DIVINITY BY THE INFUSION OF DIVINE BLOOD.
TALES OF DIVINE BLOOD HAVE BEEN PASSED DOWN IN CLANDESTINE CIRCLES... ALONG WITH THE LEGEND OF THE RULER.
ONLY THE RULER CAN LEAD HER TO THE LAND OF THE COVENANT.
?
Hee hee!
I CAN HARDLY WAIT.

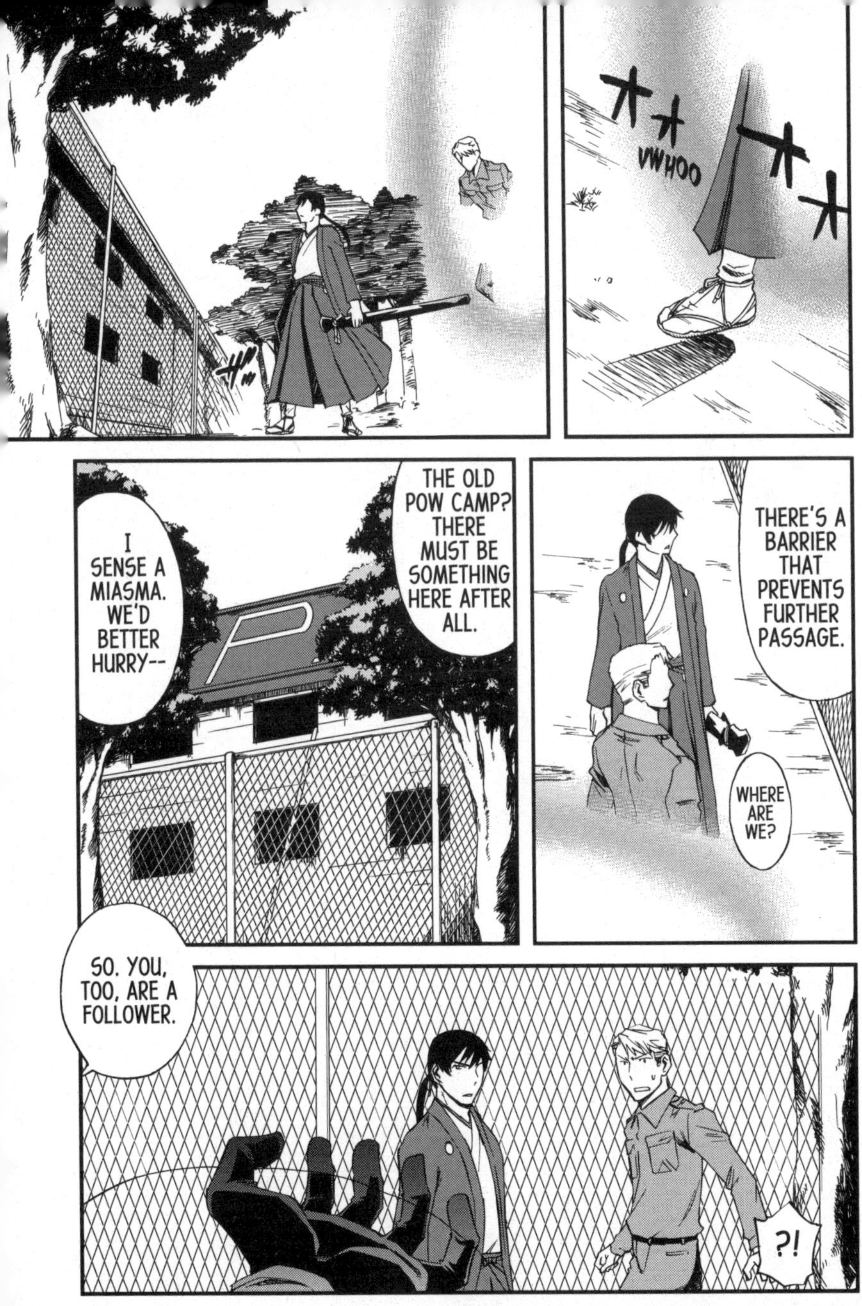
VWHOO
THERE'S A BARRIER THAT PREVENTS FURTHER PASSAGE.
WHERE ARE WE?
THE OLD POW CAMP? THERE MUST BE SOMETHING HERE AFTER ALL.
I SENSE A MIASMA. WE'D BETTER HURRY--
SO. YOU, TOO, ARE A FOLLOWER.
?!

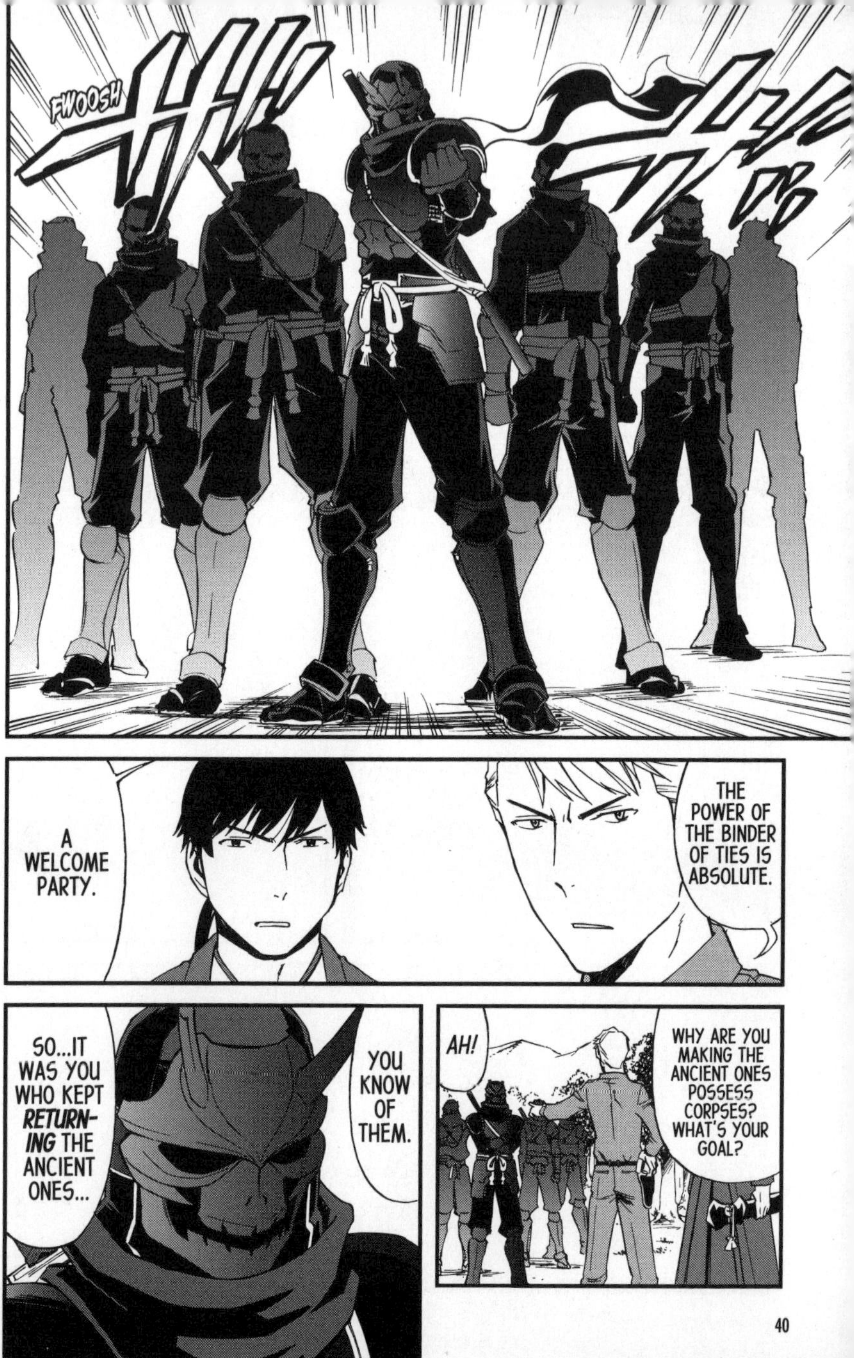
FWOOSH
THE POWER OF THE BINDER OF TIES IS ABSOLUTE.
A WELCOME PARTY.
WHY ARE YOU MAKING THE ANCIENT ONES POSSESS CORPSES? WHAT'S YOUR GOAL?
AH!
YOU KNOW OF THEM.
SO...IT WAS YOU WHO KEPT ***RETURNING*** THE ANCIENT ONES...

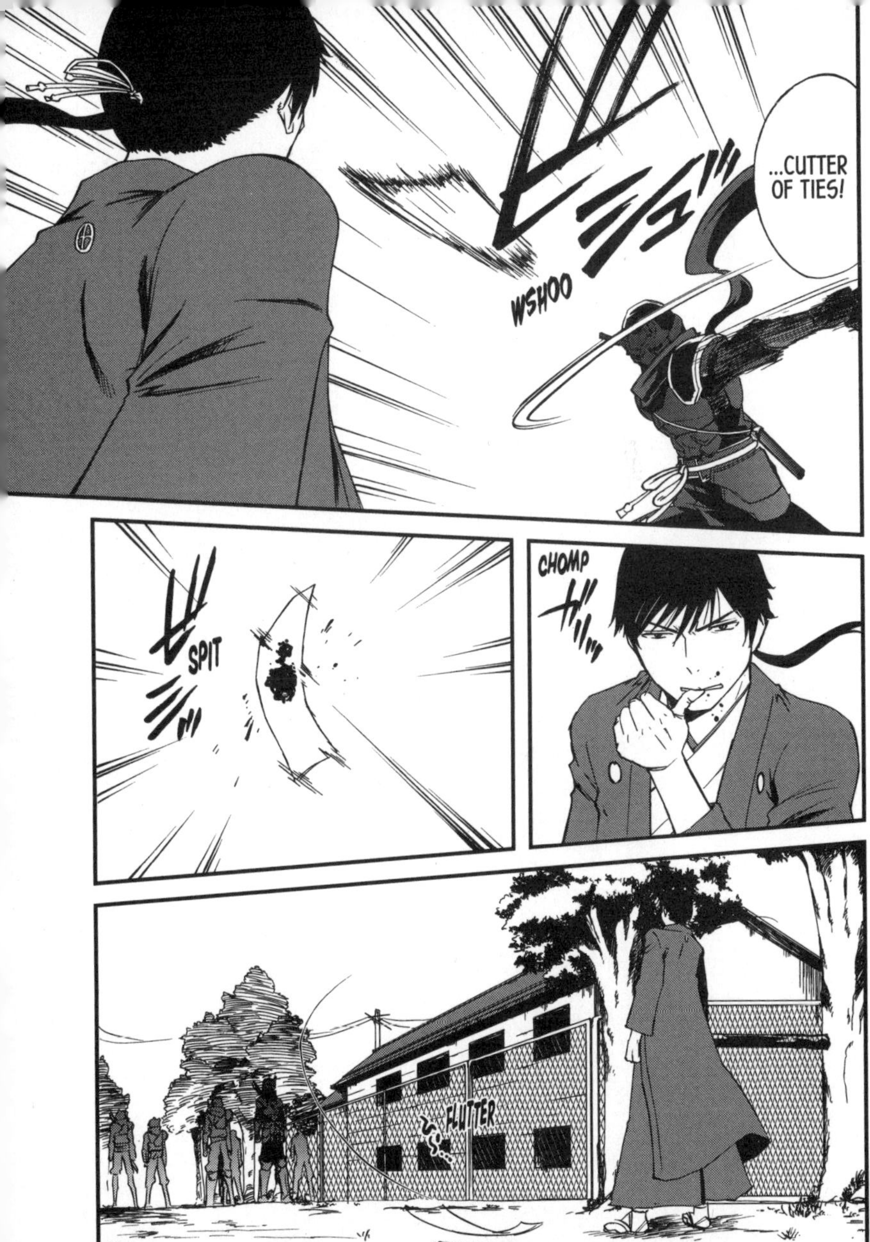
...CUTTER OF TIES!
WSHOO
CHOMP
SPIT
FLUTTER

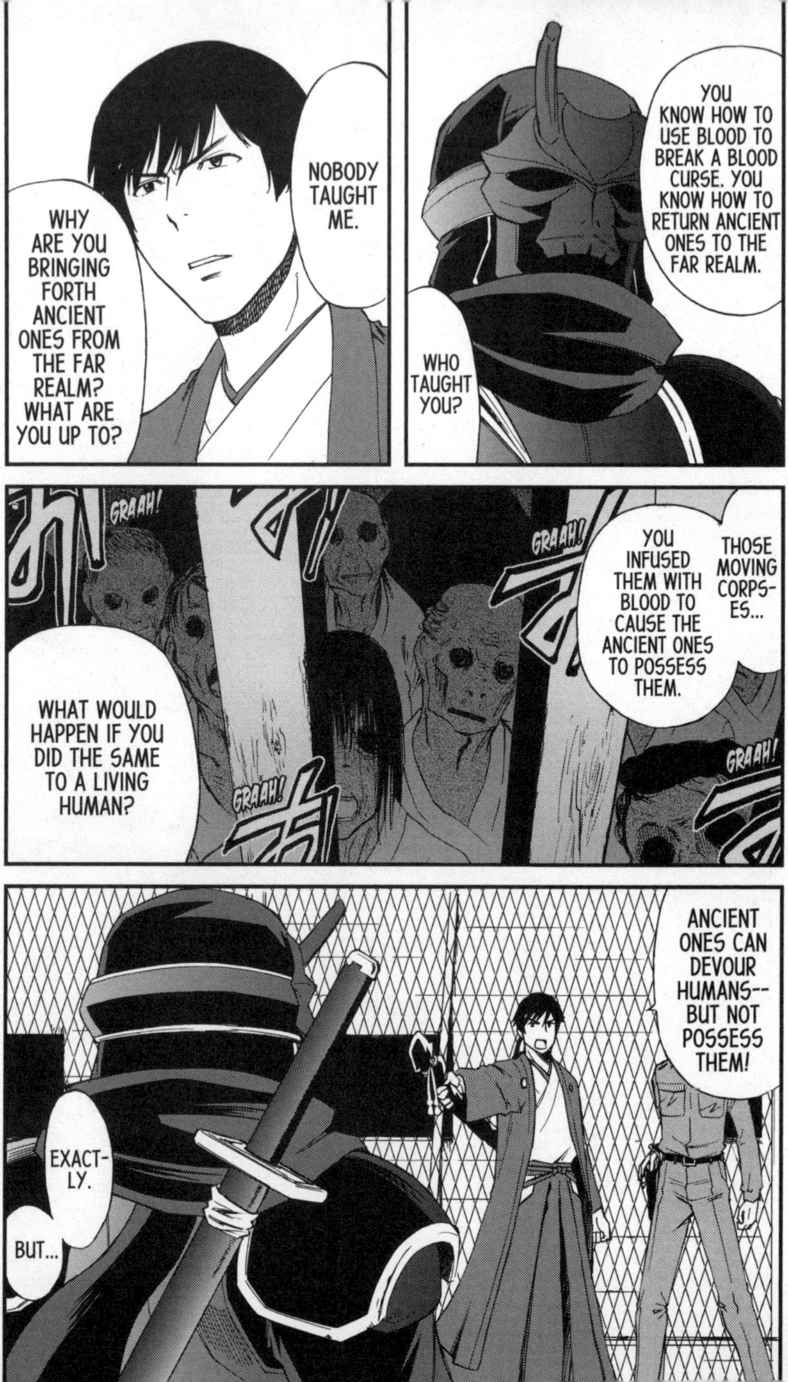
YOU KNOW HOW TO USE BLOOD TO BREAK A BLOOD CURSE. YOU KNOW HOW TO RETURN ANCIENT ONES TO THE FAR REALM.
WHO TAUGHT YOU?
NOBODY TAUGHT ME.
WHY ARE YOU BRINGING FORTH ANCIENT ONES FROM THE FAR REALM? WHAT ARE YOU UP TO?
GRAAH!
GRAAH!
THOSE MOVING CORPS-ES...
YOU INFUSED THEM WITH BLOOD TO CAUSE THE ANCIENT ONES TO POSSESS THEM.
GRAAH!
WHAT WOULD HAPPEN IF YOU DID THE SAME TO A LIVING HUMAN?
GRAAH!
ANCIENT ONES CAN DEVOUR HUMANS--BUT NOT POSSESS THEM!
EXACT-LY.
BUT...

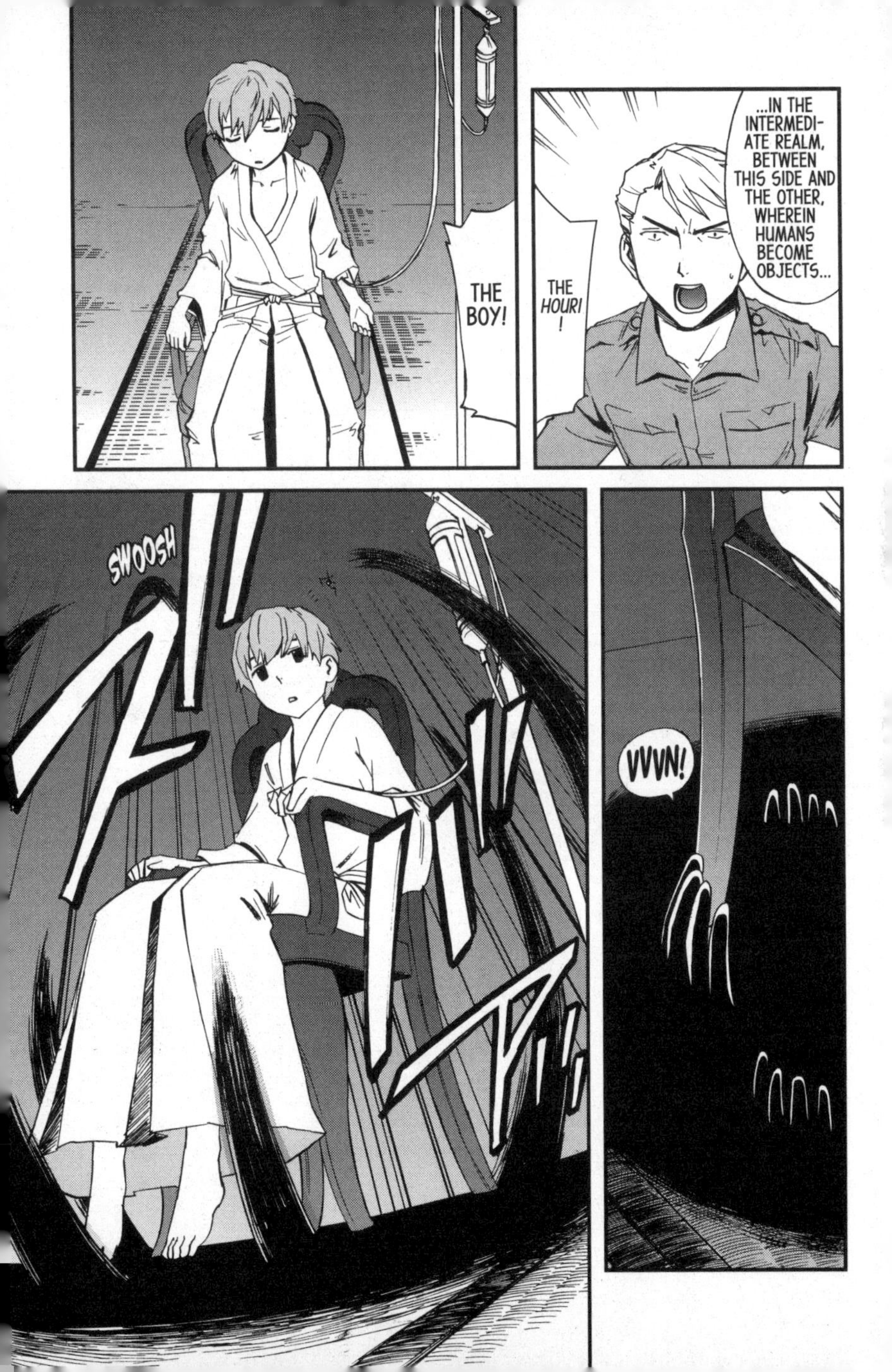
...IN THE INTERMEDIATE REALM, BETWEEN THIS SIDE AND THE OTHER, WHEREIN HUMANS BECOME OBJECTS...
THE *HOURI*!
THE BOY!
VVVN!
SWOOSH

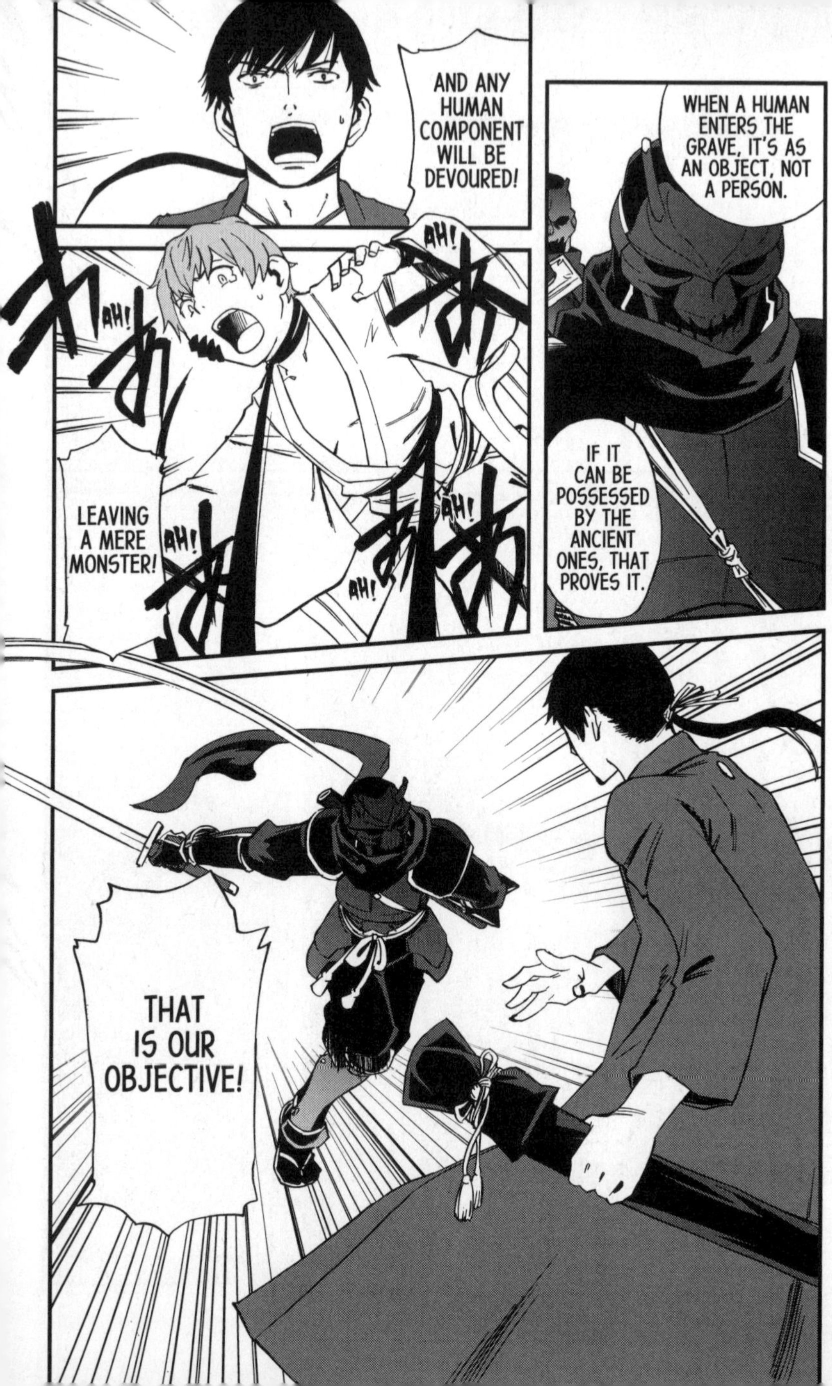

WHEN A HUMAN ENTERS THE GRAVE, IT'S AS AN OBJECT, NOT A PERSON.
IF IT CAN BE POSSESSED BY THE ANCIENT ONES, THAT PROVES IT.
AND ANY HUMAN COMPONENT WILL BE DEVOURED!
AH!
AH!
AH!
AH!
AH!
LEAVING A MERE MONSTER!
THAT IS OUR OBJECTIVE!

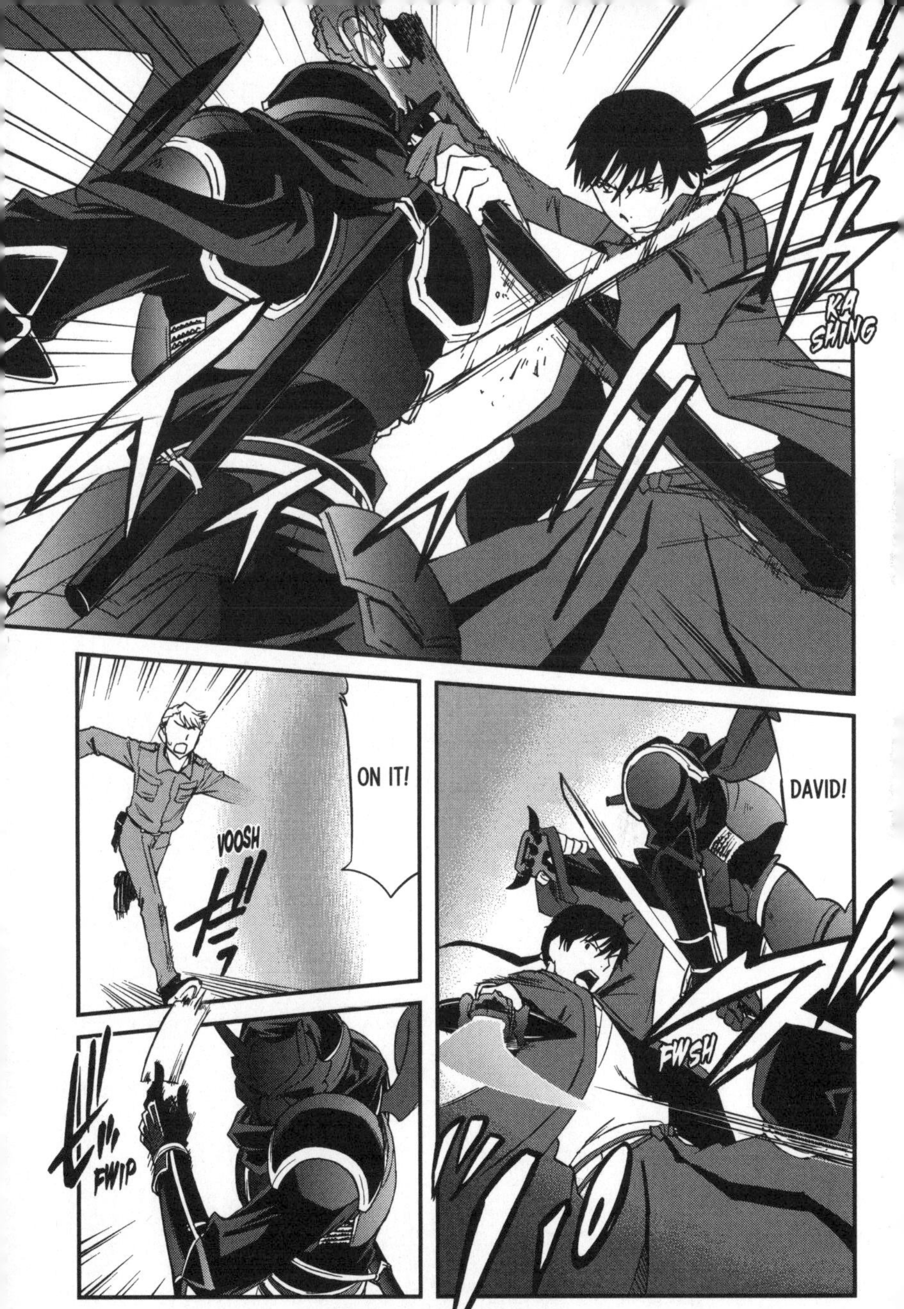
KA SHING
DAVID!
FWSH
ON IT!
VOOSH
FWIP

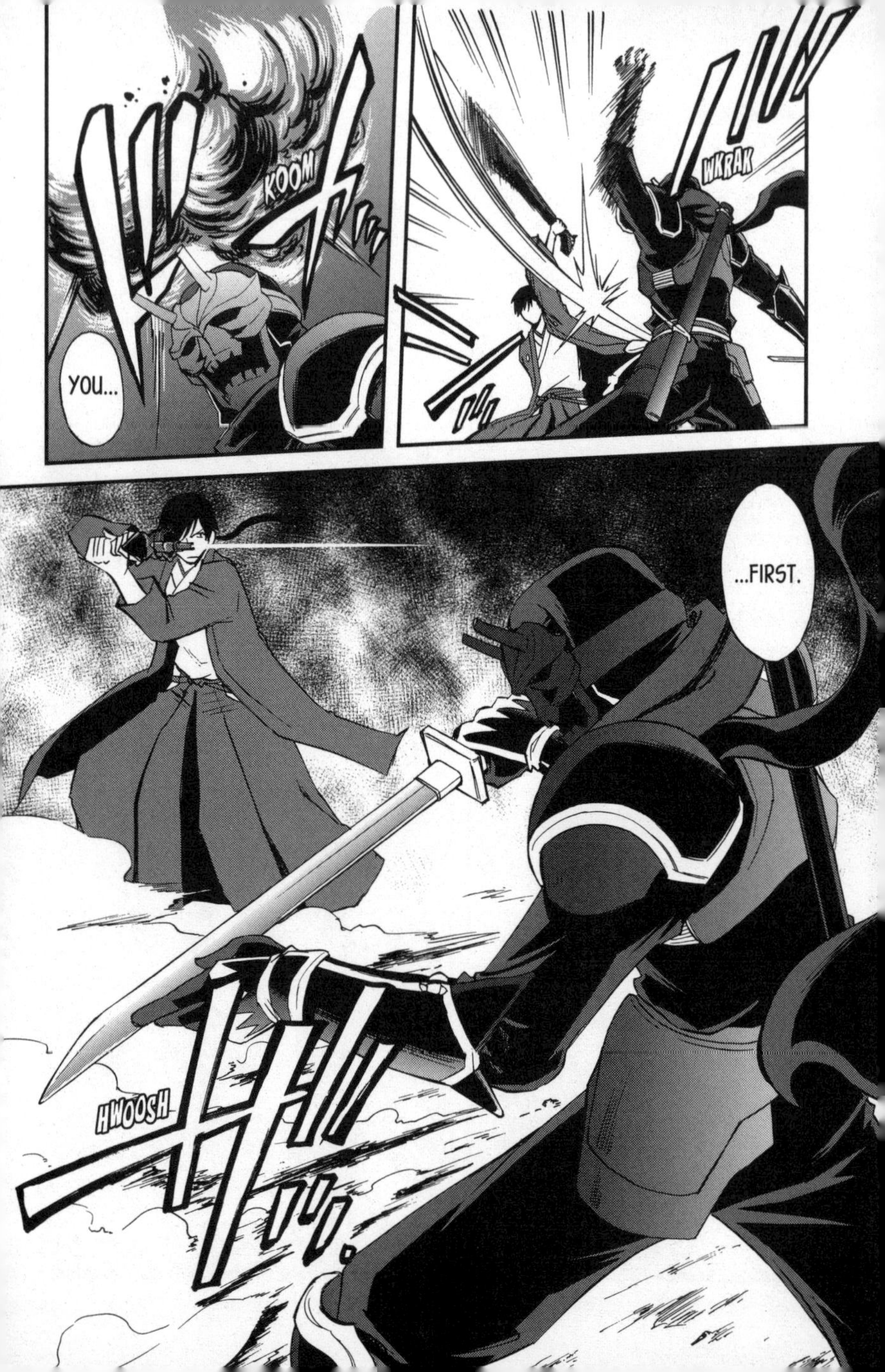
WKRAK
KOOM
YOU...
...FIRST.
HWOOSH

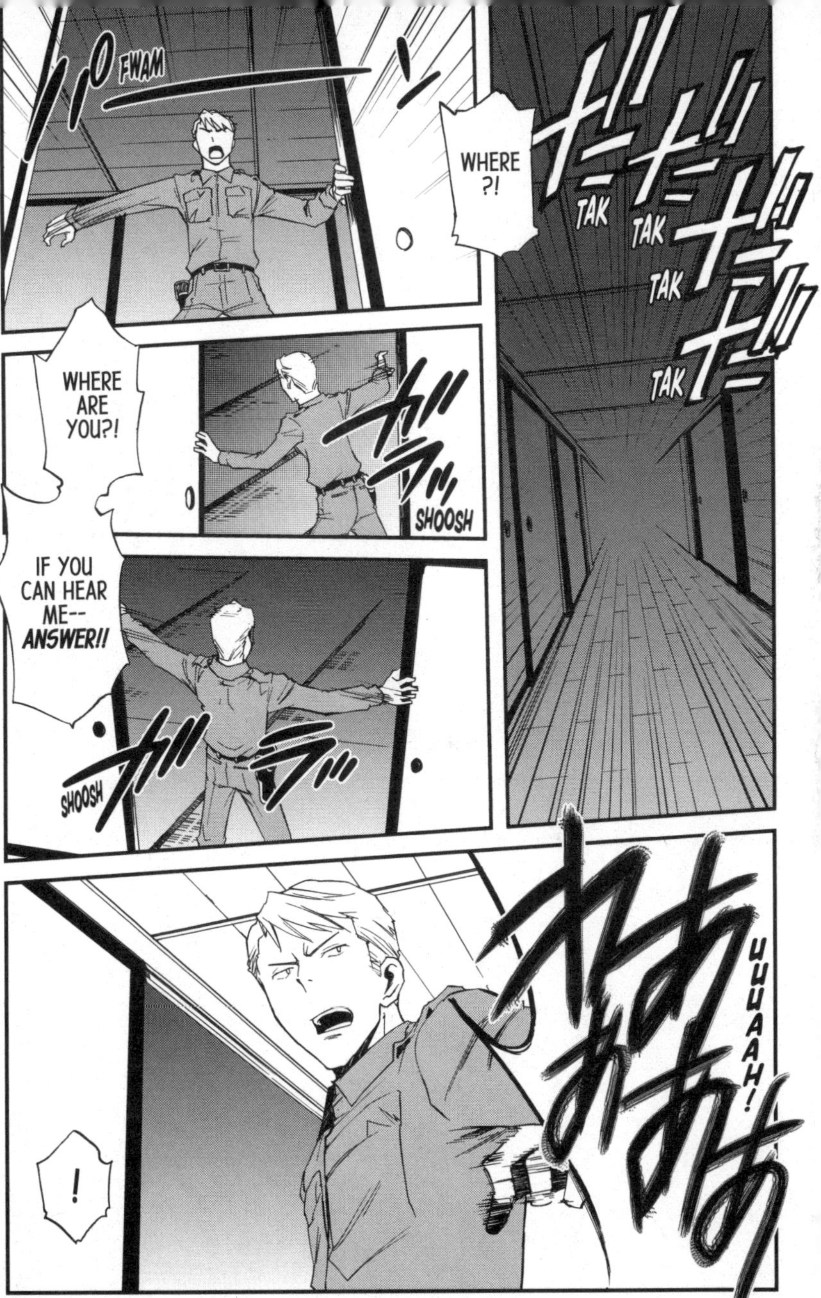

TAK
TAK
TAK
TAK
FWAM
WHERE ?!
WHERE ARE YOU?!
SHOOSH
IF YOU CAN HEAR ME-- ANSWER!!
SHOOSH
UUUUAAAH!
!

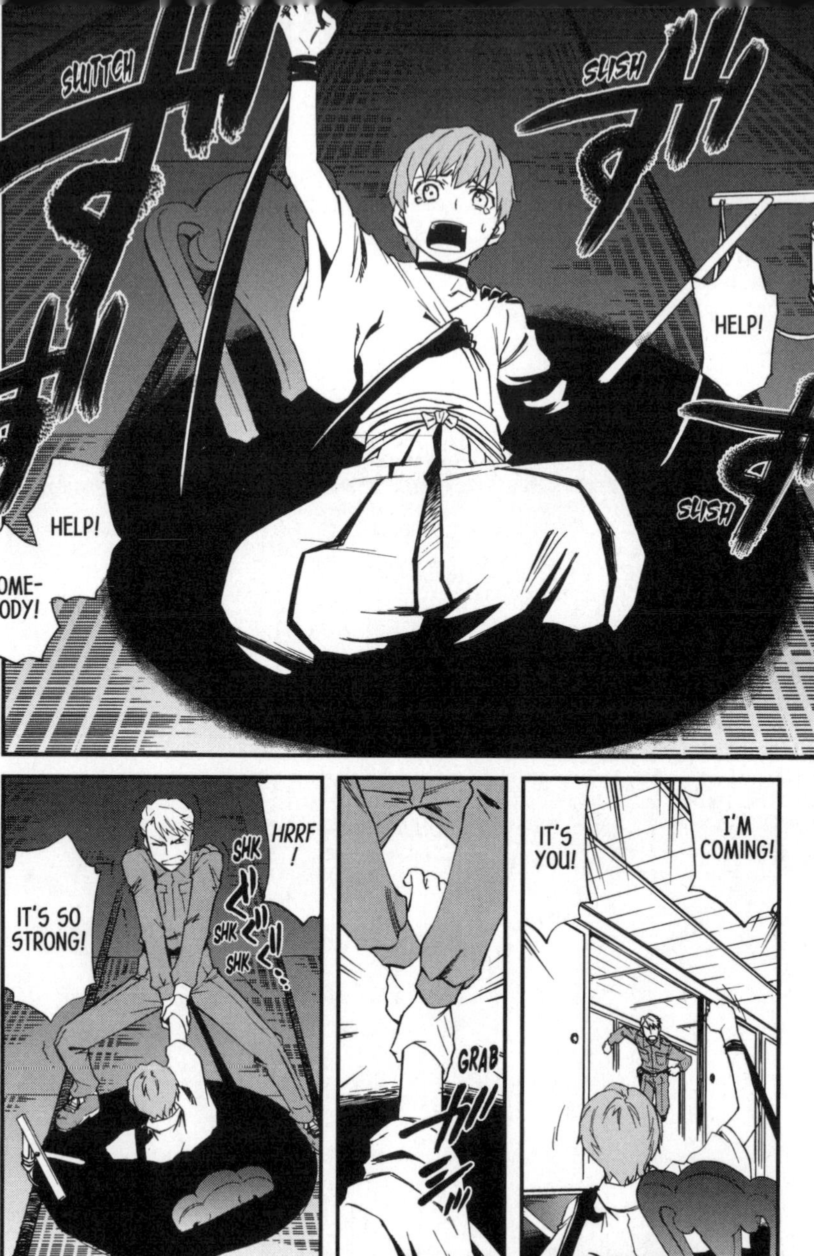
SLISH
SLUTTCH
HELP!
SLISH
HELP!
SOME-BODY!
I'M COMING!
IT'S YOU!
GRAB
HRRF!
SHK
SHK
SHK
IT'S SO STRONG!

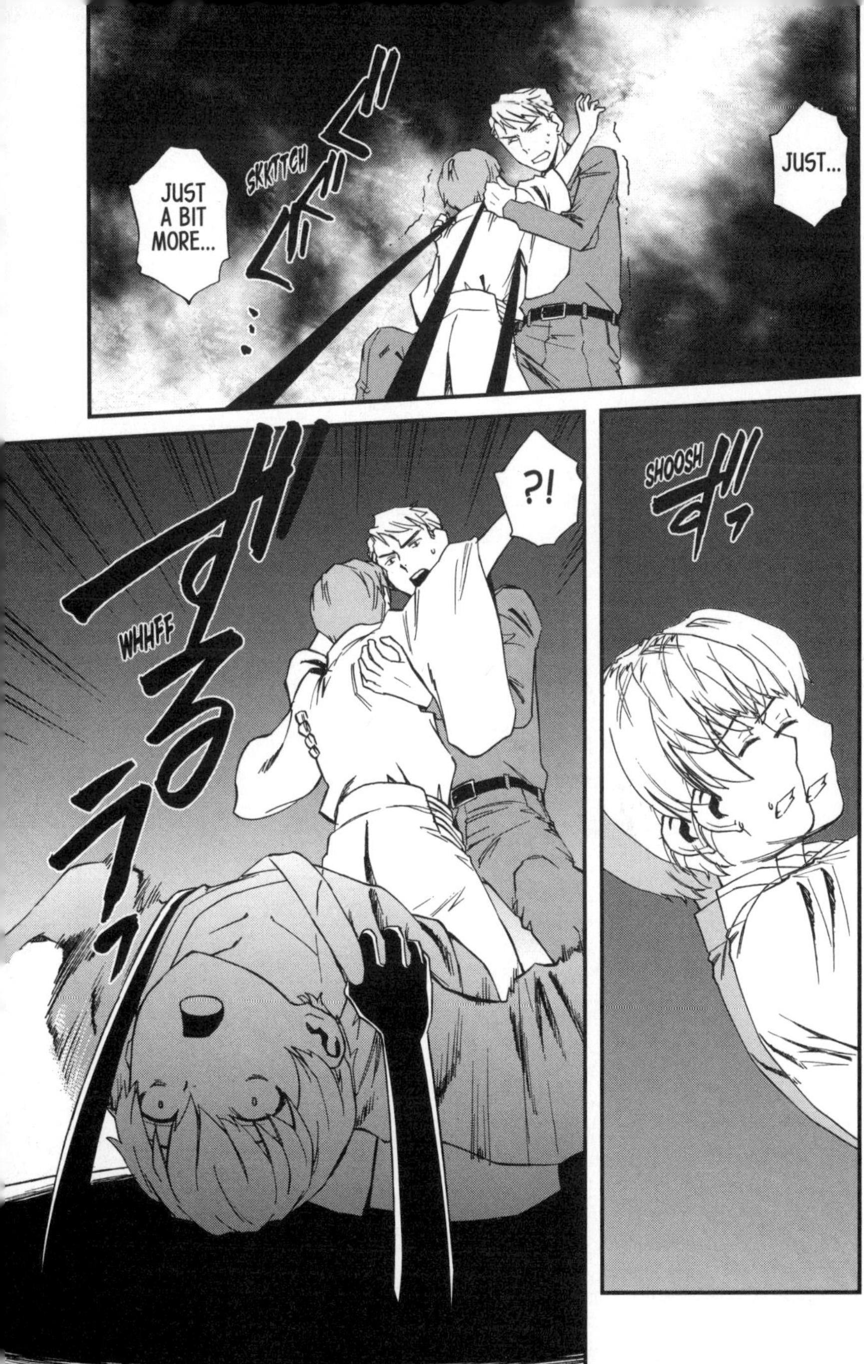
JUST...
SKKTITCH
JUST A BIT MORE...
SHOOSH
?!
WHHFF

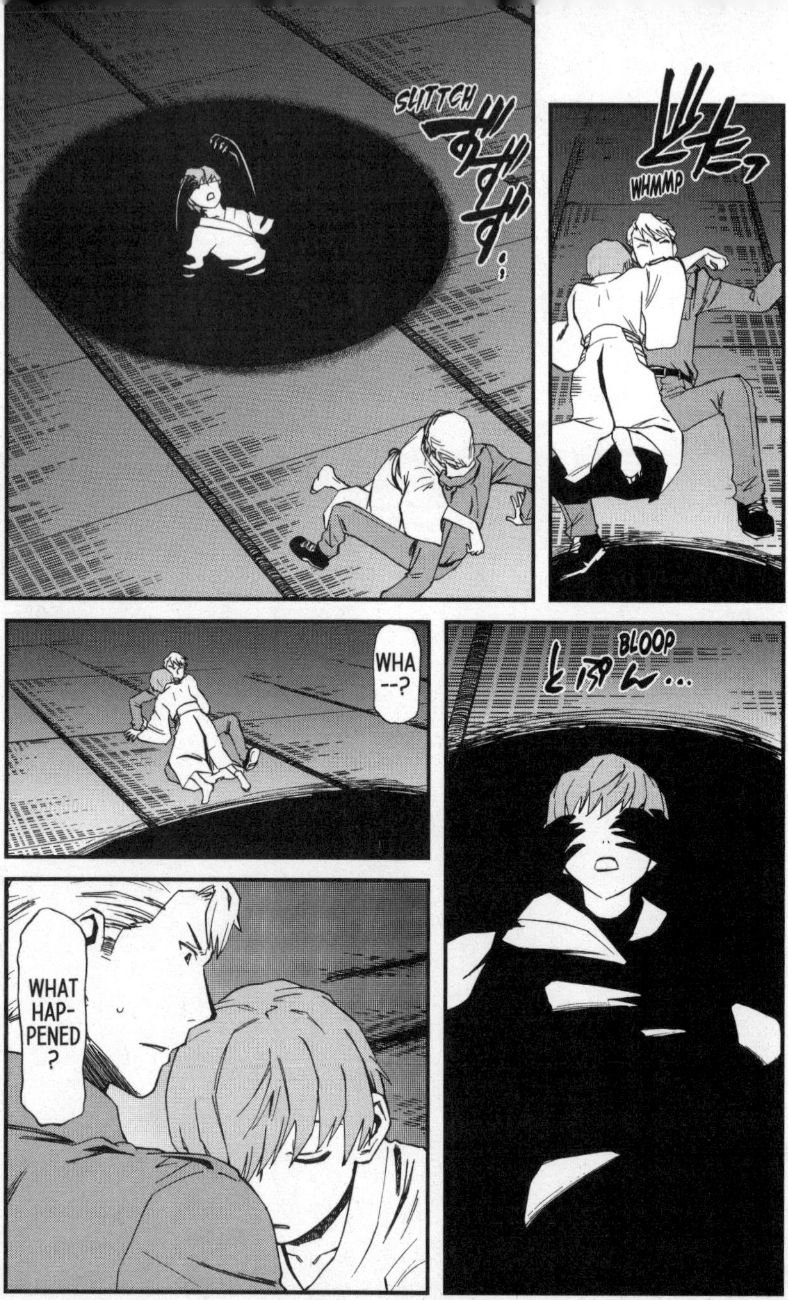

どたっ
WHMMP
SLITTCH
ずぶずぶ
BLOOP
とぷん…
WHA--?
WHAT HAP-PENED?

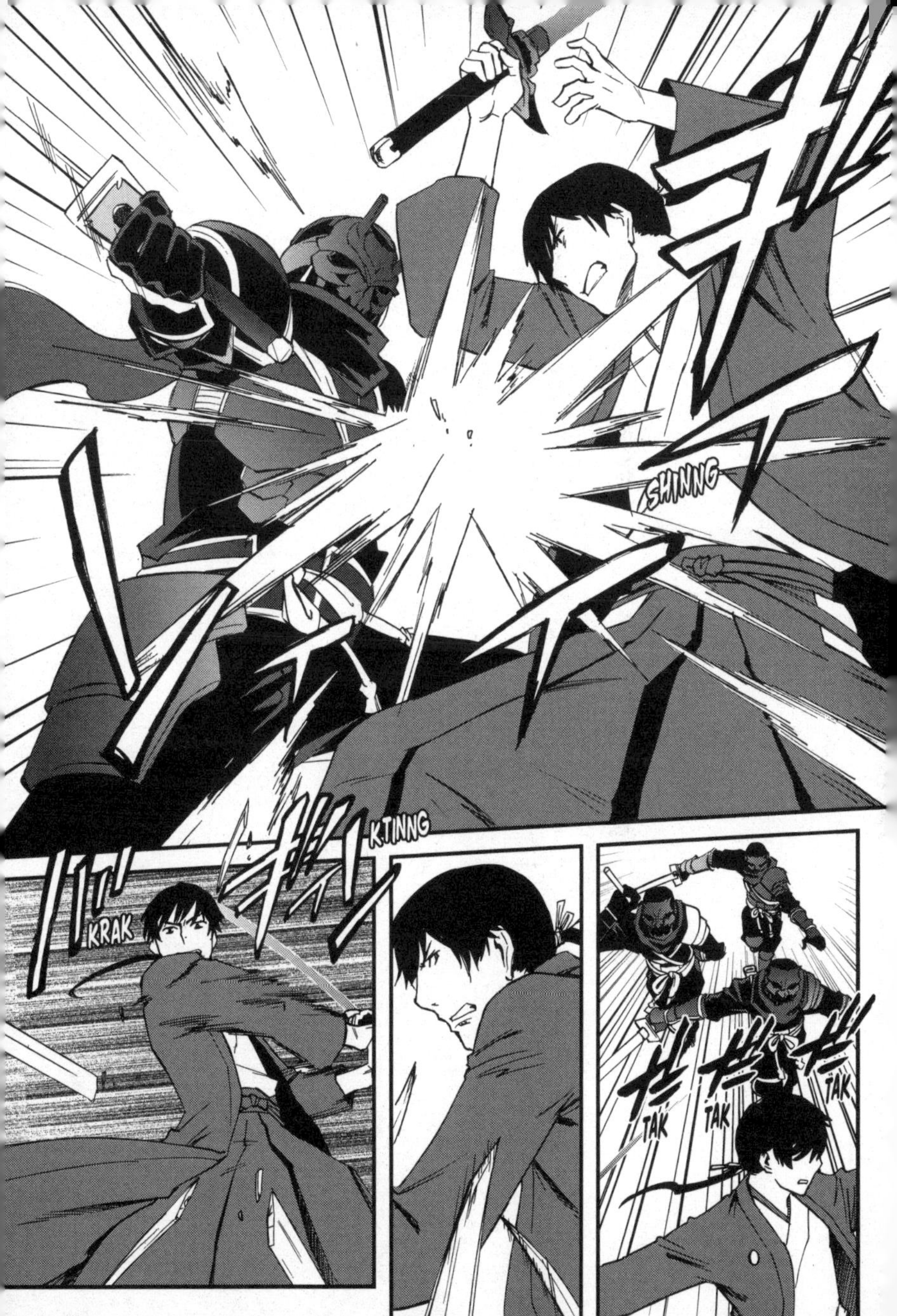
SHINNG
TAK
TAK
TAK
KTINNG
KRAK

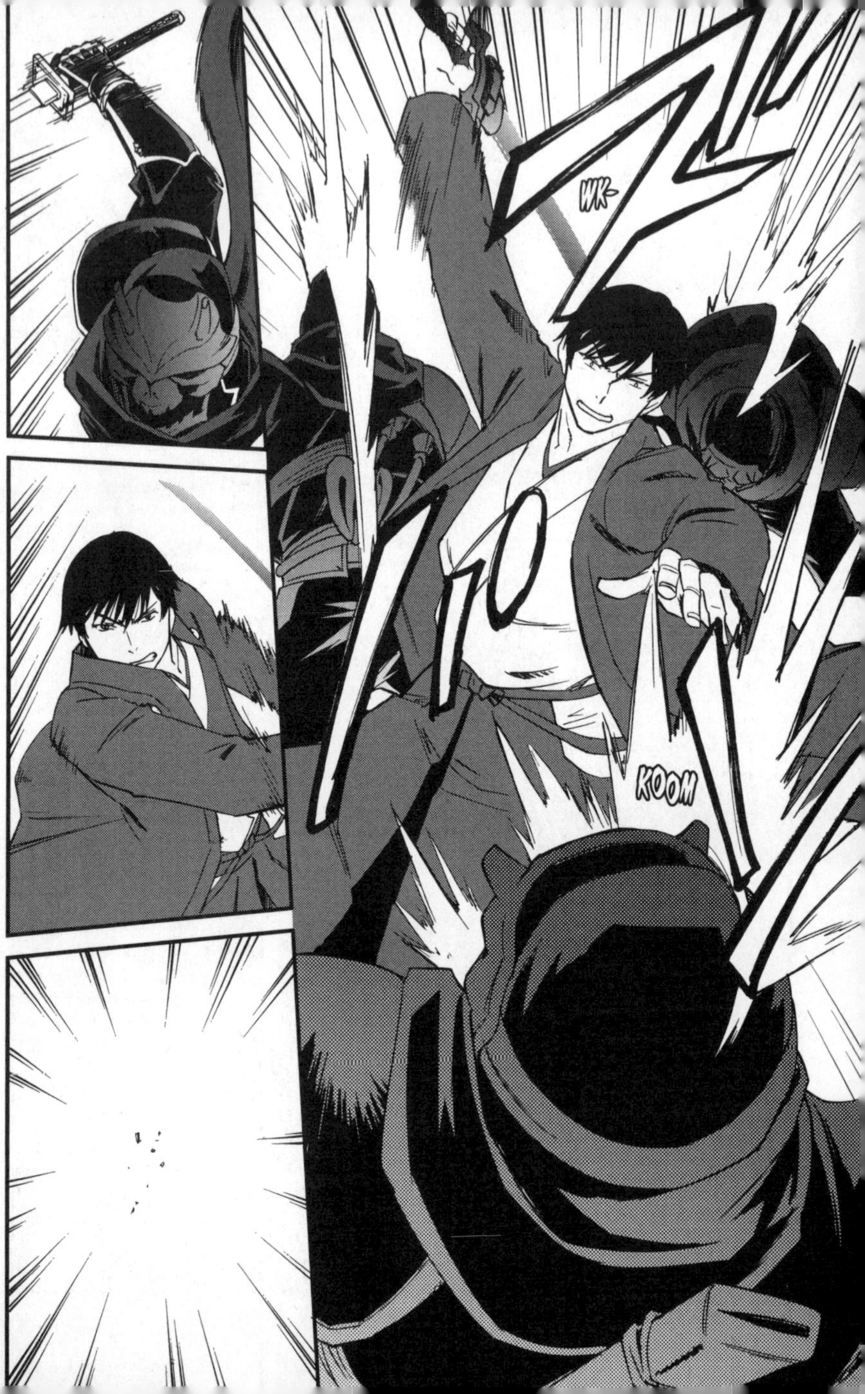
WK-
KOOM

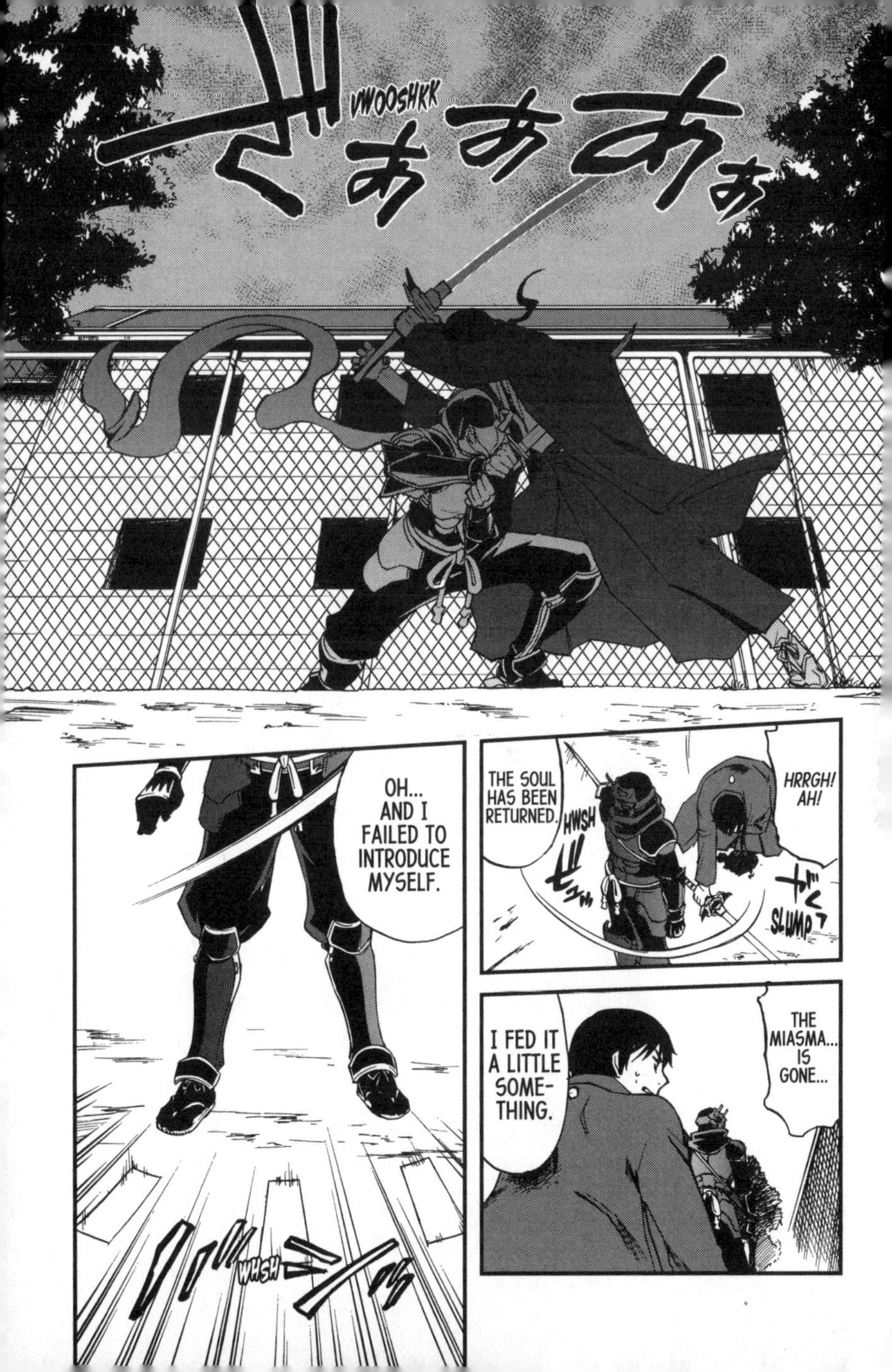
ざあああぁ
VWOOSHKK
HRRGH! AH!
THE SOUL HAS BEEN RETURNED.
HWSH
SLUMP
THE MIASMA... IS GONE...
I FED IT A LITTLE SOME-THING.
OH... AND I FAILED TO INTRODUCE MYSELF.
WHSH

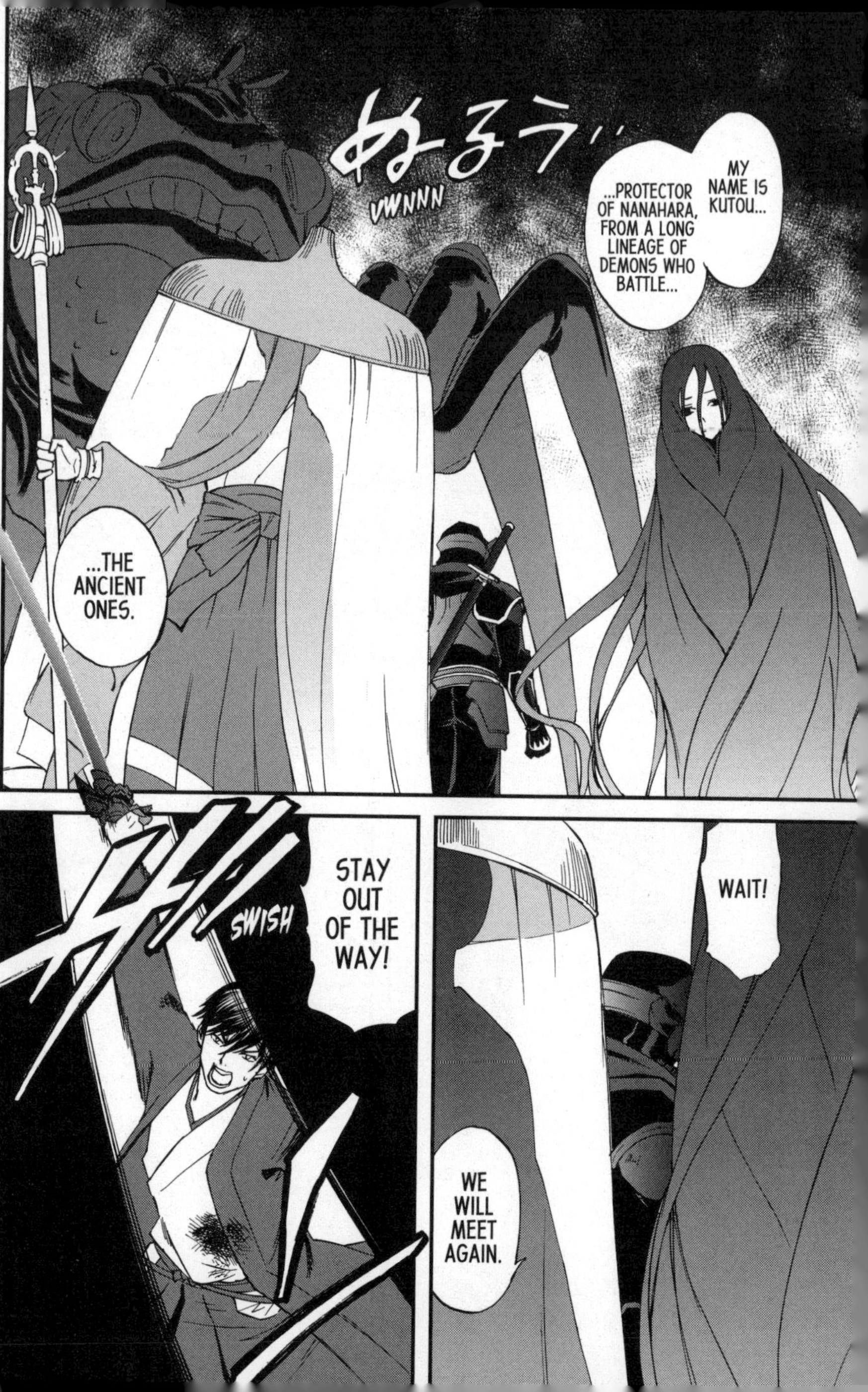
MY NAME IS KUTOU...
...PROTECTOR OF NANAHARA, FROM A LONG LINEAGE OF DEMONS WHO BATTLE...
VWNNN
...THE ANCIENT ONES.
WAIT!
WE WILL MEET AGAIN.
STAY OUT OF THE WAY!
SWISH

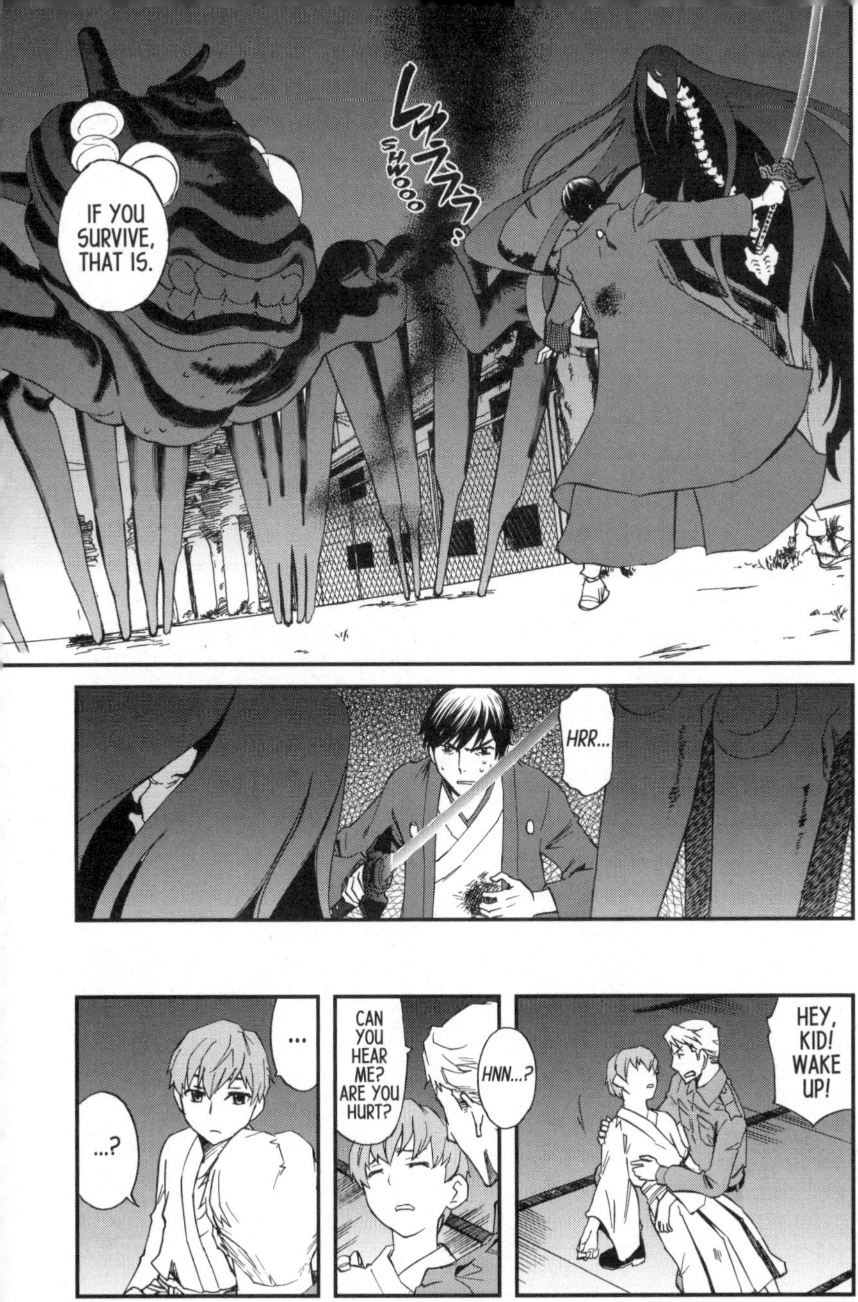
IF YOU SURVIVE, THAT IS.
SHWOOO
HRR...
HEY, KID! WAKE UP!
HNN...?
CAN YOU HEAR ME? ARE YOU HURT?
...
...?

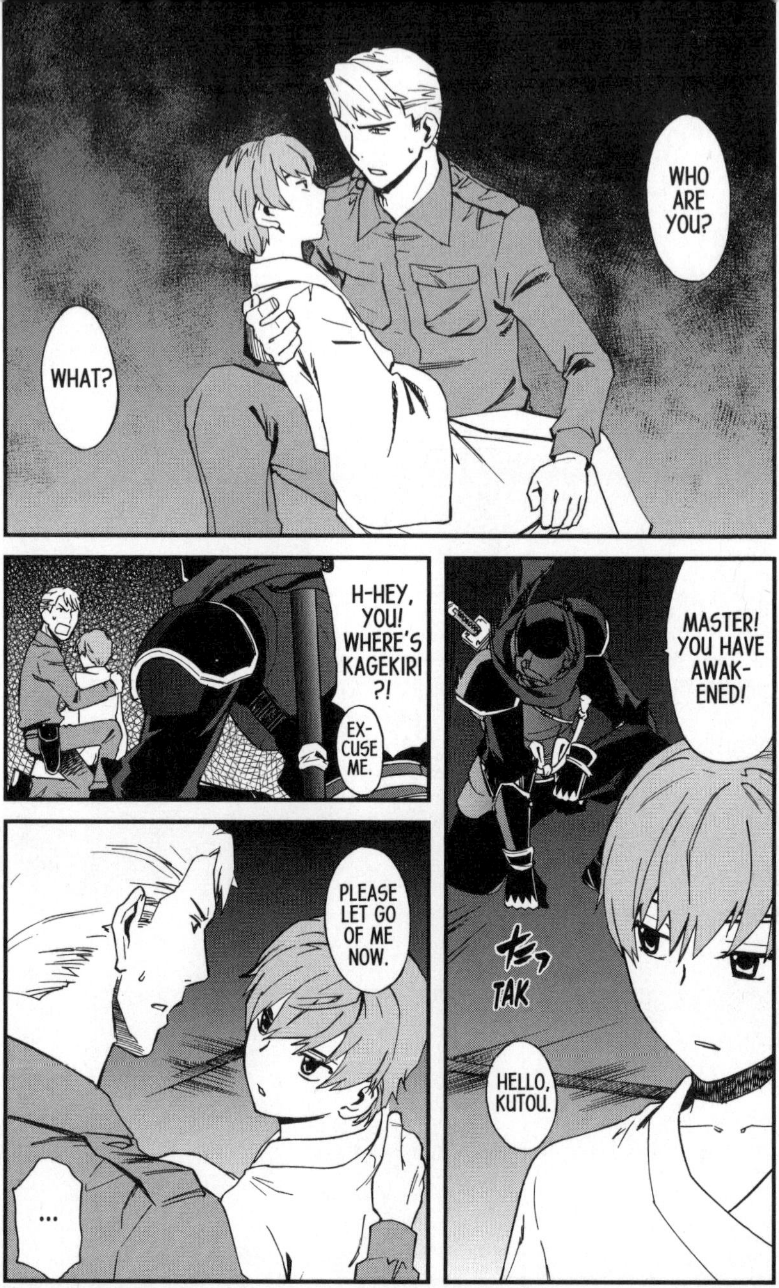
WHO ARE YOU?
WHAT?
MASTER! YOU HAVE AWAK-ENED!
TAK
HELLO, KUTOU.
H-HEY, YOU! WHERE'S KAGEKIRI ?!
EX-CUSE ME.
PLEASE LET GO OF ME NOW.
...

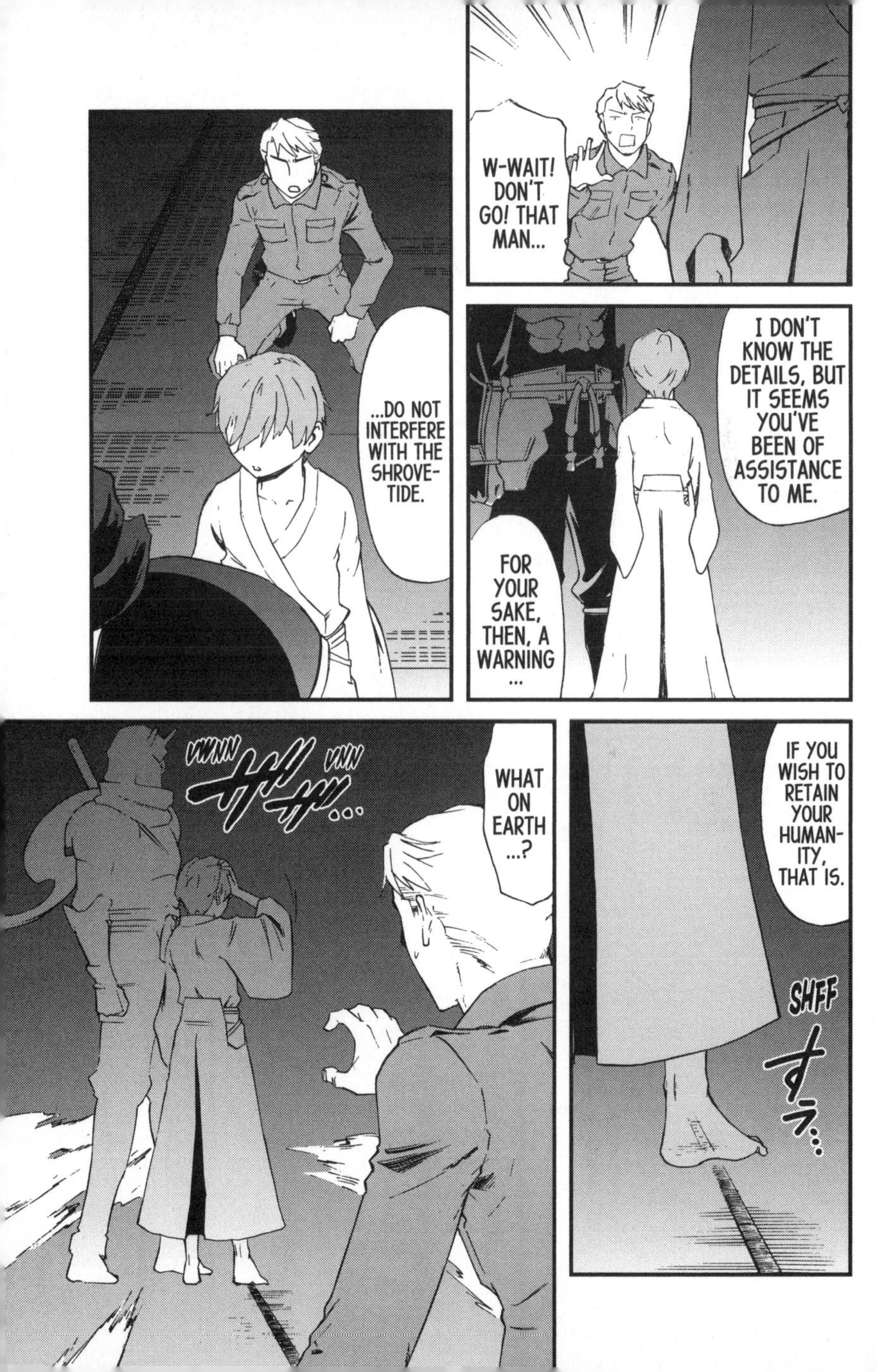

W-WAIT! DON'T GO! THAT MAN...
I DON'T KNOW THE DETAILS, BUT IT SEEMS YOU'VE BEEN OF ASSISTANCE TO ME.
FOR YOUR SAKE, THEN, A WARNING...
...DO NOT INTERFERE WITH THE SHROVE-TIDE.
IF YOU WISH TO RETAIN YOUR HUMAN-ITY, THAT IS.
SHFF
すう...
WHAT ON EARTH...?
VWNN
VNN

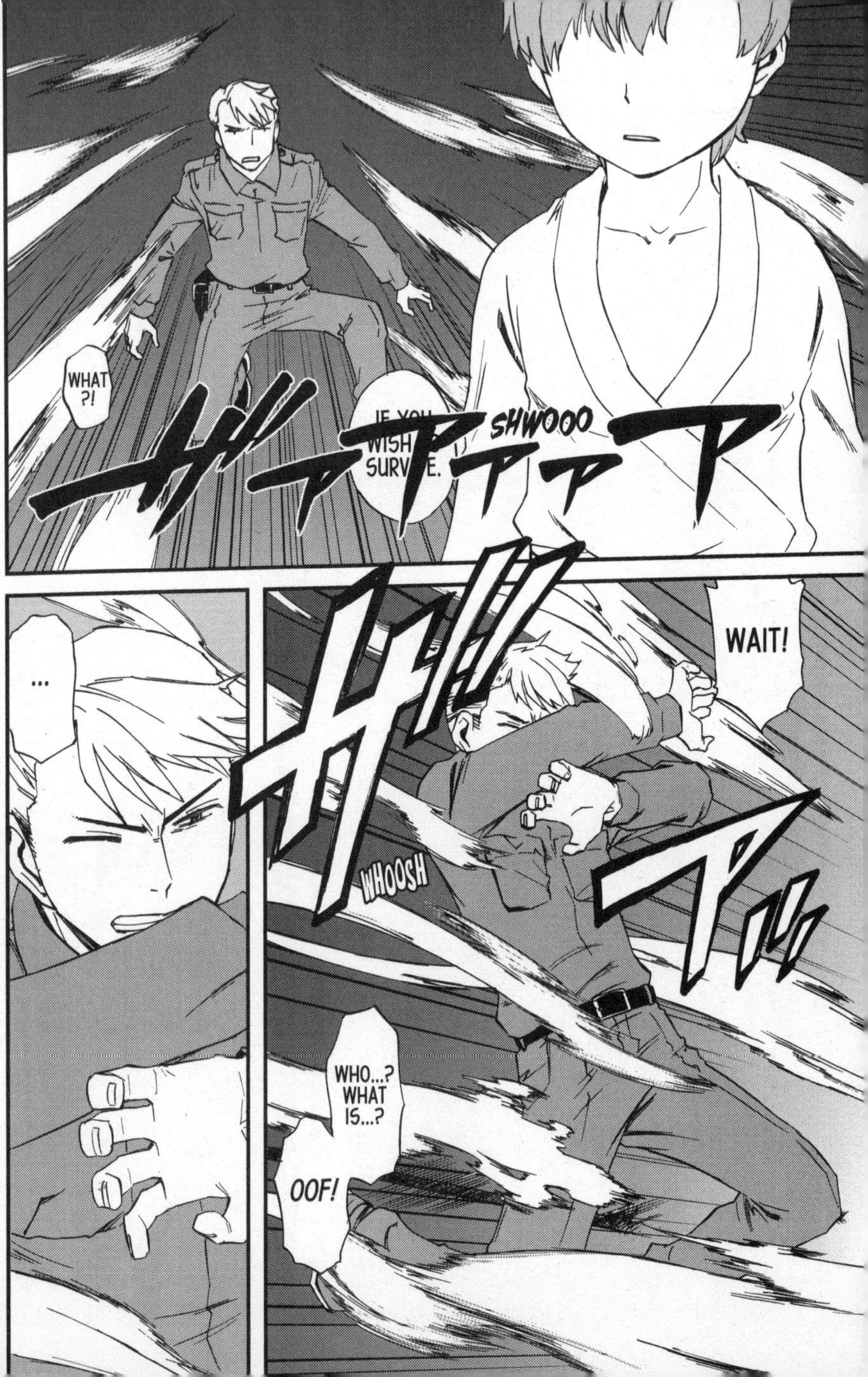
SHWOOO
IF YOU WISH TO SURVIVE.
WHAT ?!
WAIT!
WHOOSH
WHO...? WHAT IS...?
OOF!
...

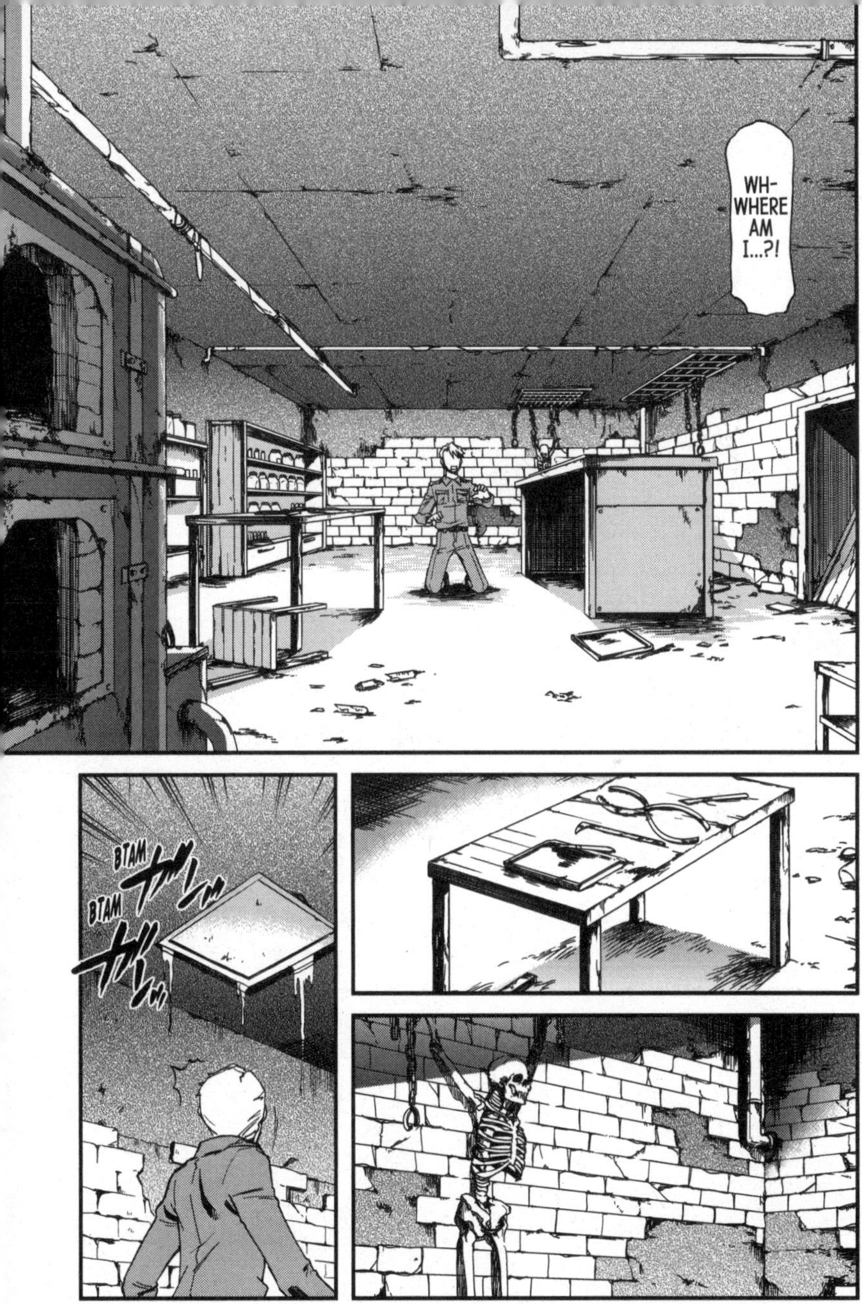
WH-WHERE AM I...?!
BTAM
BTAM

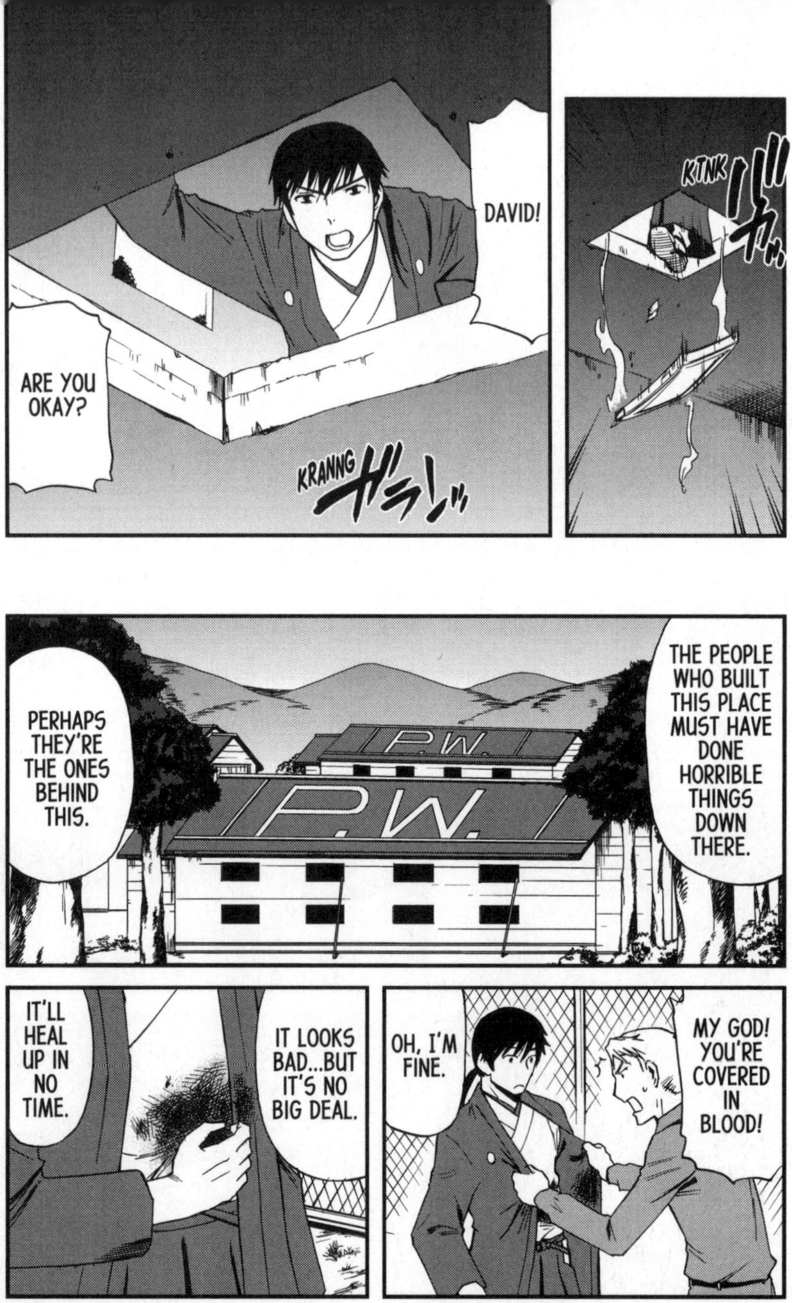
KTNK
DAVID!
ARE YOU OKAY?
KRANNG
THE PEOPLE WHO BUILT THIS PLACE MUST HAVE DONE HORRIBLE THINGS DOWN THERE.
P.W.
P.W.
PERHAPS THEY'RE THE ONES BEHIND THIS.
MY GOD! YOU'RE COVERED IN BLOOD!
OH, I'M FINE.
IT LOOKS BAD...BUT IT'S NO BIG DEAL.
IT'LL HEAL UP IN NO TIME.

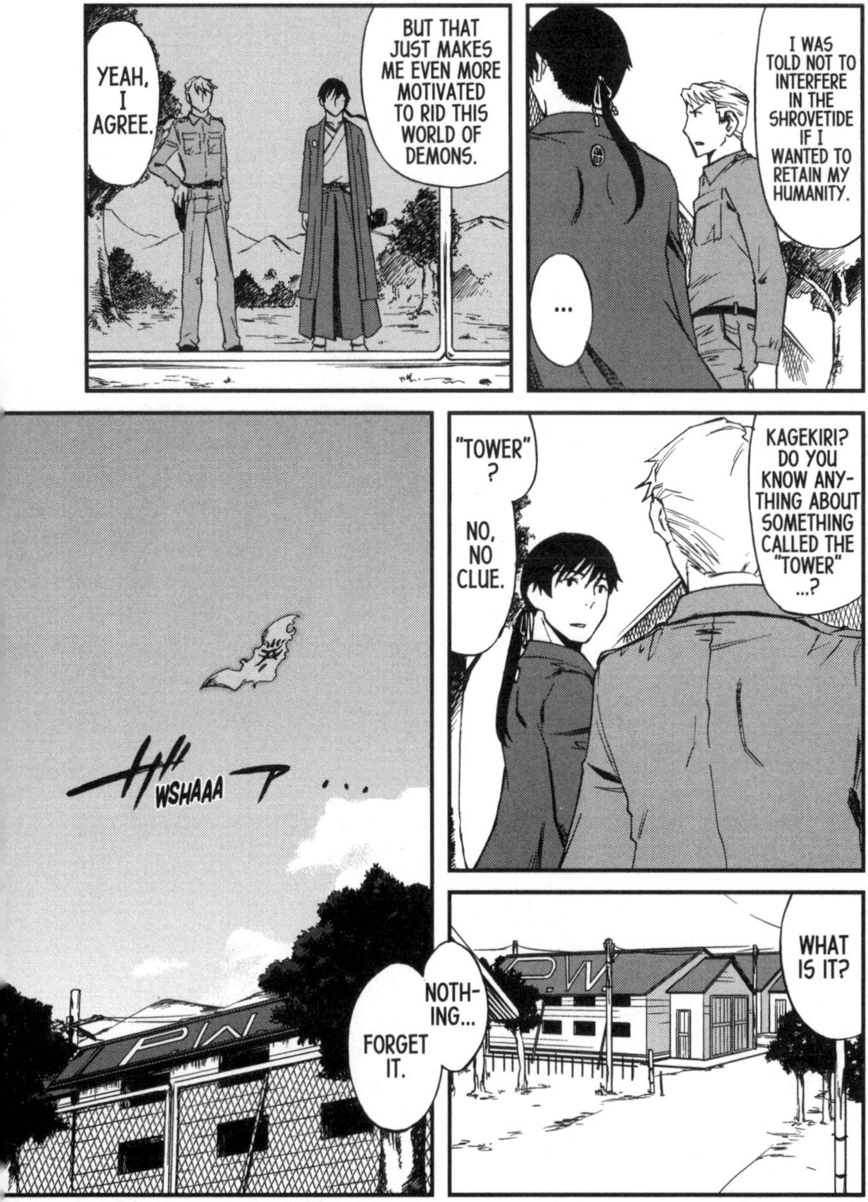
I WAS TOLD NOT TO INTERFERE IN THE SHROVETIDE IF I WANTED TO RETAIN MY HUMANITY.
...
BUT THAT JUST MAKES ME EVEN MORE MOTIVATED TO RID THIS WORLD OF DEMONS.
YEAH, I AGREE.
KAGEKIRI? DO YOU KNOW ANY-THING ABOUT SOMETHING CALLED THE "TOWER" ...?
"TOWER"?
NO, NO CLUE.
WHAT IS IT?
NOTH-ING...
FORGET IT.
WSHAAA

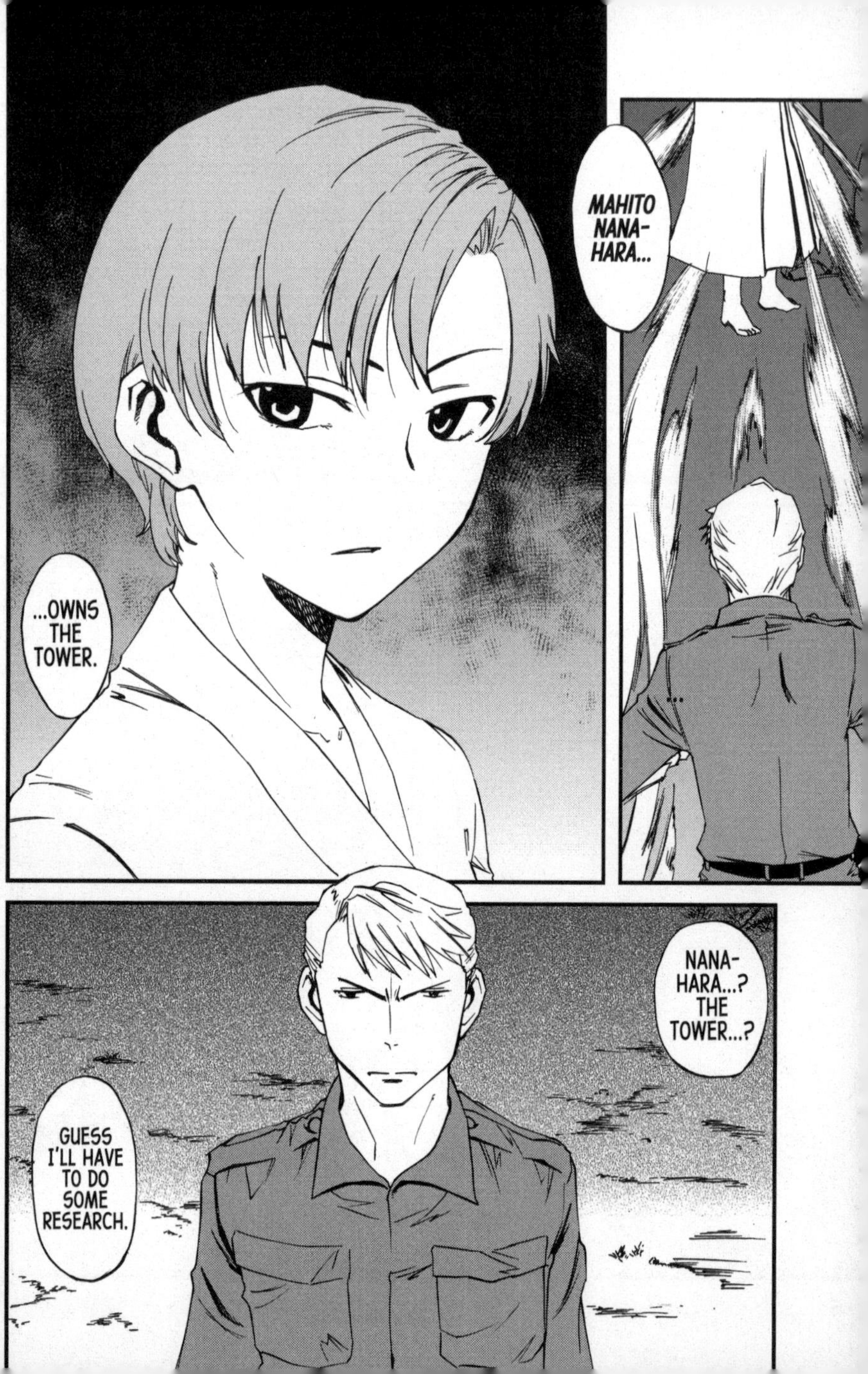
MAHITO NANA-HARA...
...
...OWNS THE TOWER.
NANA-HARA...? THE TOWER...?
GUESS I'LL HAVE TO DO SOME RESEARCH.

十六夜鬼譚

BLOOD·C

DEMONIC
MOONLIGHT

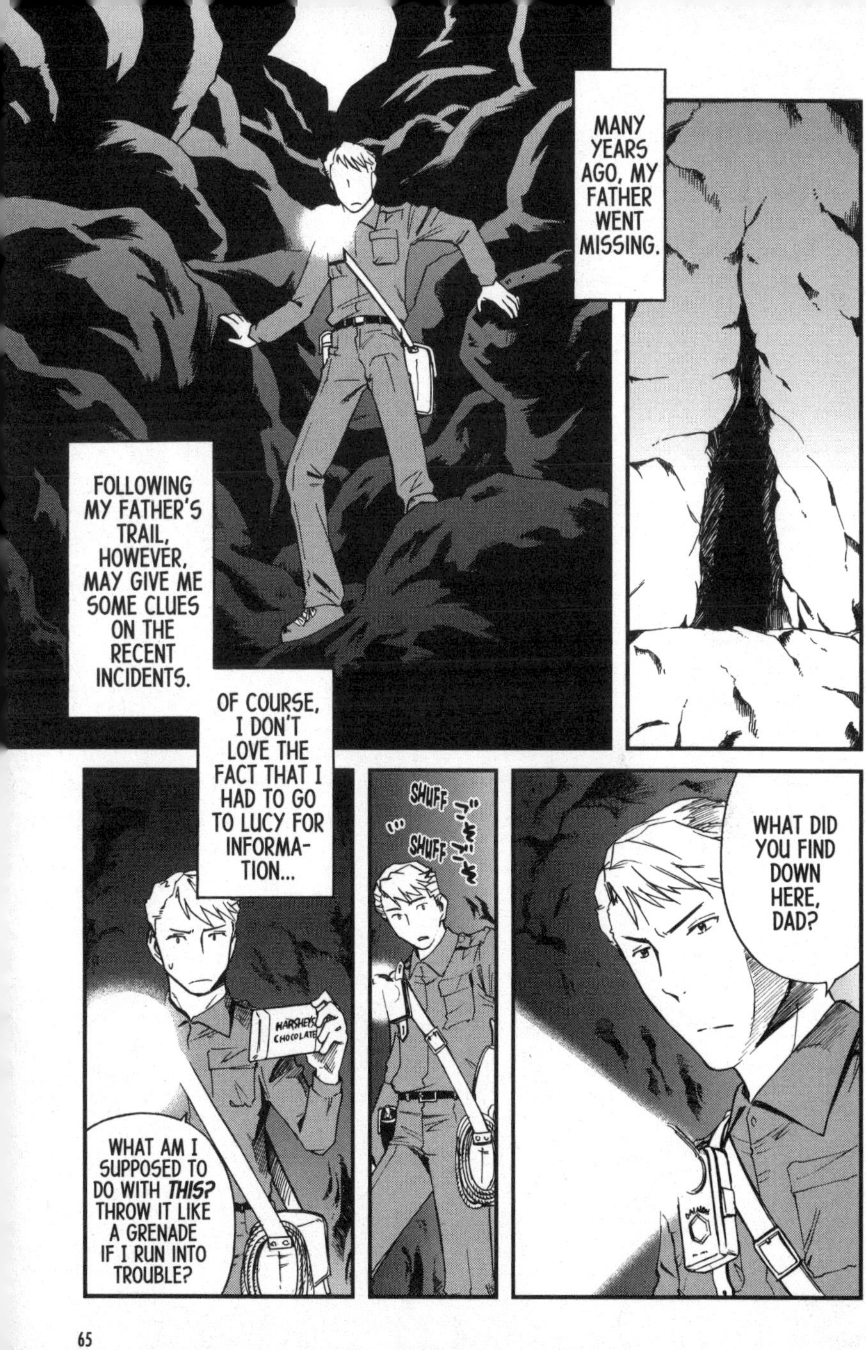

MANY YEARS AGO, MY FATHER WENT MISSING.
FOLLOWING MY FATHER'S TRAIL, HOWEVER, MAY GIVE ME SOME CLUES ON THE RECENT INCIDENTS.
OF COURSE, I DON'T LOVE THE FACT THAT I HAD TO GO TO LUCY FOR INFORMATION...
HARSHEY'S CHOCOLATE
WHAT AM I SUPPOSED TO DO WITH ***THIS?*** THROW IT LIKE A GRENADE IF I RUN INTO TROUBLE?
SHUFF
...
SHUFF
WHAT DID YOU FIND DOWN HERE, DAD?

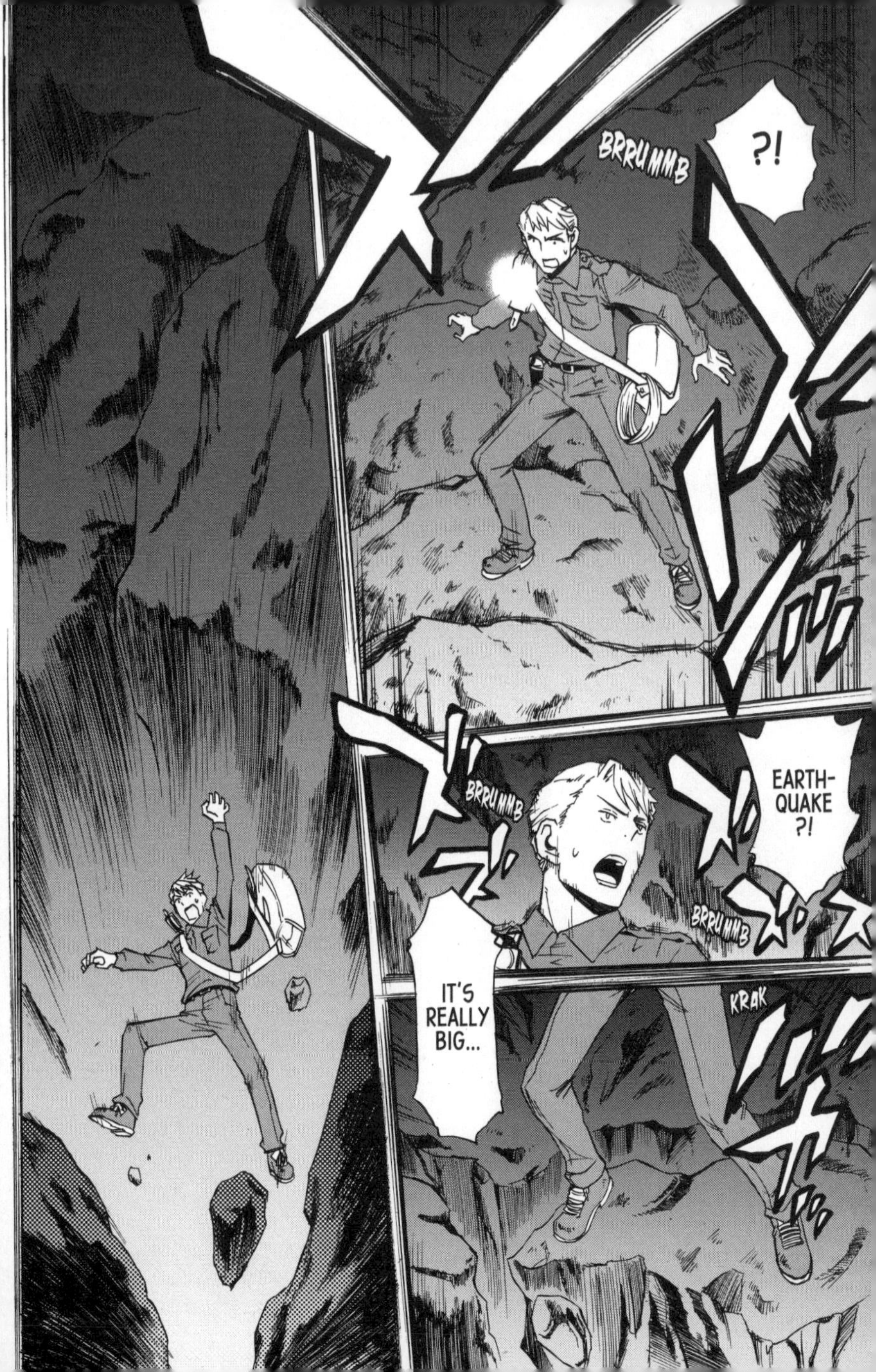
BRRUMMB
?!
EARTH-QUAKE ?!
BRRUMMB
BRRUMMB
KRAK
IT'S REALLY BIG...

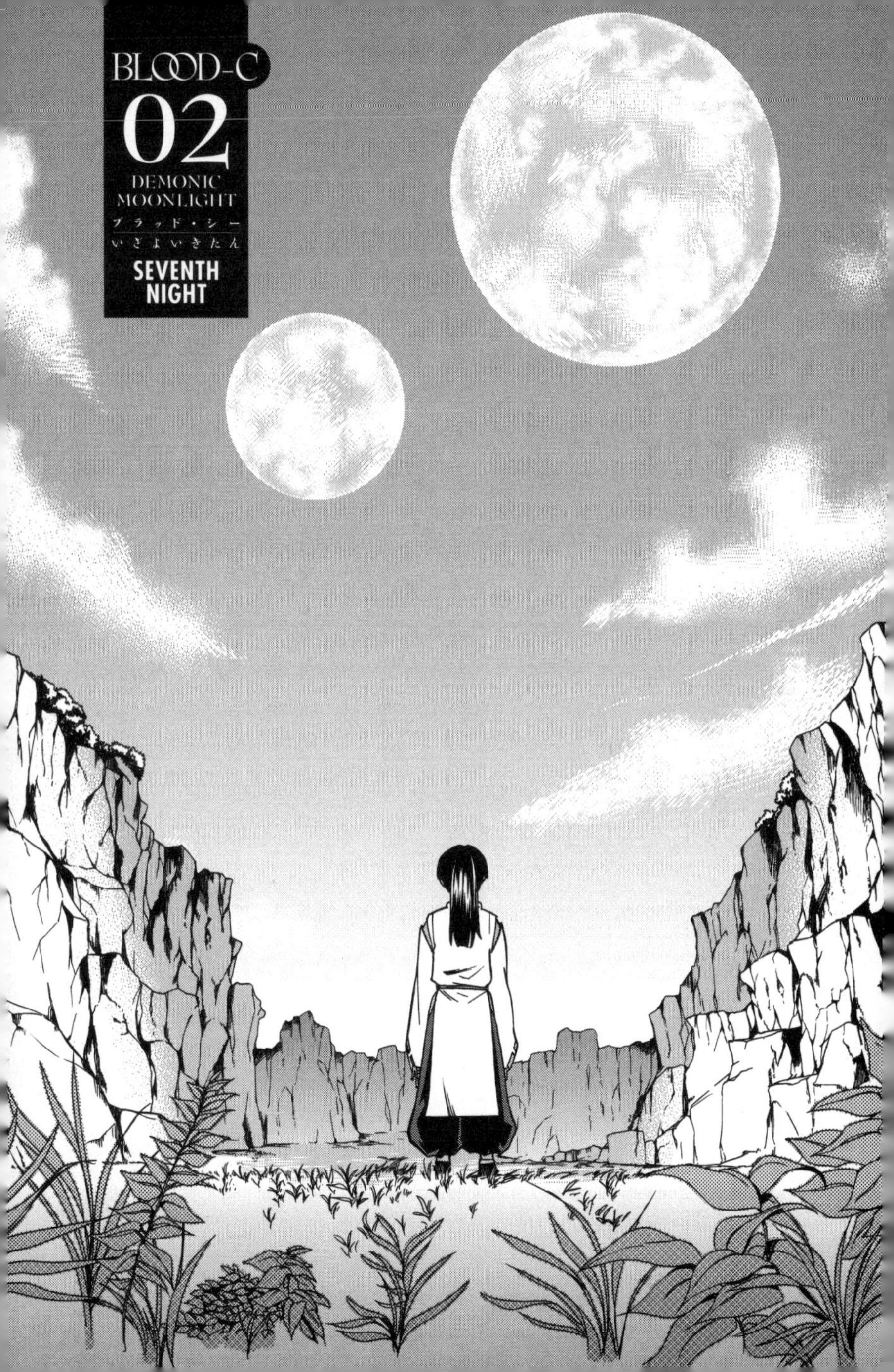
BLOOD-C
02
DEMONIC MOONLIGHT
ブラッド・シー
いざよいきたん
SEVENTH NIGHT

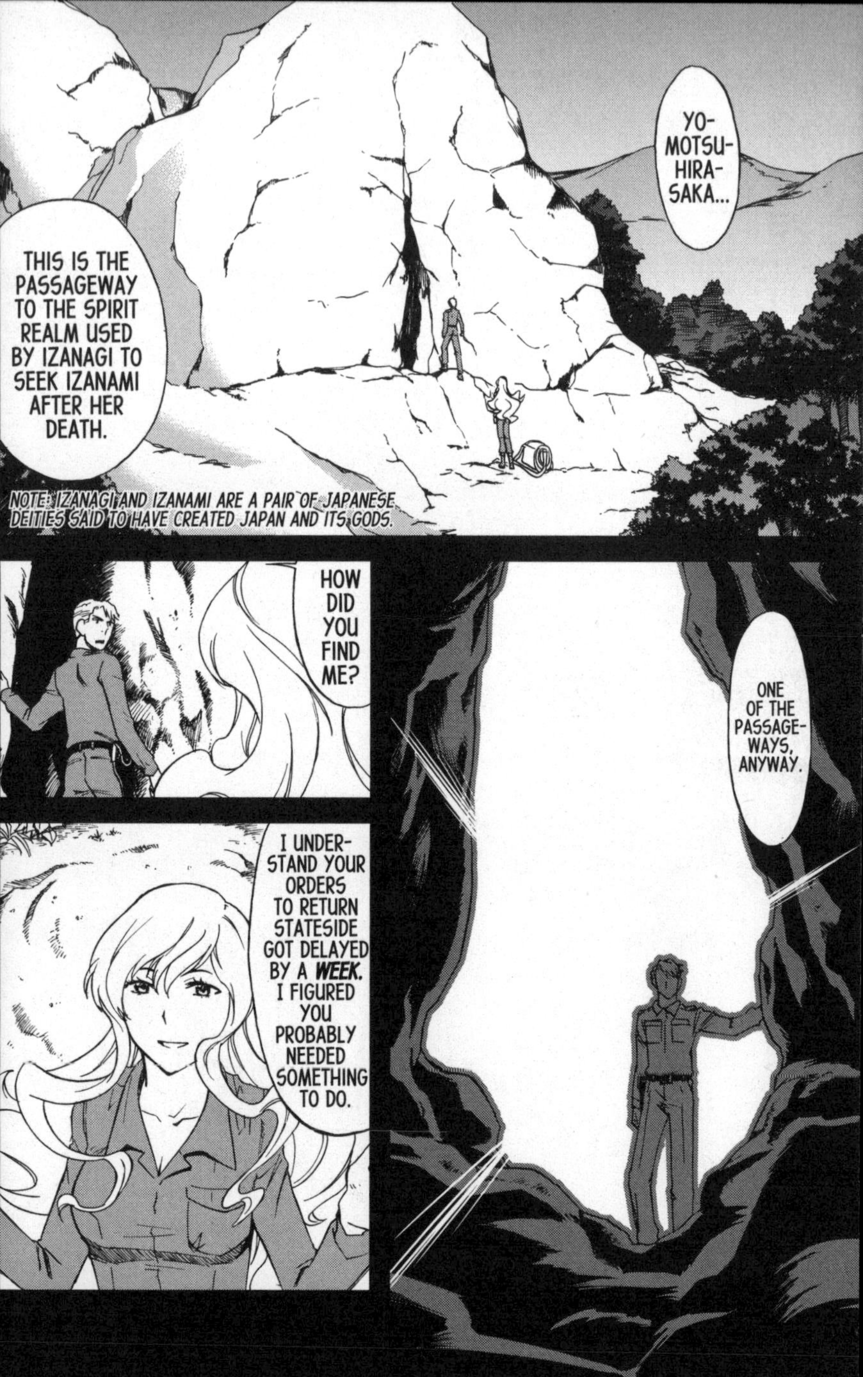
YO-MOTSU-HIRA-SAKA...
THIS IS THE PASSAGEWAY TO THE SPIRIT REALM USED BY IZANAGI TO SEEK IZANAMI AFTER HER DEATH.
NOTE: IZANAGI AND IZANAMI ARE A PAIR OF JAPANESE DEITIES SAID TO HAVE CREATED JAPAN AND ITS GODS.
ONE OF THE PASSAGE-WAYS, ANYWAY.
HOW DID YOU FIND ME?
I UNDER-STAND YOUR ORDERS TO RETURN STATESIDE GOT DELAYED BY A ***WEEK.*** I FIGURED YOU PROBABLY NEEDED SOMETHING TO DO.

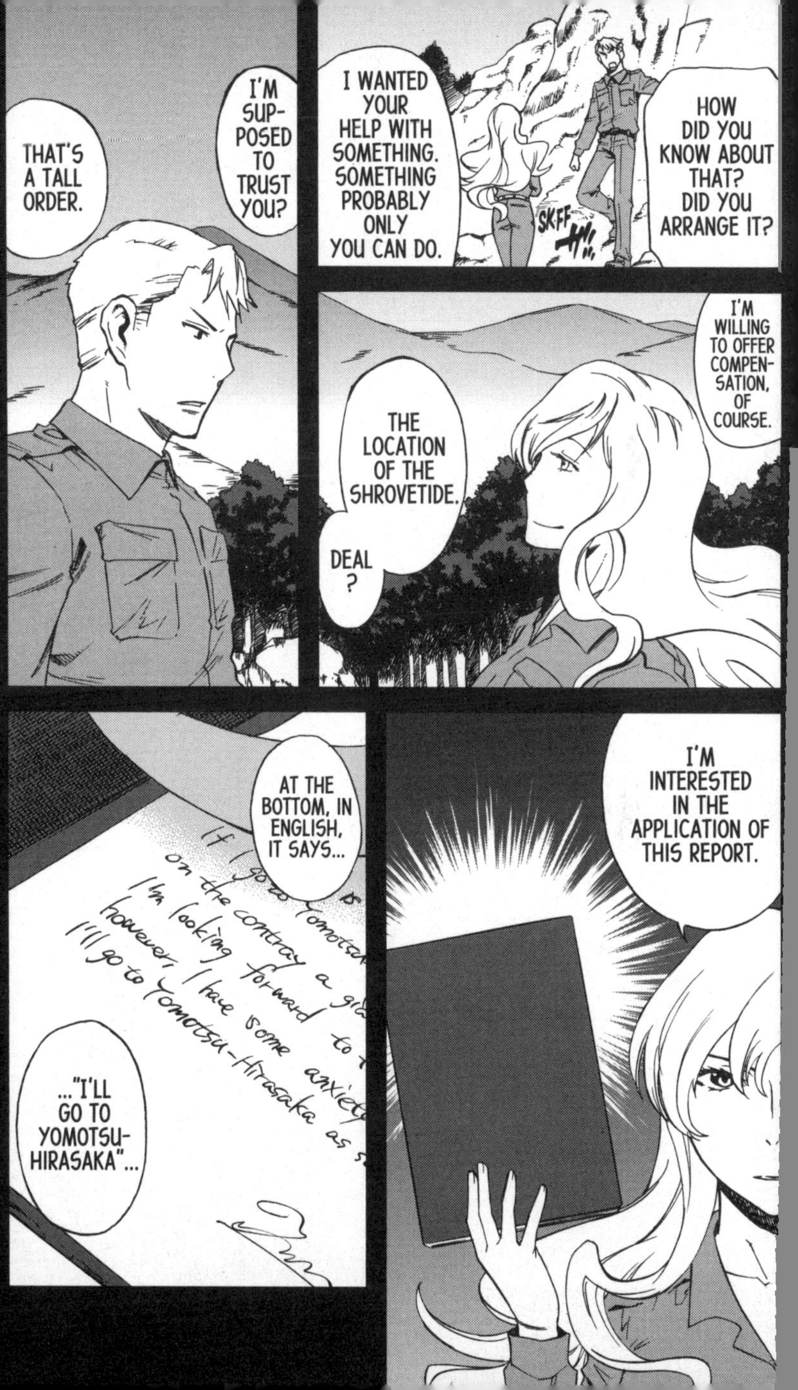
HOW DID YOU KNOW ABOUT THAT? DID YOU ARRANGE IT?
SKFF
I WANTED YOUR HELP WITH SOMETHING. SOMETHING PROBABLY ONLY YOU CAN DO.
I'M WILLING TO OFFER COMPENSATION, OF COURSE.
THE LOCATION OF THE SHROVETIDE.
DEAL?
I'M SUPPOSED TO TRUST YOU?
THAT'S A TALL ORDER.
I'M INTERESTED IN THE APPLICATION OF THIS REPORT.
AT THE BOTTOM, IN ENGLISH, IT SAYS...
on the contrary a
I'm looking forward to
however, I have some anxiety
I'll go to Yomotsu-Hirasaka as
..."I'LL GO TO YOMOTSU-HIRASAKA"...

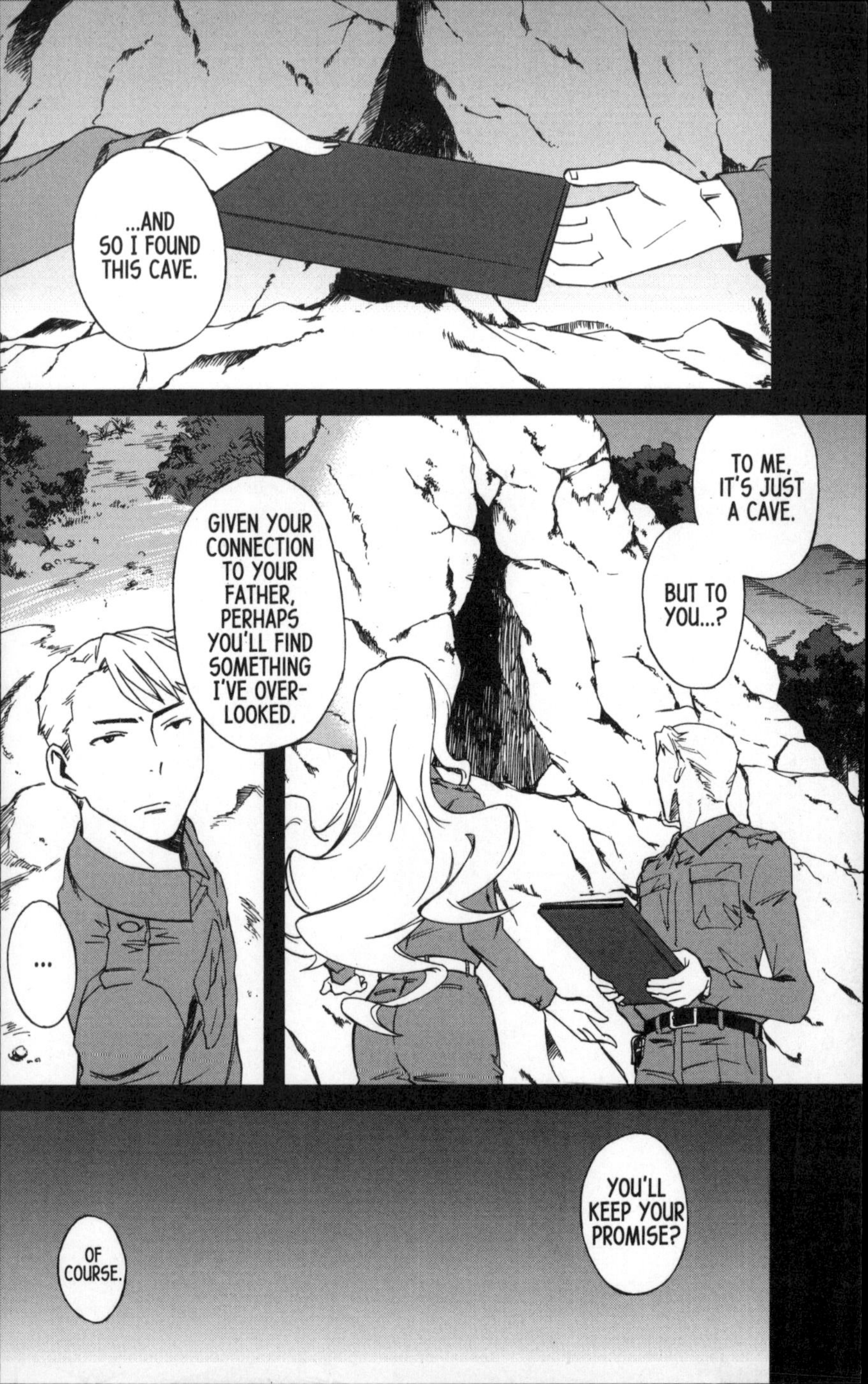
...AND SO I FOUND THIS CAVE.
TO ME, IT'S JUST A CAVE.
BUT TO YOU...?
GIVEN YOUR CONNECTION TO YOUR FATHER, PERHAPS YOU'LL FIND SOMETHING I'VE OVER-LOOKED.
...
YOU'LL KEEP YOUR PROMISE?
OF COURSE.

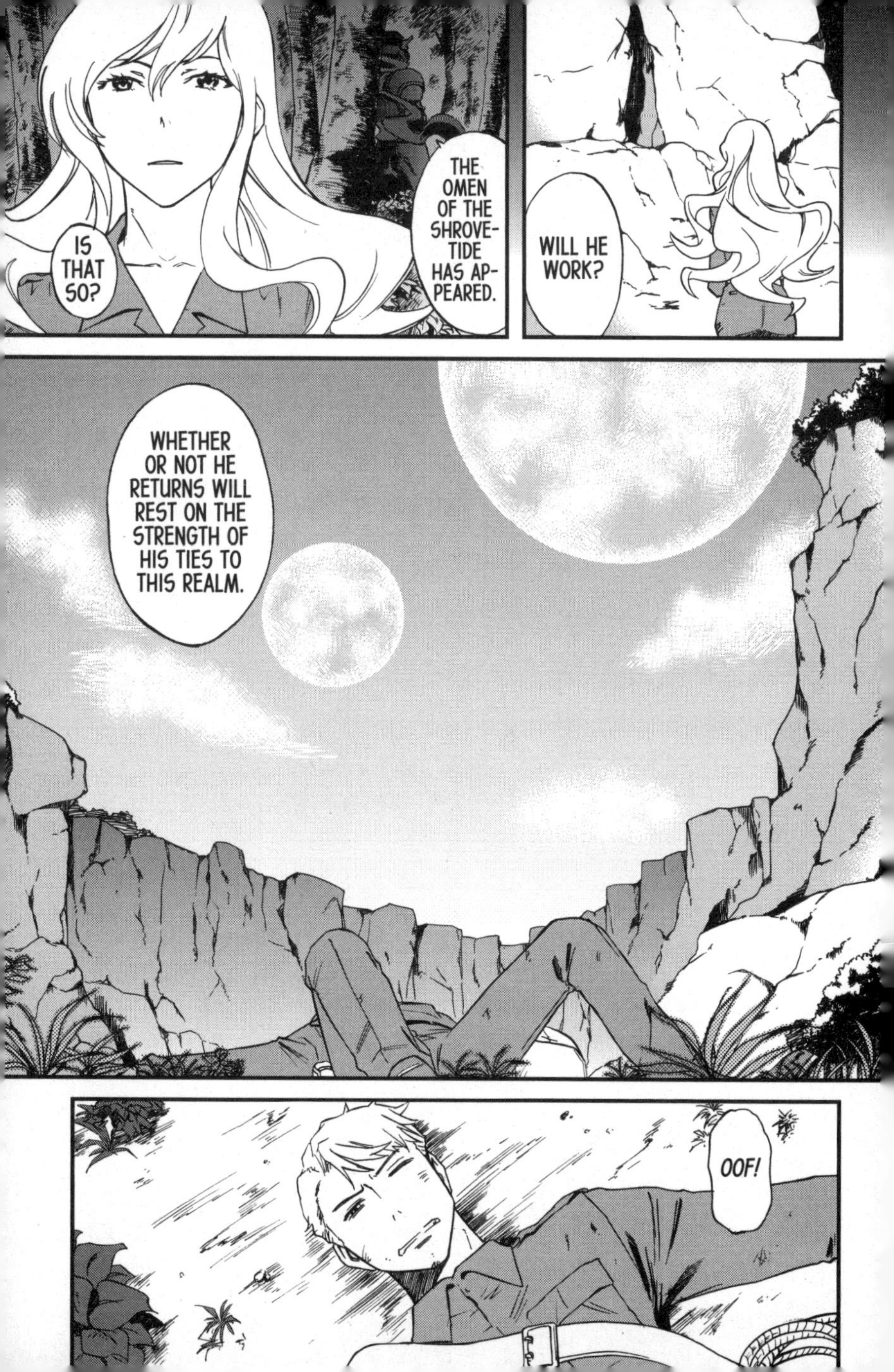
WILL HE WORK?
THE OMEN OF THE SHROVE-TIDE HAS AP-PEARED.
IS THAT SO?
WHETHER OR NOT HE RETURNS WILL REST ON THE STRENGTH OF HIS TIES TO THIS REALM.
OOF!

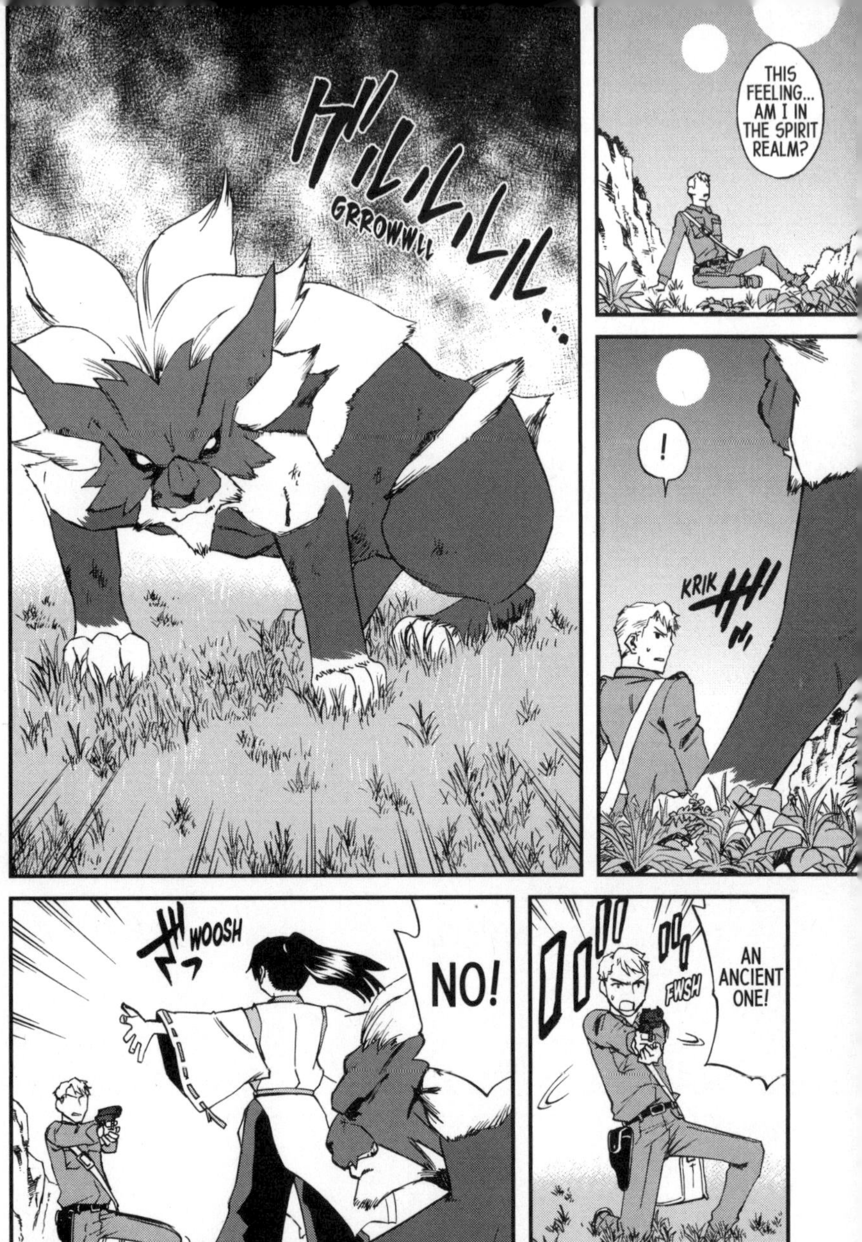
THIS FEELING... AM I IN THE SPIRIT REALM?
!
KRIK
GRROWWLL
FWSH
AN ANCIENT ONE!
WOOSH
NO!

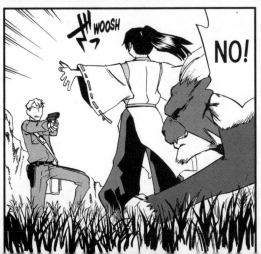

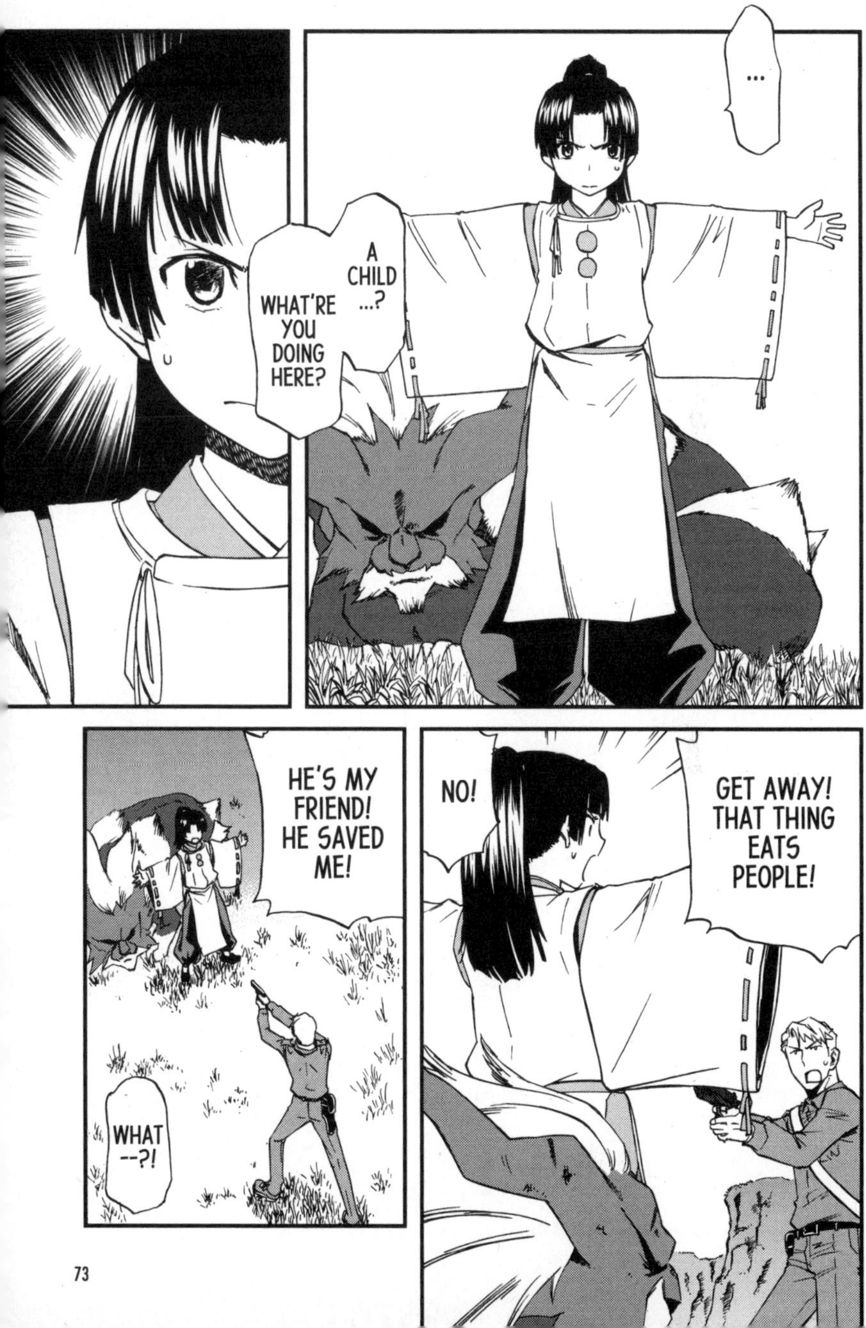
...
A CHILD ...?
WHAT'RE YOU DOING HERE?
GET AWAY! THAT THING EATS PEOPLE!
NO!
HE'S MY FRIEND! HE SAVED ME!
WHAT --?!

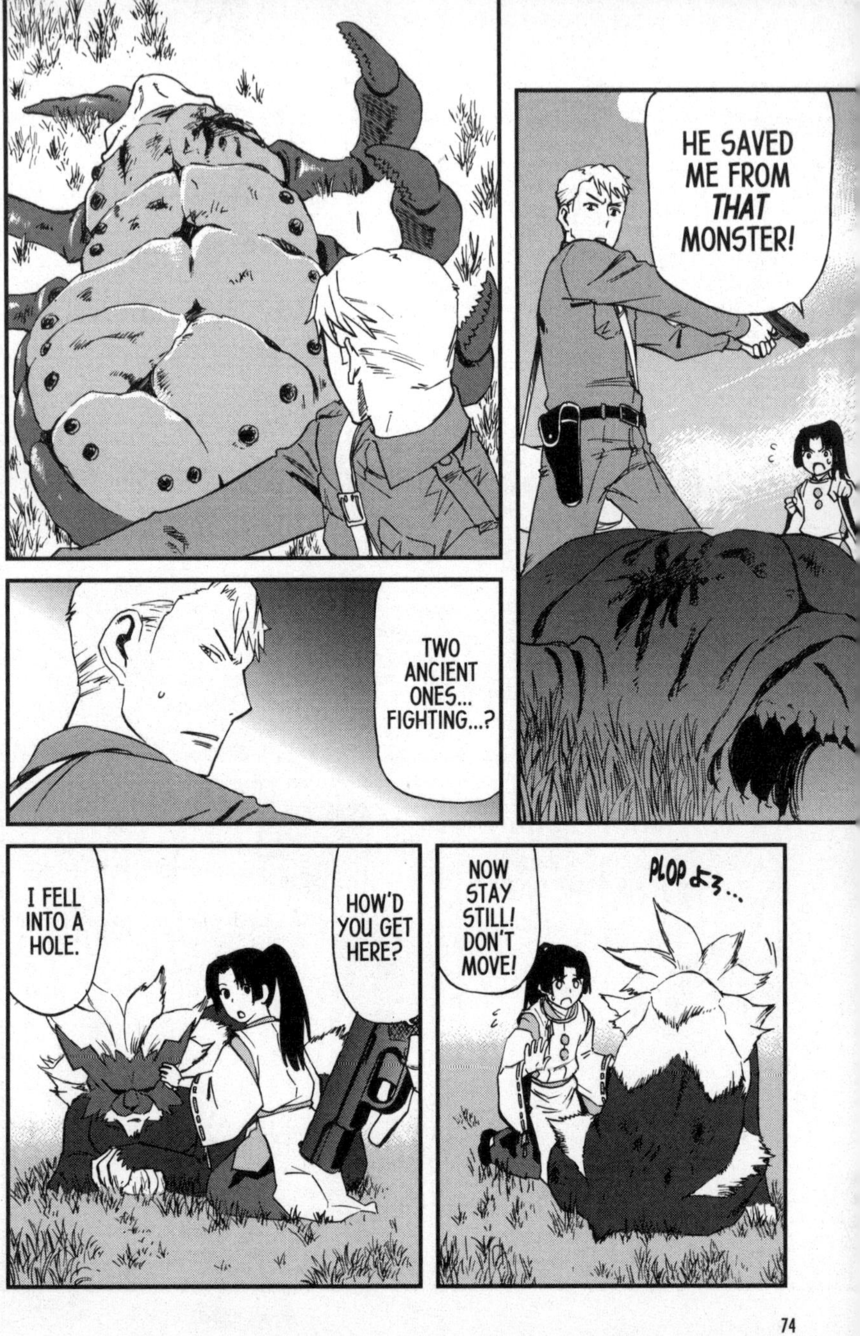
HE SAVED ME FROM *THAT* MONSTER!
TWO ANCIENT ONES... FIGHTING...?
NOW STAY STILL! DON'T MOVE!
PLOP よろ...
HOW'D YOU GET HERE?
I FELL INTO A HOLE.

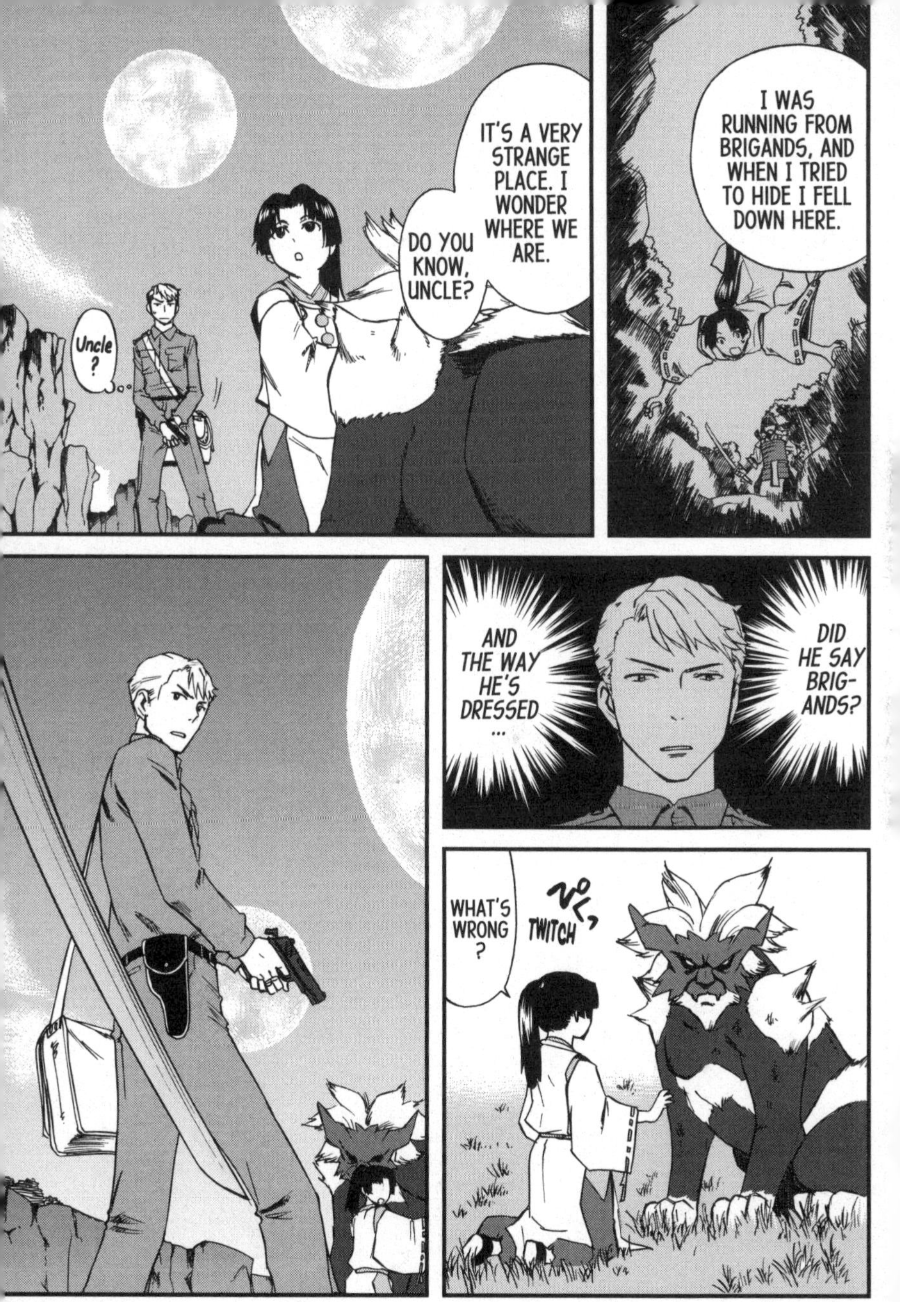
I WAS RUNNING FROM BRIGANDS, AND WHEN I TRIED TO HIDE I FELL DOWN HERE.
IT'S A VERY STRANGE PLACE. I WONDER WHERE WE ARE.
DO YOU KNOW, UNCLE?
Uncle?
DID HE SAY BRIG-ANDS?
AND THE WAY HE'S DRESSED...
TWITCH
WHAT'S WRONG?

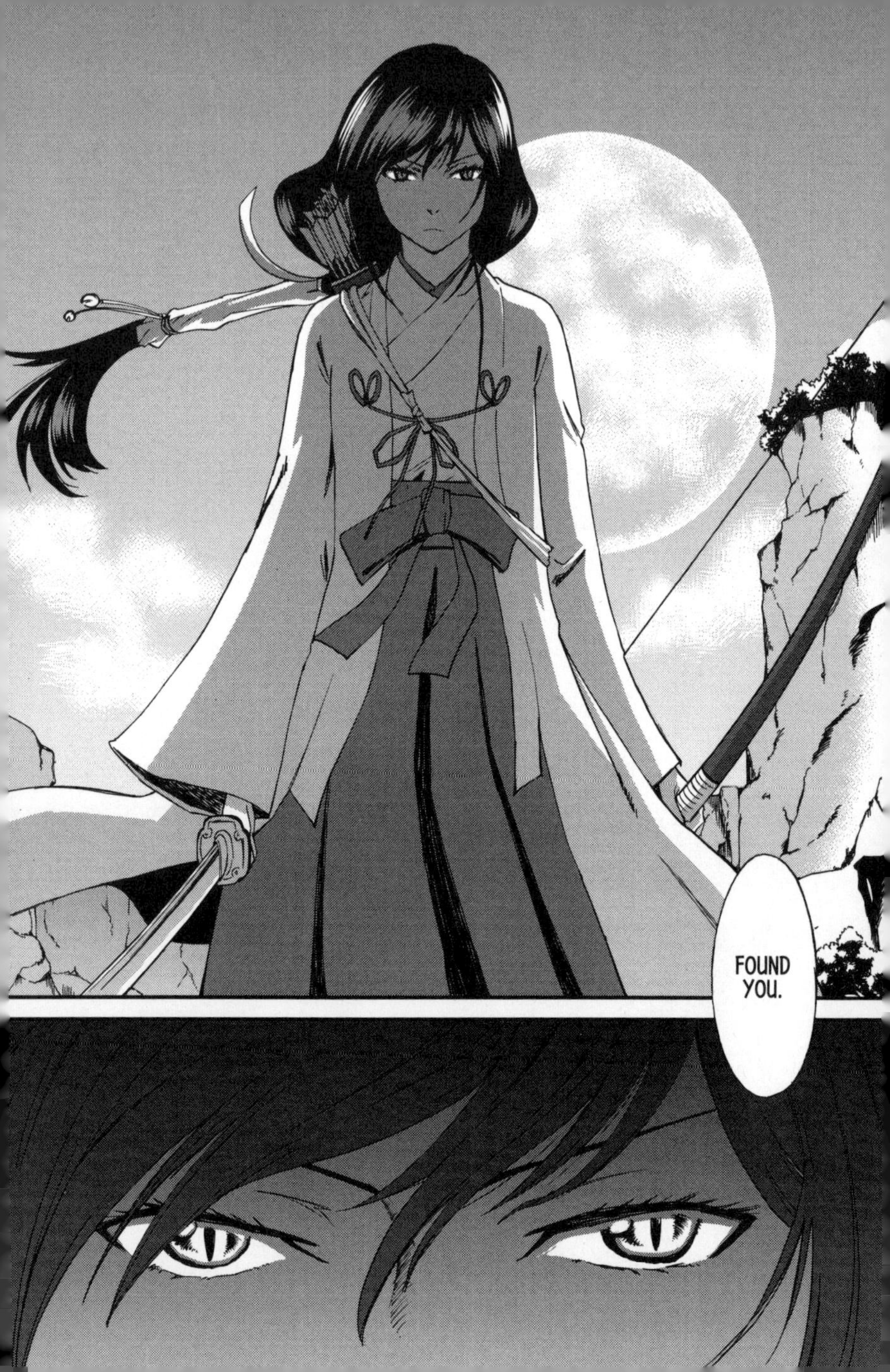
FOUND YOU.

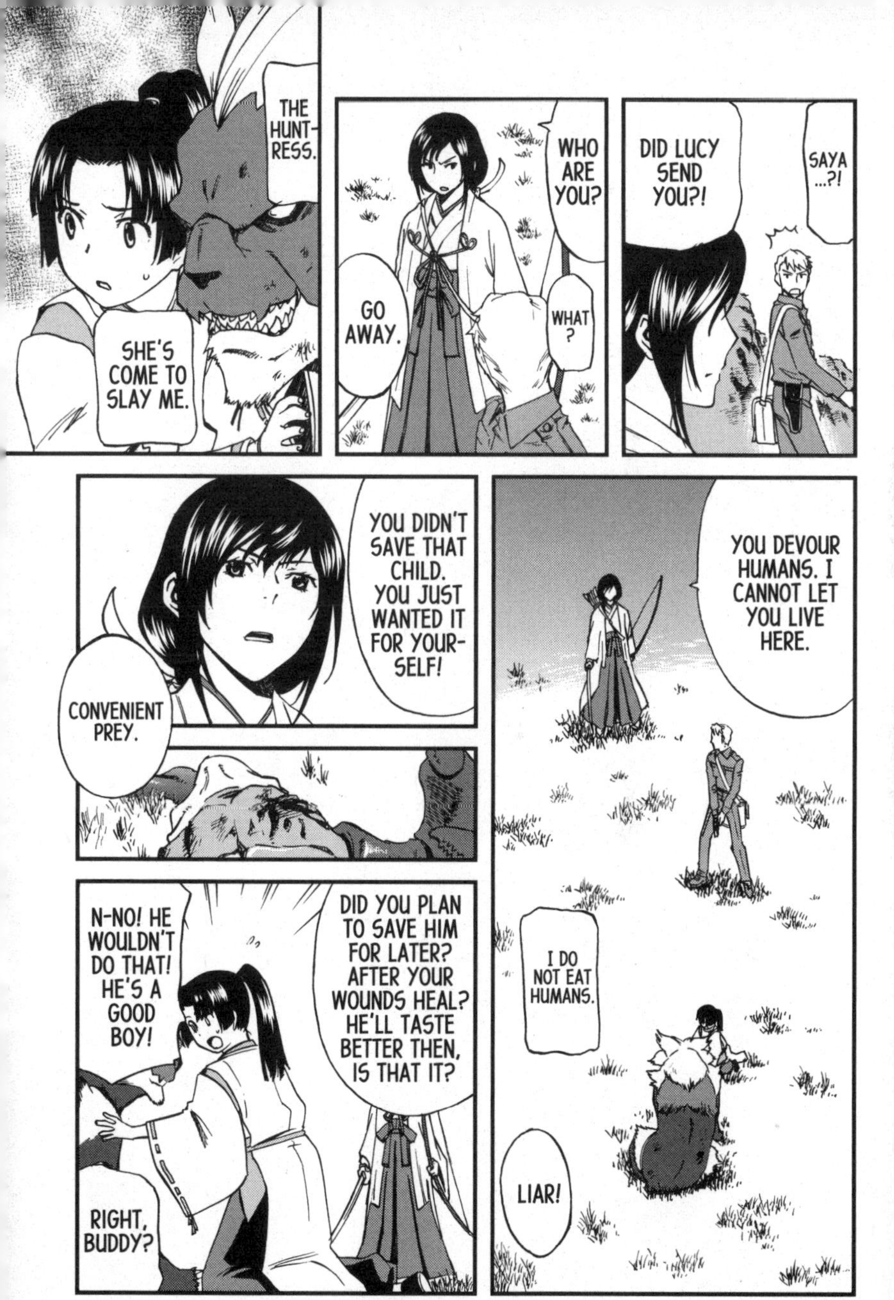
SAYA ...?!
DID LUCY SEND YOU?!
WHO ARE YOU?
WHAT?
GO AWAY.
THE HUNT-RESS.
SHE'S COME TO SLAY ME.
YOU DEVOUR HUMANS. I CANNOT LET YOU LIVE HERE.
I DO NOT EAT HUMANS.
LIAR!
YOU DIDN'T SAVE THAT CHILD. YOU JUST WANTED IT FOR YOUR-SELF!
CONVENIENT PREY.
DID YOU PLAN TO SAVE HIM FOR LATER? AFTER YOUR WOUNDS HEAL? HE'LL TASTE BETTER THEN, IS THAT IT?
N-NO! HE WOULDN'T DO THAT! HE'S A GOOD BOY!
RIGHT, BUDDY?

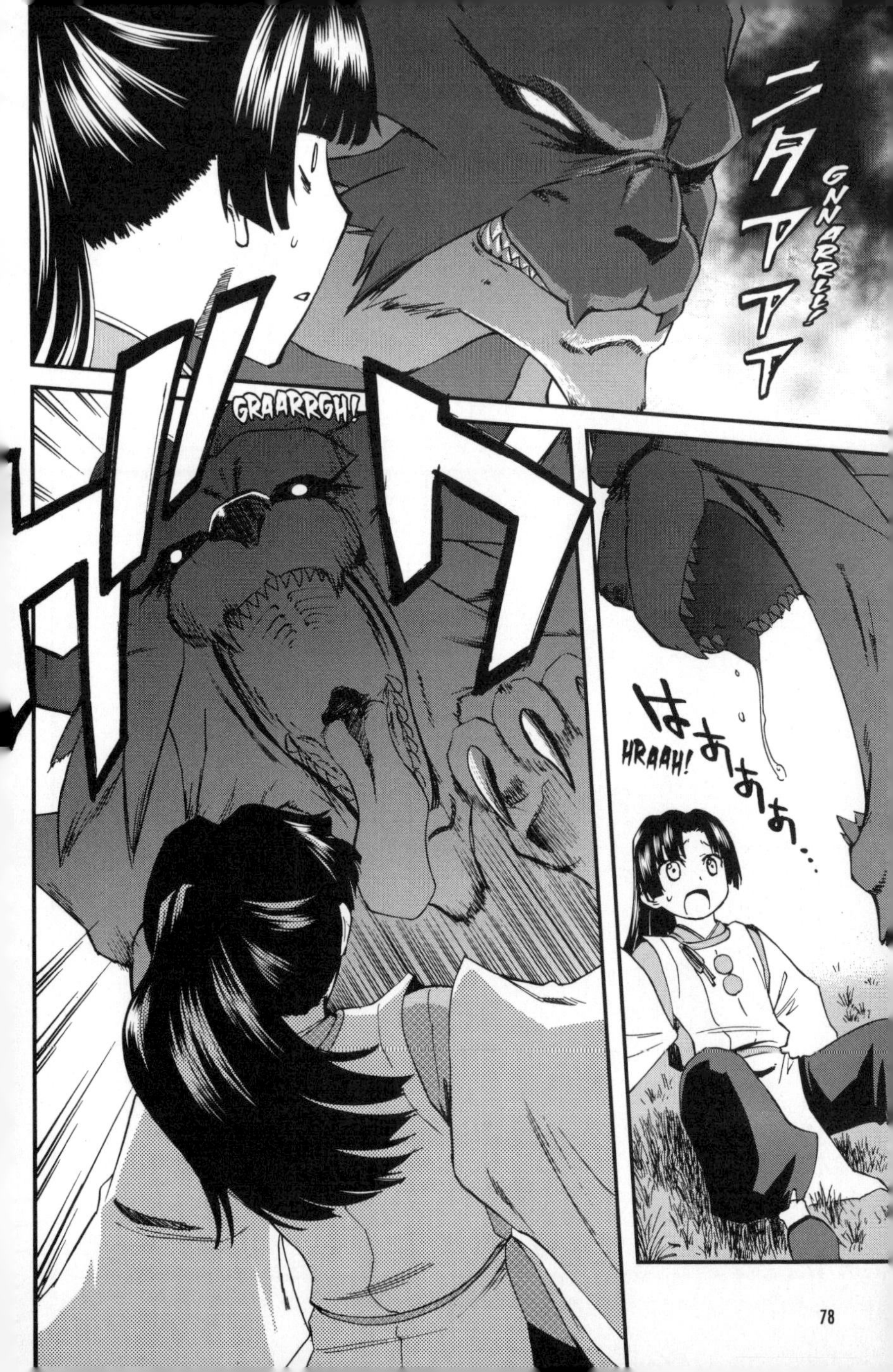
ニタァァァ
GNARRL!
はあぁぁ…
HRAAH!
GRAARRGH!

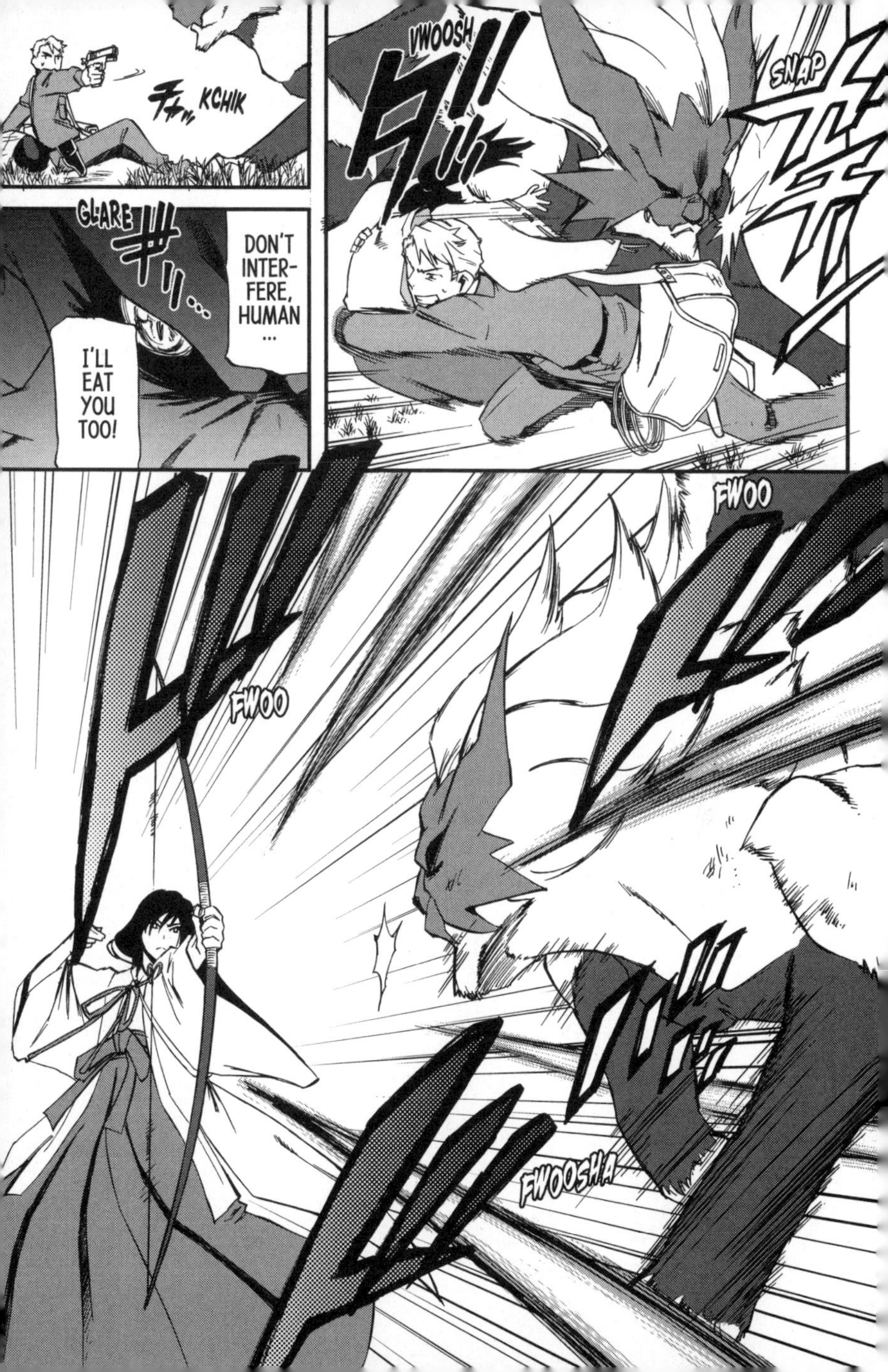
VWOOSH
SNAP
KCHIK
GLARE
DON'T INTER-FERE, HUMAN ...
I'LL EAT YOU TOO!
FWOO
FWOO
FWOOSHA

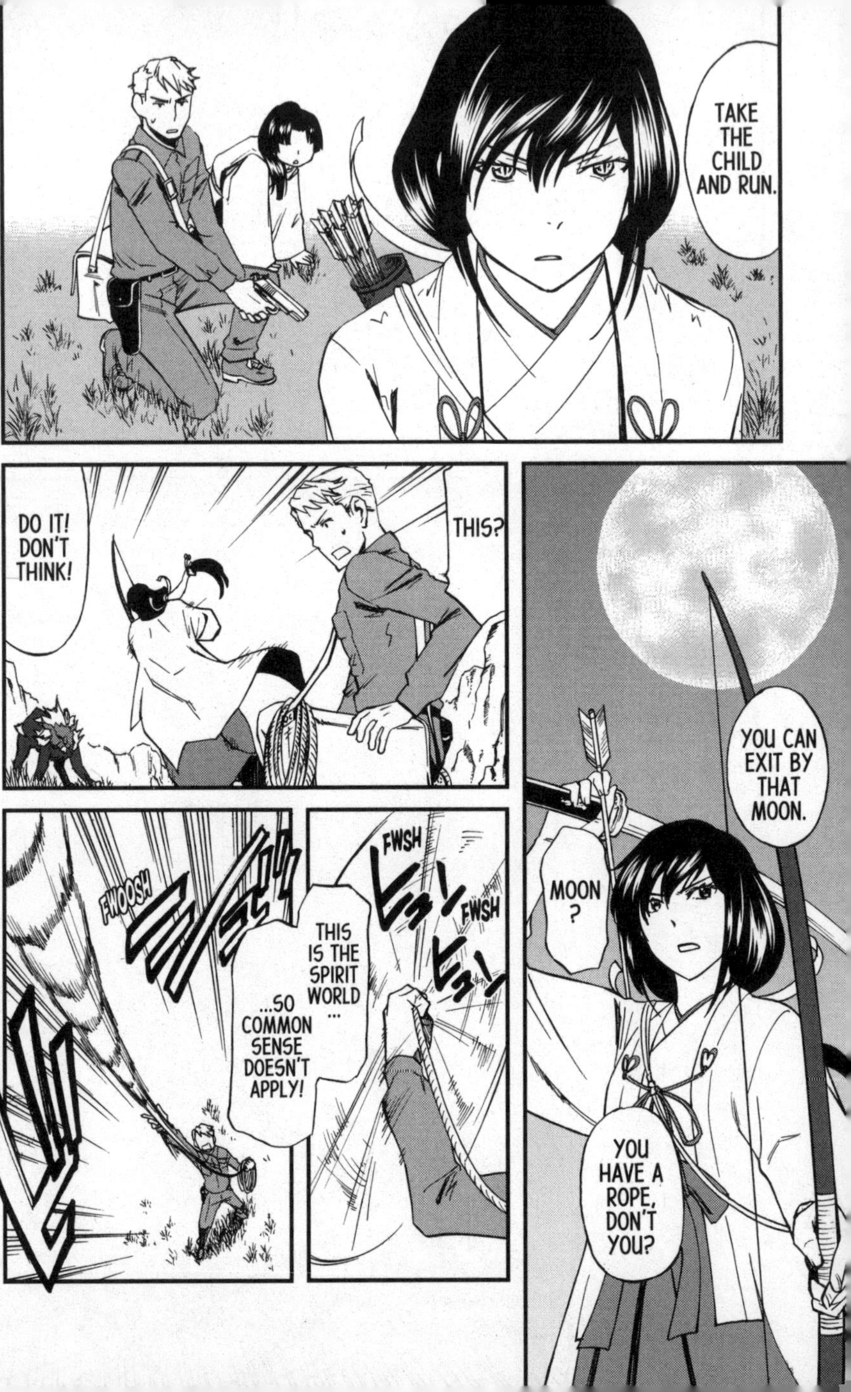
TAKE THE CHILD AND RUN.
YOU CAN EXIT BY THAT MOON.
MOON ?
YOU HAVE A ROPE, DON'T YOU?
THIS?
DO IT! DON'T THINK!
FWSH
FWSH
THIS IS THE SPIRIT WORLD ...
...SO COMMON SENSE DOESN'T APPLY!
FWOOSH

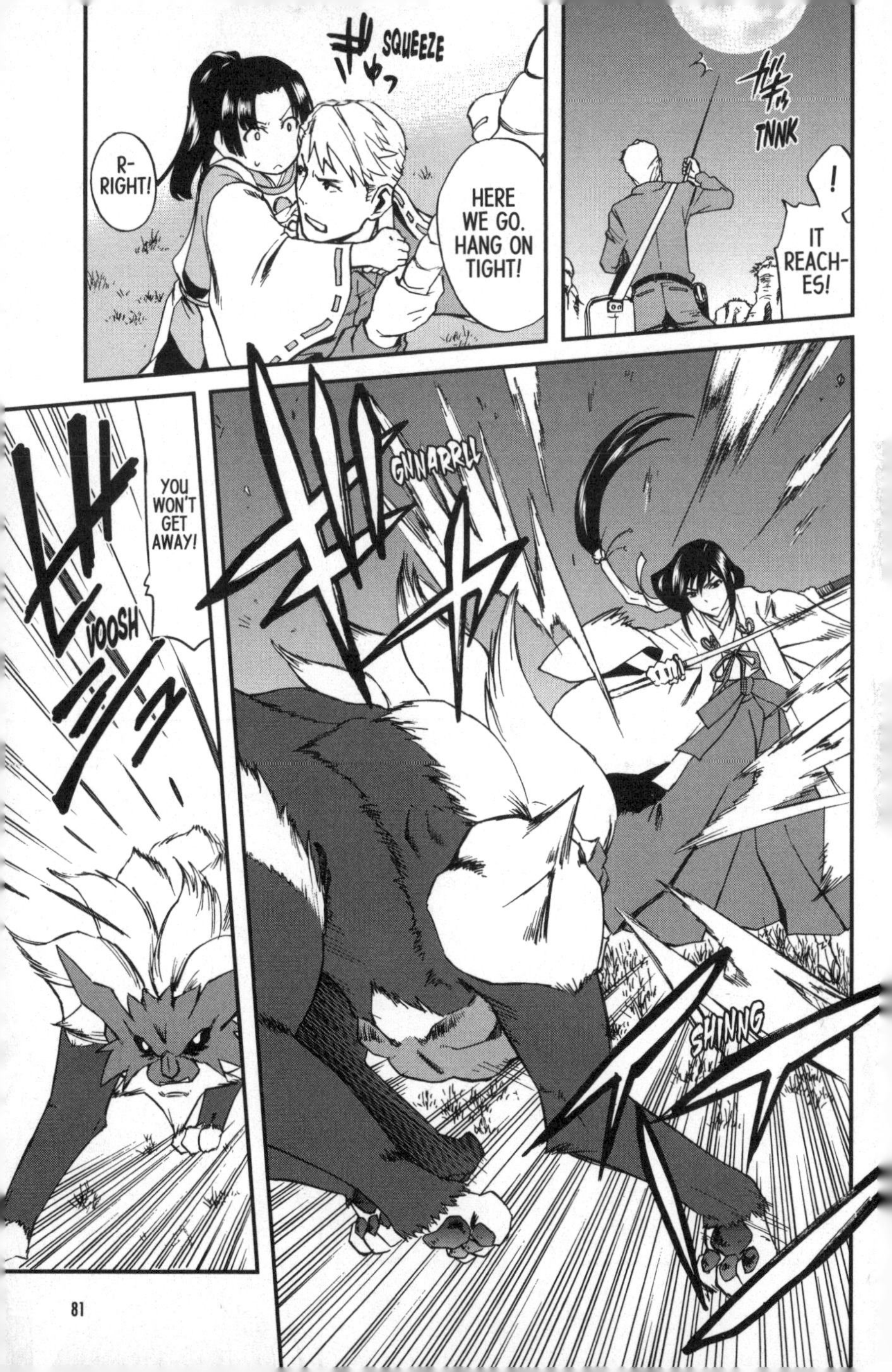
TNNK
!
IT REACHES!
SQUEEZE
HERE WE GO. HANG ON TIGHT!
R-RIGHT!
GNNARRLL
SHINNG
YOU WON'T GET AWAY!
VOOSH

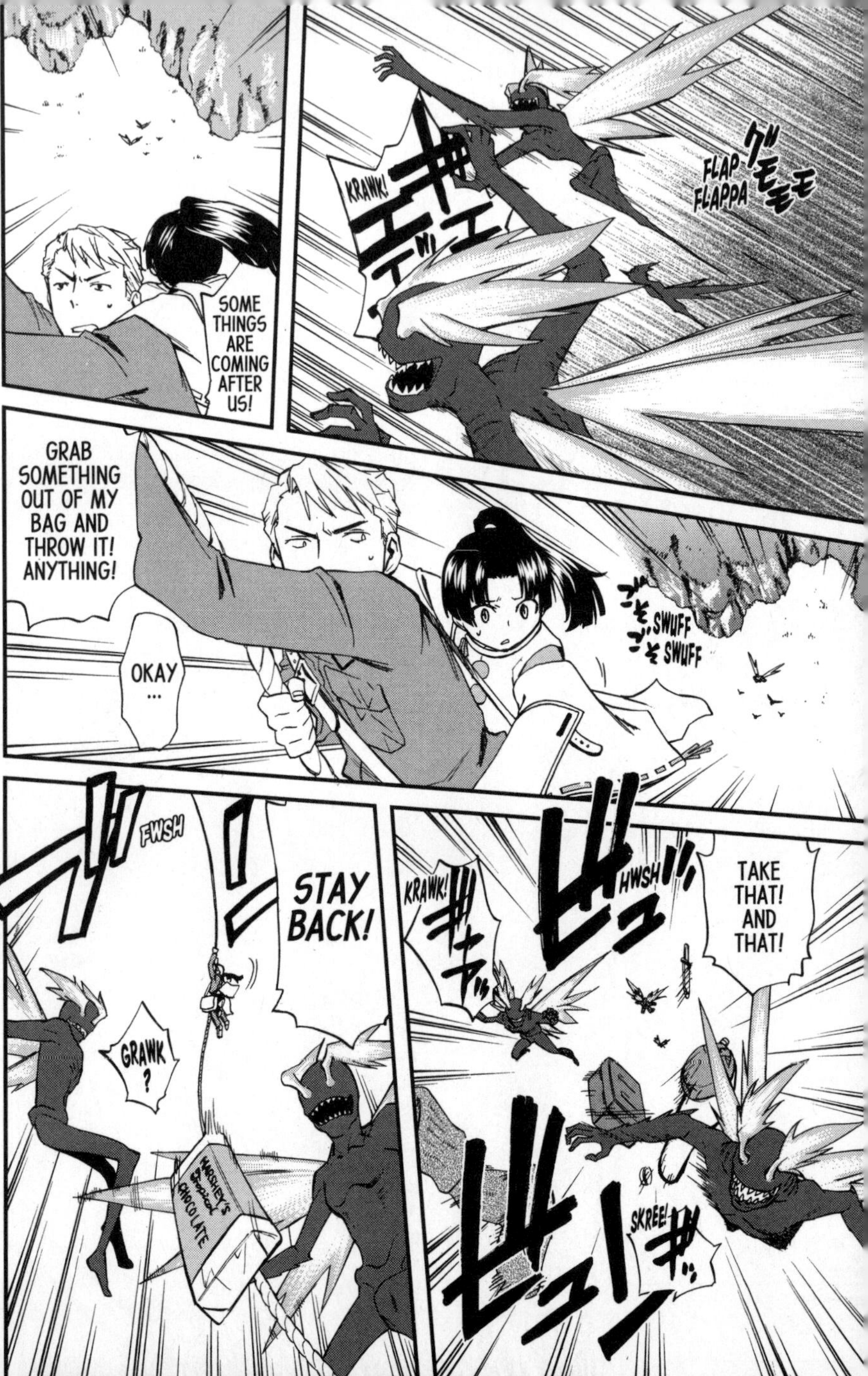
FLAP FLAPPA
KRAWK!
SOME THINGS ARE COMING AFTER US!
SWUFF SWUFF
GRAB SOMETHING OUT OF MY BAG AND THROW IT! ANYTHING!
OKAY ...
TAKE THAT! AND THAT!
HWSH
KRAWK!
SKREE!
STAY BACK!
FWSH
GRAWK ?
HARSHEY'S Tropical CHOCOLATE

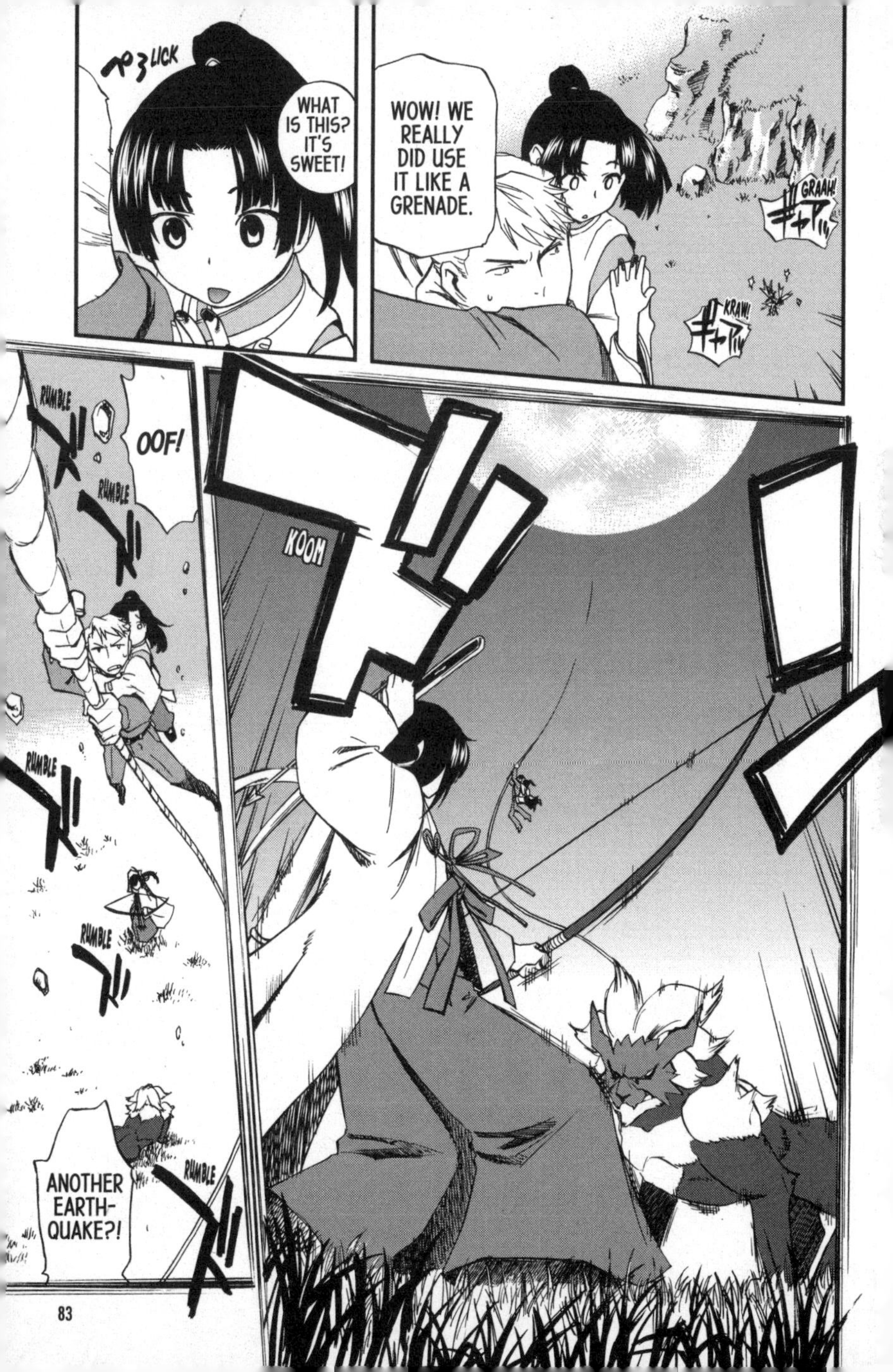
WOW! WE REALLY DID USE IT LIKE A GRENADE.
GRAAH!
KRAW!
LICK
WHAT IS THIS? IT'S SWEET!
KOOM
RUMBLE
OOF!
RUMBLE
RUMBLE
RUMBLE
ANOTHER EARTH-QUAKE?!
RUMBLE

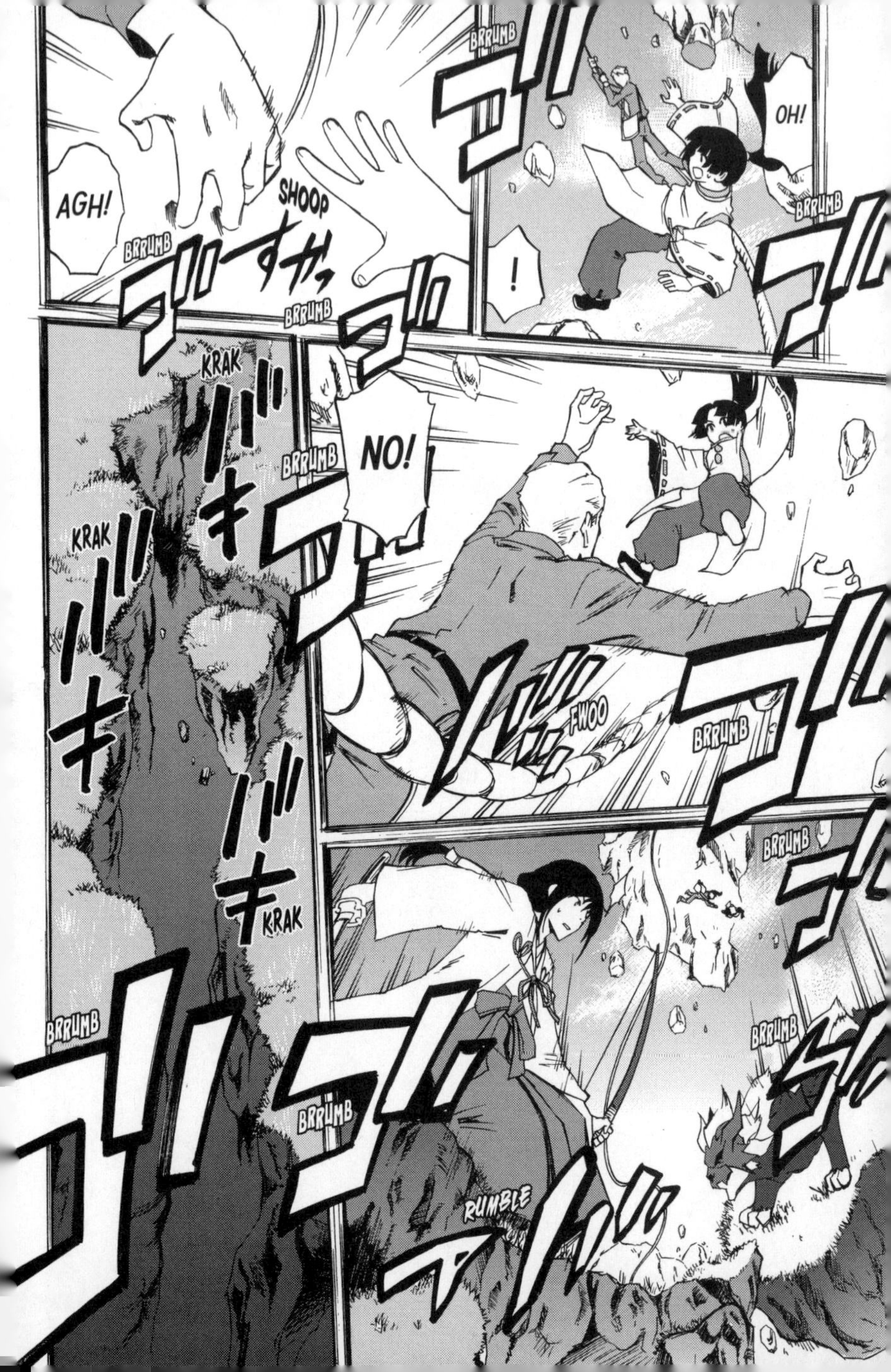

BRRUMB
OH!
!
BRRUMB
AGH!
SHOOP
BRRUMB
BRRUMB
NO!
BRRUMB
FWOO
BRRUMB
BRRUMB
BRRUMB
RUMBLE
KRAK
KRAK
KRAK
BRRUMB
BRRUMB

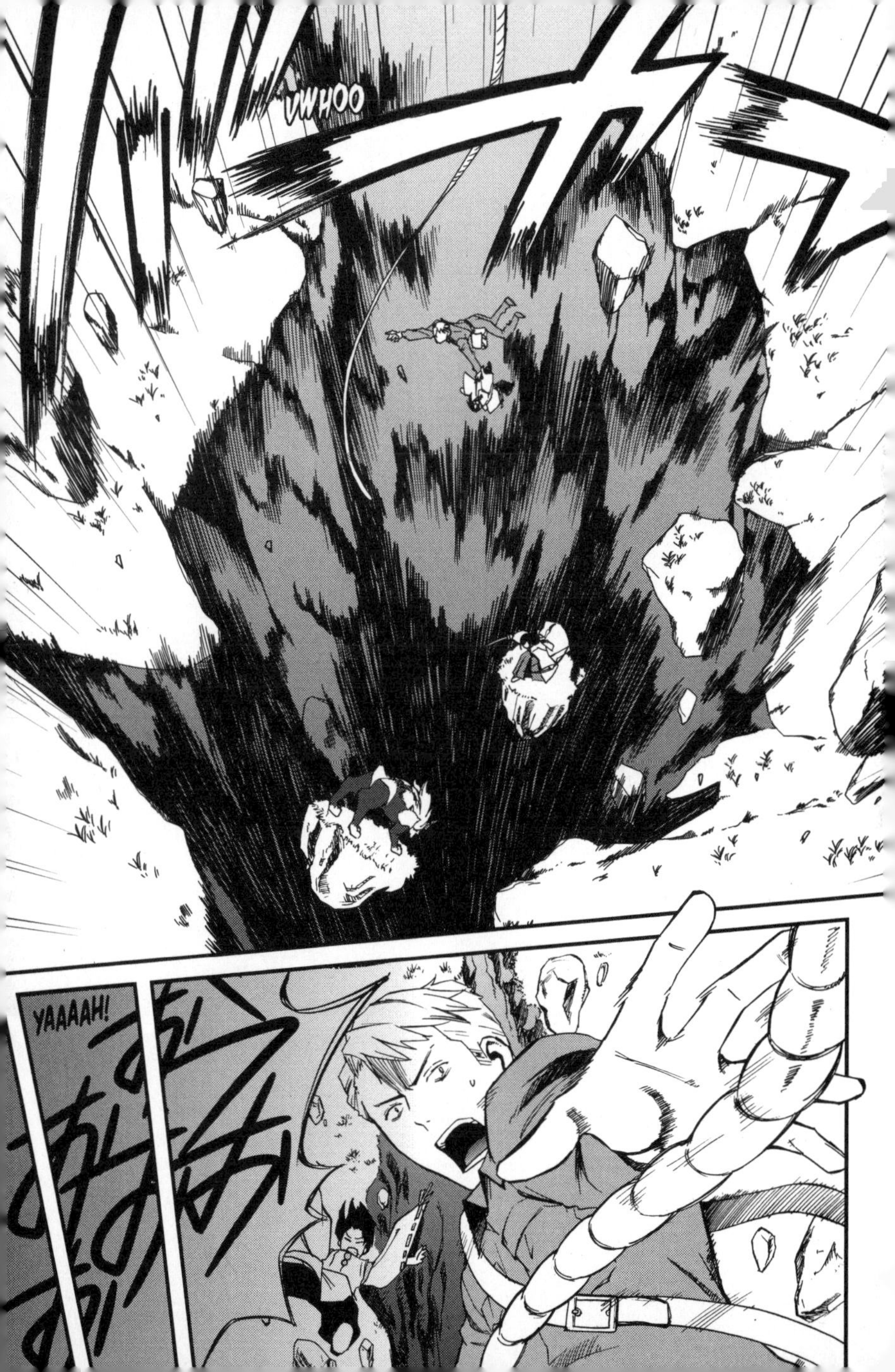
VWHOO
YAAAAH!

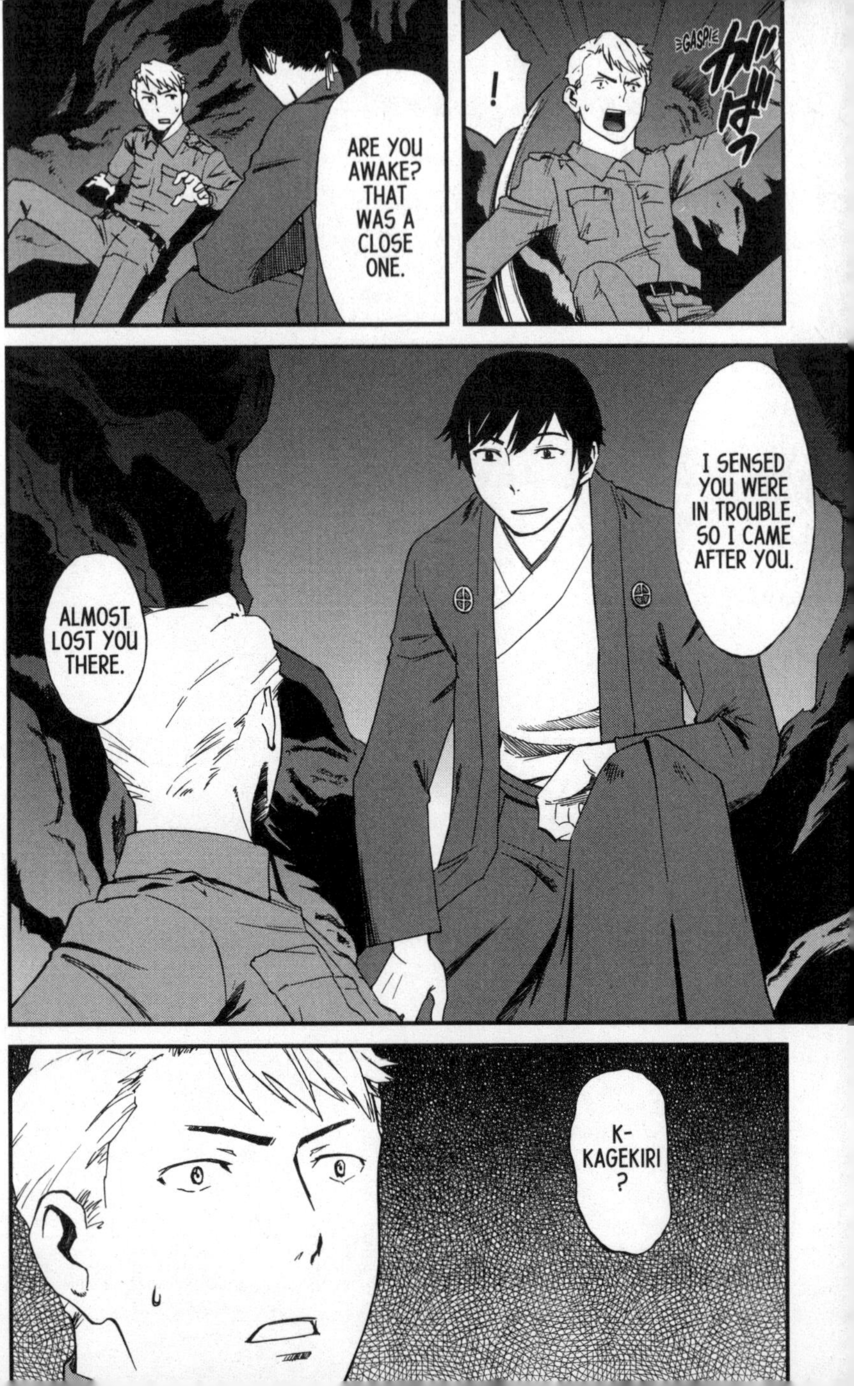
GASP!
がばっ
!
ARE YOU AWAKE? THAT WAS A CLOSE ONE.
I SENSED YOU WERE IN TROUBLE, SO I CAME AFTER YOU.
ALMOST LOST YOU THERE.
K-KAGEKIRI?

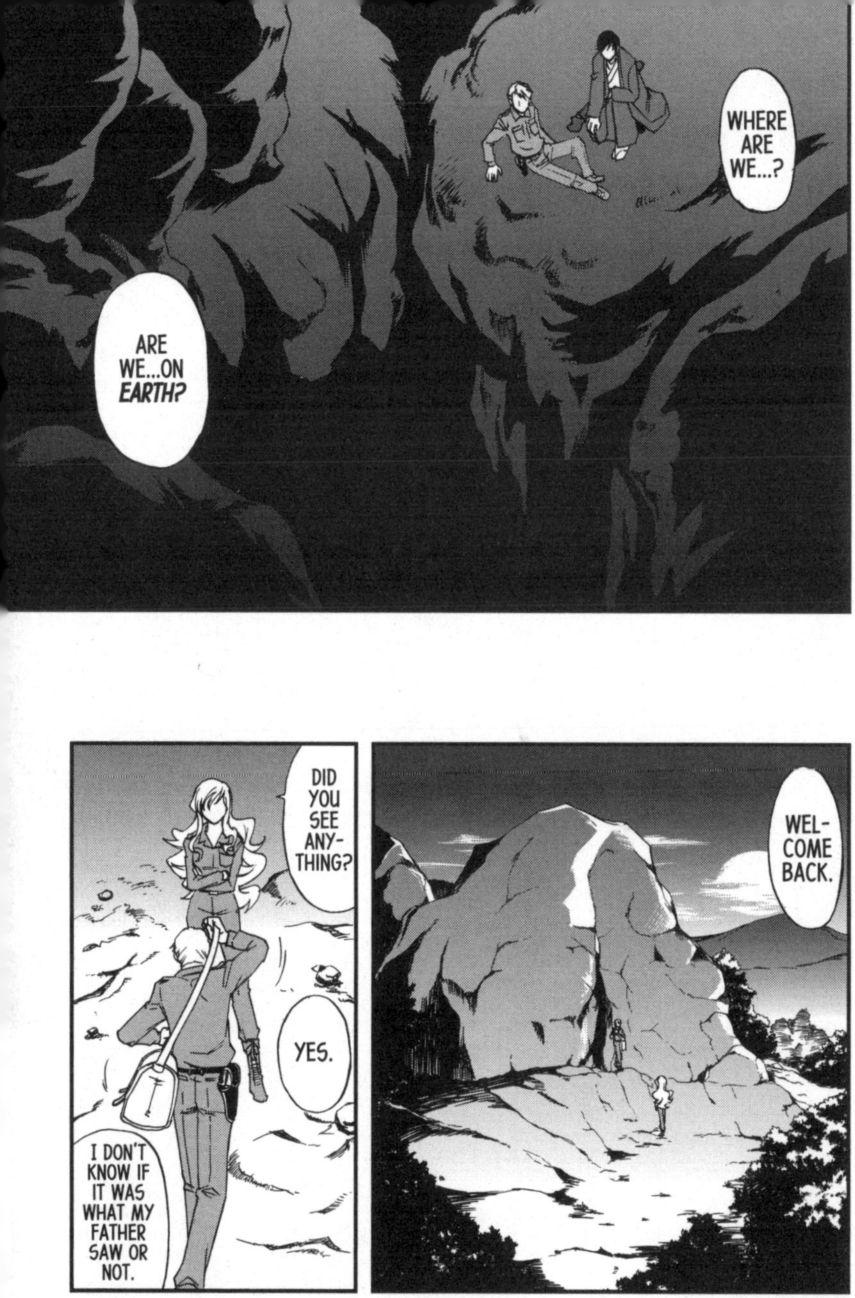
WHERE ARE WE...?
ARE WE...ON *EARTH?*
WEL-COME BACK.
DID YOU SEE ANY-THING?
YES.
I DON'T KNOW IF IT WAS WHAT MY FATHER SAW OR NOT.

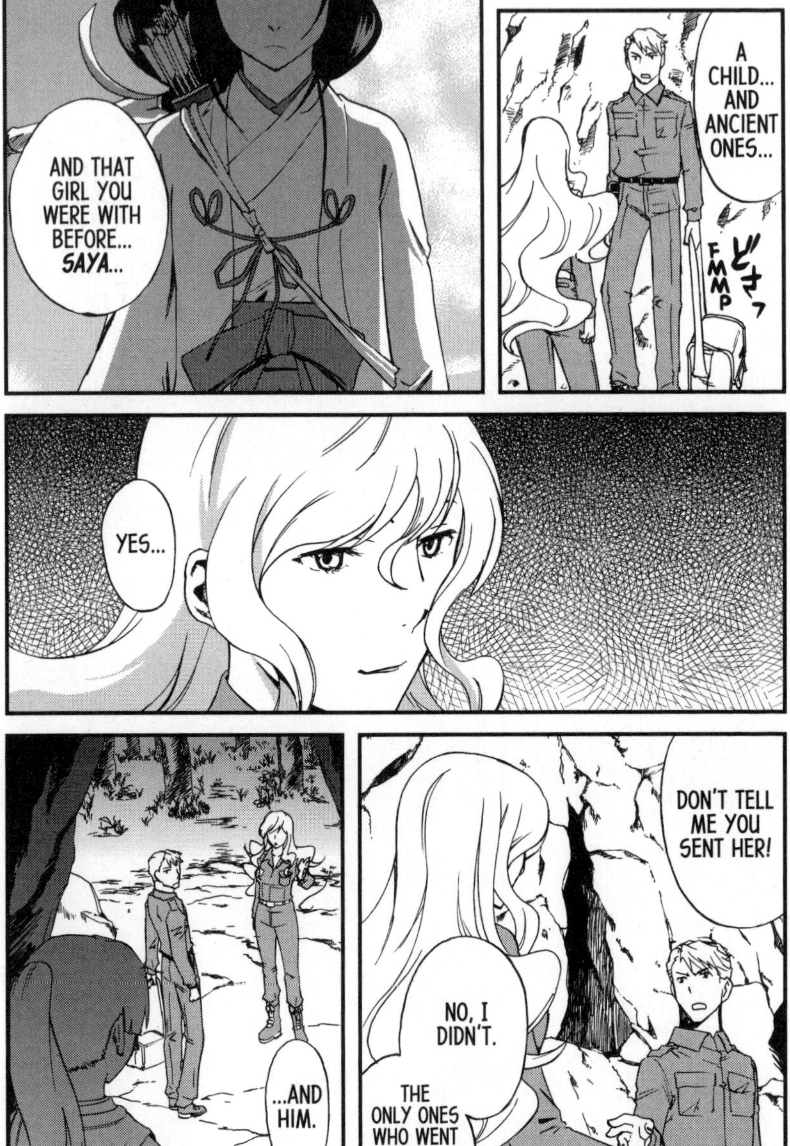
A CHILD... AND ANCIENT ONES...
FMMP
どさっ
AND THAT GIRL YOU WERE WITH BEFORE... SAYA...
YES...
DON'T TELL ME YOU SENT HER!
NO, I DIDN'T.
THE ONLY ONES WHO WENT INSIDE WERE YOU...
...AND HIM.

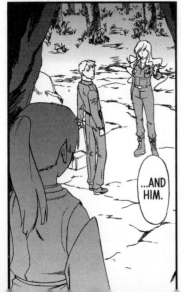

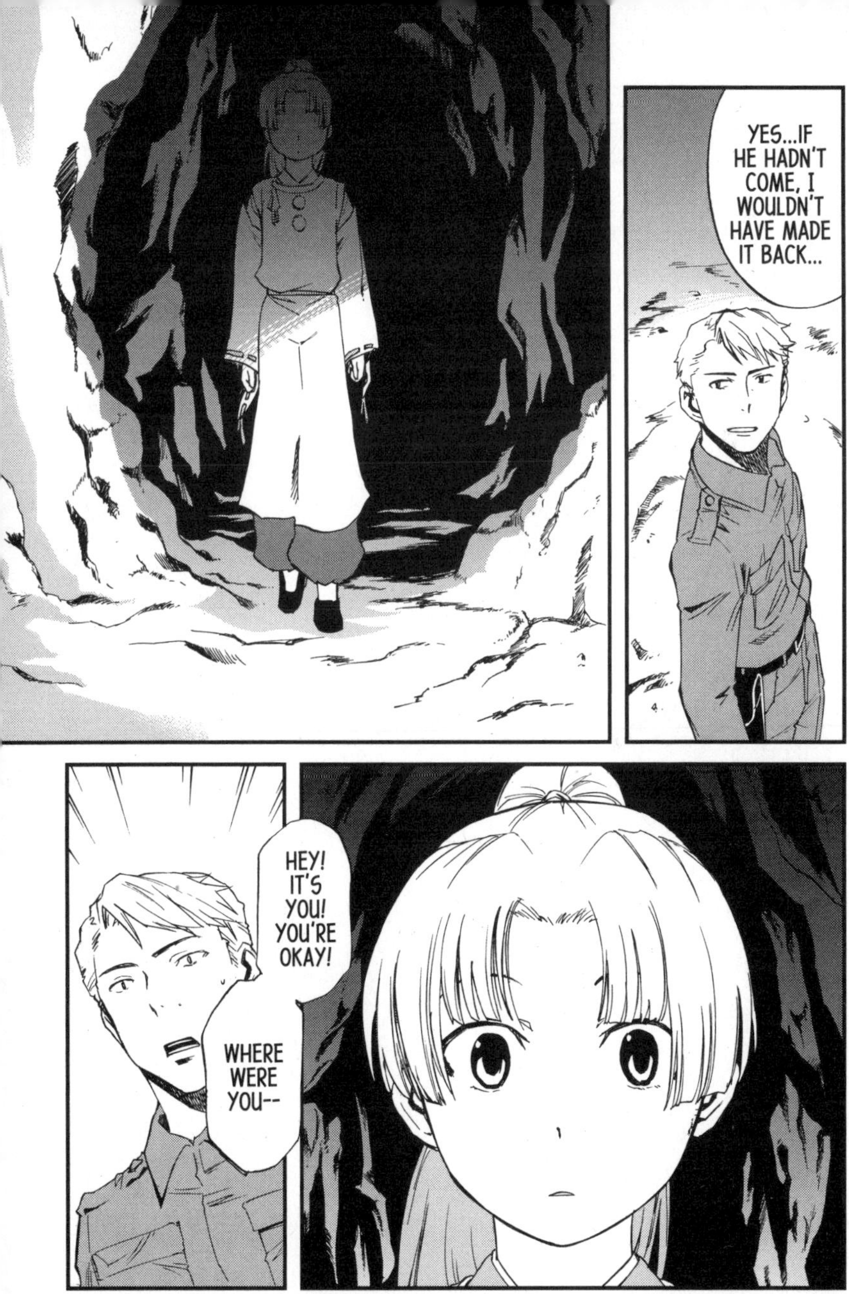
YES...IF HE HADN'T COME, I WOULDN'T HAVE MADE IT BACK...
HEY! IT'S YOU! YOU'RE OKAY!
WHERE WERE YOU--

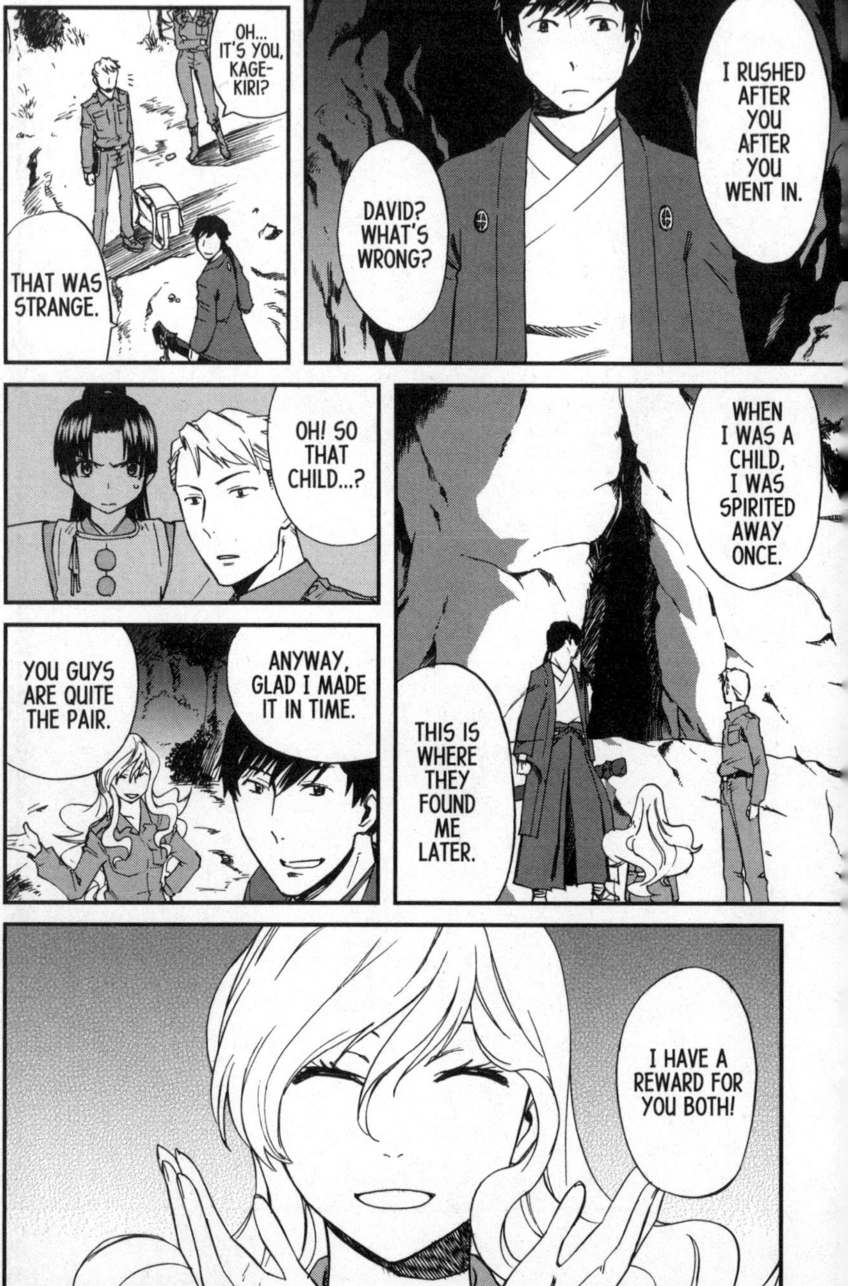
I RUSHED AFTER YOU AFTER YOU WENT IN.
DAVID? WHAT'S WRONG?
OH... IT'S YOU, KAGE-KIRI?
THAT WAS STRANGE.
WHEN I WAS A CHILD, I WAS SPIRITED AWAY ONCE.
THIS IS WHERE THEY FOUND ME LATER.
OH! SO THAT CHILD...?
ANYWAY, GLAD I MADE IT IN TIME.
YOU GUYS ARE QUITE THE PAIR.
I HAVE A REWARD FOR YOU BOTH!

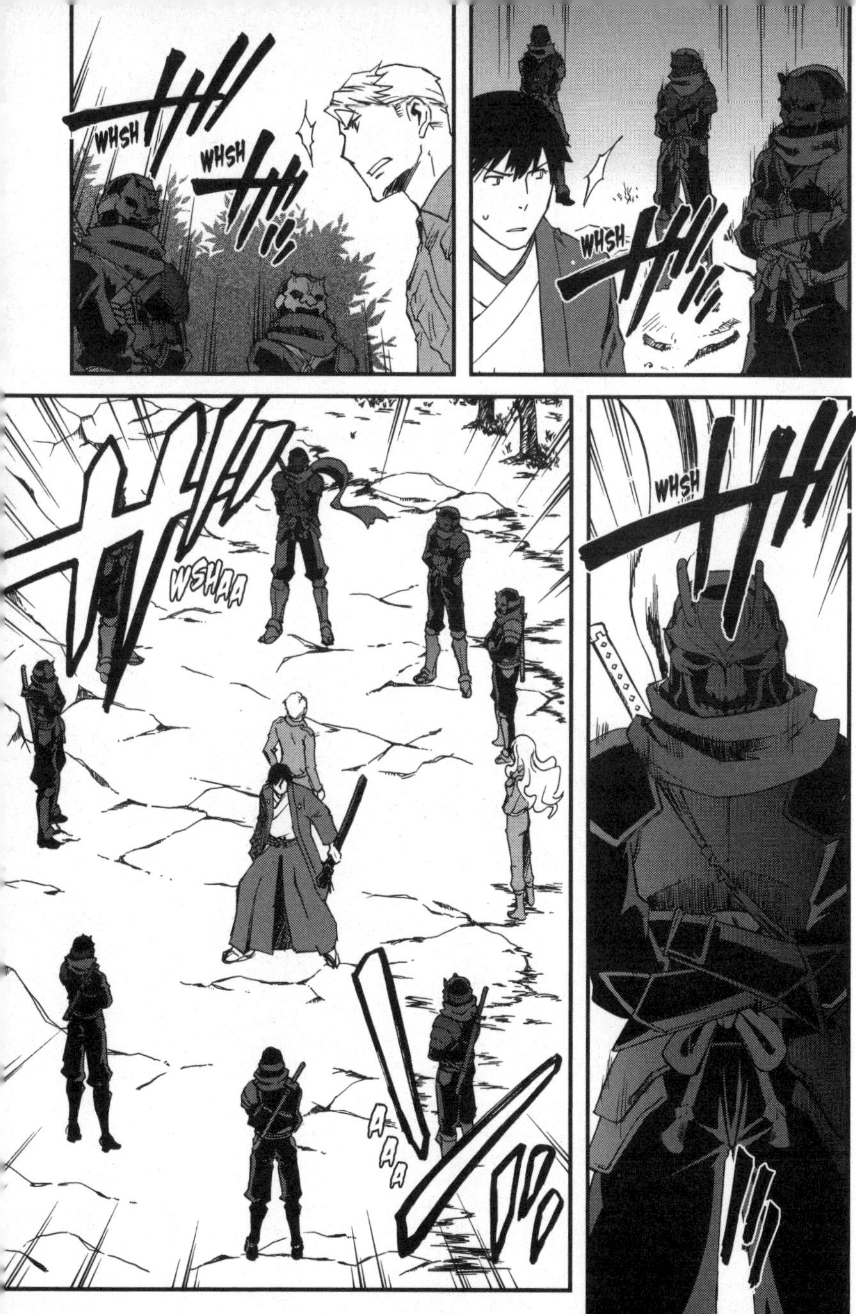
WHSH
WHSH
WHSH
WHSH
WSHAA
AAA

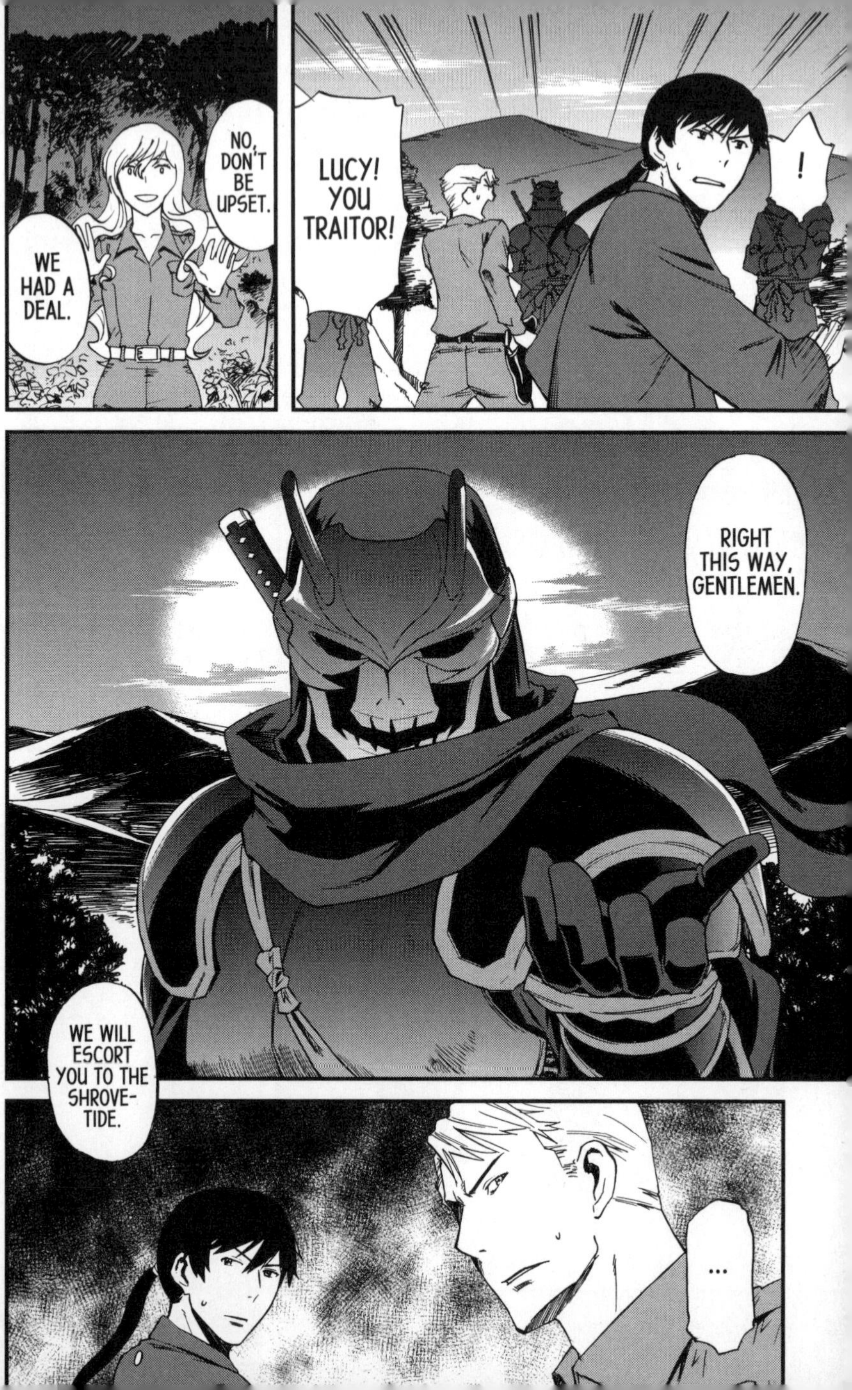
!
LUCY! YOU TRAITOR!
NO, DON'T BE UPSET.
WE HAD A DEAL.
RIGHT THIS WAY, GENTLEMEN.
WE WILL ESCORT YOU TO THE SHROVE-TIDE.
...

十六夜鬼譚

BLOOD-C
DEMONIC
MOONLIGHT

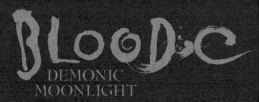

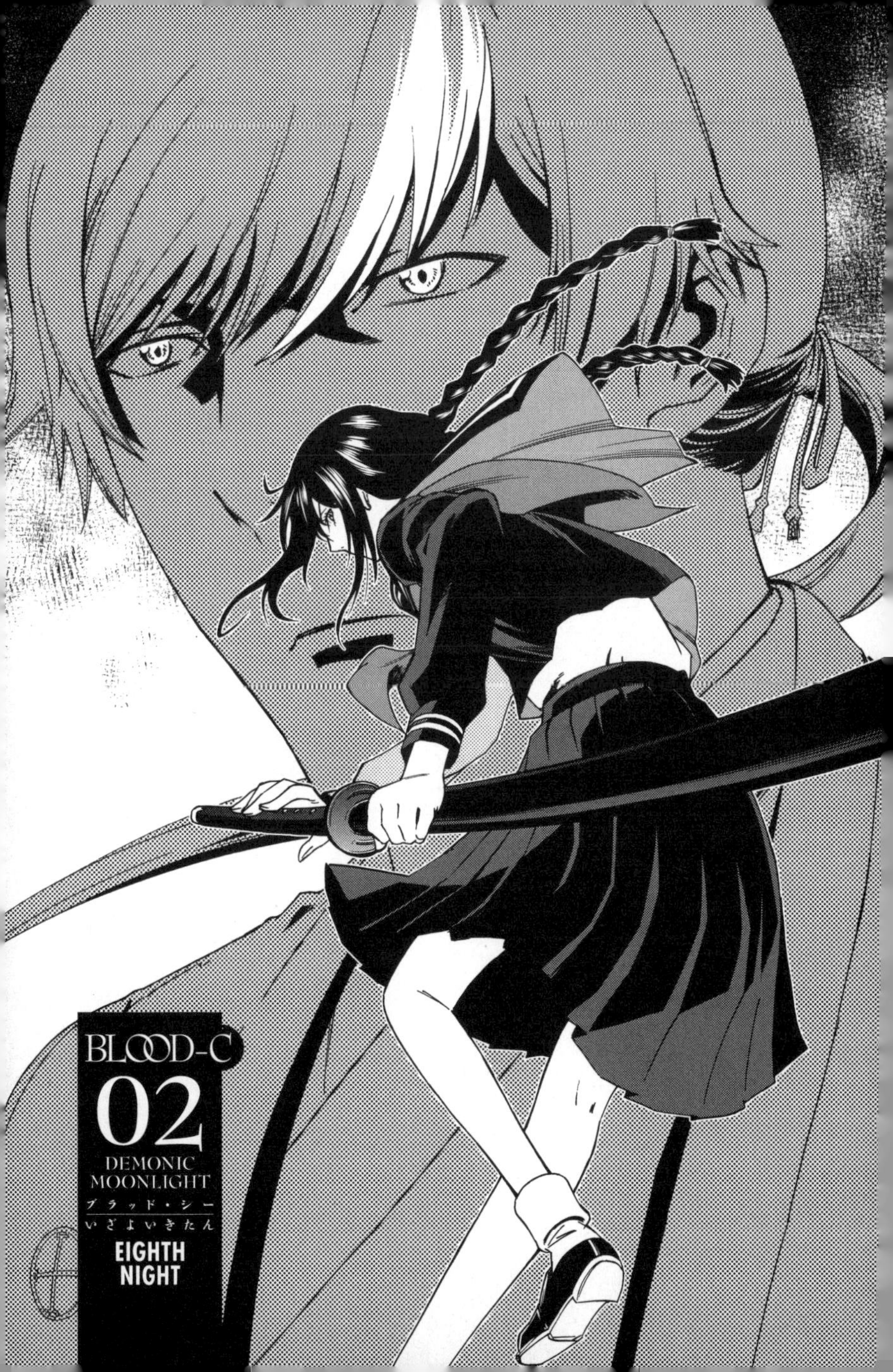
BLOOD-C
02
DEMONIC
MOONLIGHT
ブラッド・シー
いざよいきたん
EIGHTH
NIGHT

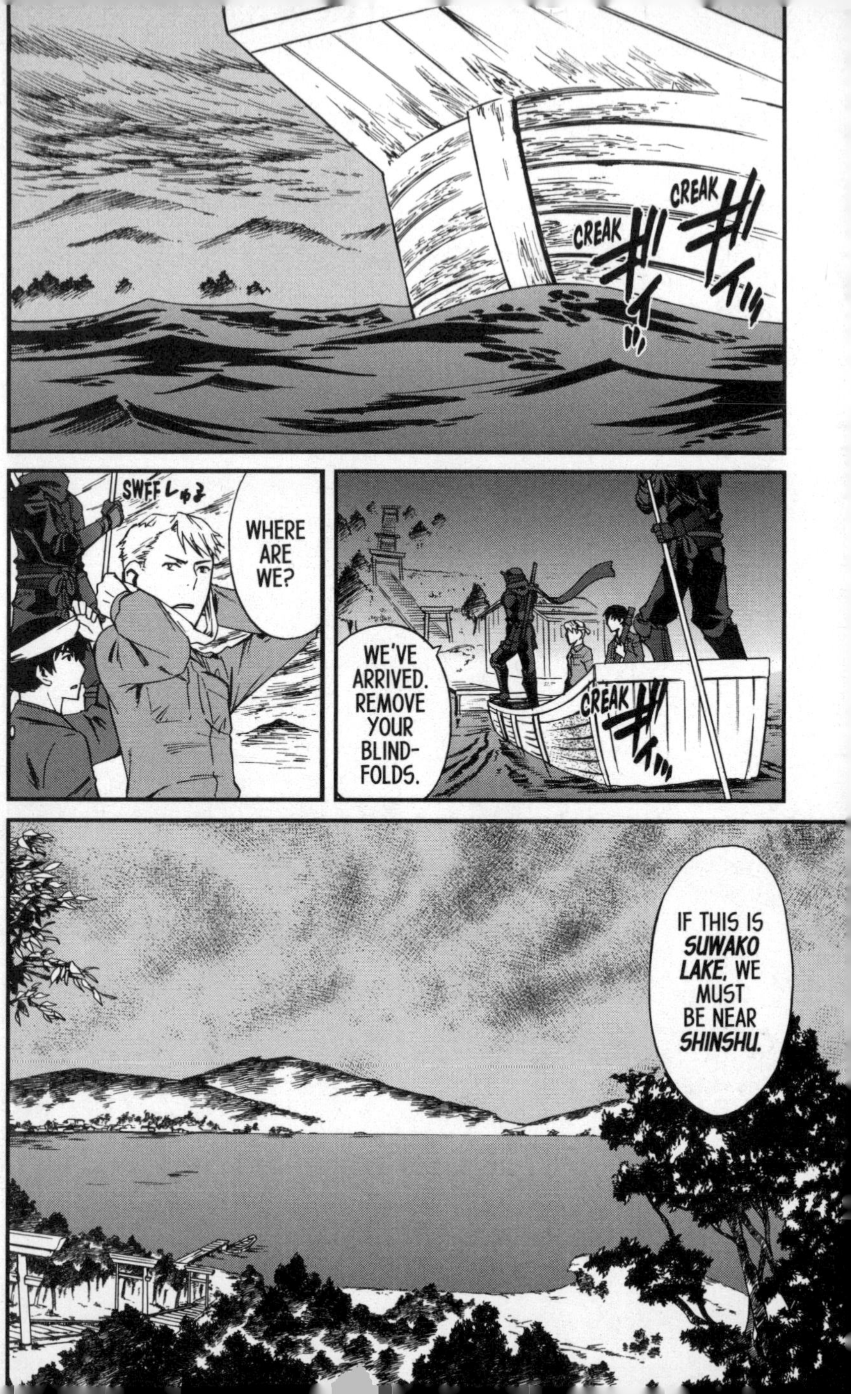
CREAK
CREAK
CREAK
WE'VE ARRIVED. REMOVE YOUR BLIND-FOLDS.
SWFF
WHERE ARE WE?
IF THIS IS SUWAKO LAKE, WE MUST BE NEAR SHINSHU.

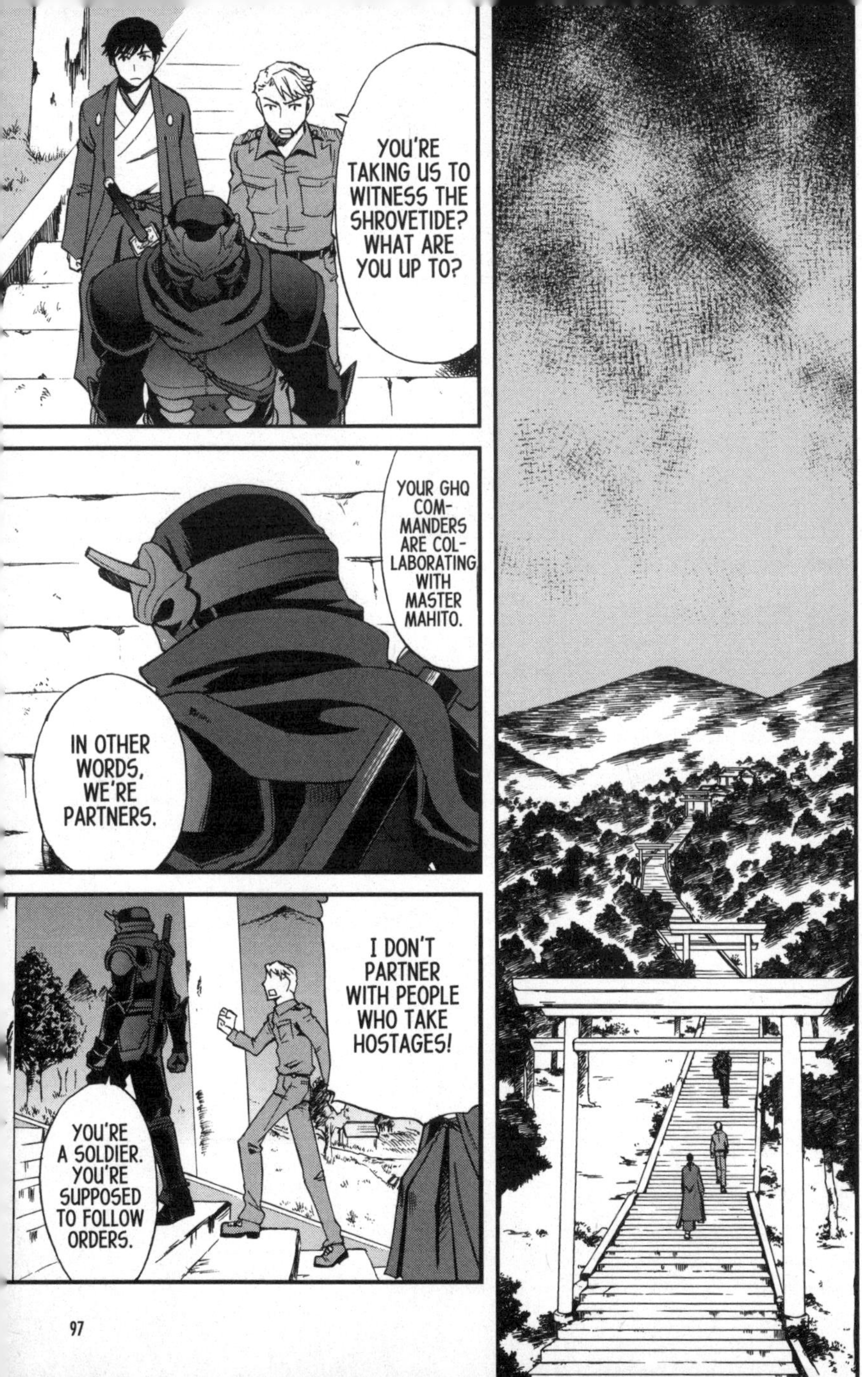
YOU'RE TAKING US TO WITNESS THE SHROVETIDE? WHAT ARE YOU UP TO?
YOUR GHQ COM-MANDERS ARE COL-LABORATING WITH MASTER MAHITO.
IN OTHER WORDS, WE'RE PARTNERS.
I DON'T PARTNER WITH PEOPLE WHO TAKE HOSTAGES!
YOU'RE A SOLDIER. YOU'RE SUPPOSED TO FOLLOW ORDERS.

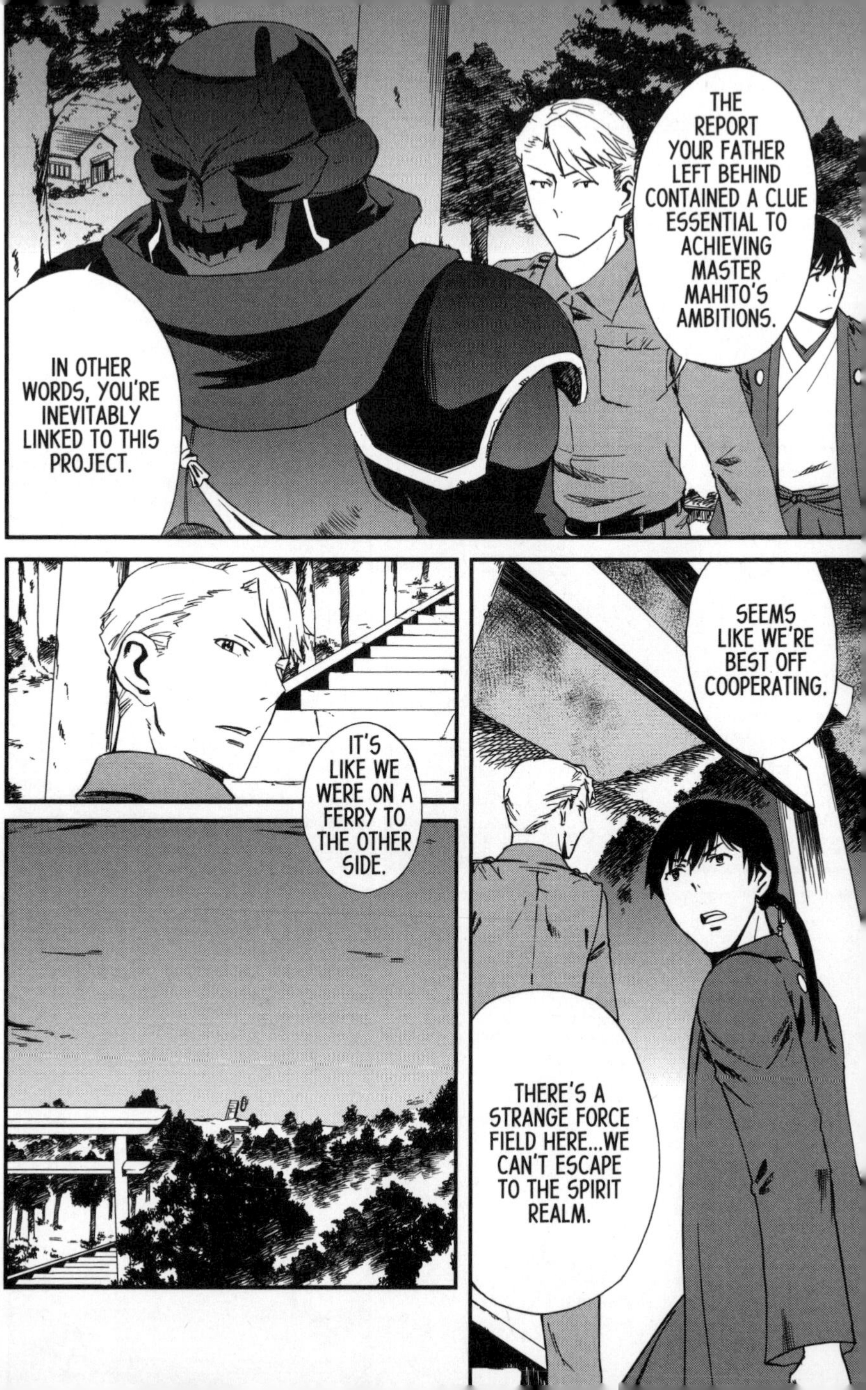
THE REPORT YOUR FATHER LEFT BEHIND CONTAINED A CLUE ESSENTIAL TO ACHIEVING MASTER MAHITO'S AMBITIONS.
IN OTHER WORDS, YOU'RE INEVITABLY LINKED TO THIS PROJECT.
SEEMS LIKE WE'RE BEST OFF COOPERATING.
THERE'S A STRANGE FORCE FIELD HERE...WE CAN'T ESCAPE TO THE SPIRIT REALM.
IT'S LIKE WE WERE ON A FERRY TO THE OTHER SIDE.

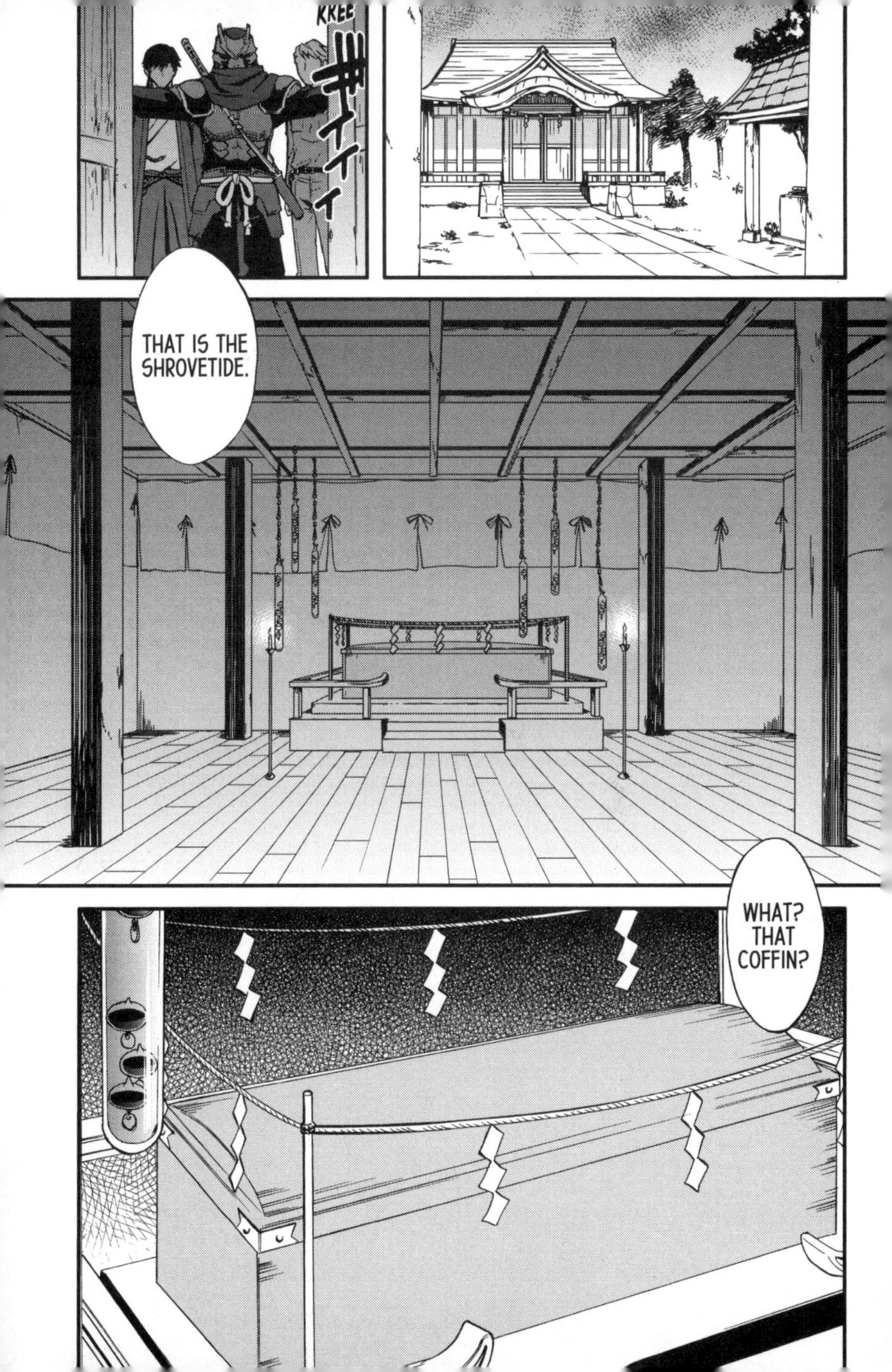
KREE
THAT IS THE SHROVETIDE.
WHAT? THAT COFFIN?

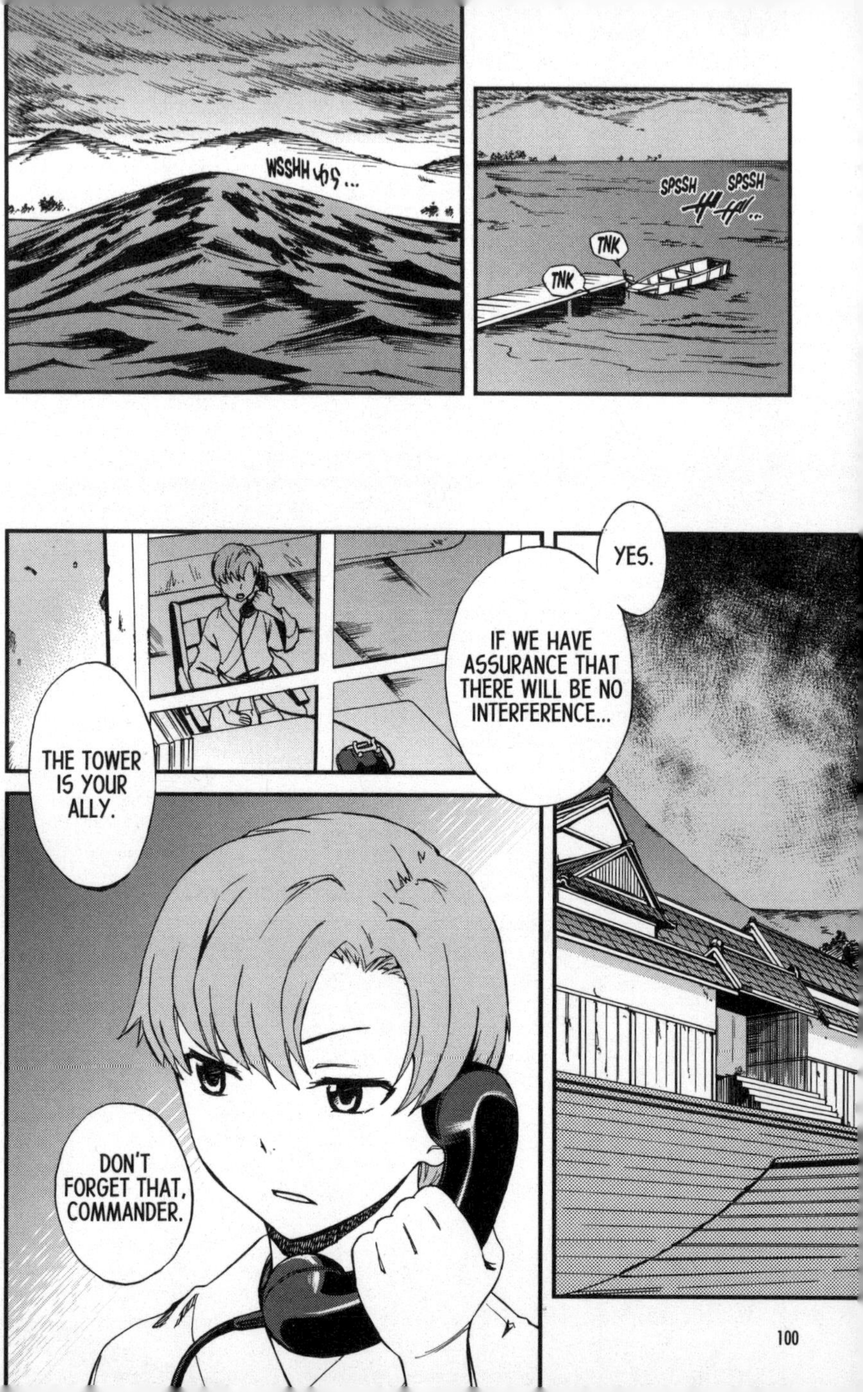
SPSSH
SPSSH
TNK
TNK
WSSHH
YES.
IF WE HAVE ASSURANCE THAT THERE WILL BE NO INTERFERENCE...
THE TOWER IS YOUR ALLY.
DON'T FORGET THAT, COMMANDER.

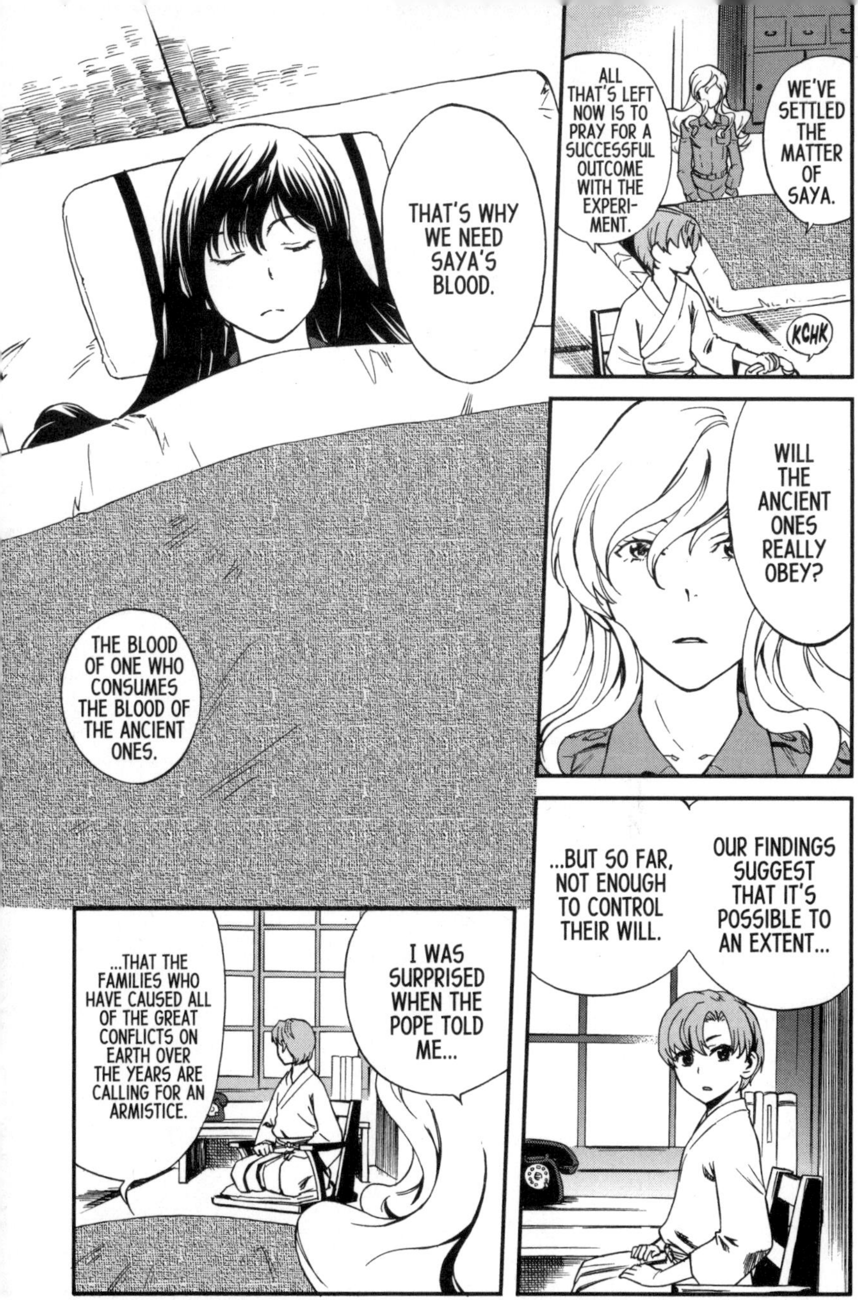

WE'VE SETTLED THE MATTER OF SAYA.
ALL THAT'S LEFT NOW IS TO PRAY FOR A SUCCESSFUL OUTCOME WITH THE EXPERI-MENT.
KCHK
WILL THE ANCIENT ONES REALLY OBEY?
THAT'S WHY WE NEED SAYA'S BLOOD.
THE BLOOD OF ONE WHO CONSUMES THE BLOOD OF THE ANCIENT ONES.
OUR FINDINGS SUGGEST THAT IT'S POSSIBLE TO AN EXTENT...
...BUT SO FAR, NOT ENOUGH TO CONTROL THEIR WILL.
I WAS SURPRISED WHEN THE POPE TOLD ME...
...THAT THE FAMILIES WHO HAVE CAUSED ALL OF THE GREAT CONFLICTS ON EARTH OVER THE YEARS ARE CALLING FOR AN ARMISTICE.

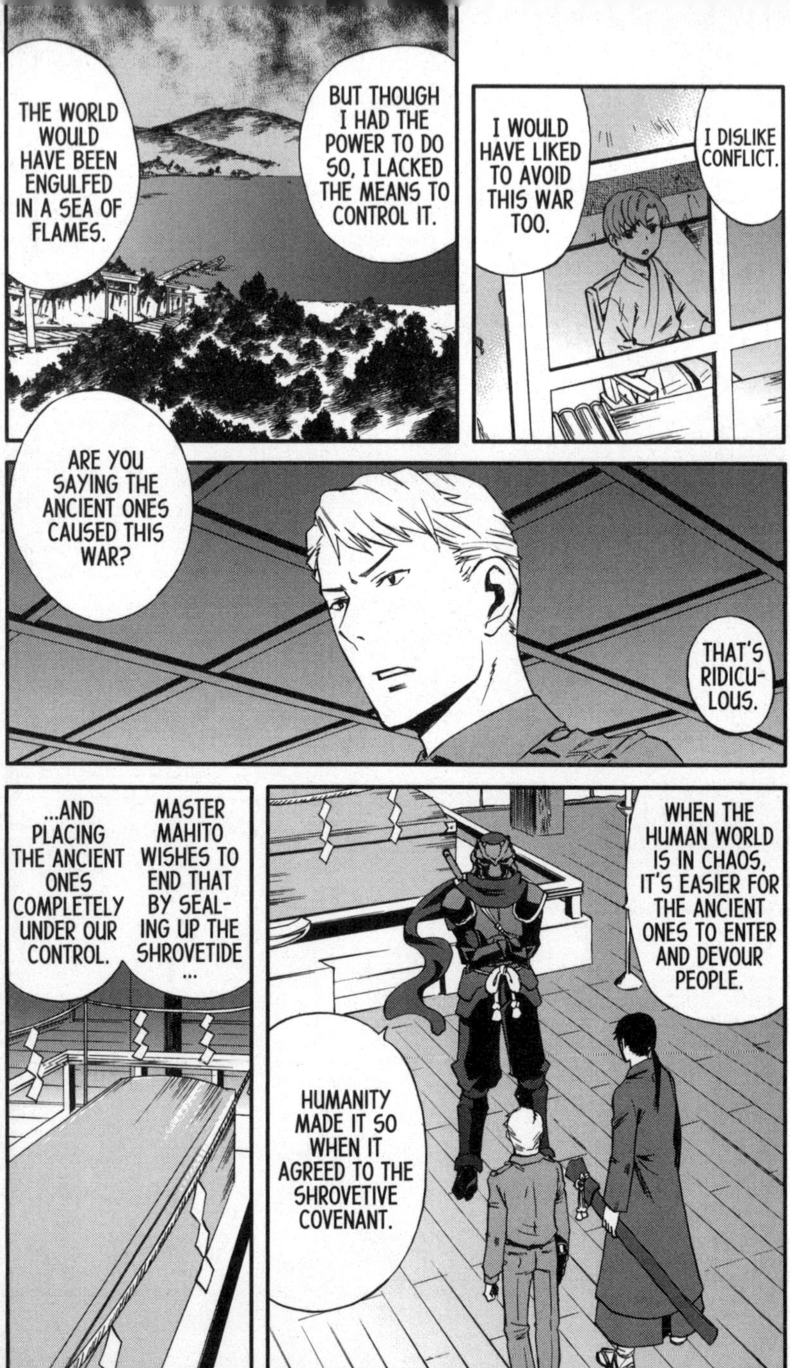
I DISLIKE CONFLICT.
I WOULD HAVE LIKED TO AVOID THIS WAR TOO.
BUT THOUGH I HAD THE POWER TO DO SO, I LACKED THE MEANS TO CONTROL IT.
THE WORLD WOULD HAVE BEEN ENGULFED IN A SEA OF FLAMES.
ARE YOU SAYING THE ANCIENT ONES CAUSED THIS WAR?
THAT'S RIDICU-LOUS.
WHEN THE HUMAN WORLD IS IN CHAOS, IT'S EASIER FOR THE ANCIENT ONES TO ENTER AND DEVOUR PEOPLE.
HUMANITY MADE IT SO WHEN IT AGREED TO THE SHROVETIVE COVENANT.
MASTER MAHITO WISHES TO END THAT BY SEAL-ING UP THE SHROVETIDE ...
...AND PLACING THE ANCIENT ONES COMPLETELY UNDER OUR CONTROL.

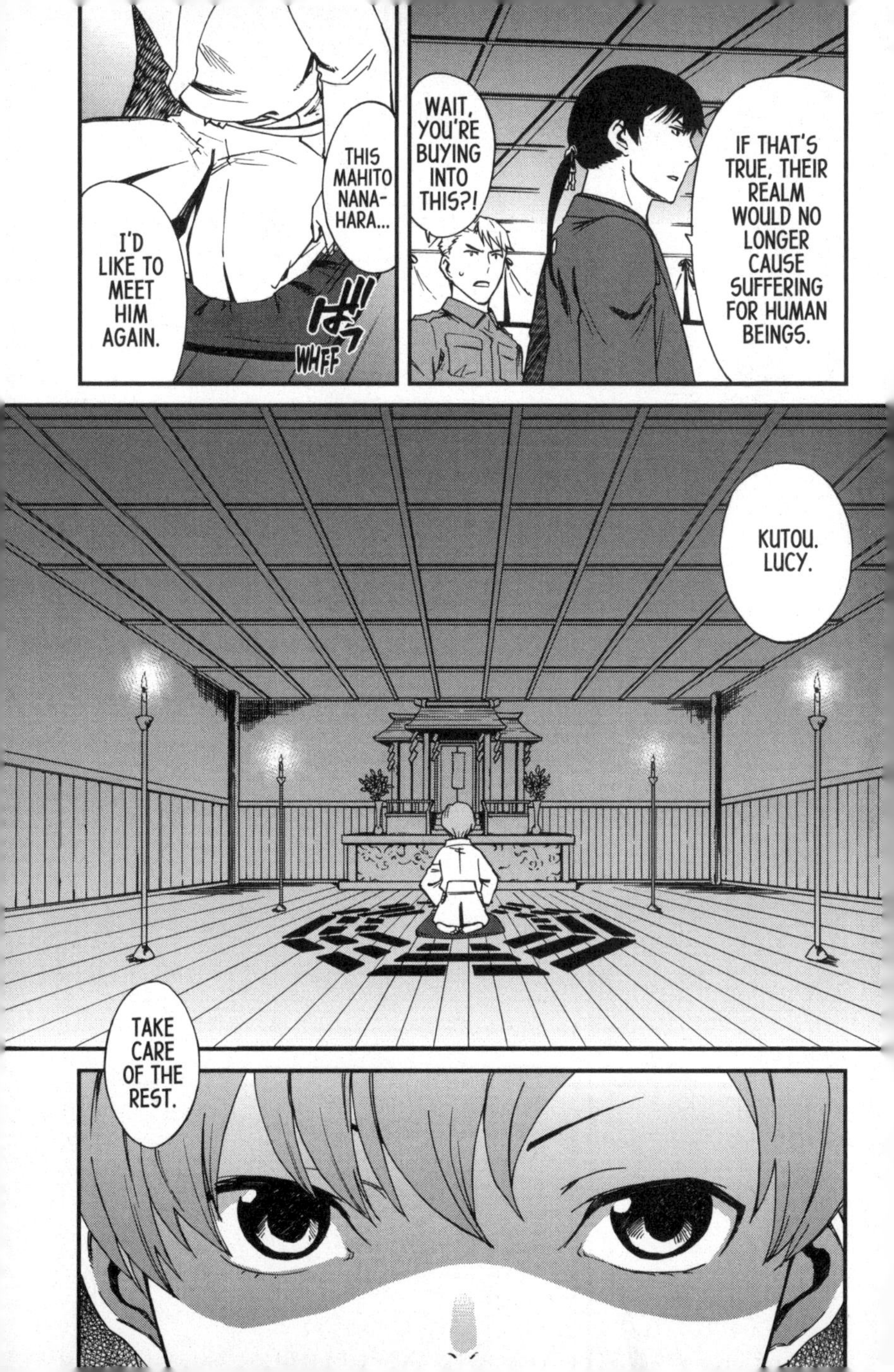
IF THAT'S TRUE, THEIR REALM WOULD NO LONGER CAUSE SUFFERING FOR HUMAN BEINGS.
WAIT, YOU'RE BUYING INTO THIS?!
THIS MAHITO NANA-HARA...
I'D LIKE TO MEET HIM AGAIN.
ばっ
WHFF
KUTOU. LUCY.
TAKE CARE OF THE REST.

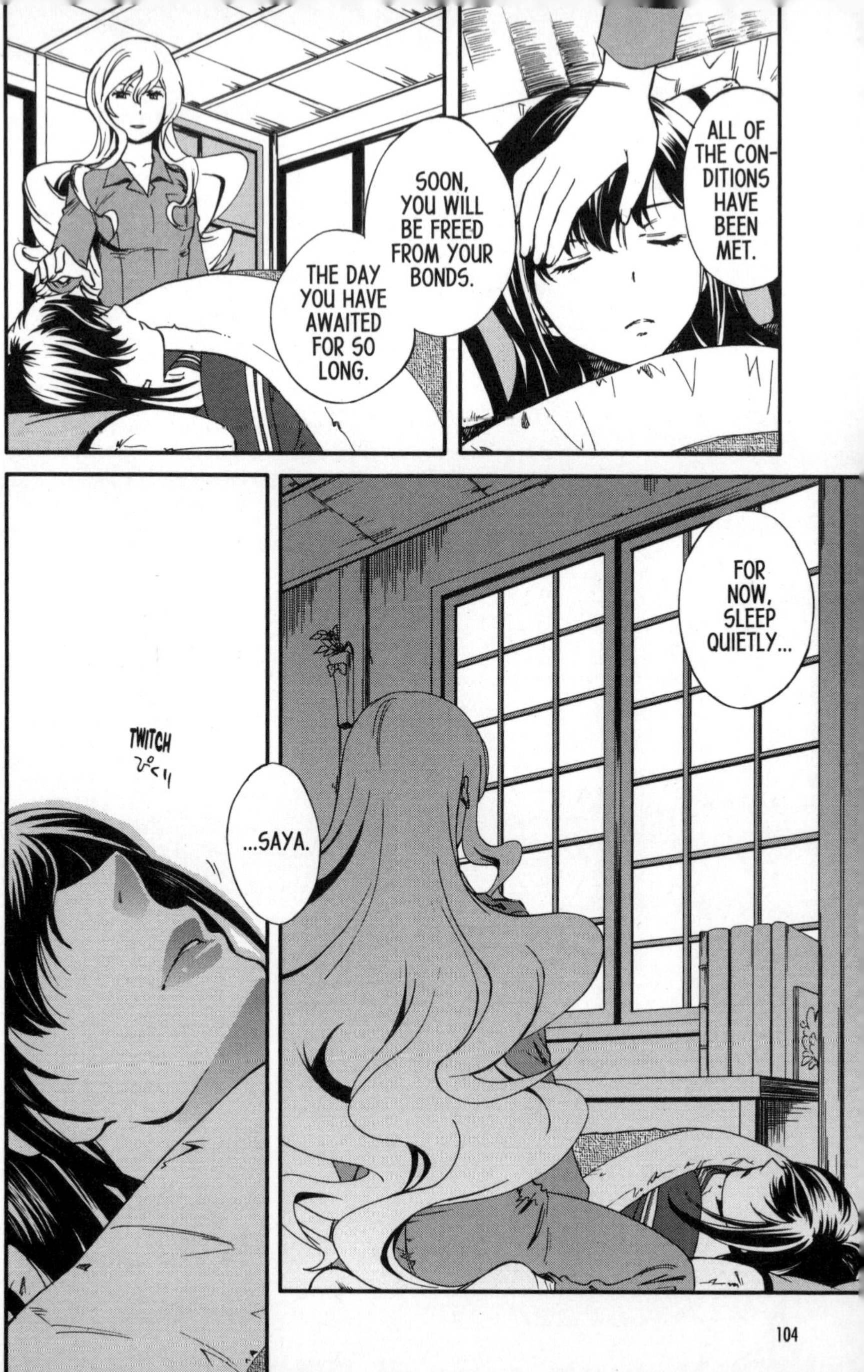
ALL OF THE CON-DITIONS HAVE BEEN MET.
SOON, YOU WILL BE FREED FROM YOUR BONDS.
THE DAY YOU HAVE AWAITED FOR SO LONG.
FOR NOW, SLEEP QUIETLY...
...SAYA.
TWITCH
ぴくり

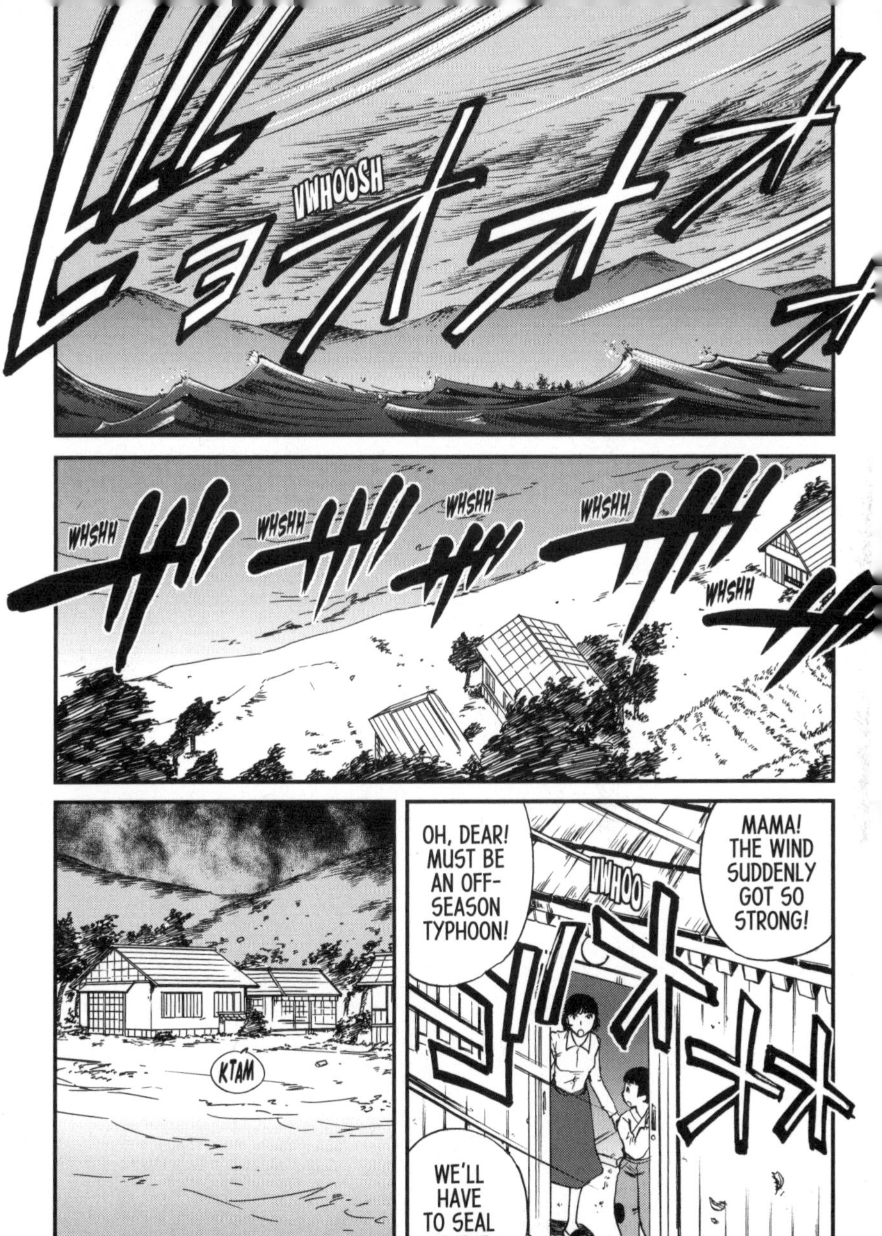
VWHOOSH
WHSHH
WHSHH
WHSHH
WHSHH
WHSHH
MAMA! THE WIND SUDDENLY GOT SO STRONG!
VWHOO
OH, DEAR! MUST BE AN OFF-SEASON TYPHOON!
WE'LL HAVE TO SEAL UP THE HOUSE.
KTAM

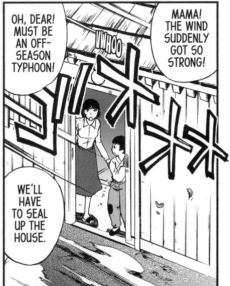

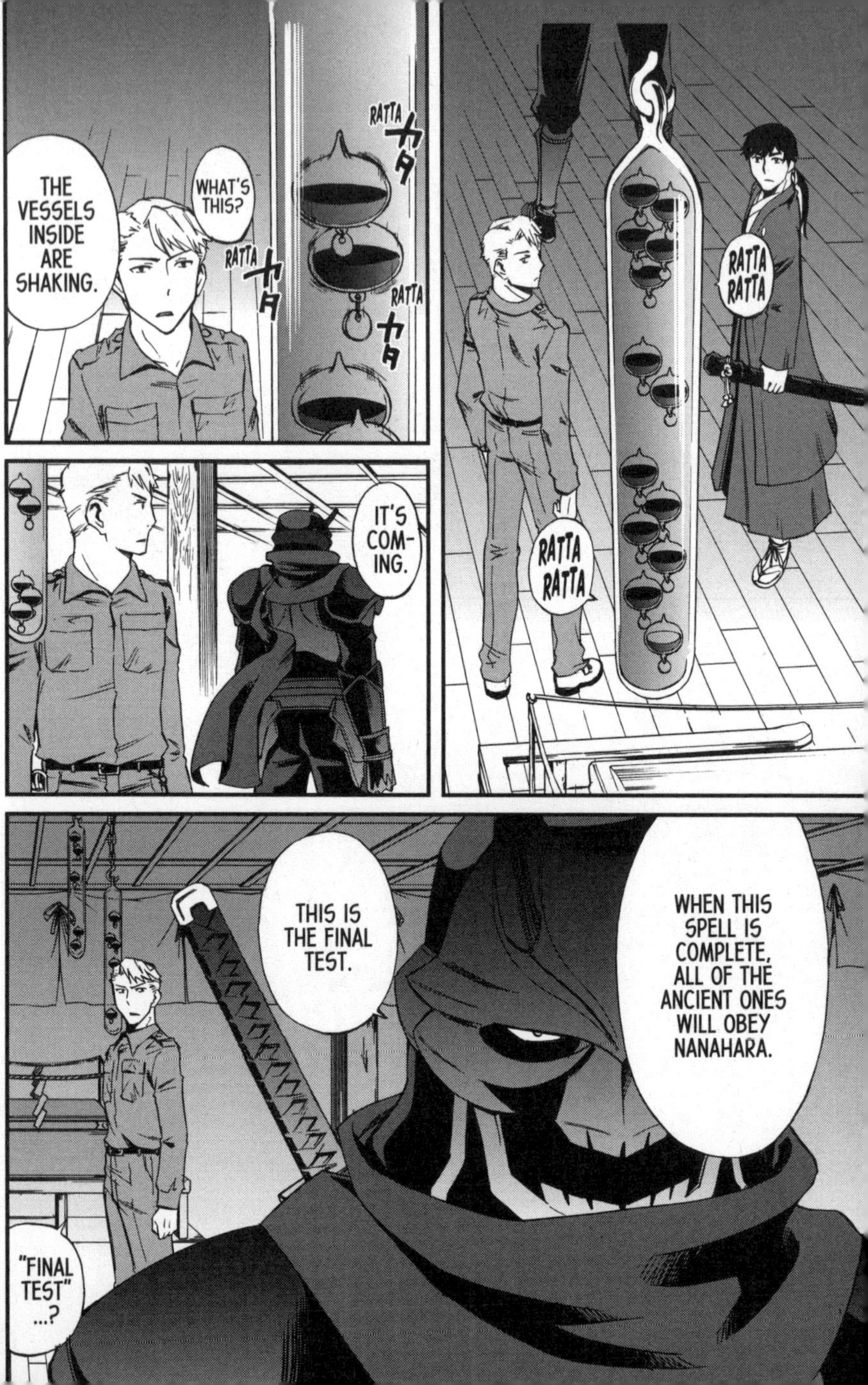
RATTA RATTA
RATTA RATTA
RATTA
WHAT'S THIS?
RATTA
RATTA
THE VESSELS INSIDE ARE SHAKING.
IT'S COM-ING.
WHEN THIS SPELL IS COMPLETE, ALL OF THE ANCIENT ONES WILL OBEY NANAHARA.
THIS IS THE FINAL TEST.
"FINAL TEST" ...?

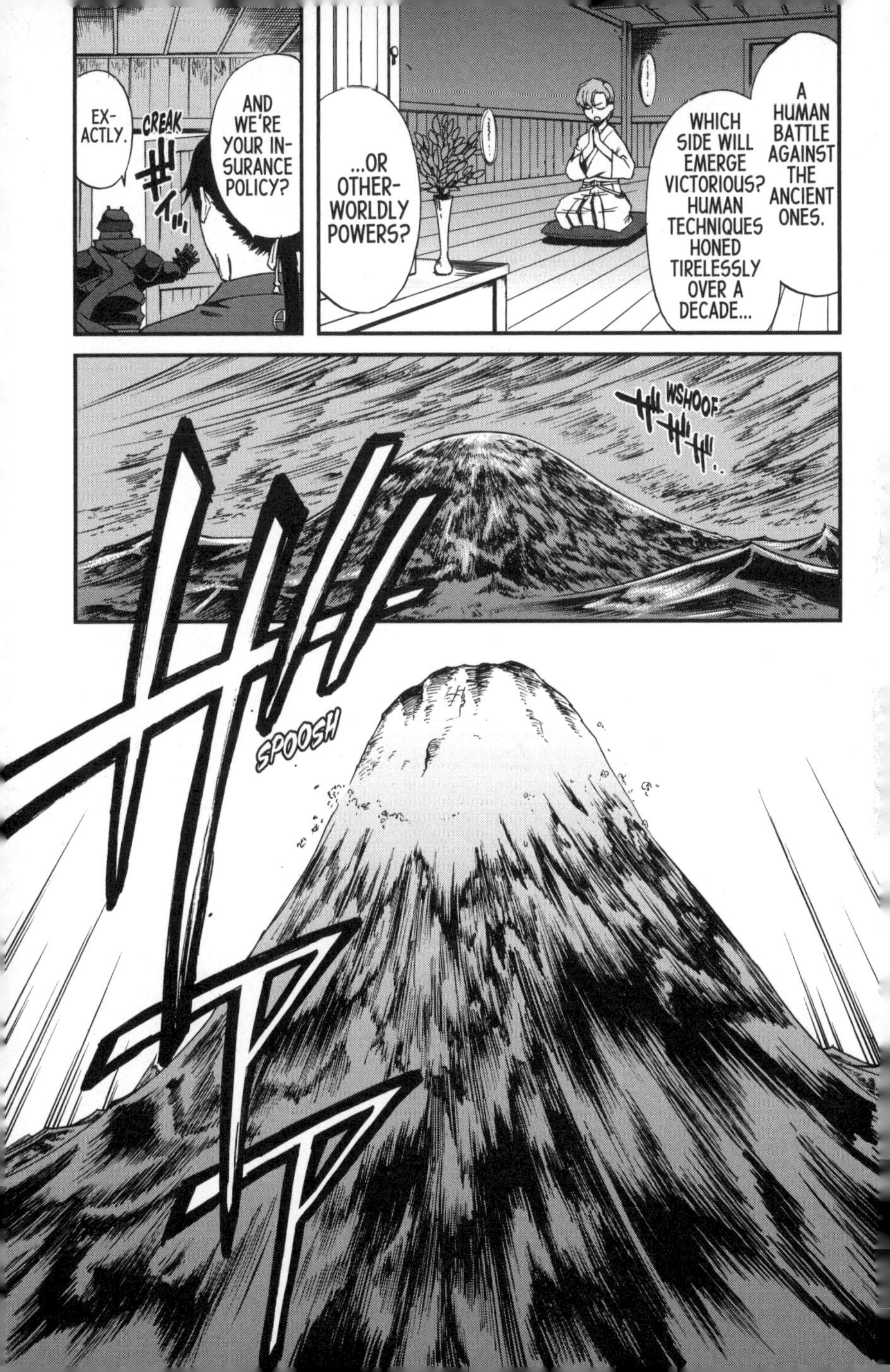

A HUMAN BATTLE AGAINST THE ANCIENT ONES.
WHICH SIDE WILL EMERGE VICTORIOUS? HUMAN TECHNIQUES HONED TIRELESSLY OVER A DECADE...
...OR OTHER-WORLDLY POWERS?
AND WE'RE YOUR IN-SURANCE POLICY?
CREAK
EX-ACTLY.
WSHOOF
SPOOSH

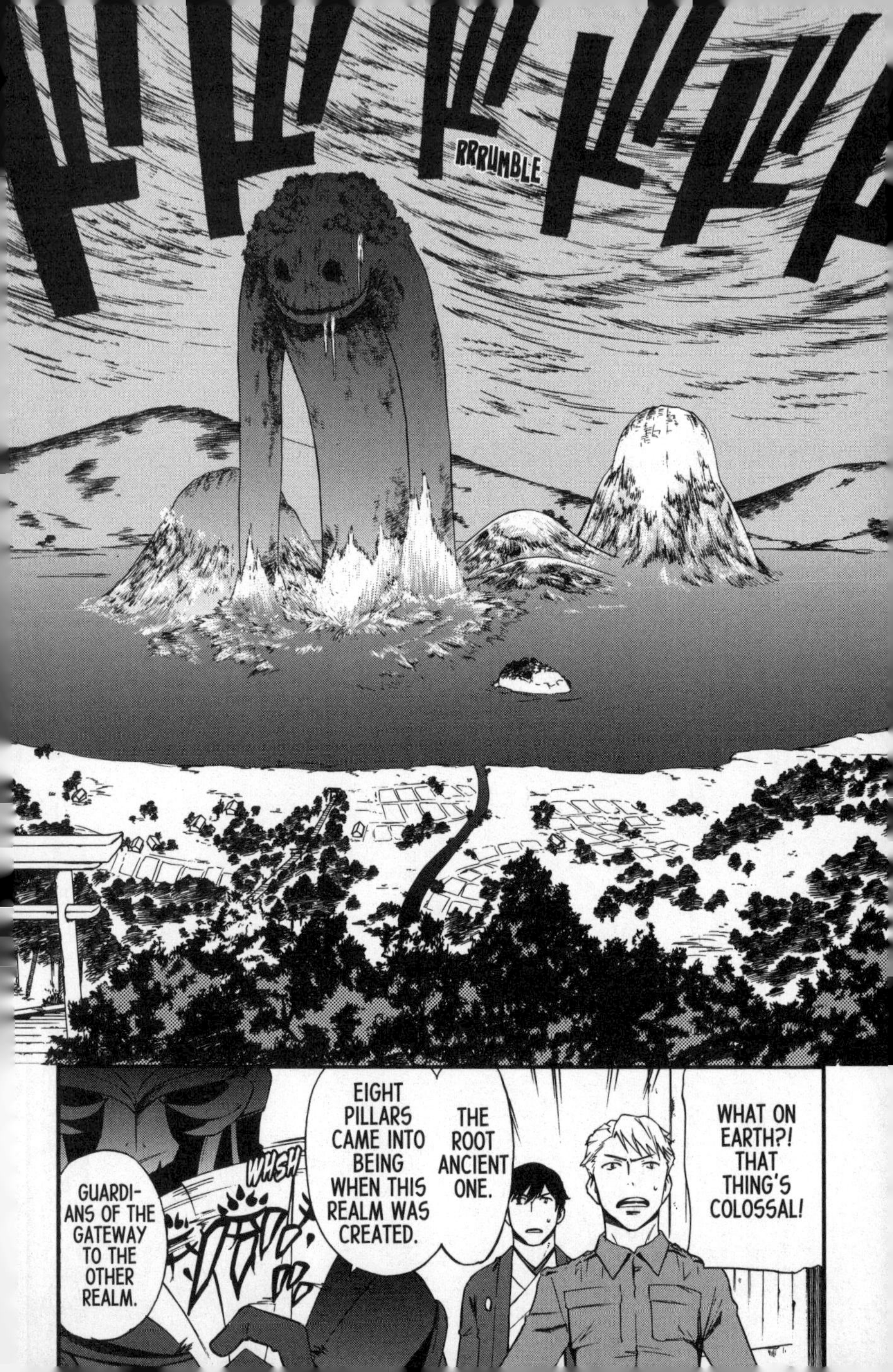
RRRUMBLE
WHAT ON EARTH?! THAT THING'S COLOSSAL!
THE ROOT ANCIENT ONE.
EIGHT PILLARS CAME INTO BEING WHEN THIS REALM WAS CREATED.
WHSH
GUARDI-ANS OF THE GATEWAY TO THE OTHER REALM.

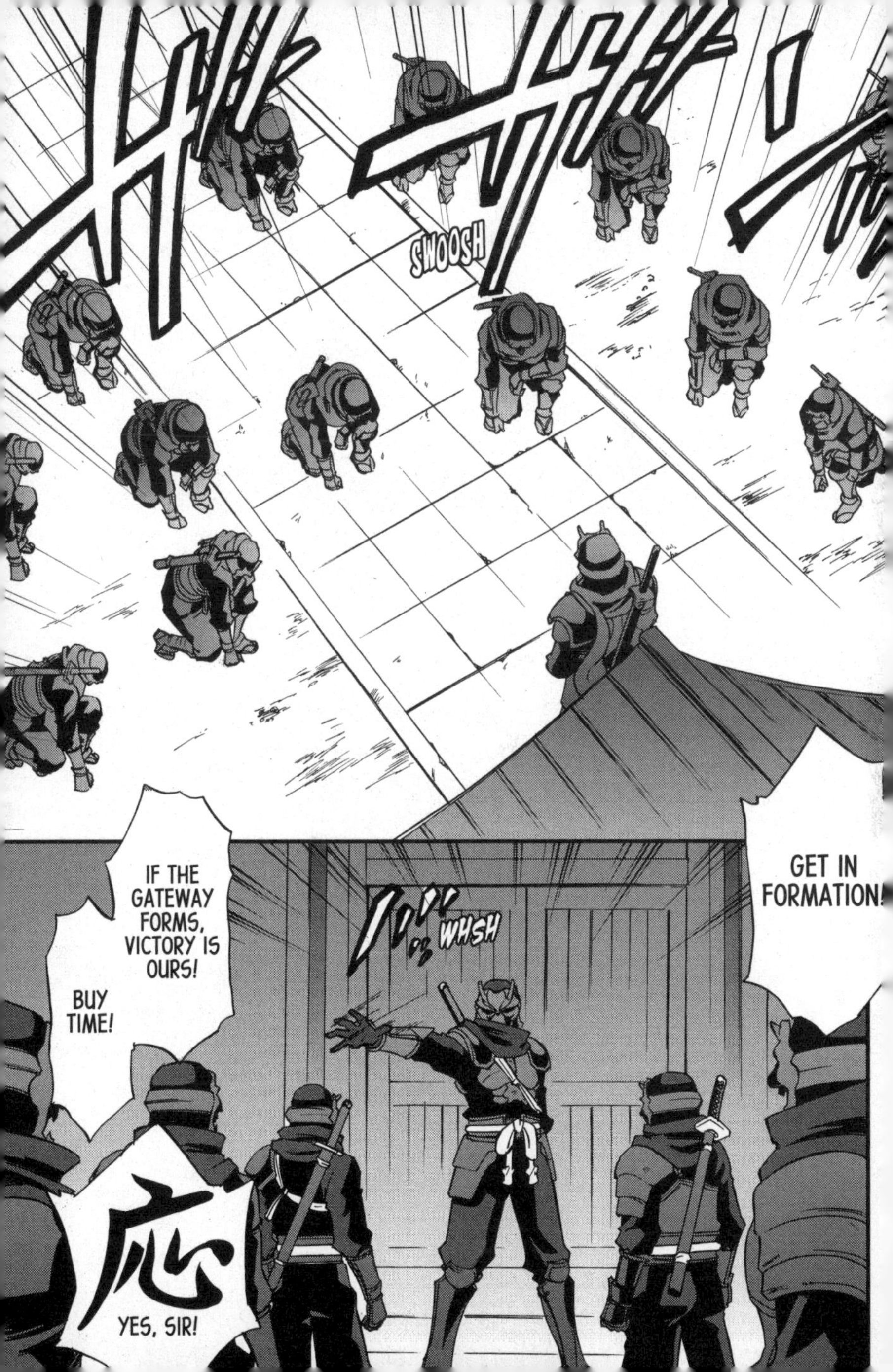
SWOOSH
GET IN FORMATION!
WHSH
IF THE GATEWAY FORMS, VICTORY IS OURS!
BUY TIME!
応
YES, SIR!

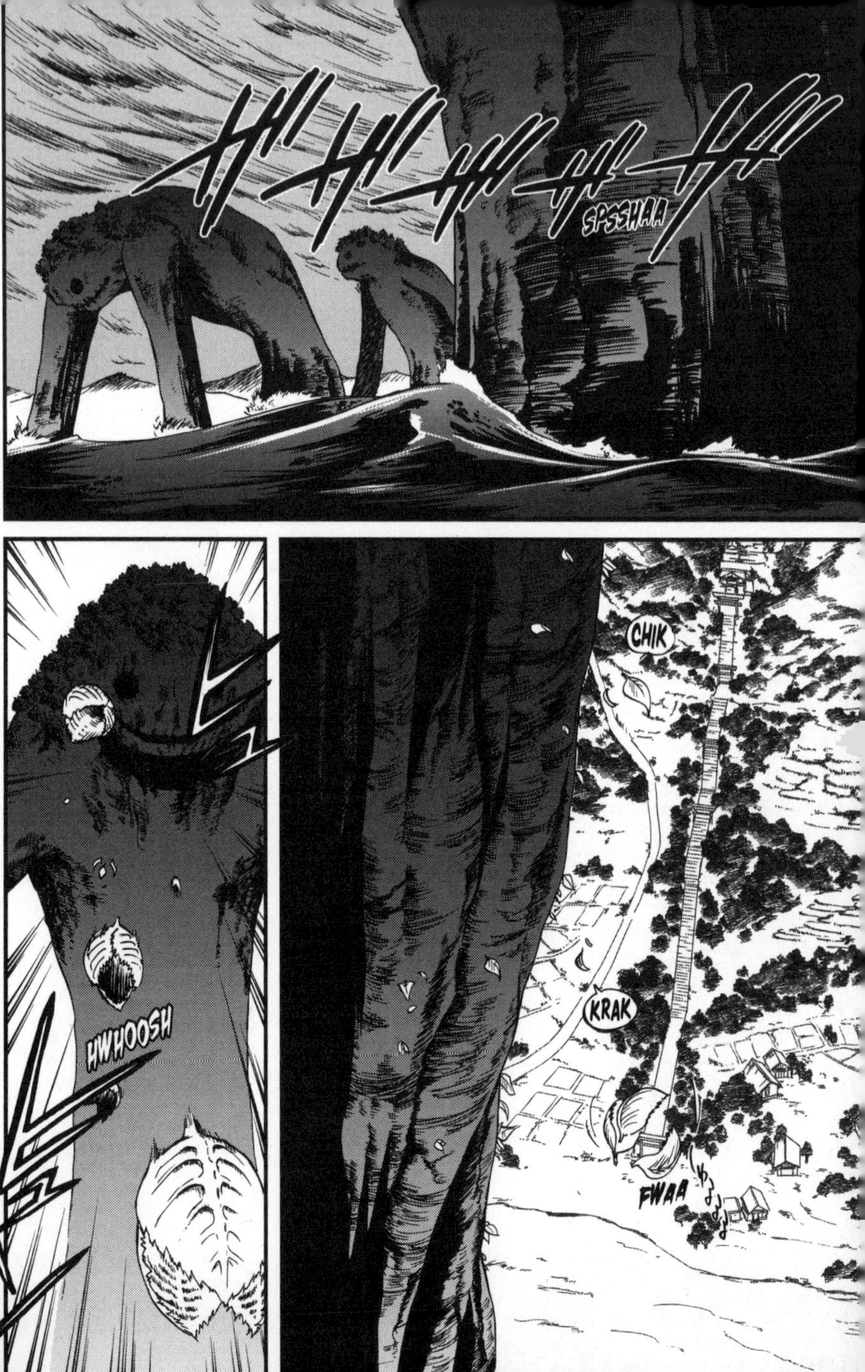
SPSSHAA
CHIK
KRAK
FWAA
HWHOOSH

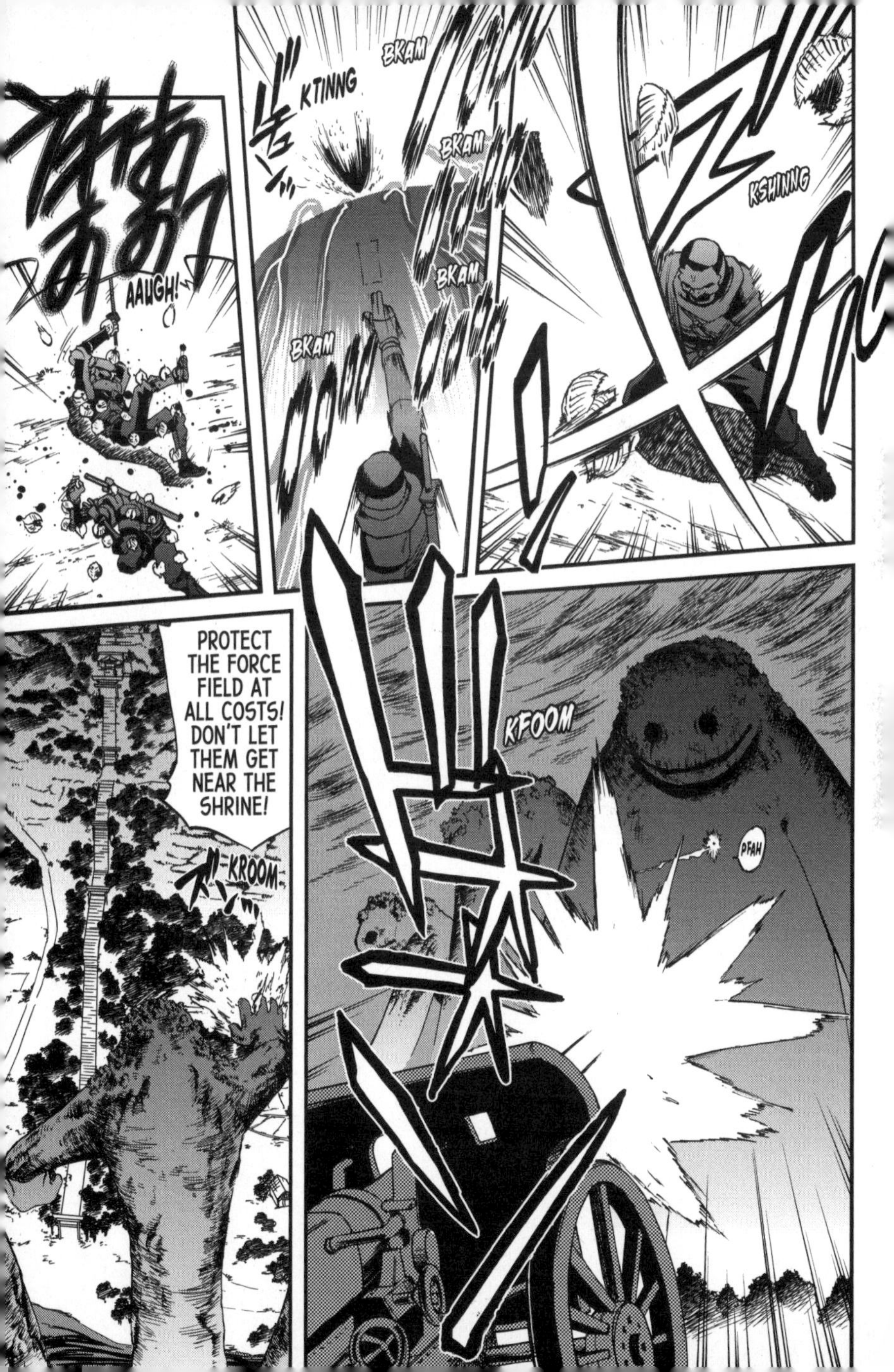
KSHINNG
BKAM
KTINNG
BKAM
BKAM
BKAM
AAUGH!
KFOOM
PFAH
PROTECT THE FORCE FIELD AT ALL COSTS! DON'T LET THEM GET NEAR THE SHRINE!
KROOM

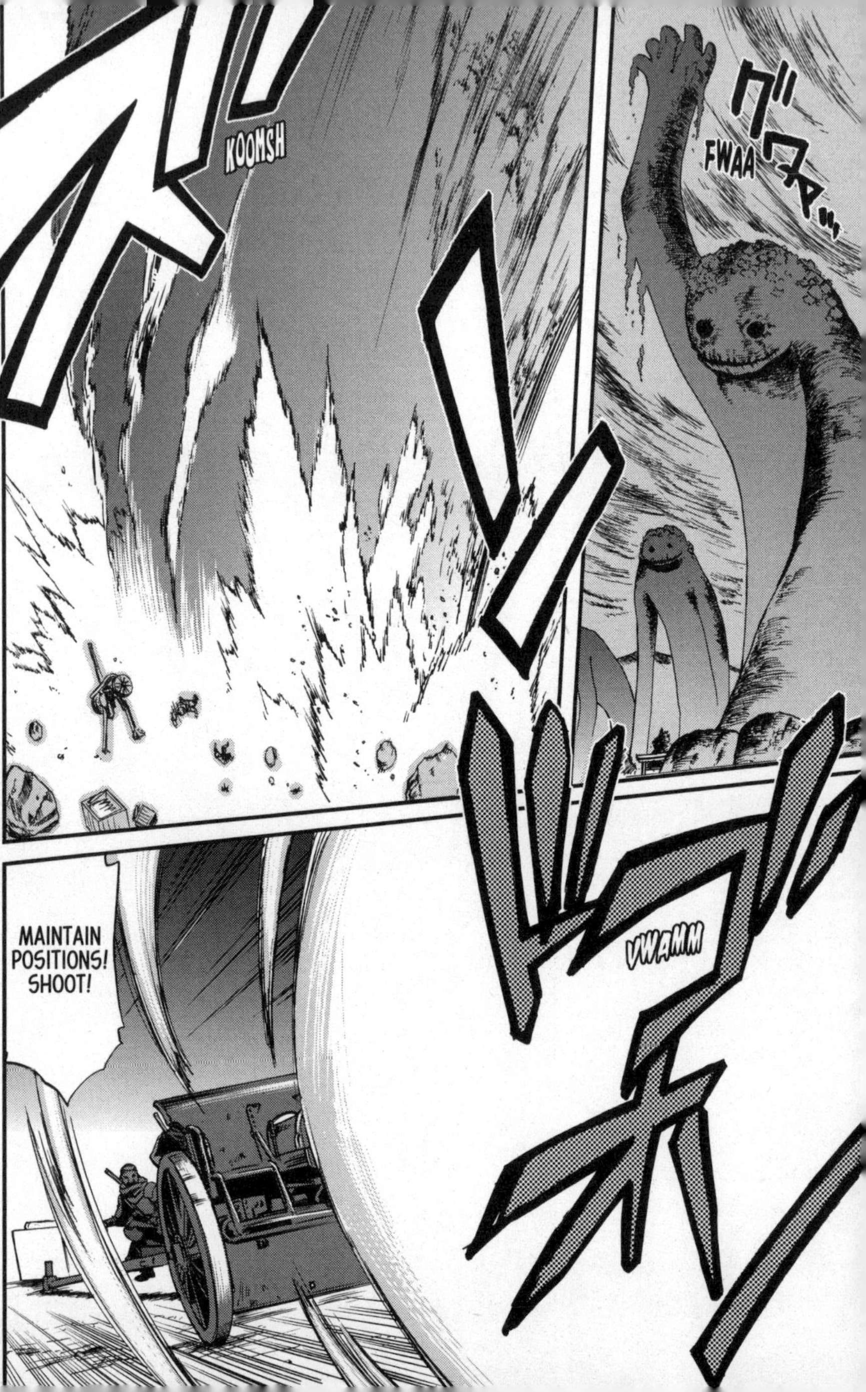
グワァ…
FWAA
KOOMSH
MAINTAIN POSITIONS! SHOOT!
VWAMM

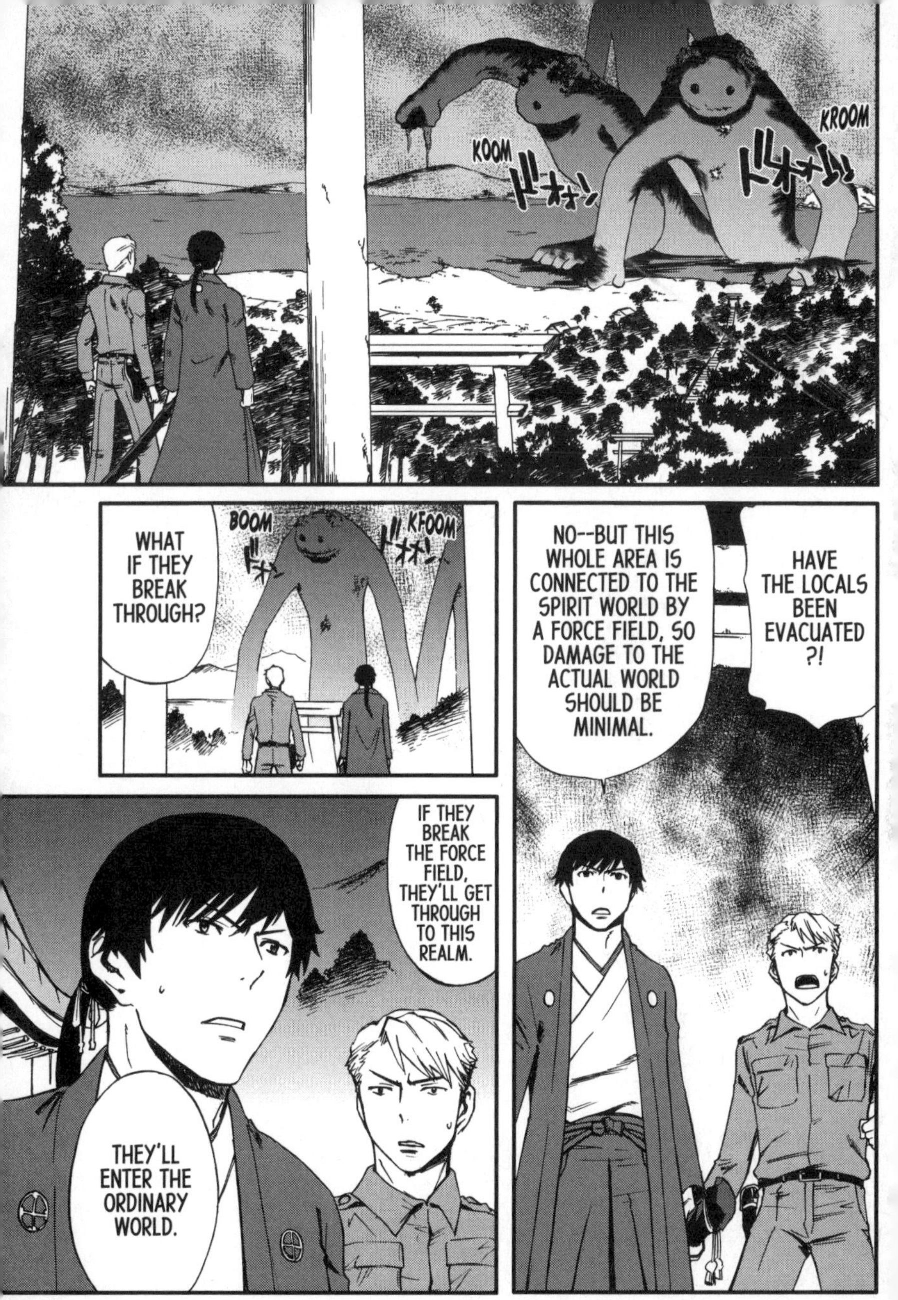
KROOM
KOOM
HAVE THE LOCALS BEEN EVACUATED ?!
NO--BUT THIS WHOLE AREA IS CONNECTED TO THE SPIRIT WORLD BY A FORCE FIELD, SO DAMAGE TO THE ACTUAL WORLD SHOULD BE MINIMAL.
KFOOM
BOOM
WHAT IF THEY BREAK THROUGH?
IF THEY BREAK THE FORCE FIELD, THEY'LL GET THROUGH TO THIS REALM.
THEY'LL ENTER THE ORDINARY WORLD.

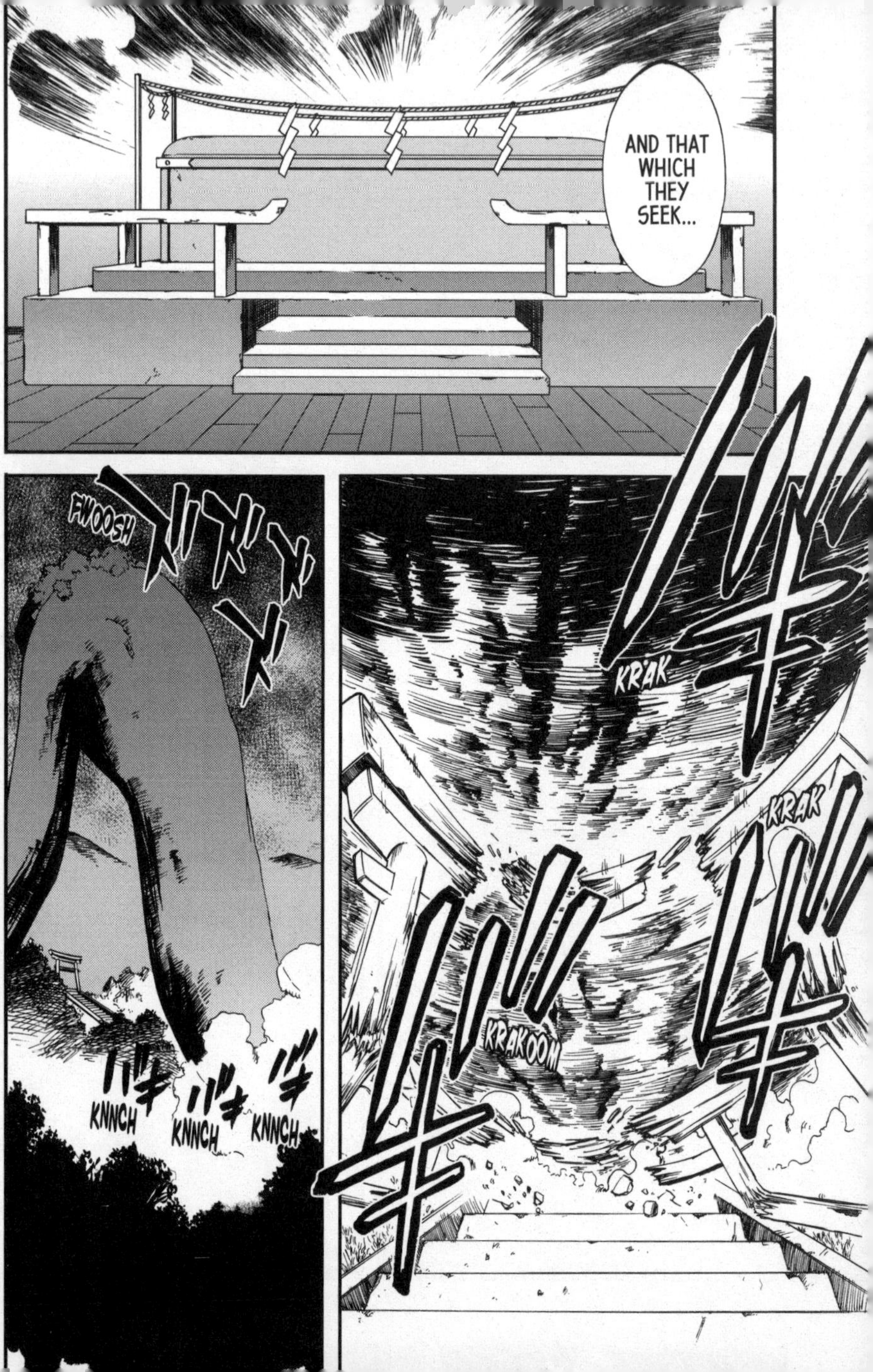
AND THAT WHICH THEY SEEK...
KRAK
KRAK
KRAKOOM
FWOOSH
KNNCH
KNNCH
KNNCH

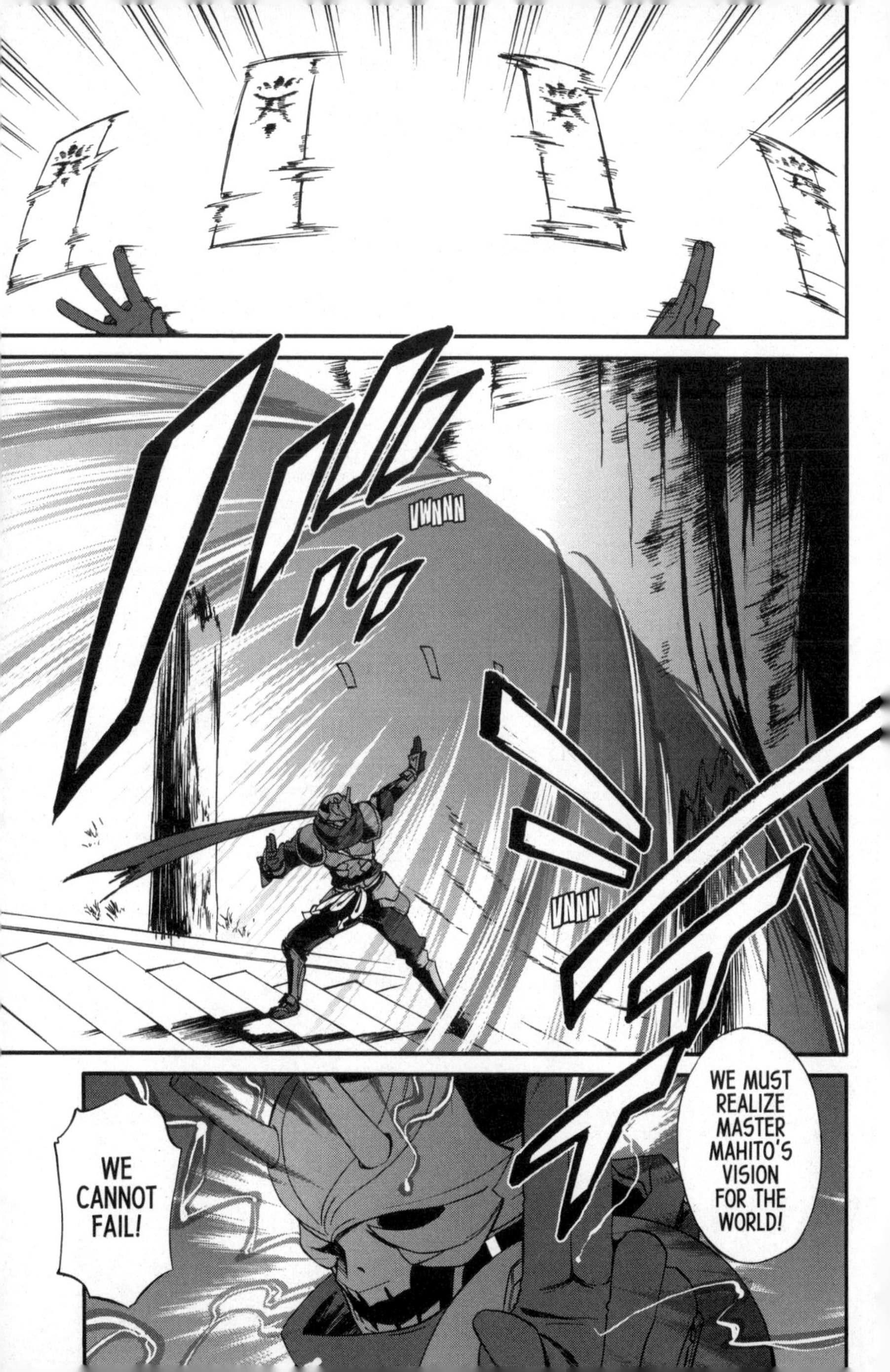
VWNNN
VNNN
WE MUST REALIZE MASTER MAHITO'S VISION FOR THE WORLD!
WE CANNOT FAIL!

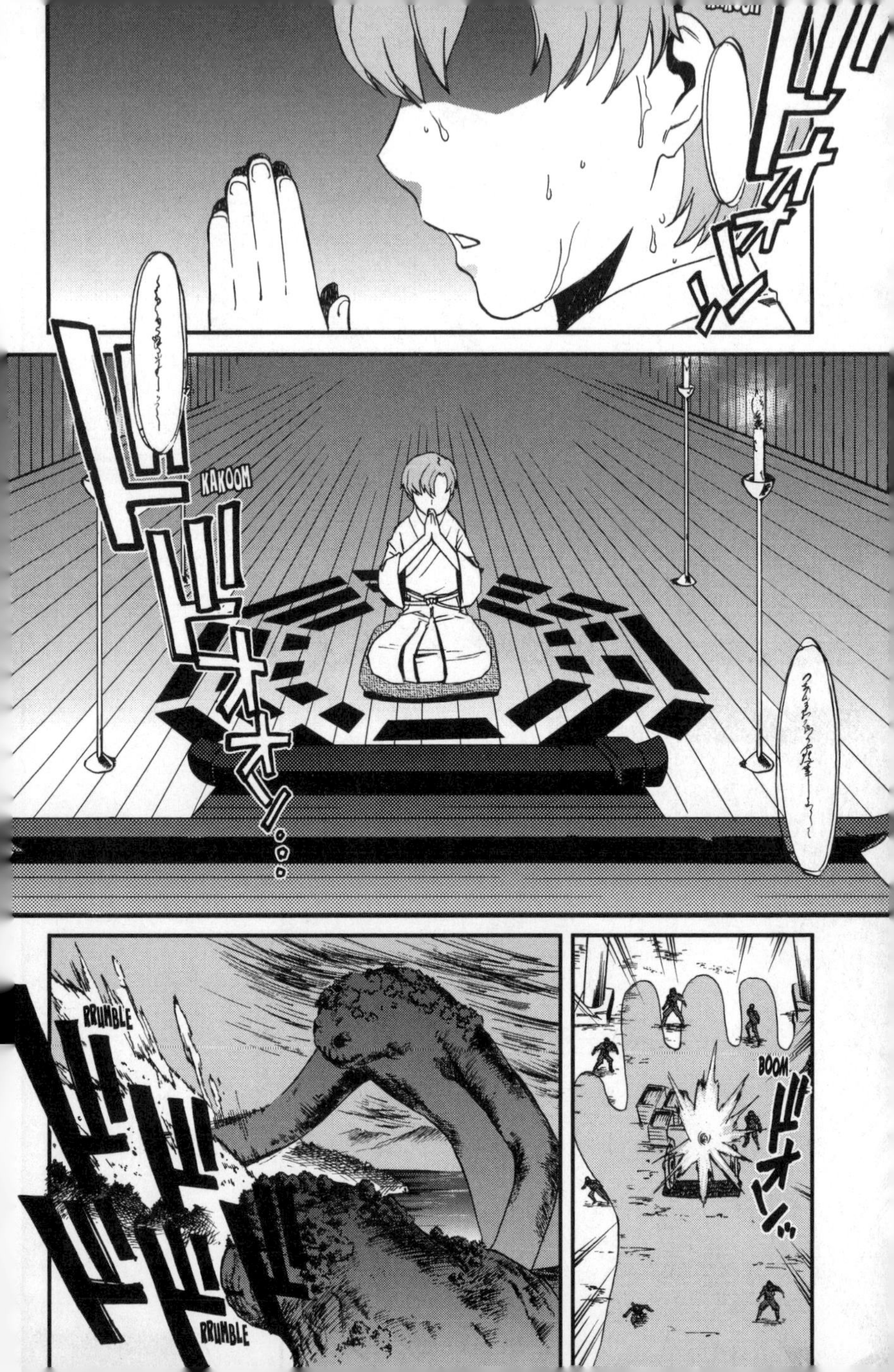
KAKOOM
BOOM
RRUMBLE
RRUMBLE

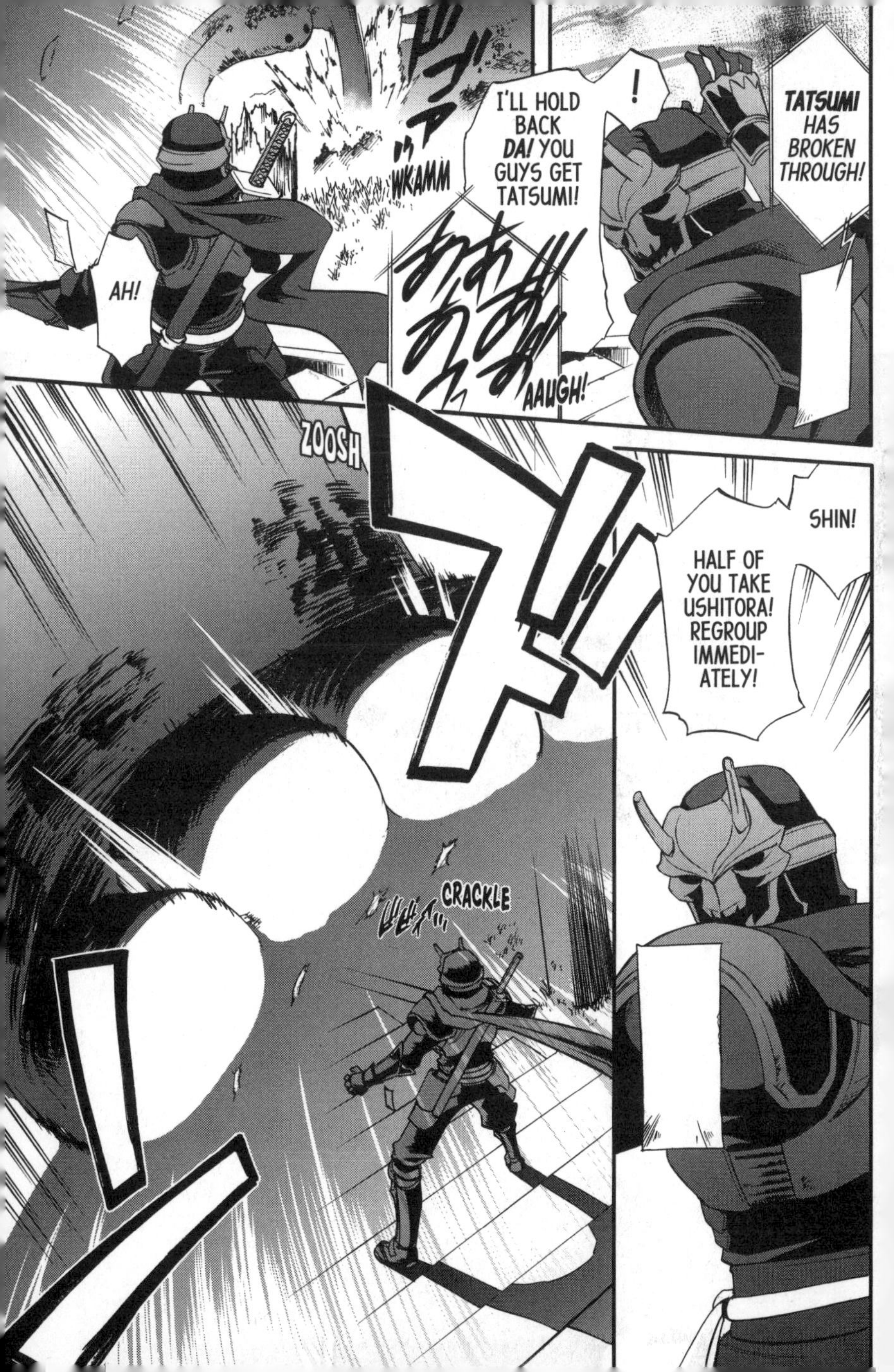
TATSUMI HAS BROKEN THROUGH!
!
I'LL HOLD BACK DA! YOU GUYS GET TATSUMI!
WKAMM
AAUGH!
AH!
SHIN!
HALF OF YOU TAKE USHITORA! REGROUP IMMEDI-ATELY!
ZOOSH
CRACKLE

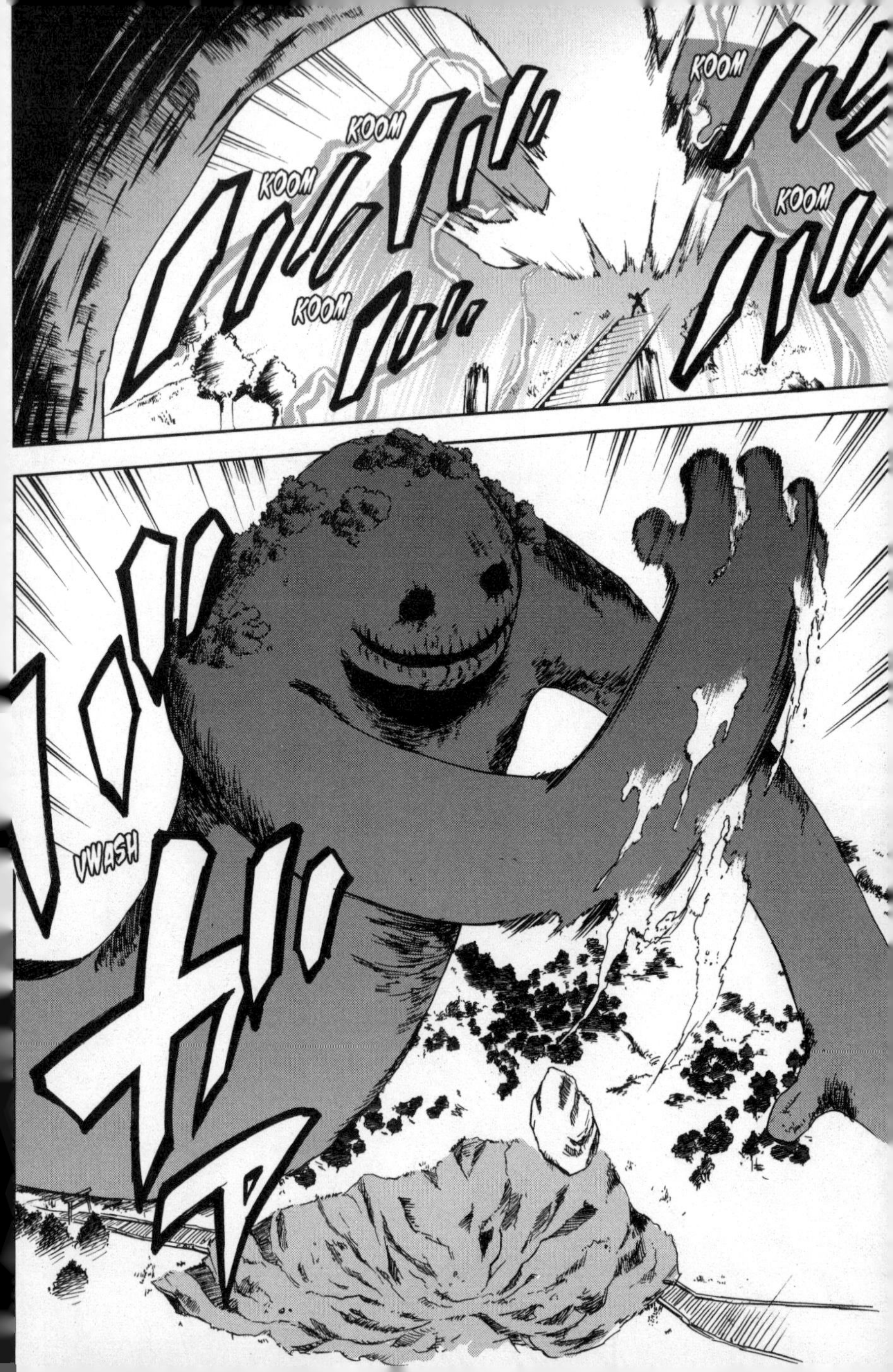
KOOM
KOOM
KOOM
KOOM
KOOM
VWASH

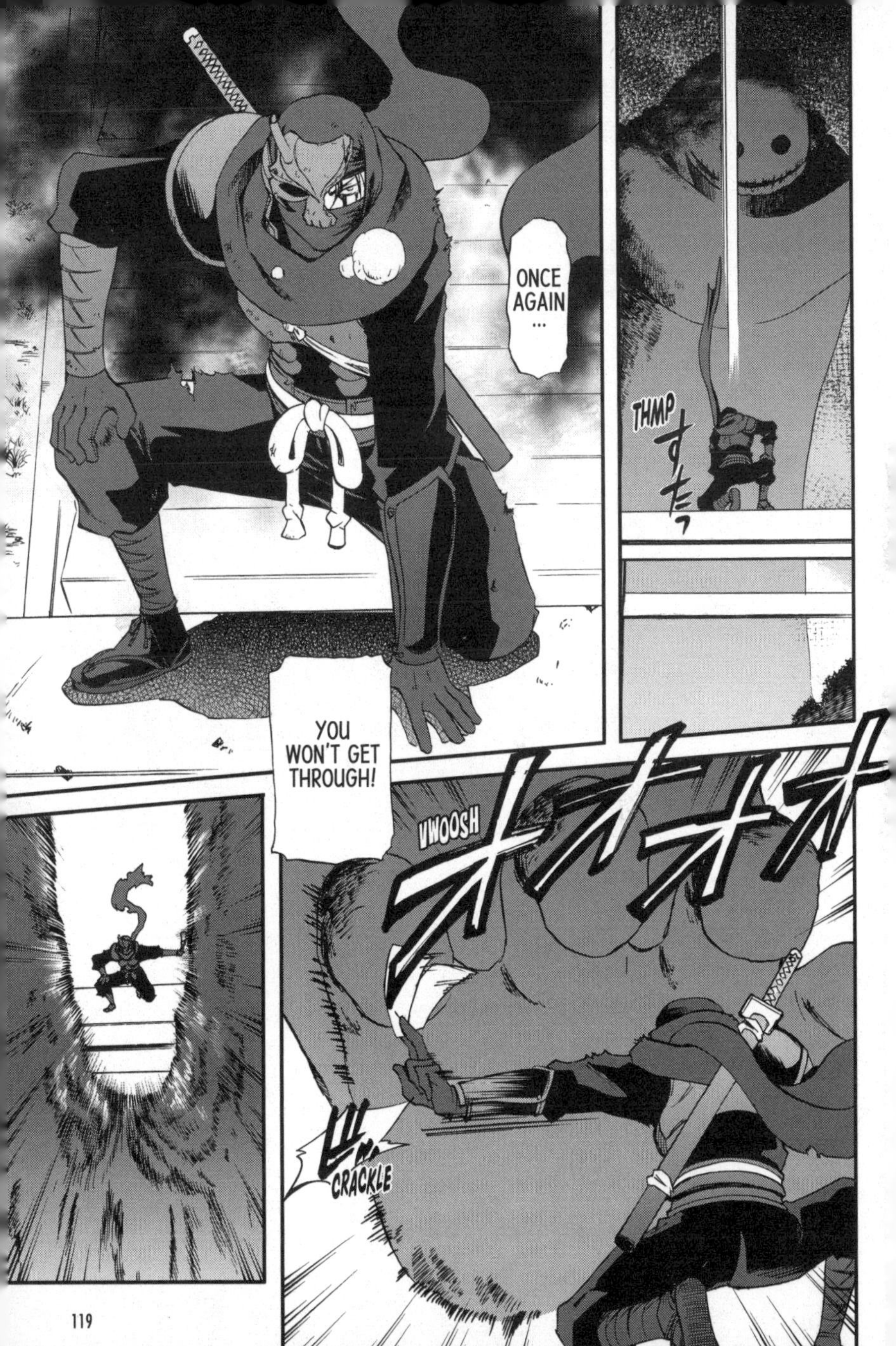
THMP
すたっ
ONCE AGAIN...
YOU WON'T GET THROUGH!
VWOOSH
オオオオ
CRACKLE

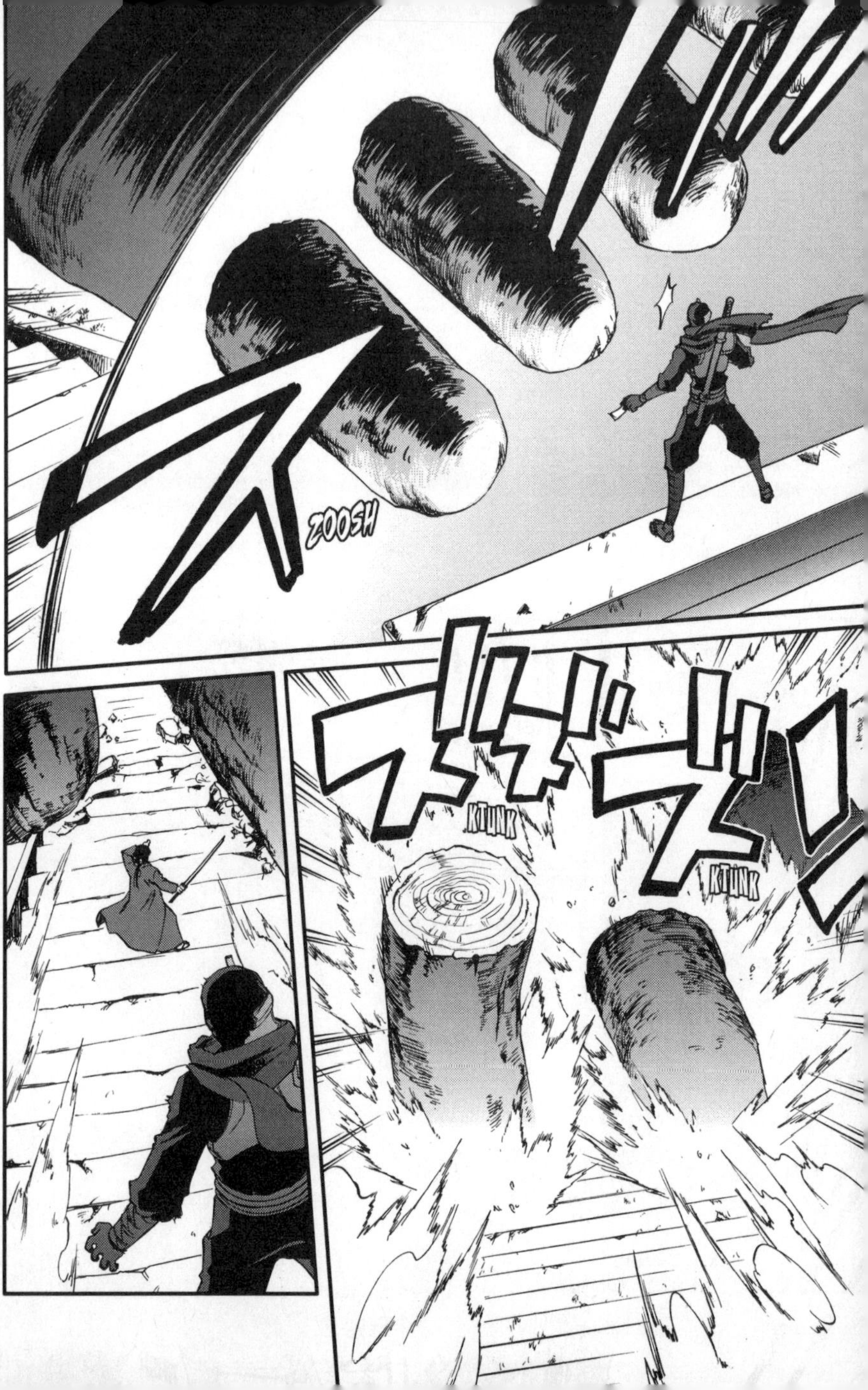

ZOOSH
KTUNK
KTUNK

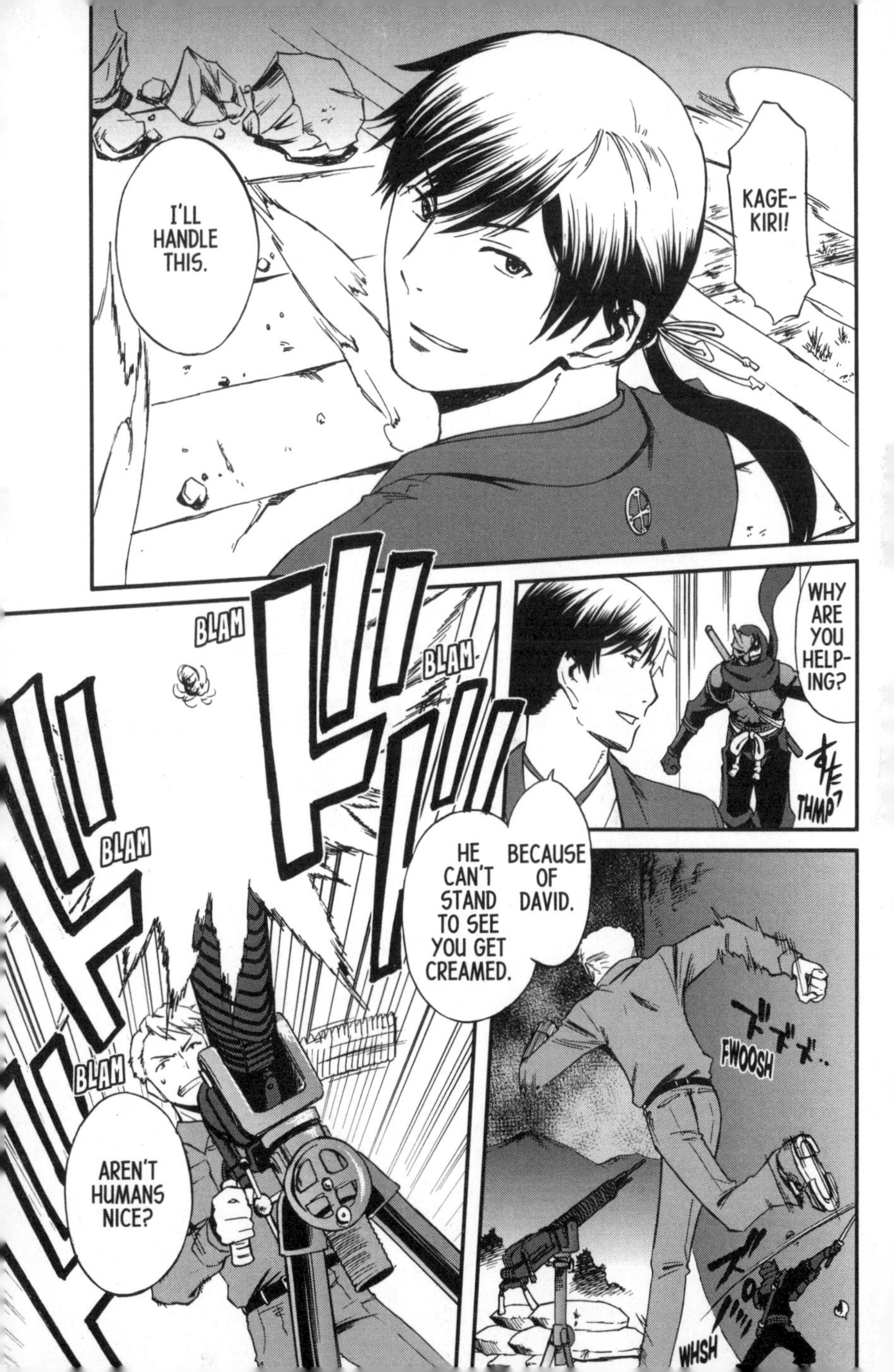
KAGE-KIRI!
I'LL HANDLE THIS.
WHY ARE YOU HELPING?
THMP
BECAUSE OF DAVID.
HE CAN'T STAND TO SEE YOU GET CREAMED.
FWOOSH
WHSH
BLAM
BLAM
BLAM
BLAM
AREN'T HUMANS NICE?

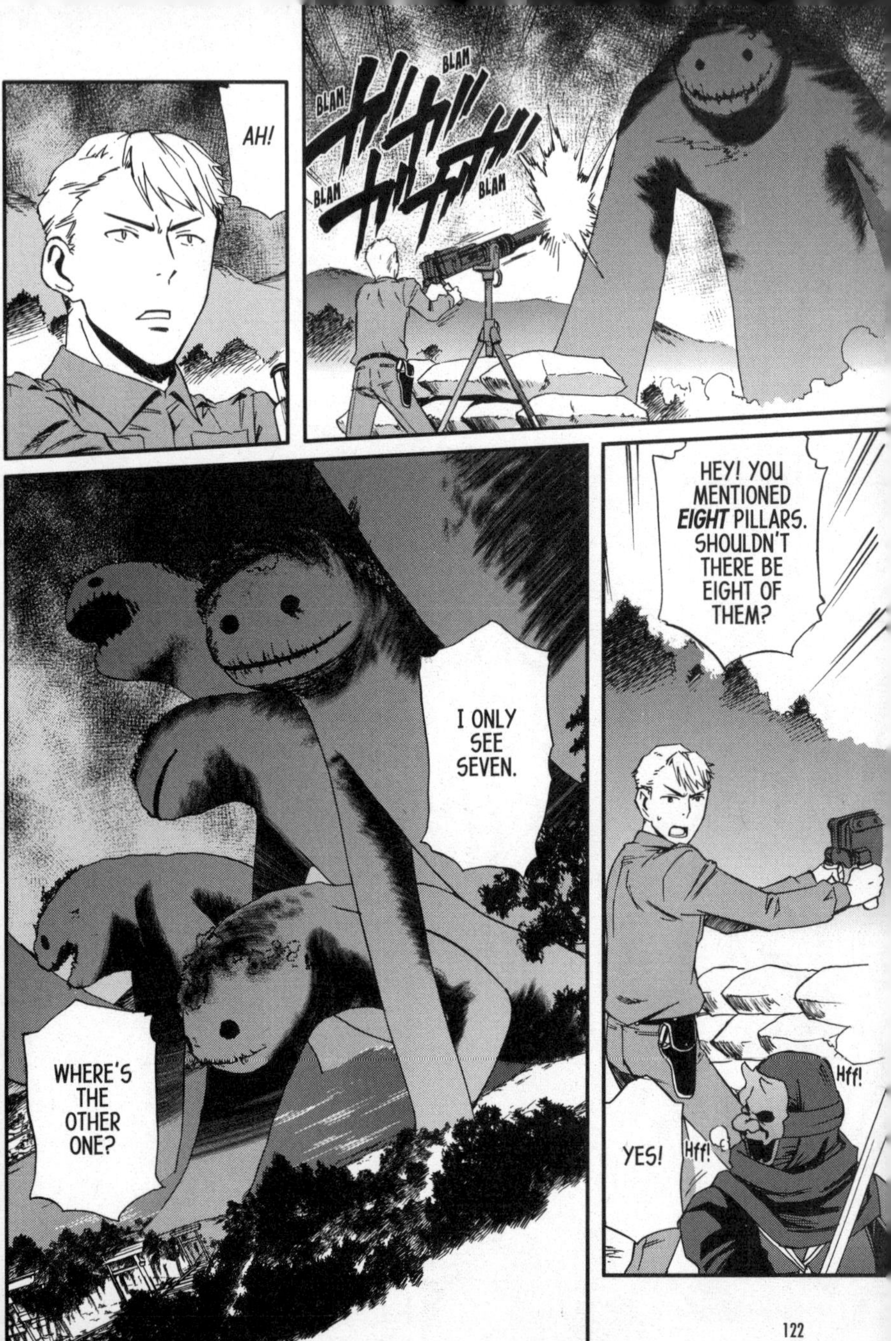
BLAM
BLAM
BLAM
BLAM
AH!
HEY! YOU MENTIONED *EIGHT* PILLARS. SHOULDN'T THERE BE EIGHT OF THEM?
Hff!
YES!
Hff!
I ONLY SEE SEVEN.
WHERE'S THE OTHER ONE?

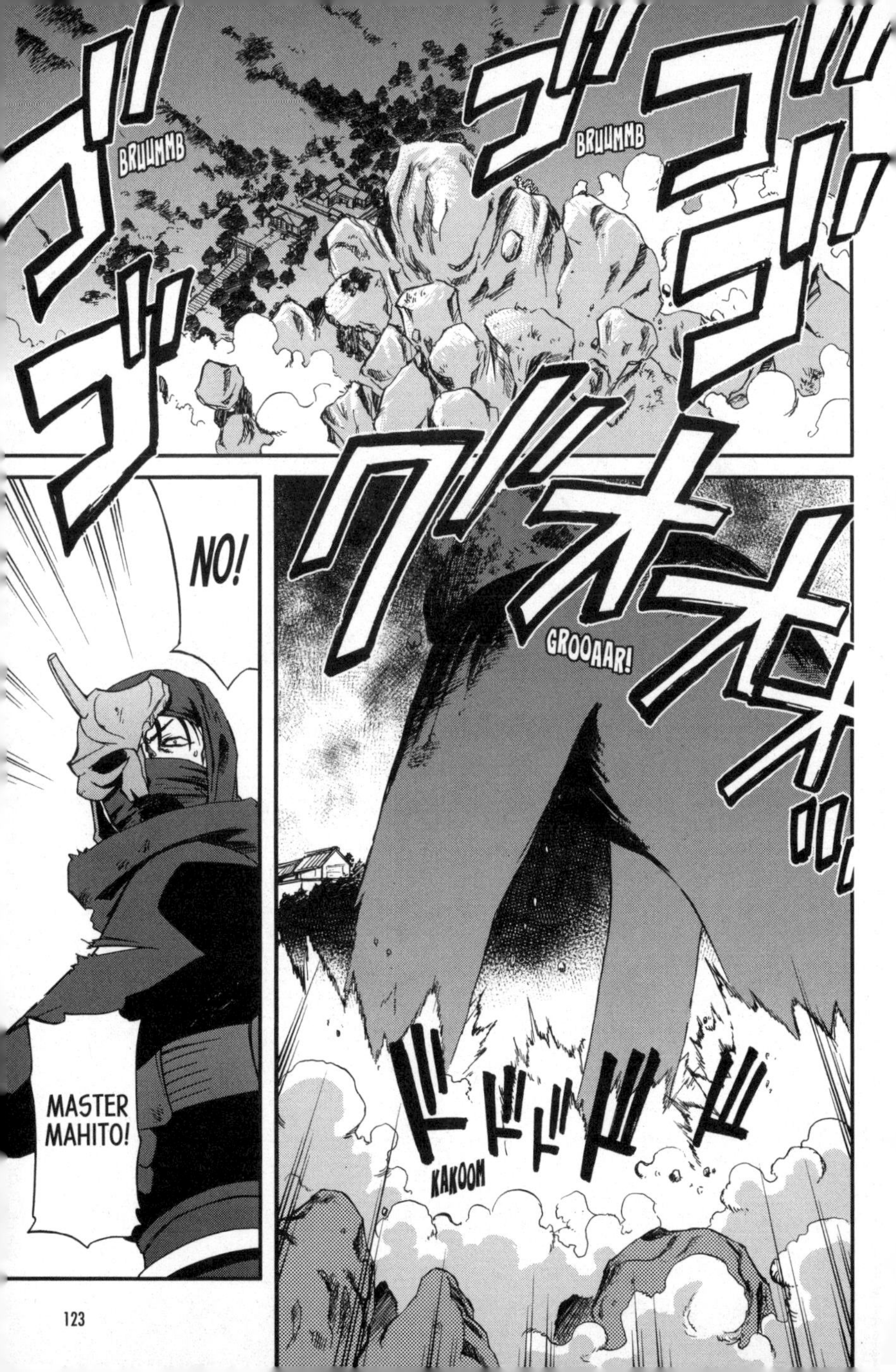
BRUUMMB
BRUUMMB
GROOAAR!
KAKOOM
NO!
MASTER MAHITO!

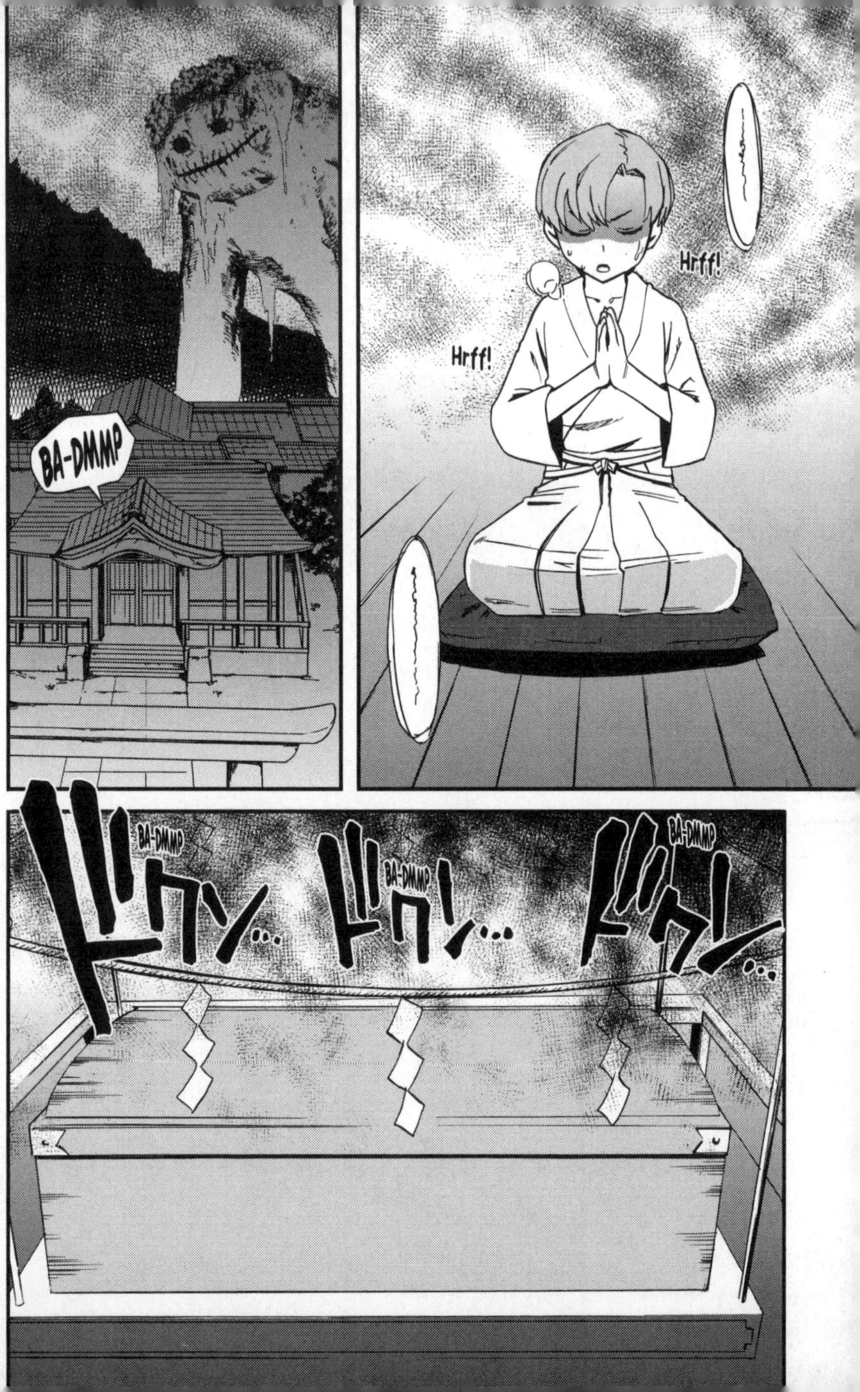
Hrff!
Hrff!
BA-DMMP
ドクン…
BA-DMMP
ドクン…
BA-DMMP
ドクン…
BA-DMMP

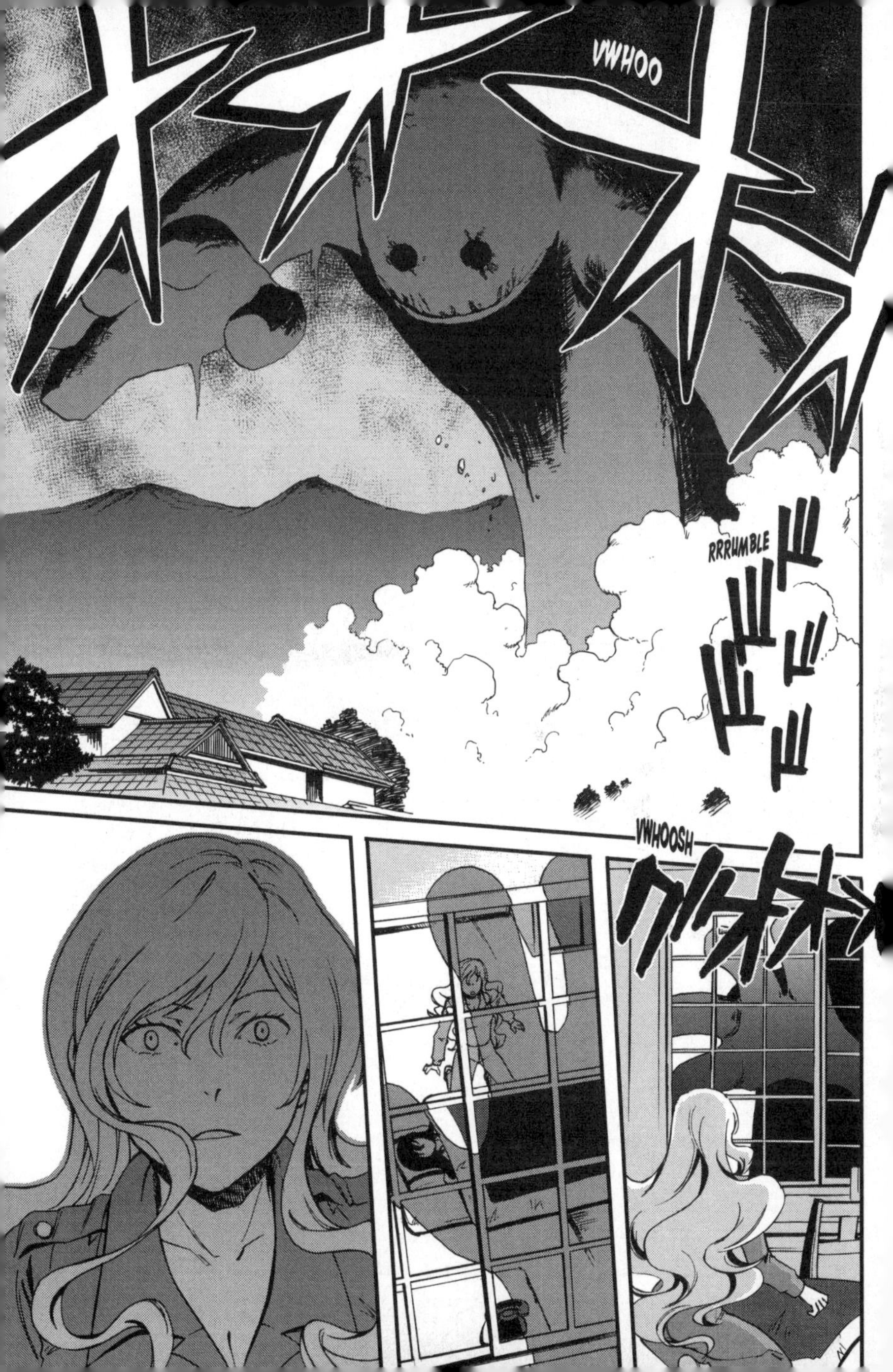
VWHOO
RRRUMBLE
VWHOOSH

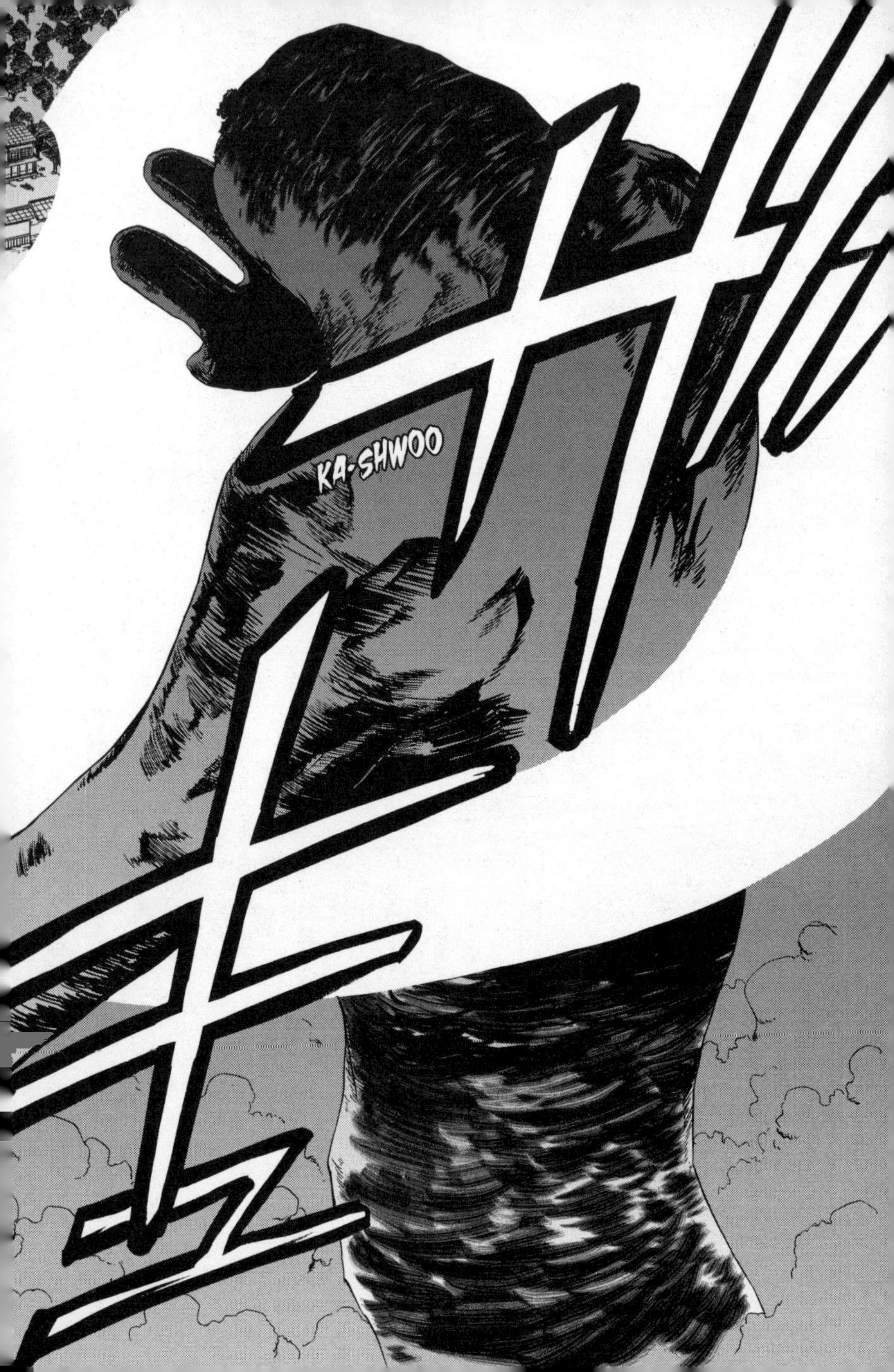
KA-SHWOO

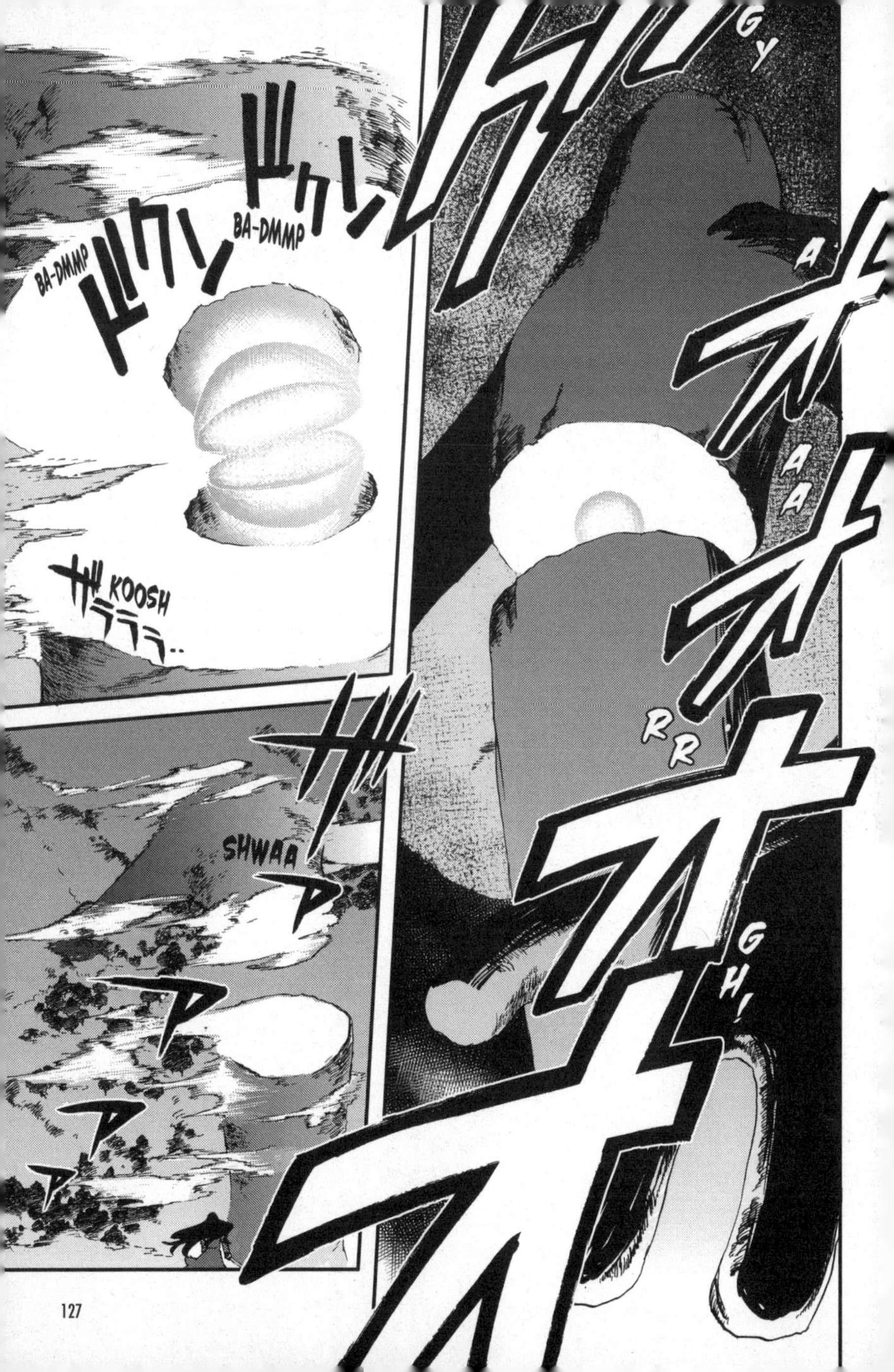
GYAAAARRGH!
BA-DMMP
BA-DMMP
KOOSH
SHWAAP

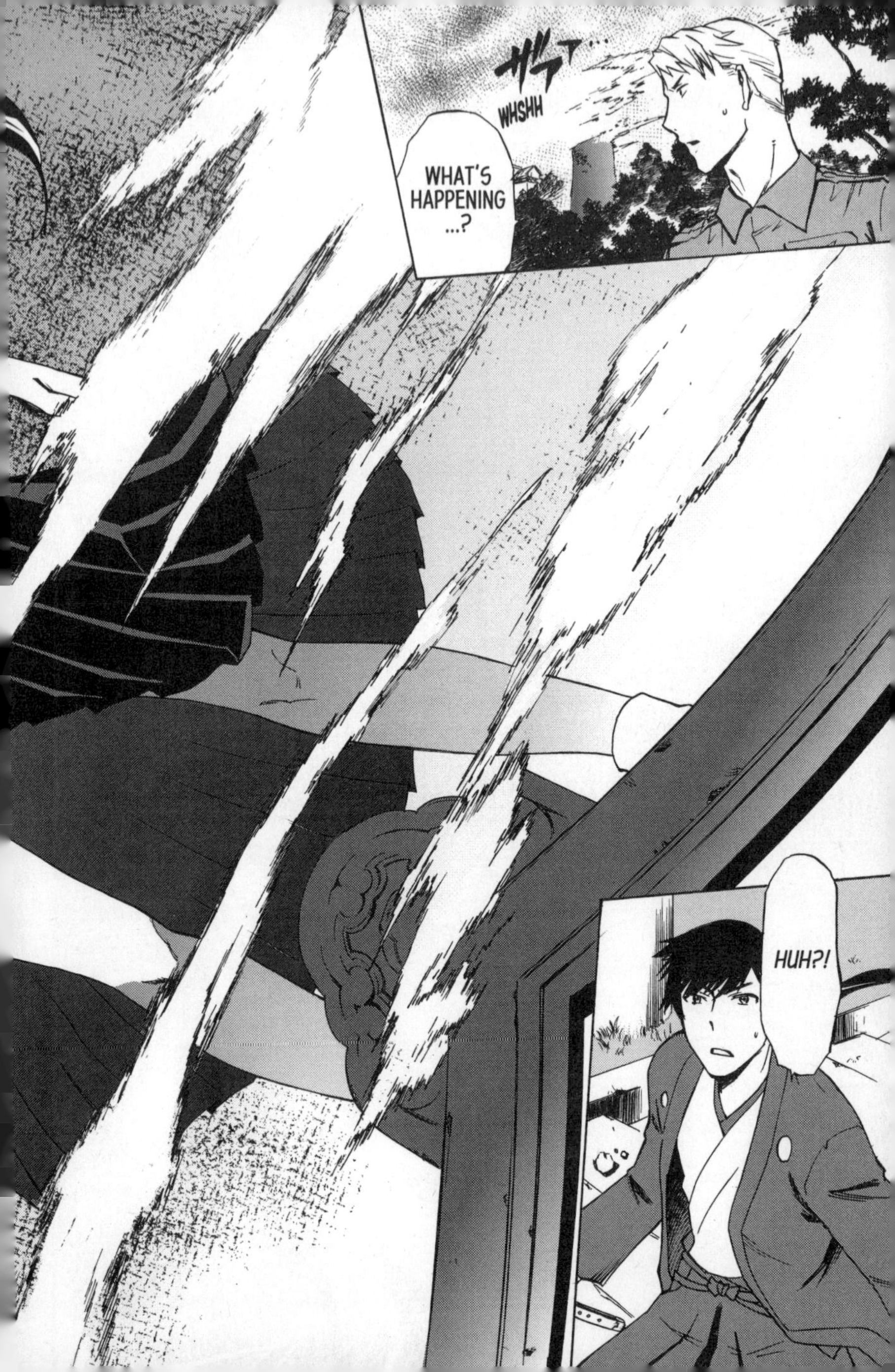
ザザァ…
WHSHH
WHAT'S HAPPENING ...?
HUH?!

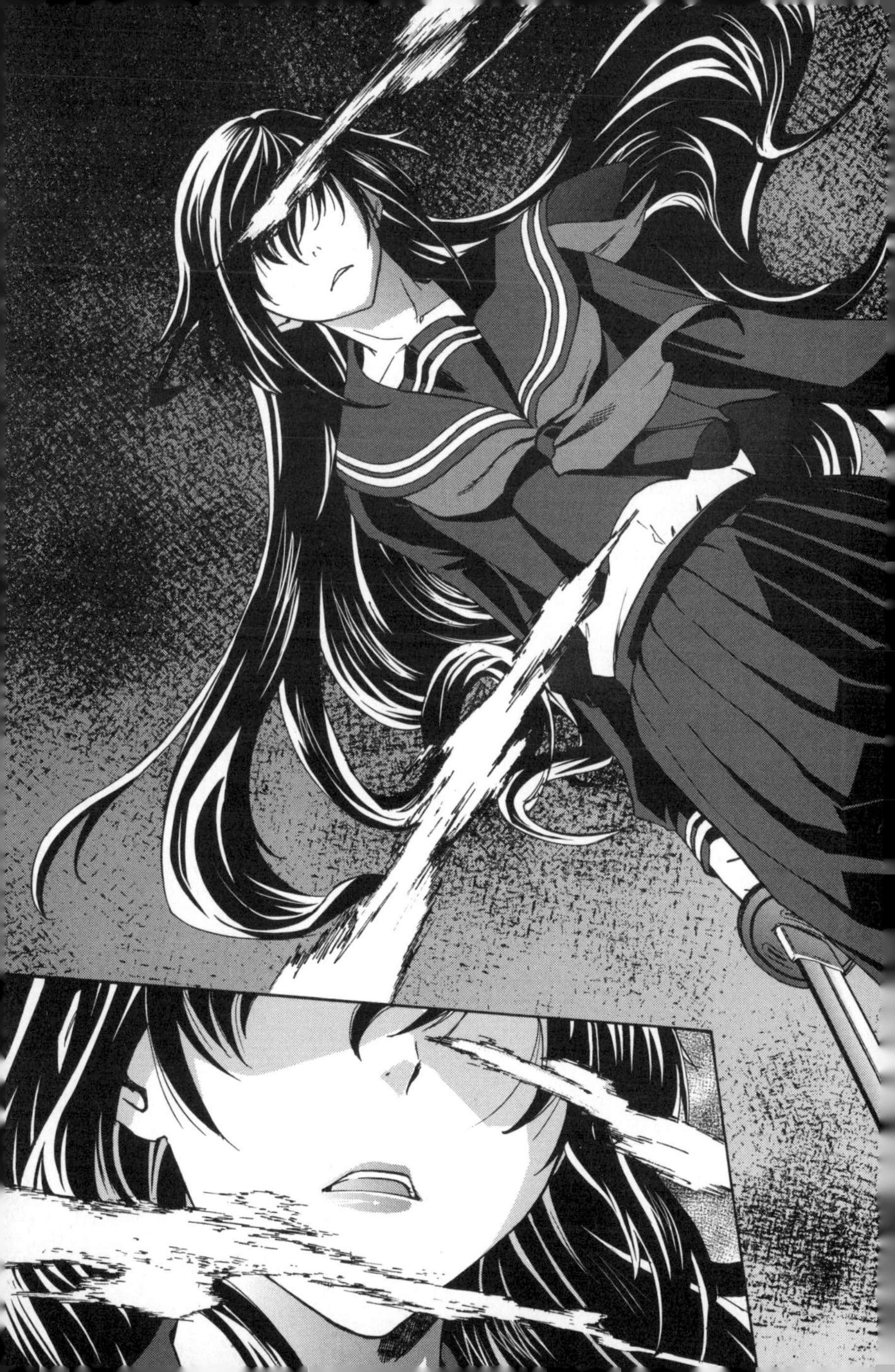

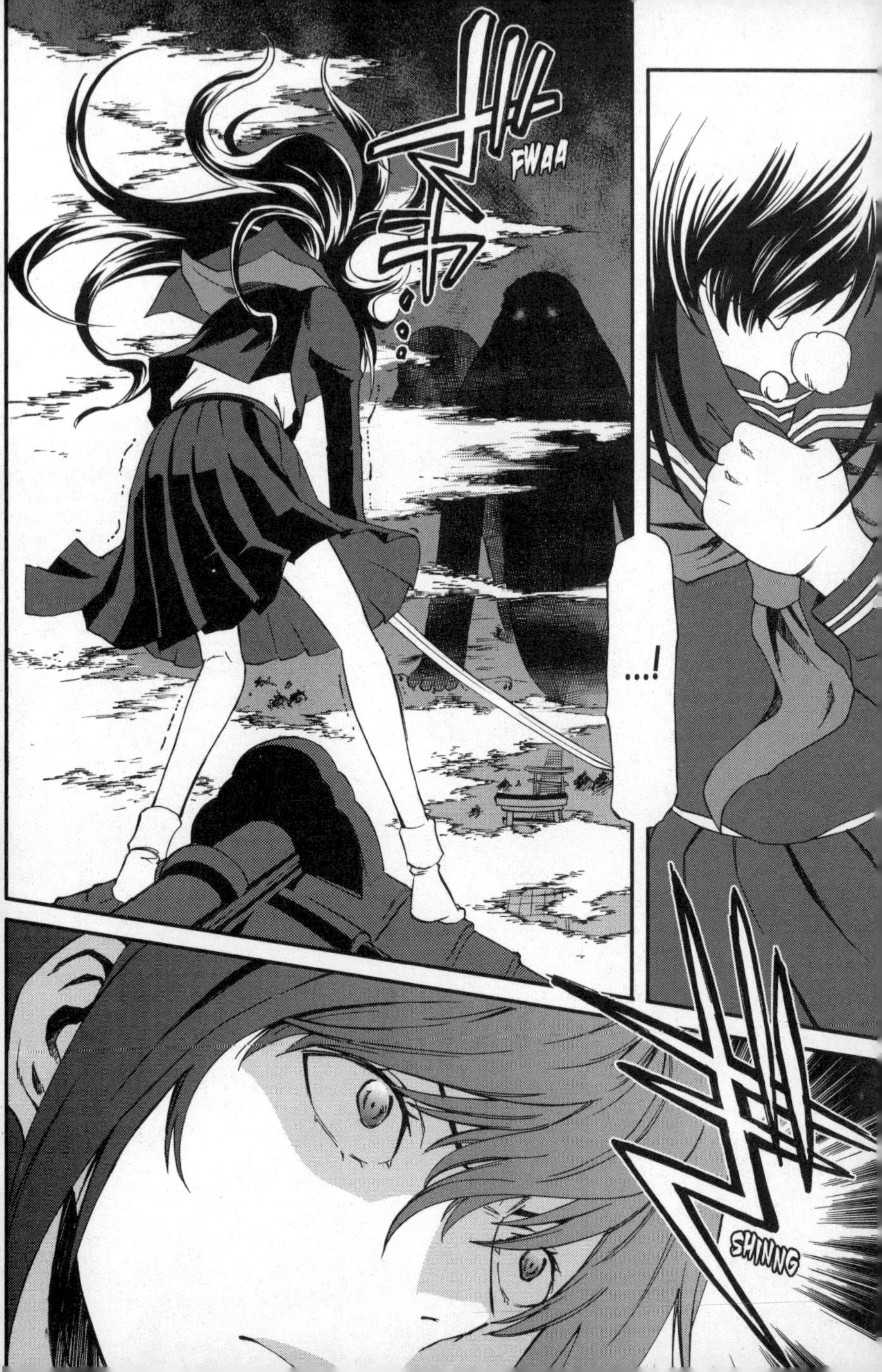
...!
FWAA
SHINNG

十六夜鬼譚

BLOOD-C
DEMONIC
MOONLIGHT

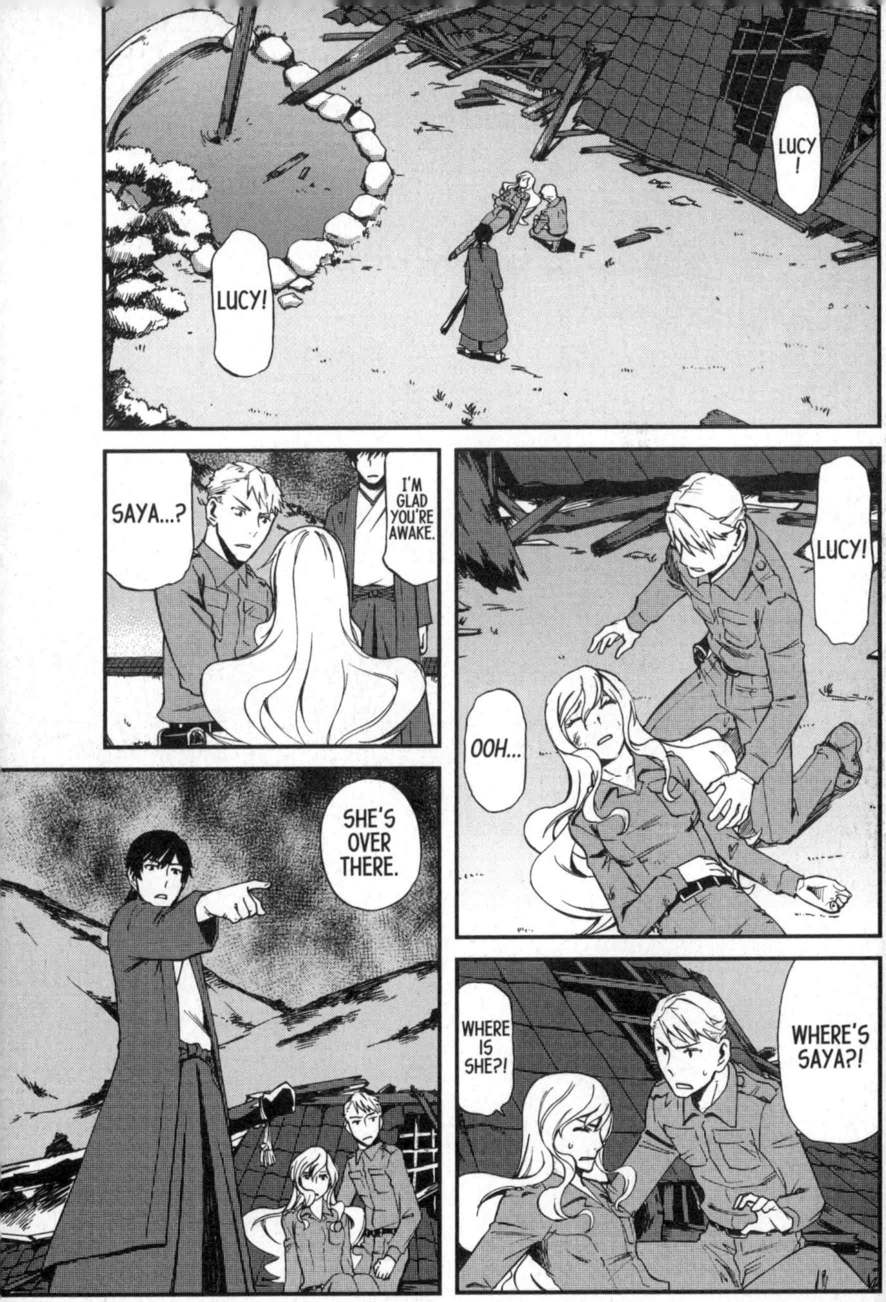
LUCY !
LUCY!
LUCY!
OOH...
I'M GLAD YOU'RE AWAKE.
SAYA...?
WHERE'S SAYA?!
WHERE IS SHE?!
SHE'S OVER THERE.

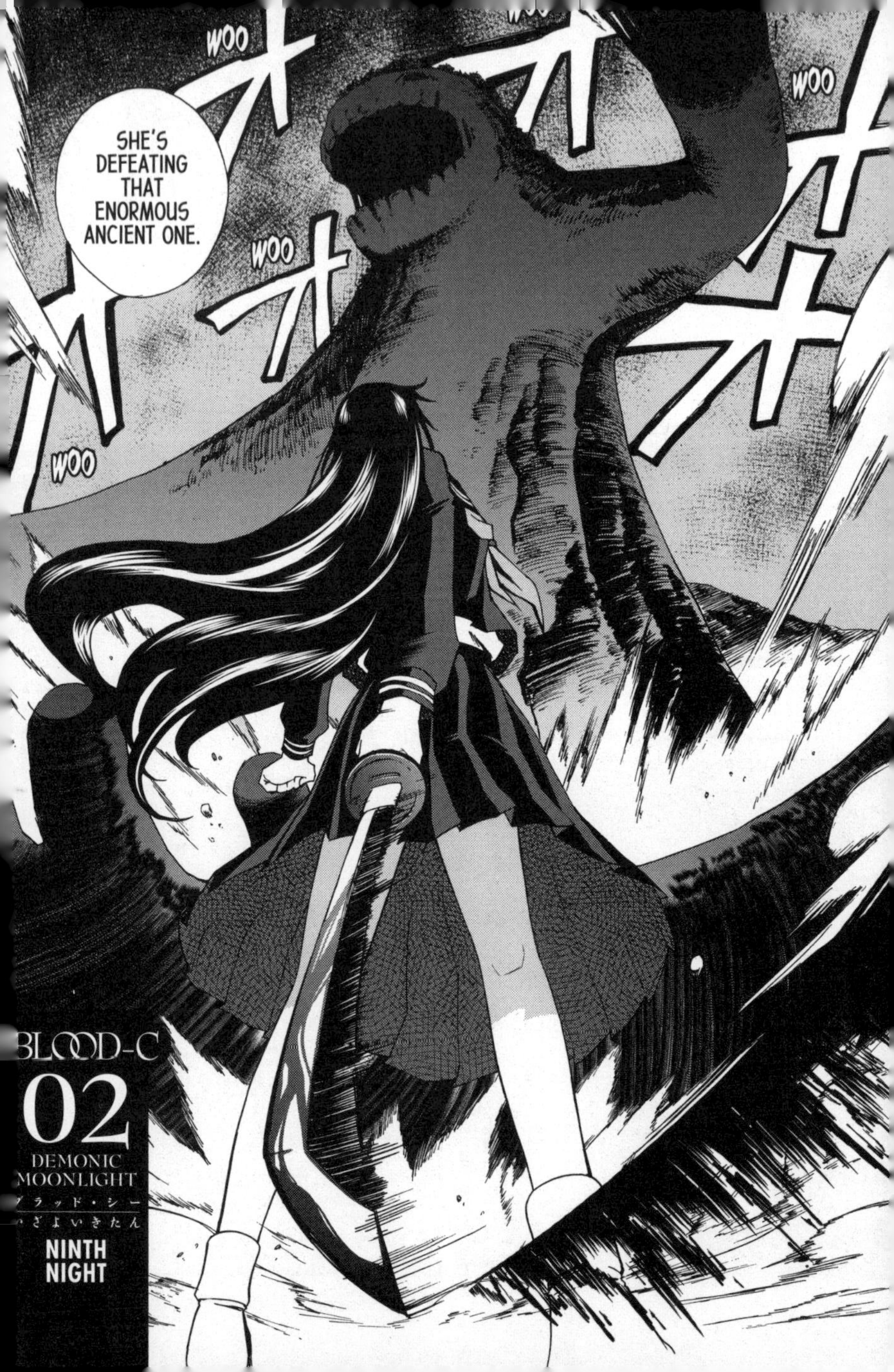
WOO
WOO
SHE'S DEFEATING THAT ENORMOUS ANCIENT ONE.
WOO
WOO
BLOOD-C
02
DEMONIC MOONLIGHT
NINTH NIGHT

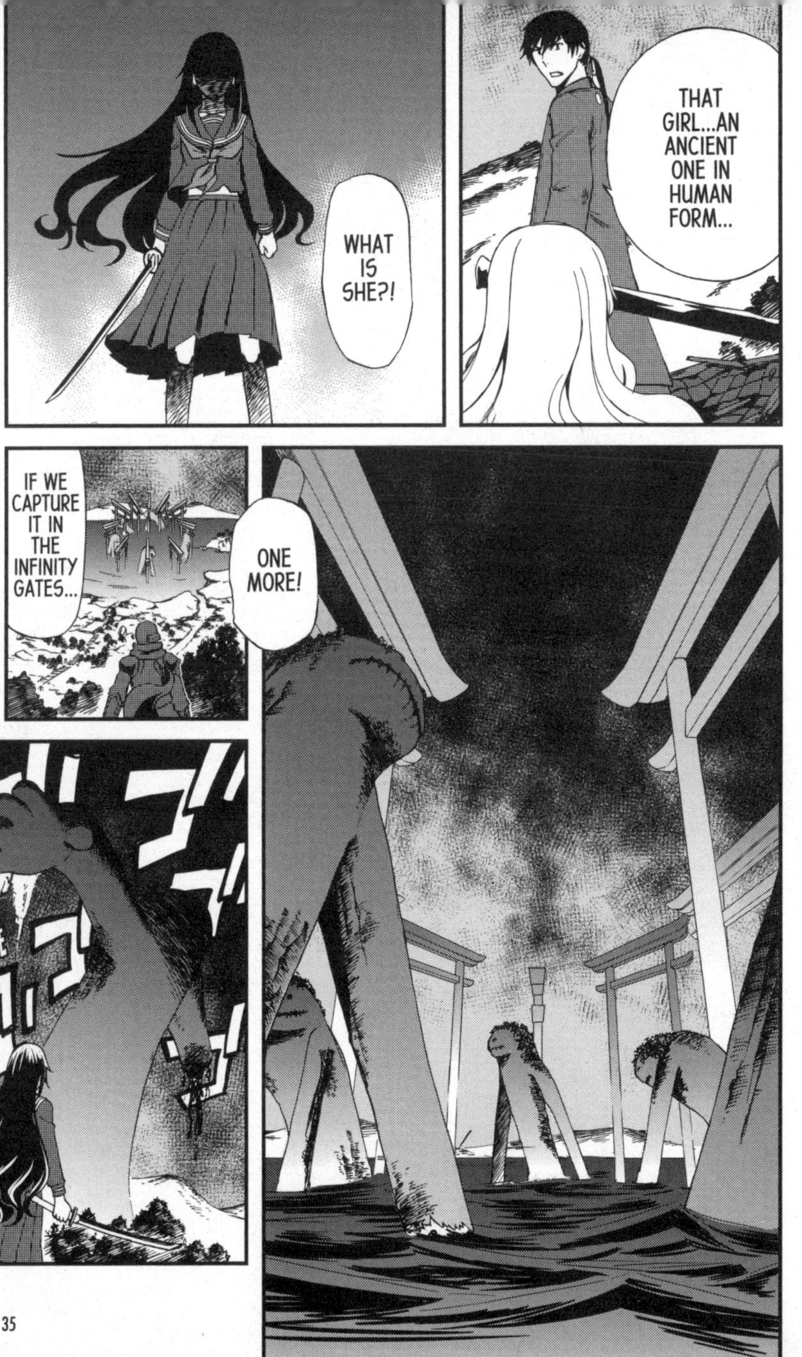
THAT GIRL...AN ANCIENT ONE IN HUMAN FORM...
WHAT IS SHE?!
ONE MORE!
IF WE CAPTURE IT IN THE INFINITY GATES...
RRUMBLE

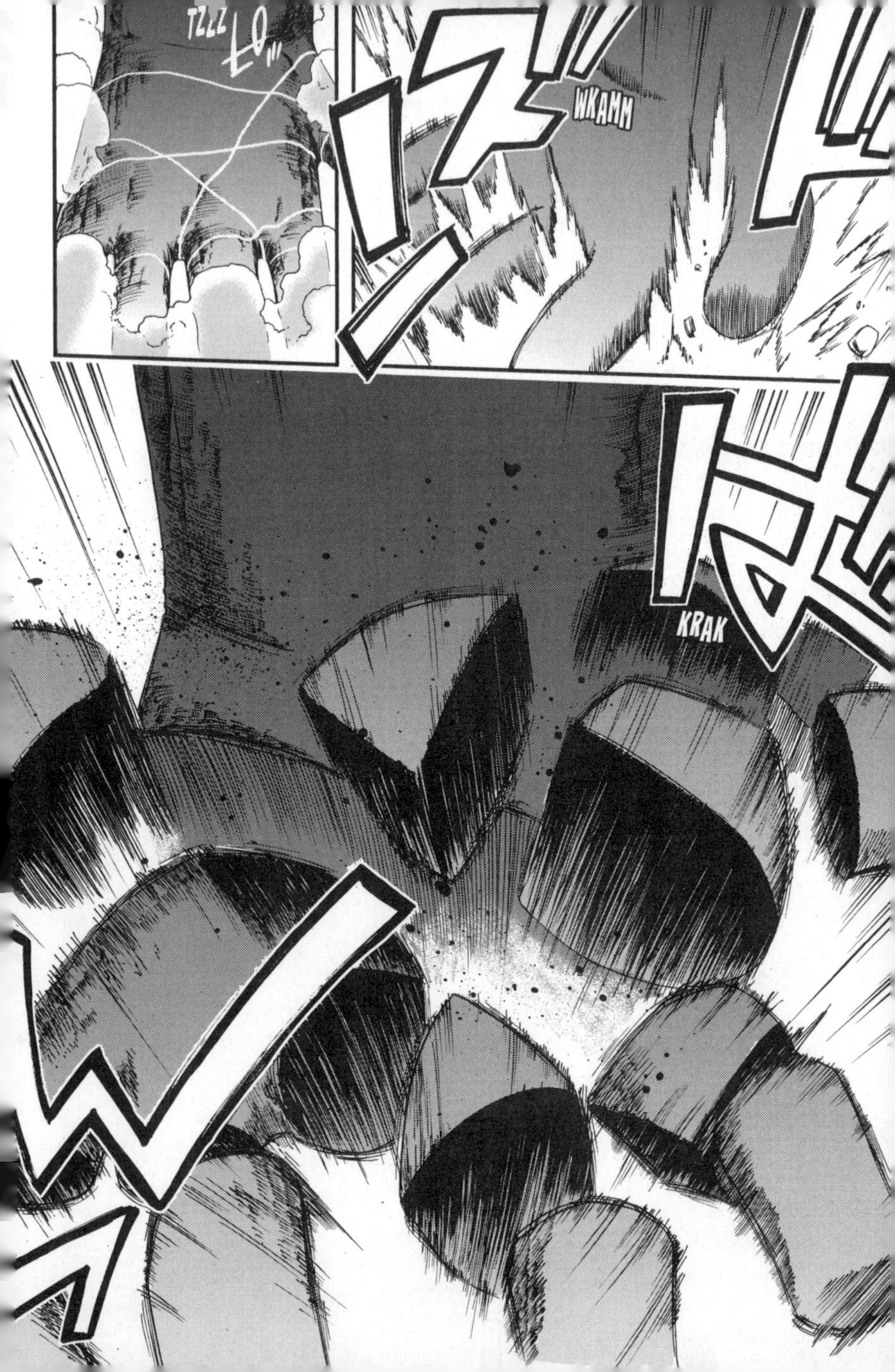
WKAMM
TZZZ
KRAK

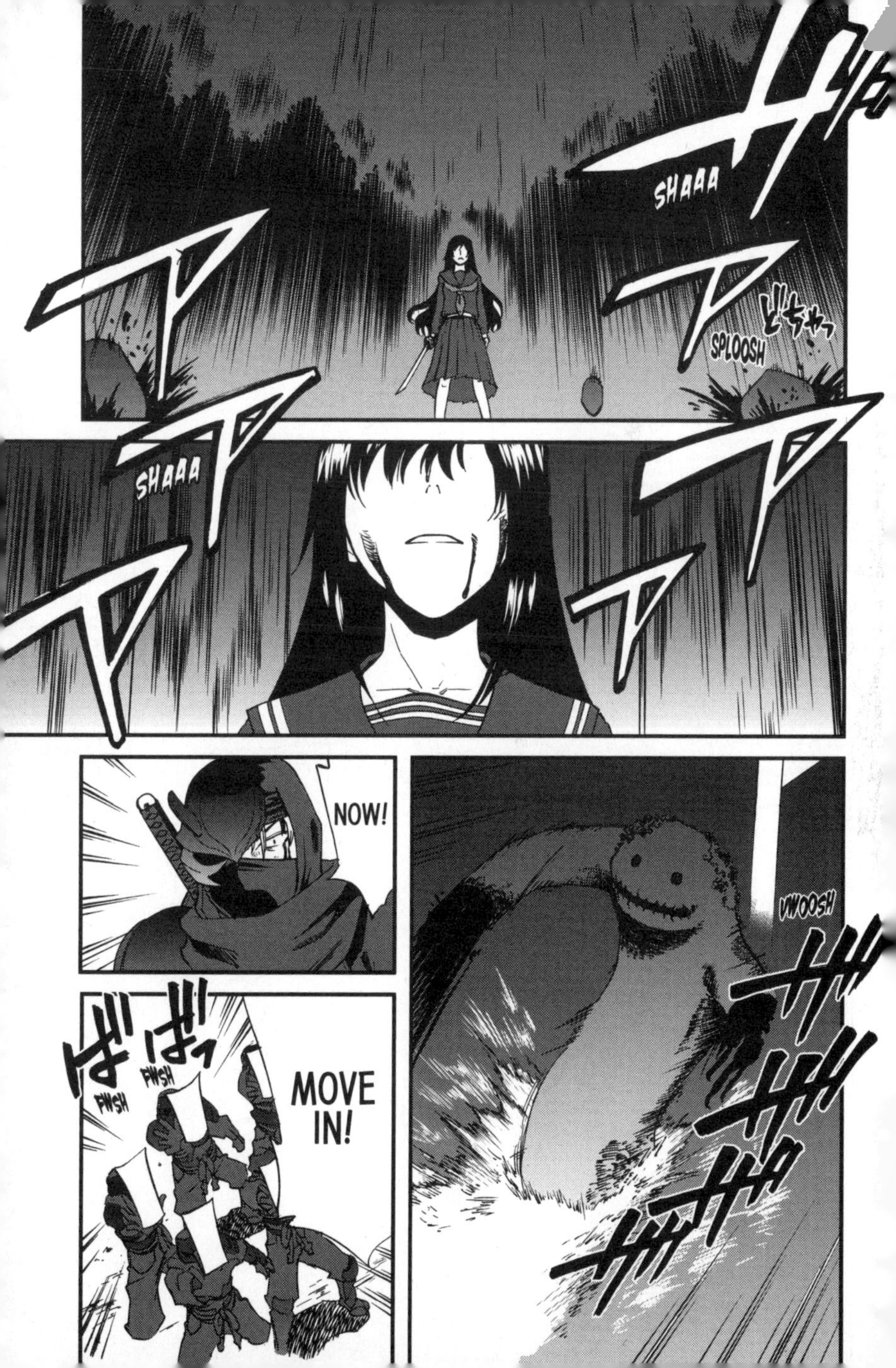
SHAAA
どちゃっ
SPLOOSH
SHAAA
VWOOSH
NOW!
ばばっ
PWSH
PWSH
MOVE IN!

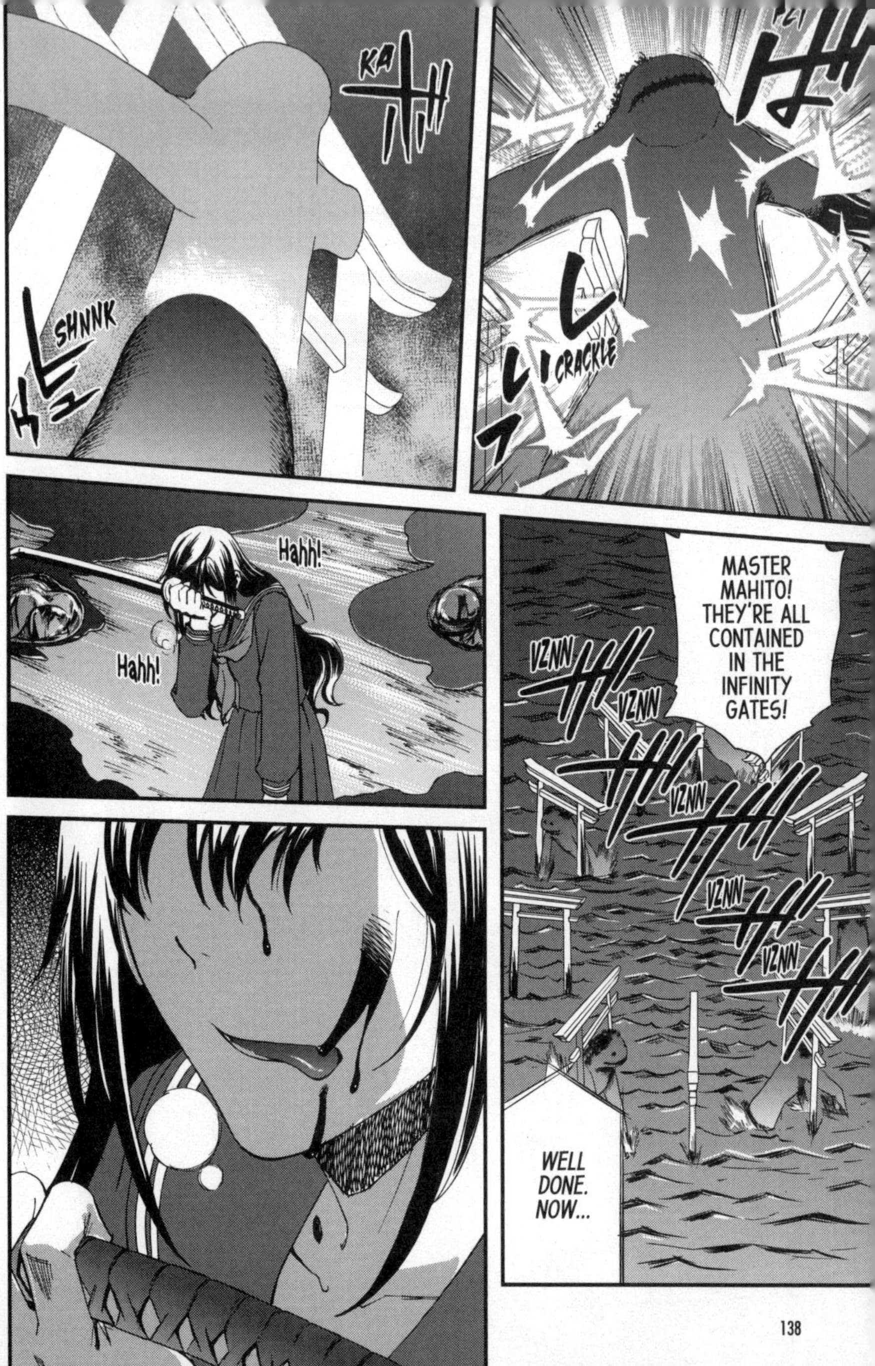
CRACKLE
KA
SHNNK
MASTER MAHITO! THEY'RE ALL CONTAINED IN THE INFINITY GATES!
VZNN
VZNN
VZNN
VZNN
VZNN
WELL DONE. NOW...
Hahh!
Hahh!

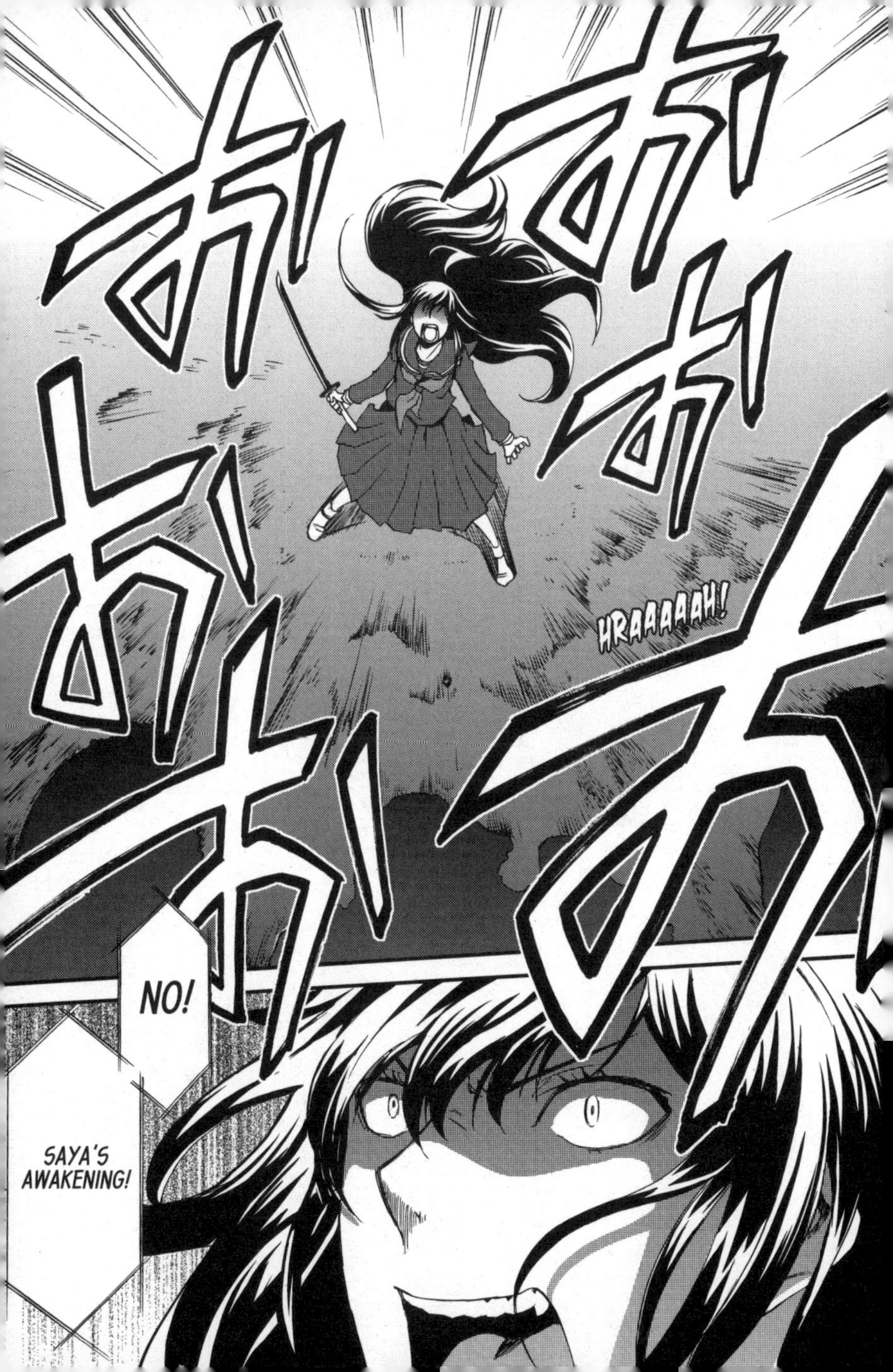
HRAAAAAH!
NO!
SAYA'S AWAKENING!

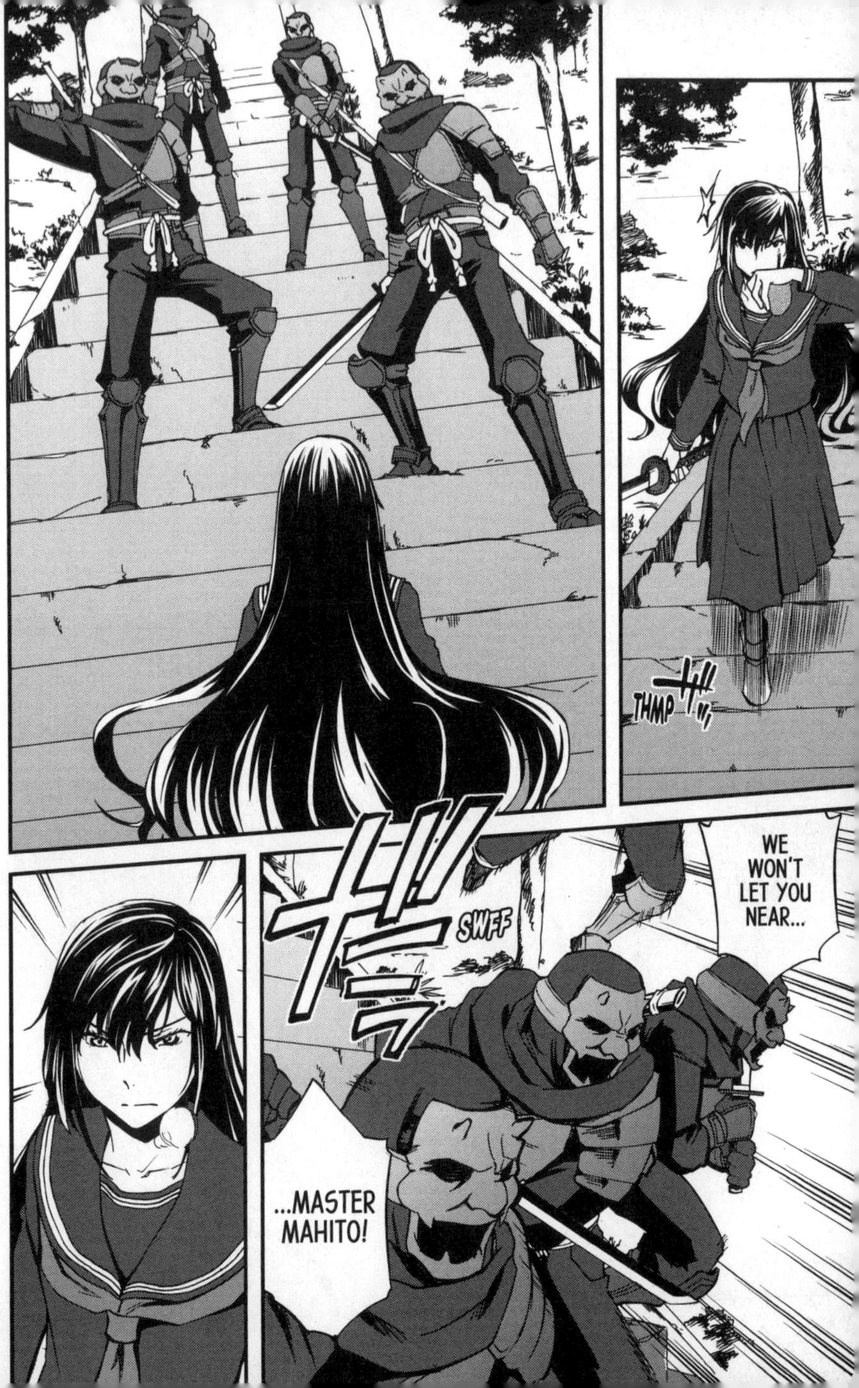
THMP
WE WON'T LET YOU NEAR...
SWFF
...MASTER MAHITO!

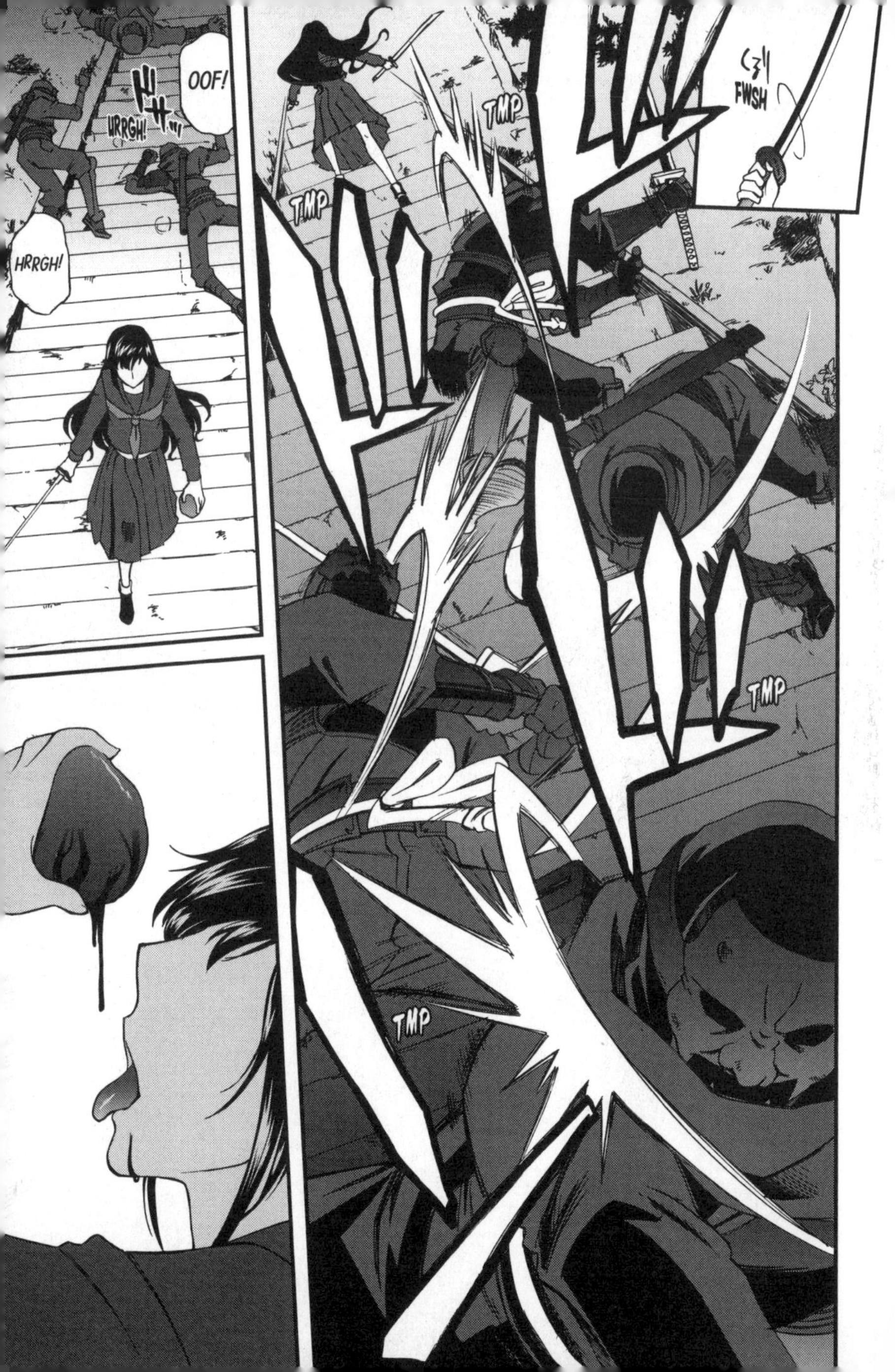
くるり
FWSH
TMP
TMP
TMP
TMP
OOF!
URRGH!
HRRGH!

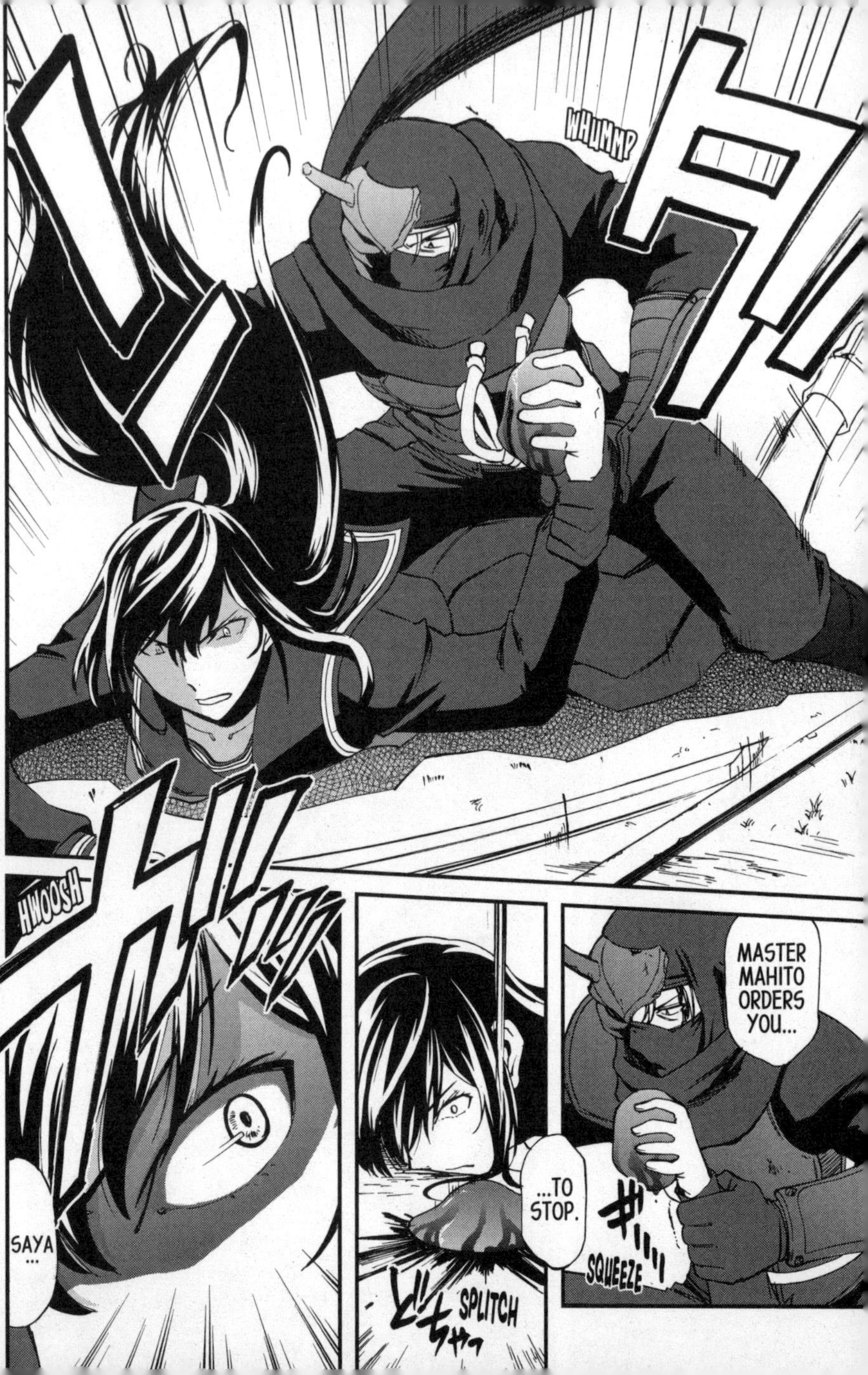
WHUMMP
HWOOSH
MASTER MAHITO ORDERS YOU...
SQUEEZE
...TO STOP.
SPLITCH
SAYA...

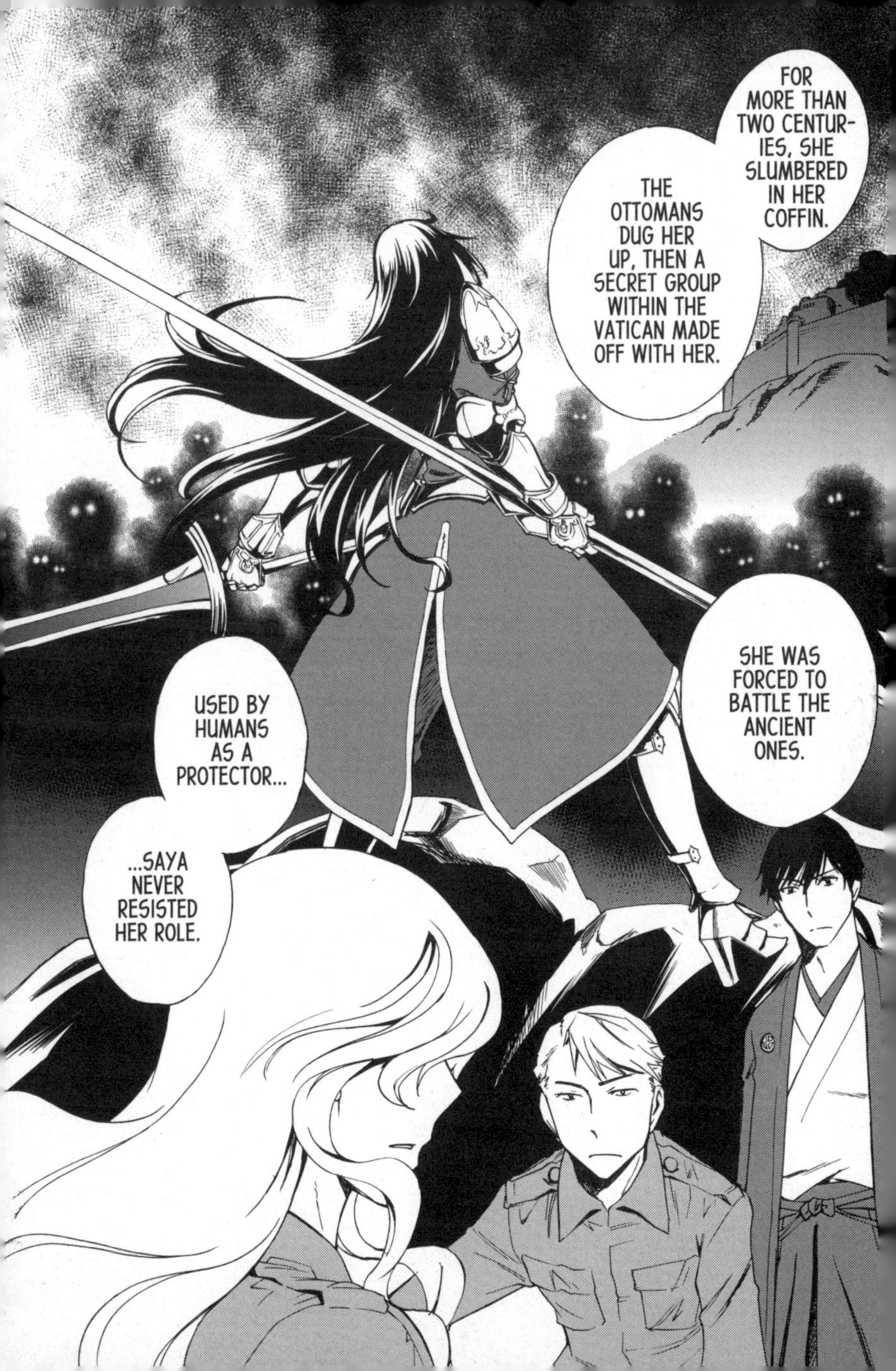
FOR MORE THAN TWO CENTURIES, SHE SLUMBERED IN HER COFFIN.
THE OTTOMANS DUG HER UP, THEN A SECRET GROUP WITHIN THE VATICAN MADE OFF WITH HER.
SHE WAS FORCED TO BATTLE THE ANCIENT ONES.
USED BY HUMANS AS A PROTECTOR...
...SAYA NEVER RESISTED HER ROLE.

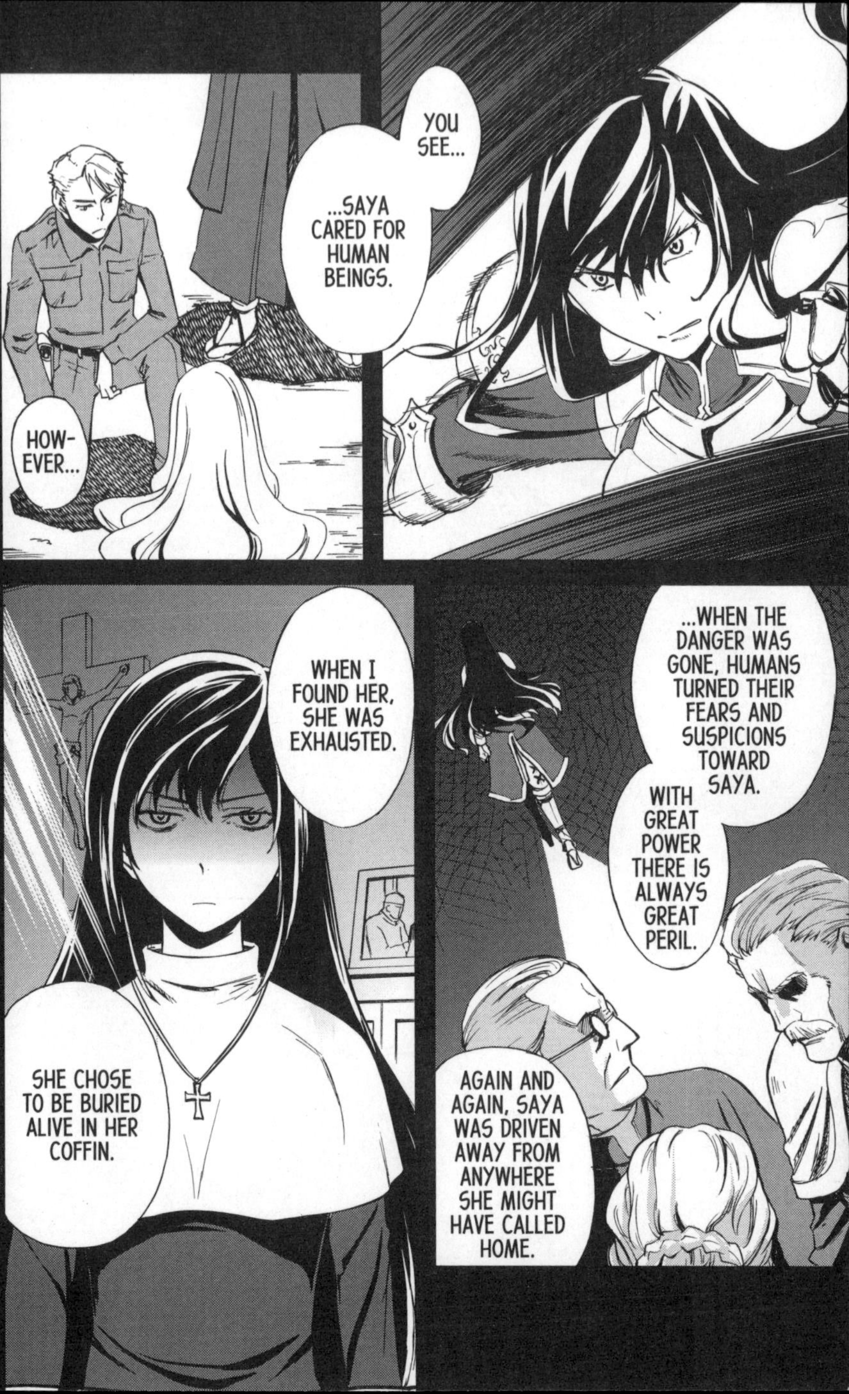
YOU SEE...
...SAYA CARED FOR HUMAN BEINGS.
HOW-EVER...
...WHEN THE DANGER WAS GONE, HUMANS TURNED THEIR FEARS AND SUSPICIONS TOWARD SAYA.
WITH GREAT POWER THERE IS ALWAYS GREAT PERIL.
AGAIN AND AGAIN, SAYA WAS DRIVEN AWAY FROM ANYWHERE SHE MIGHT HAVE CALLED HOME.
WHEN I FOUND HER, SHE WAS EXHAUSTED.
SHE CHOSE TO BE BURIED ALIVE IN HER COFFIN.

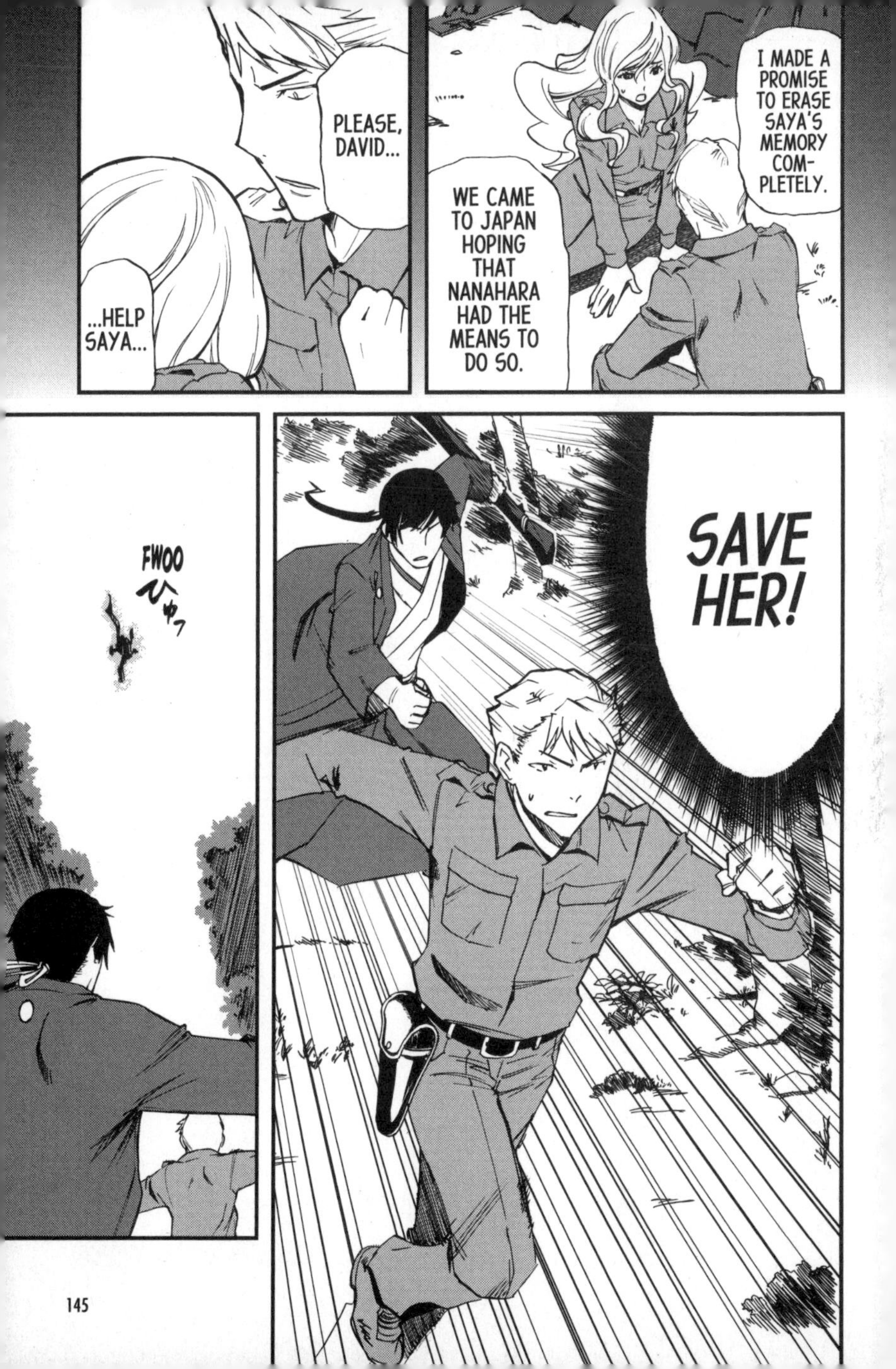
I MADE A PROMISE TO ERASE SAYA'S MEMORY COMPLETELY.
WE CAME TO JAPAN HOPING THAT NANAHARA HAD THE MEANS TO DO SO.
PLEASE, DAVID...
...HELP SAYA...
SAVE HER!
FWOO
ひゅっ

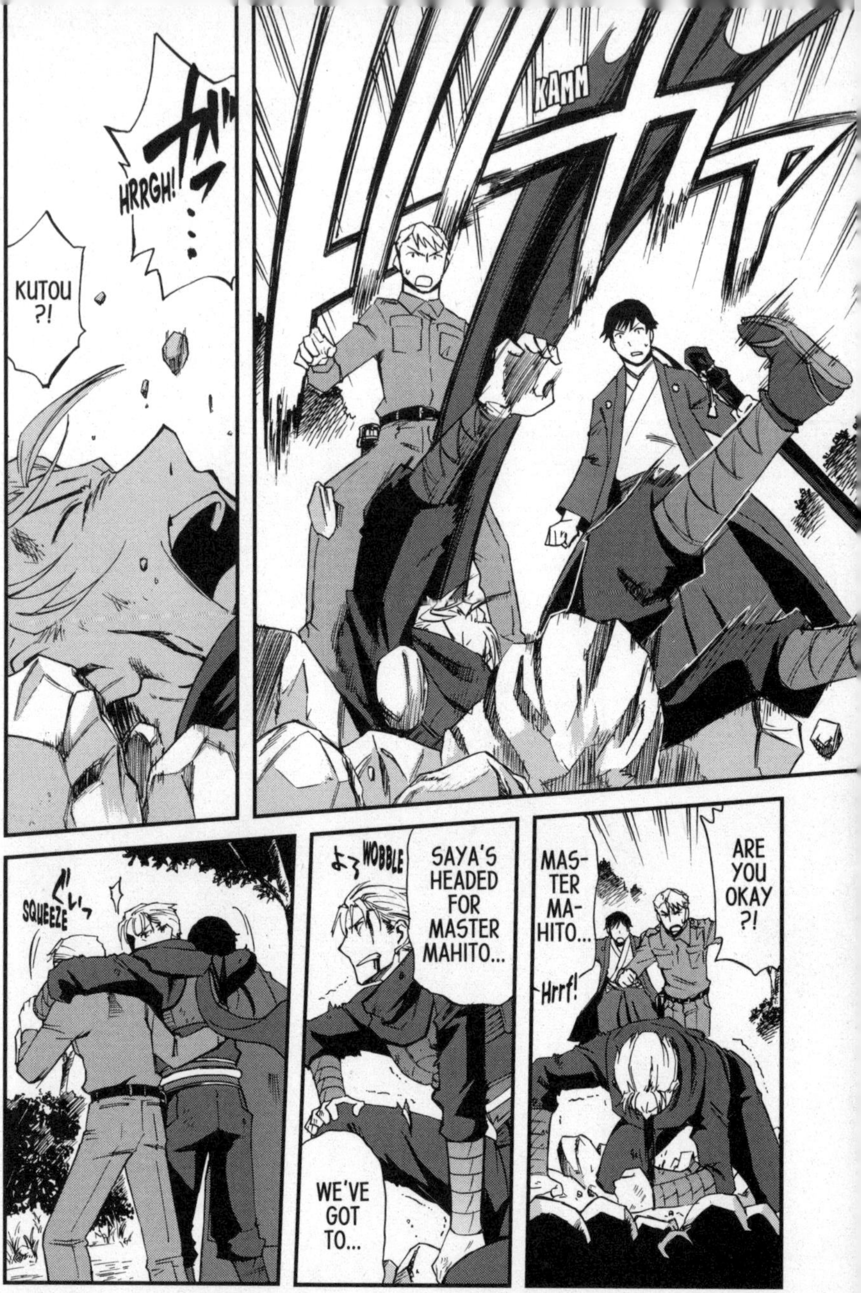
KAMM
HRRGH!
KUTOU ?!
ARE YOU OKAY ?!
MAS- TER MA- HITO...
Hrrf!
SAYA'S HEADED FOR MASTER MAHITO...
WOBBLE
WE'VE GOT TO...
SQUEEZE

WE NEED YOU.

LEAVE ME...

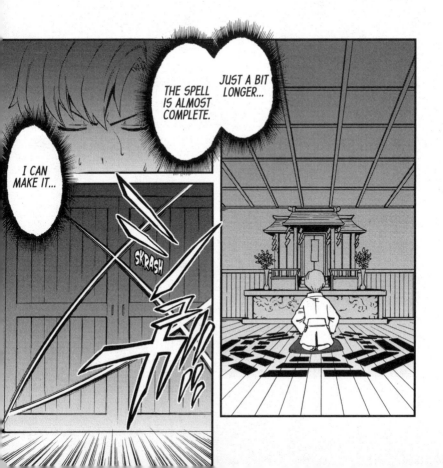

JUST A BIT LONGER...

THE SPELL IS ALMOST COMPLETE.

I CAN MAKE IT...

SKRASH

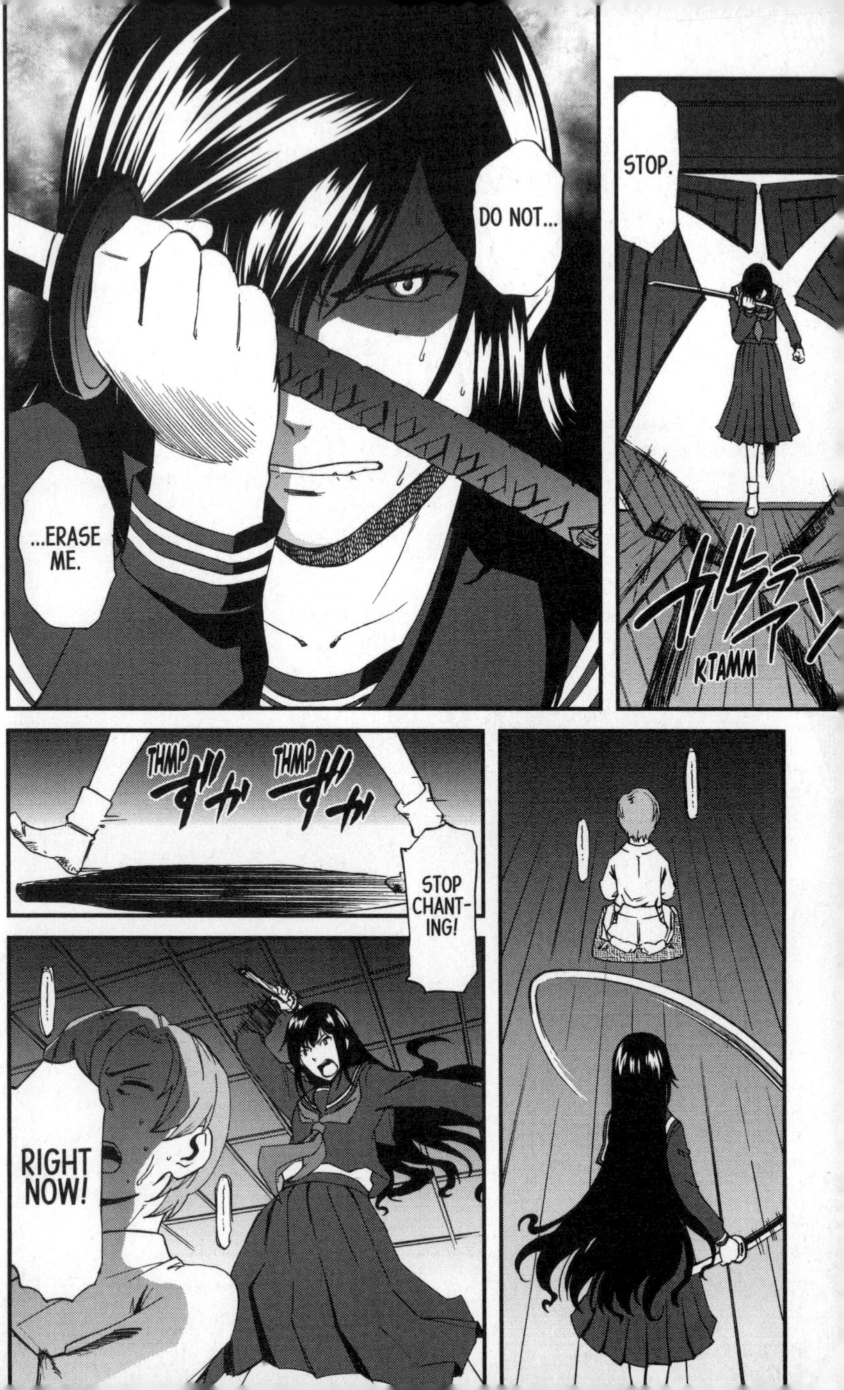
STOP.
KTAMM
DO NOT...
...ERASE ME.
THMP
THMP
STOP CHANTING!
RIGHT NOW!

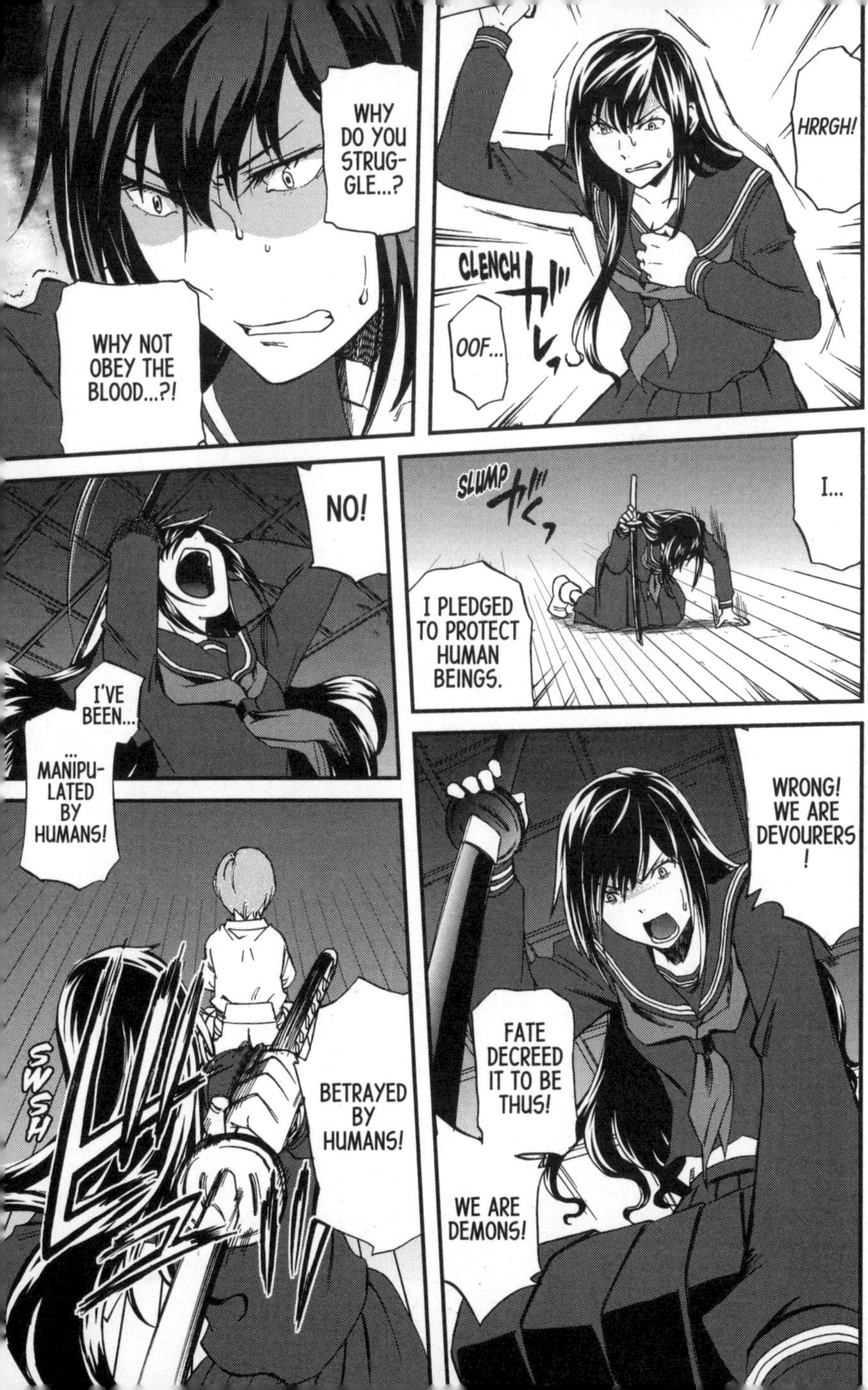
HRRGH!
CLENCH
OOF...
WHY DO YOU STRUGGLE...?
WHY NOT OBEY THE BLOOD...?!
SLUMP
I...
I PLEDGED TO PROTECT HUMAN BEINGS.
NO!
I'VE BEEN...
... MANIPULATED BY HUMANS!
WRONG! WE ARE DEVOURERS!
FATE DECREED IT TO BE THUS!
WE ARE DEMONS!
BETRAYED BY HUMANS!
SWSH

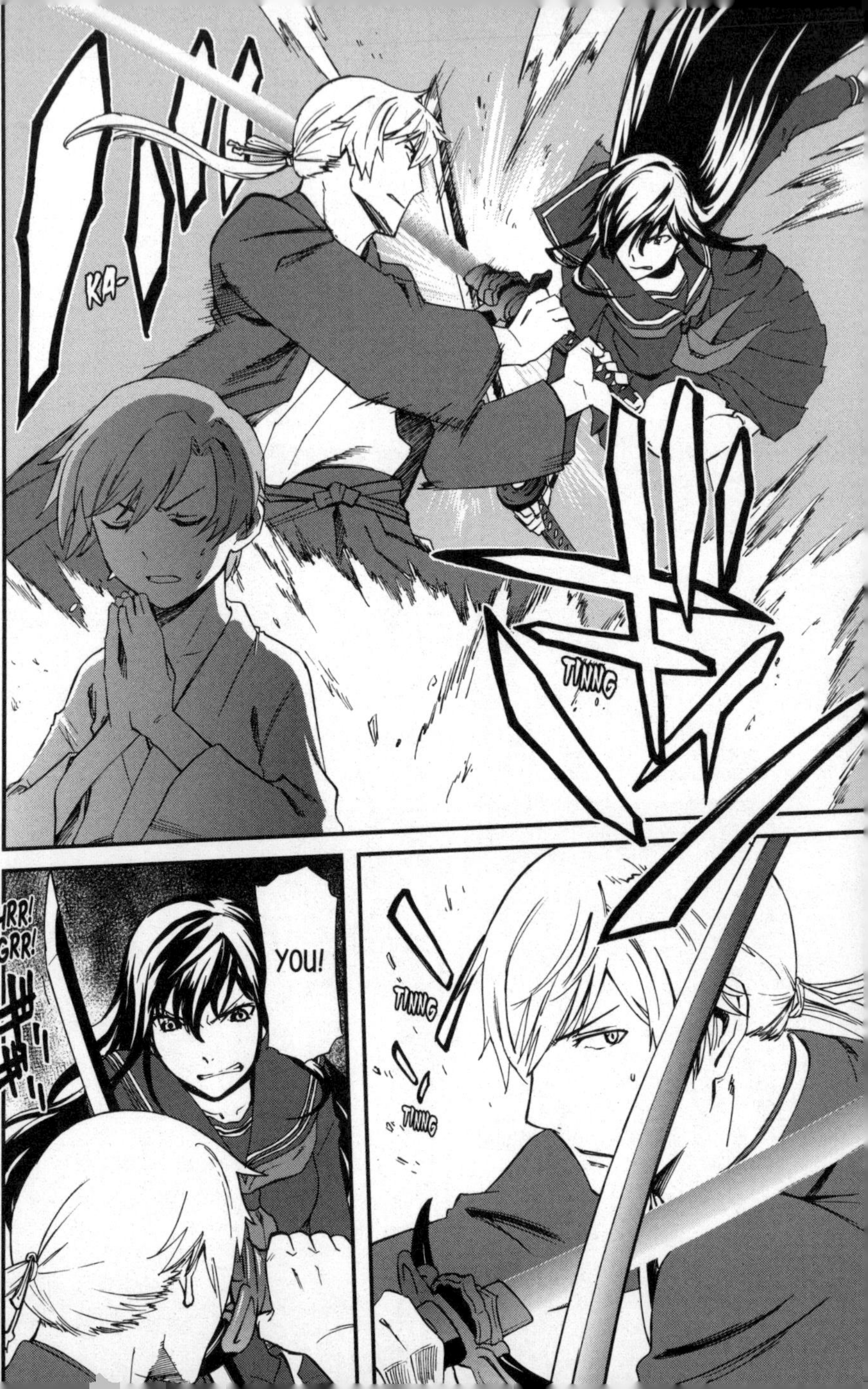
KA-
TINNG
TINNG
TINNG
YOU!
HRR! GRR!

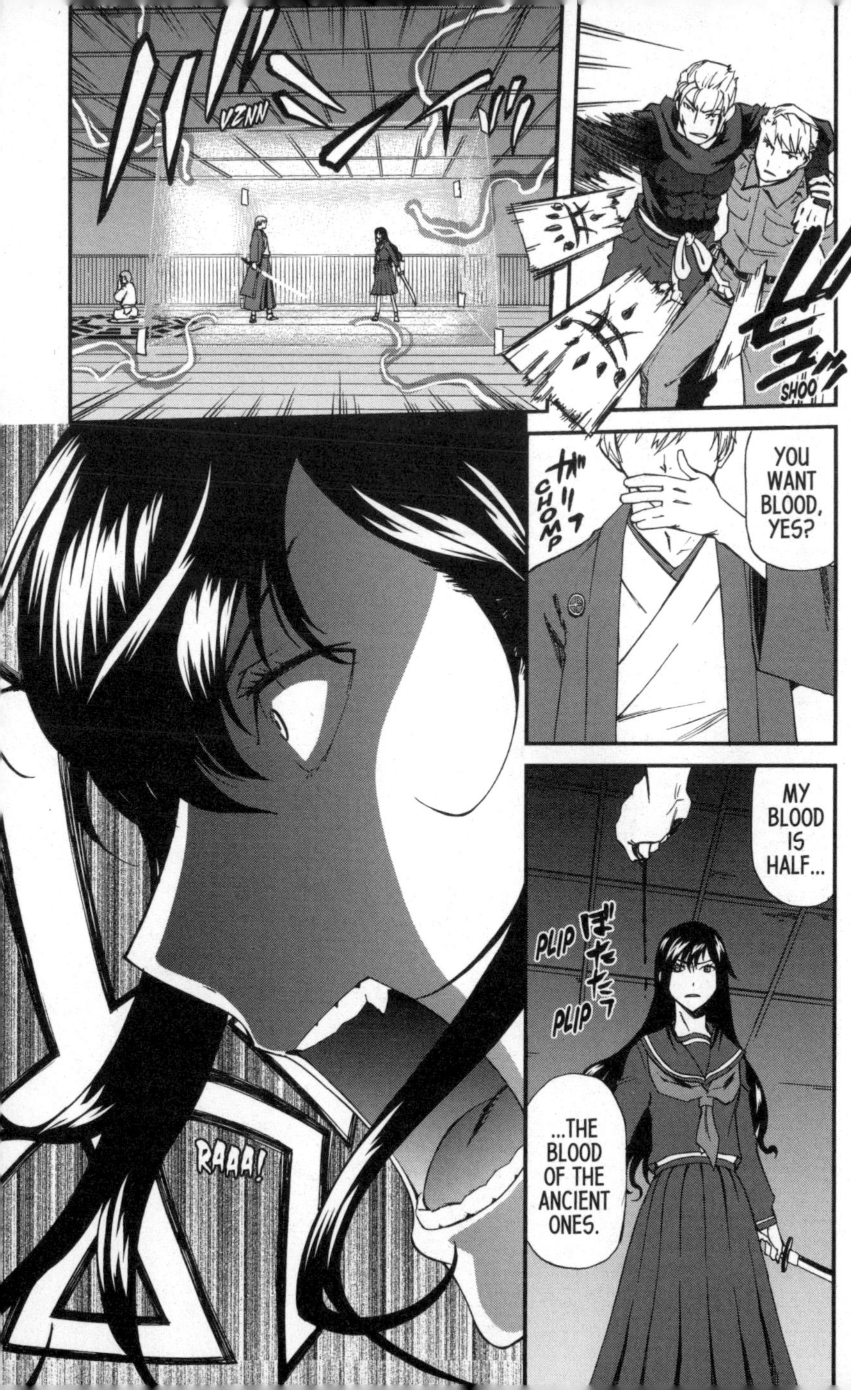
SHOO
VZNN
CHOMP
YOU WANT BLOOD, YES?
MY BLOOD IS HALF...
PLIP
PLIP
...THE BLOOD OF THE ANCIENT ONES.
RAAA!

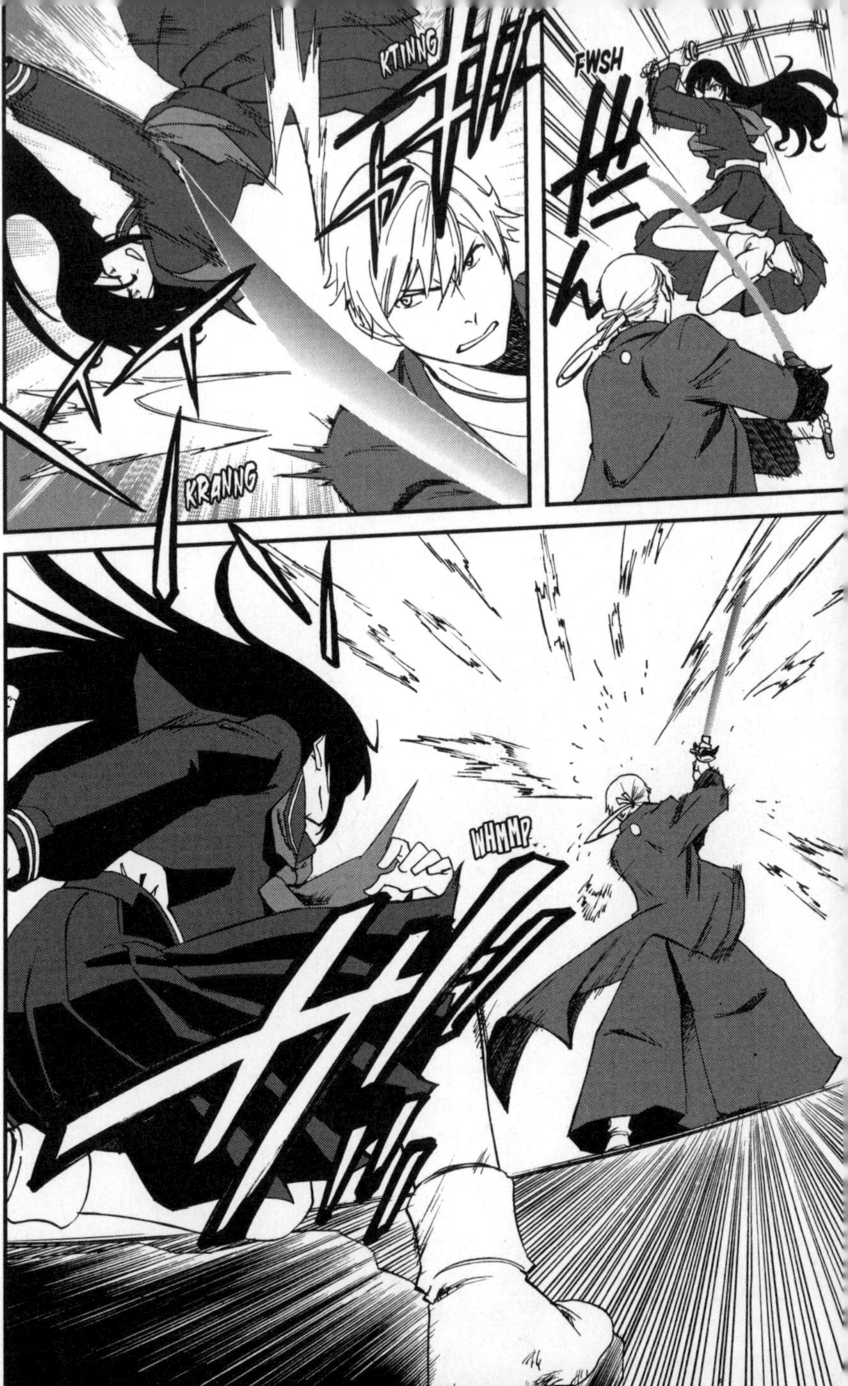
FWSH
KTINNG
KRANNG
WHMMP

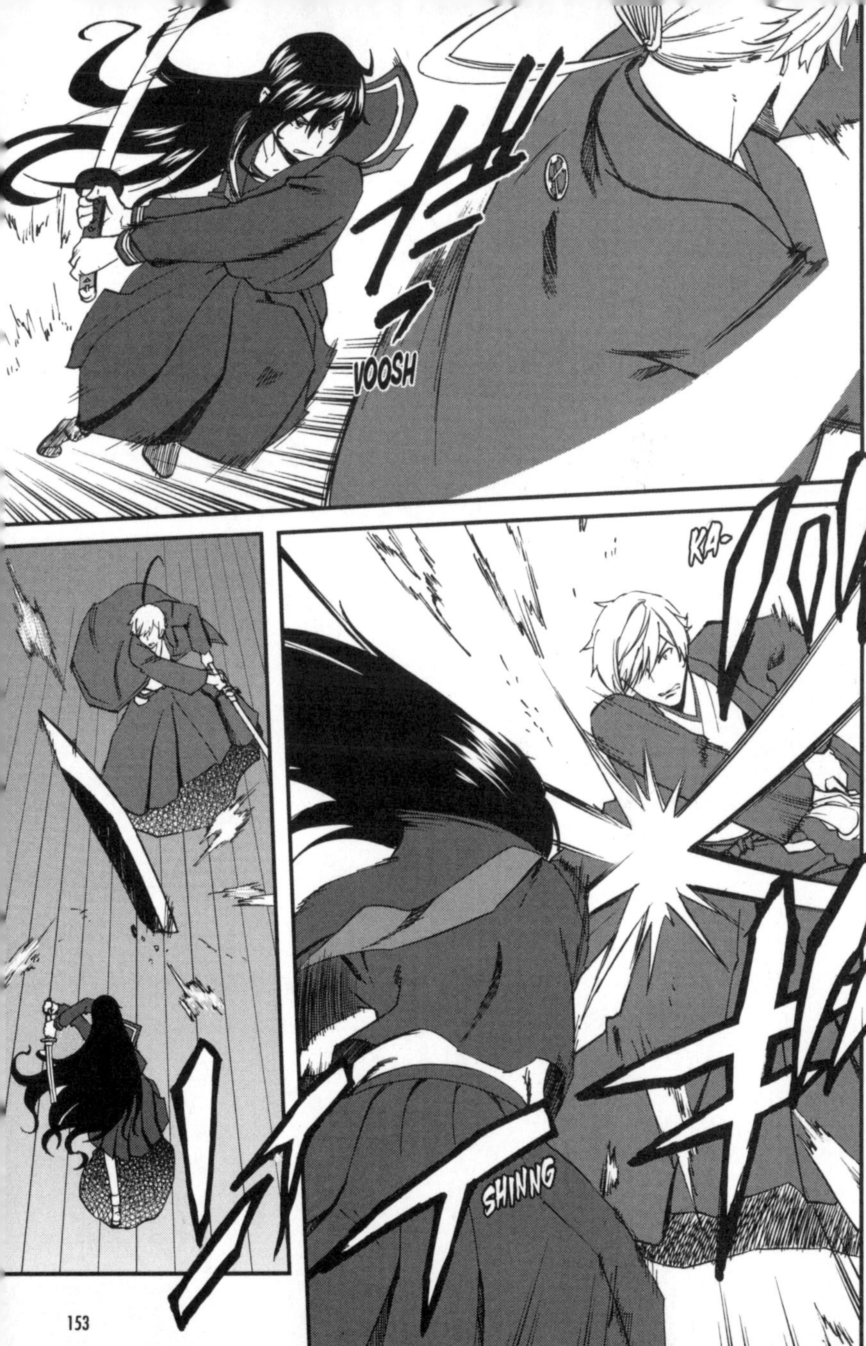
VOOSH
KA-
SHINNG

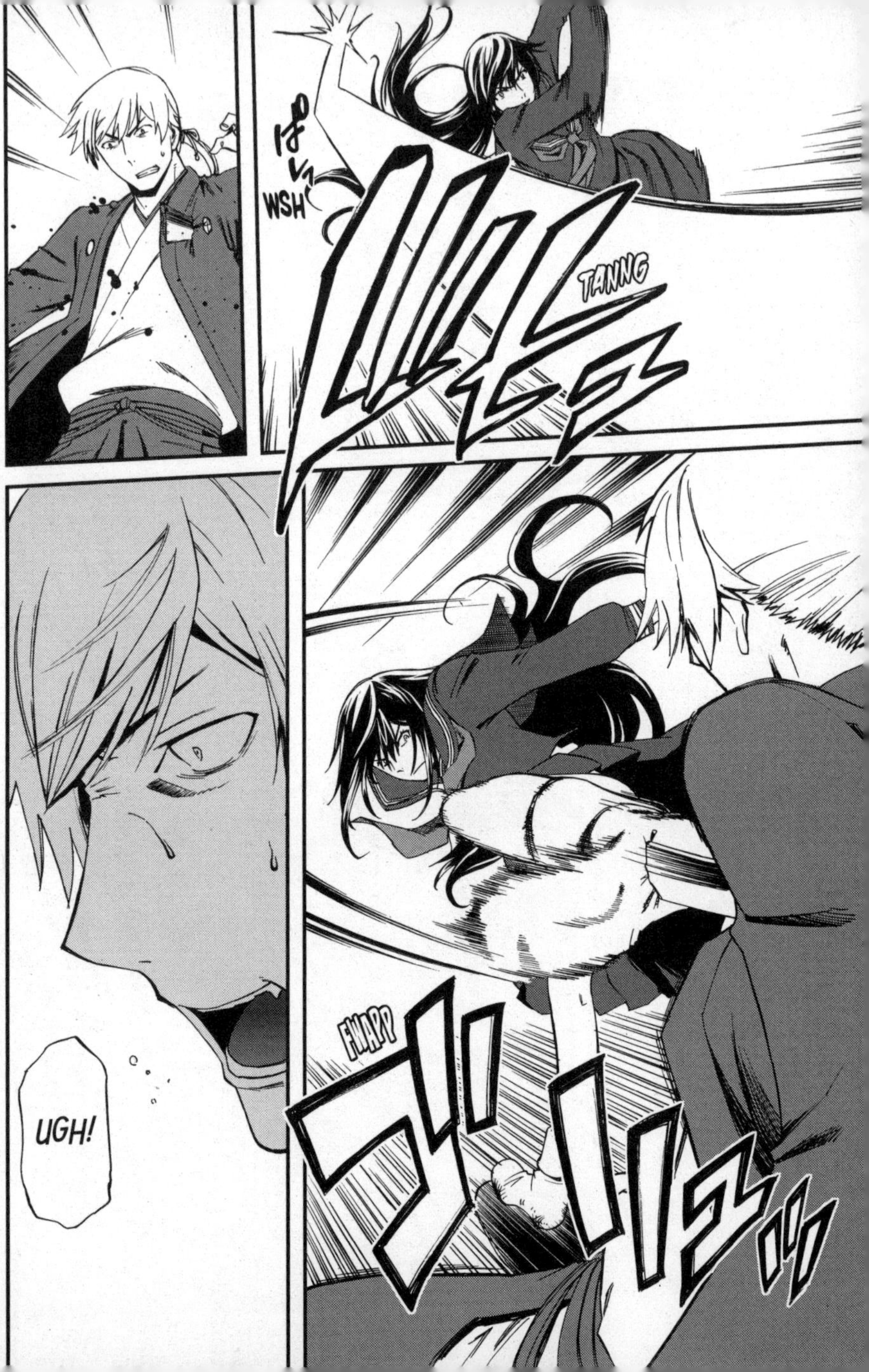
WSH
TANNG
FWAPP
UGH!

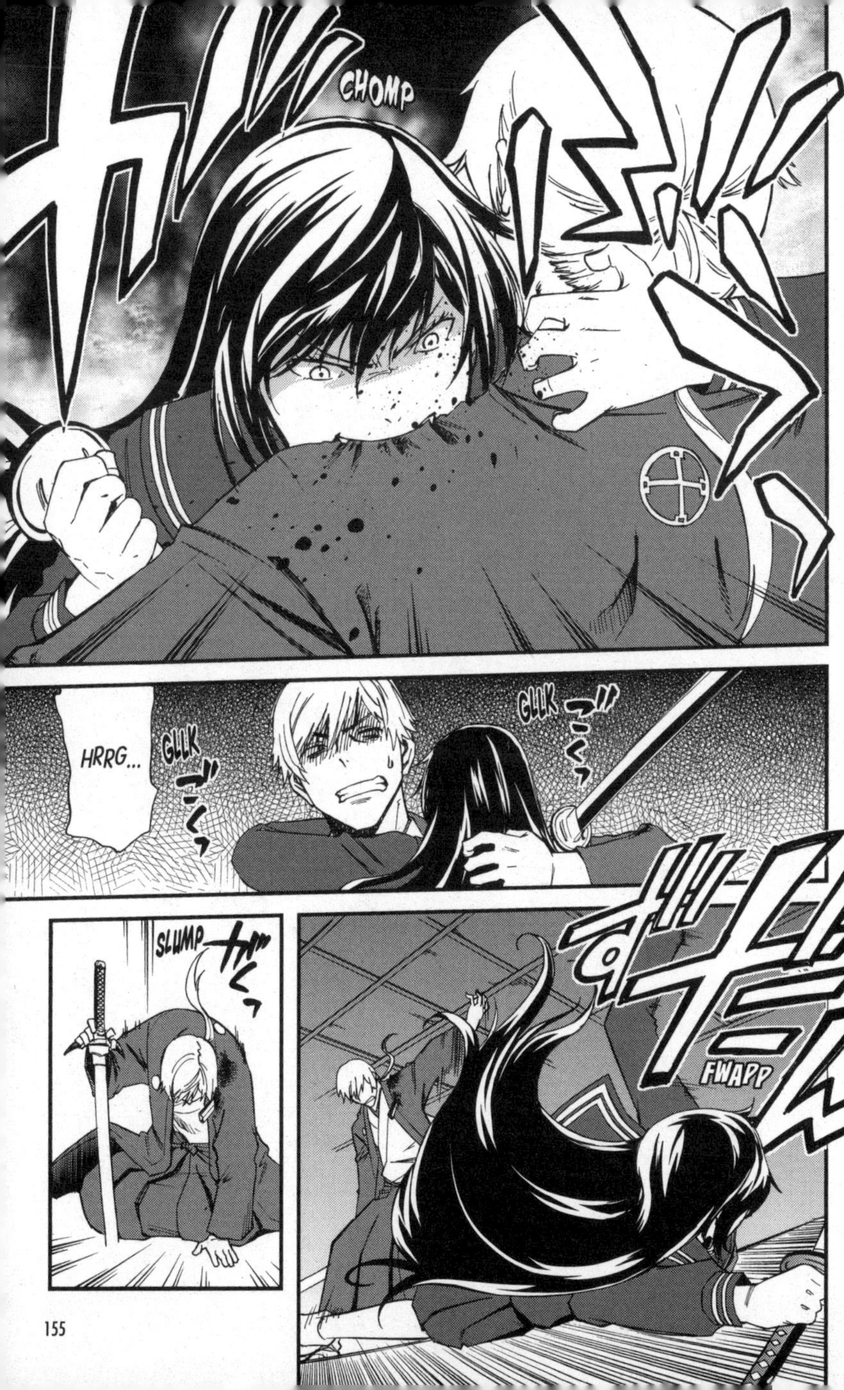
CHOMP
GLLK
HRRG...
GLLK
FWAPP
SLUMP

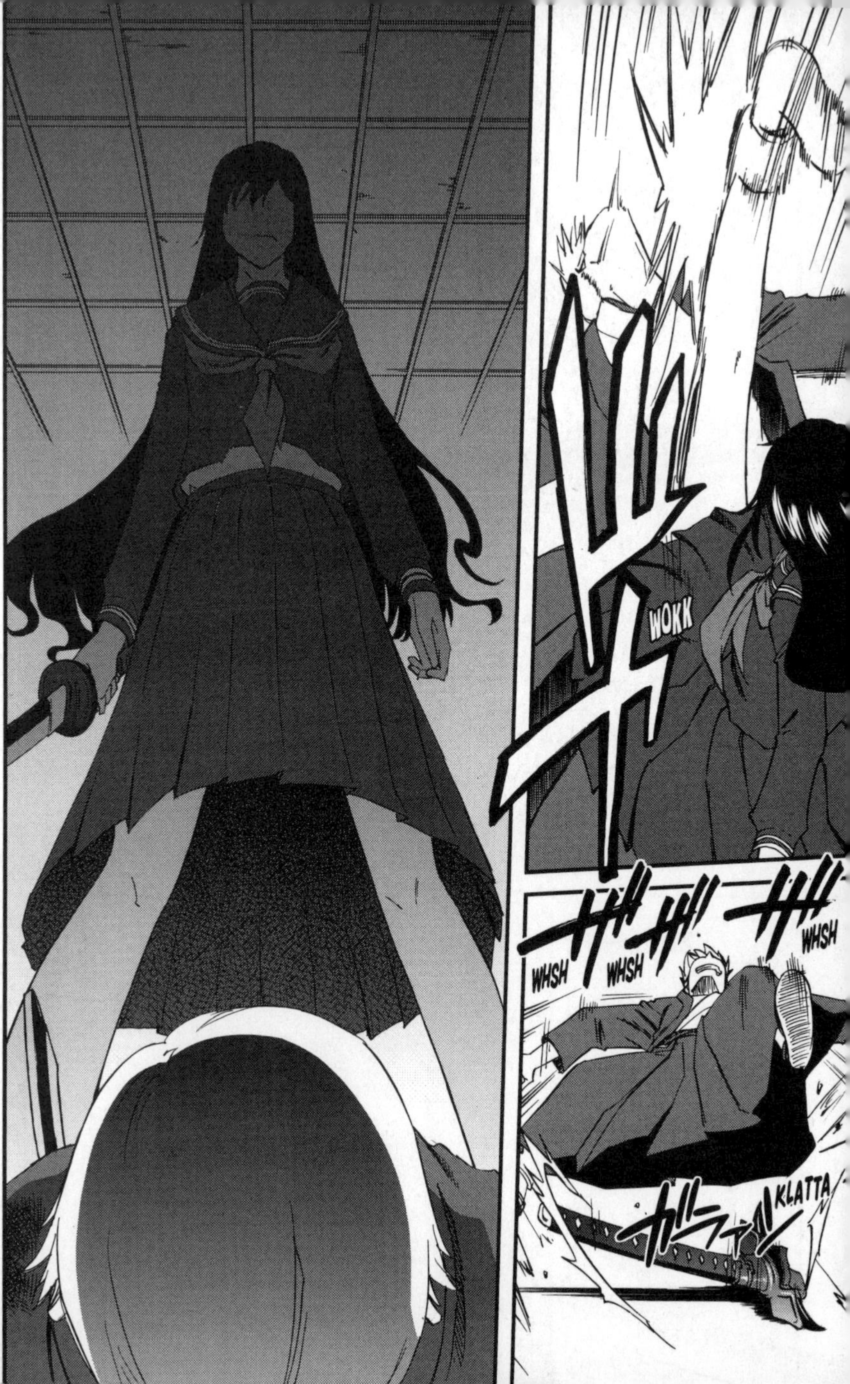
WOKK
WHSH
WHSH
WHSH
KLATTA

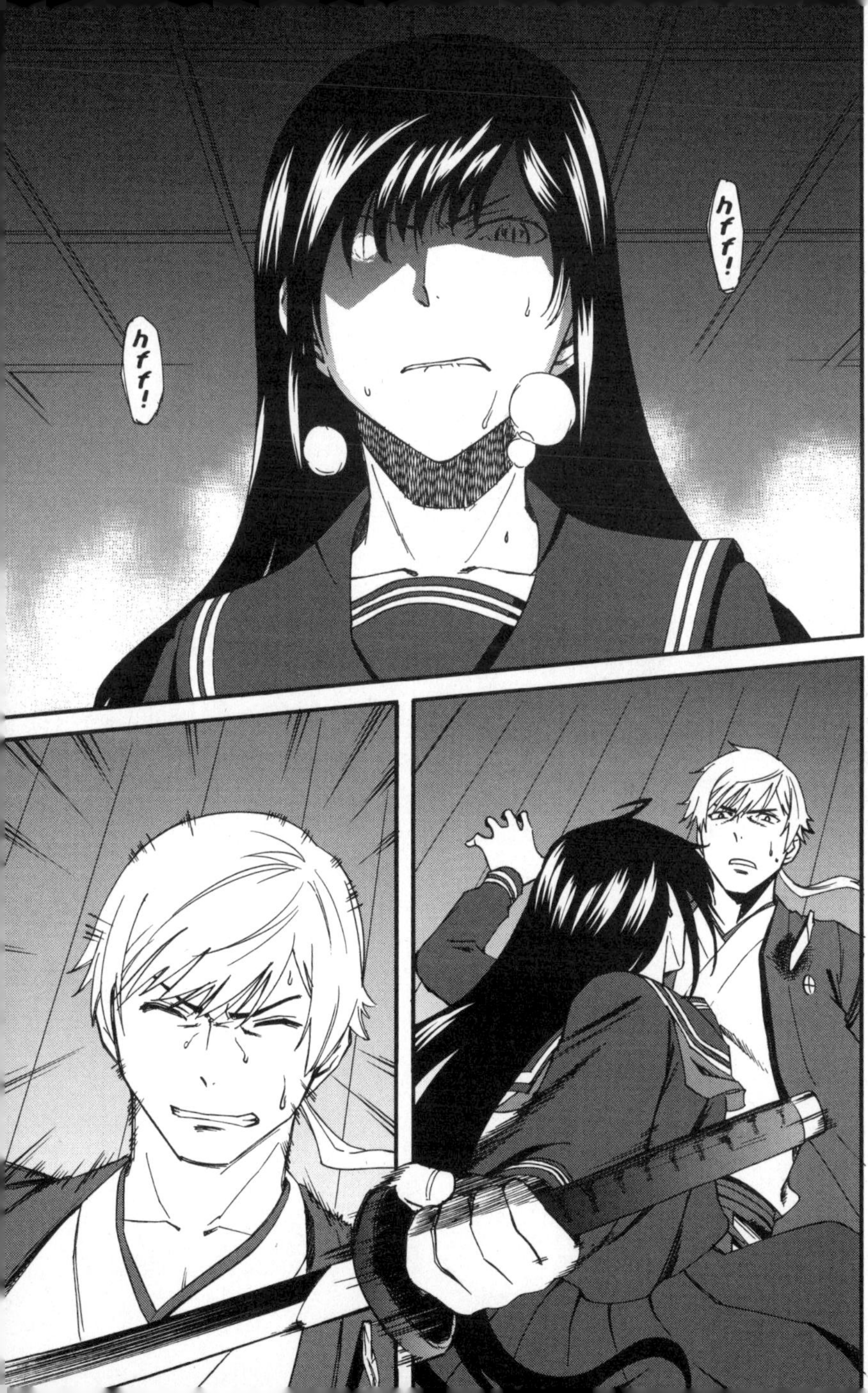
hff!
hff!

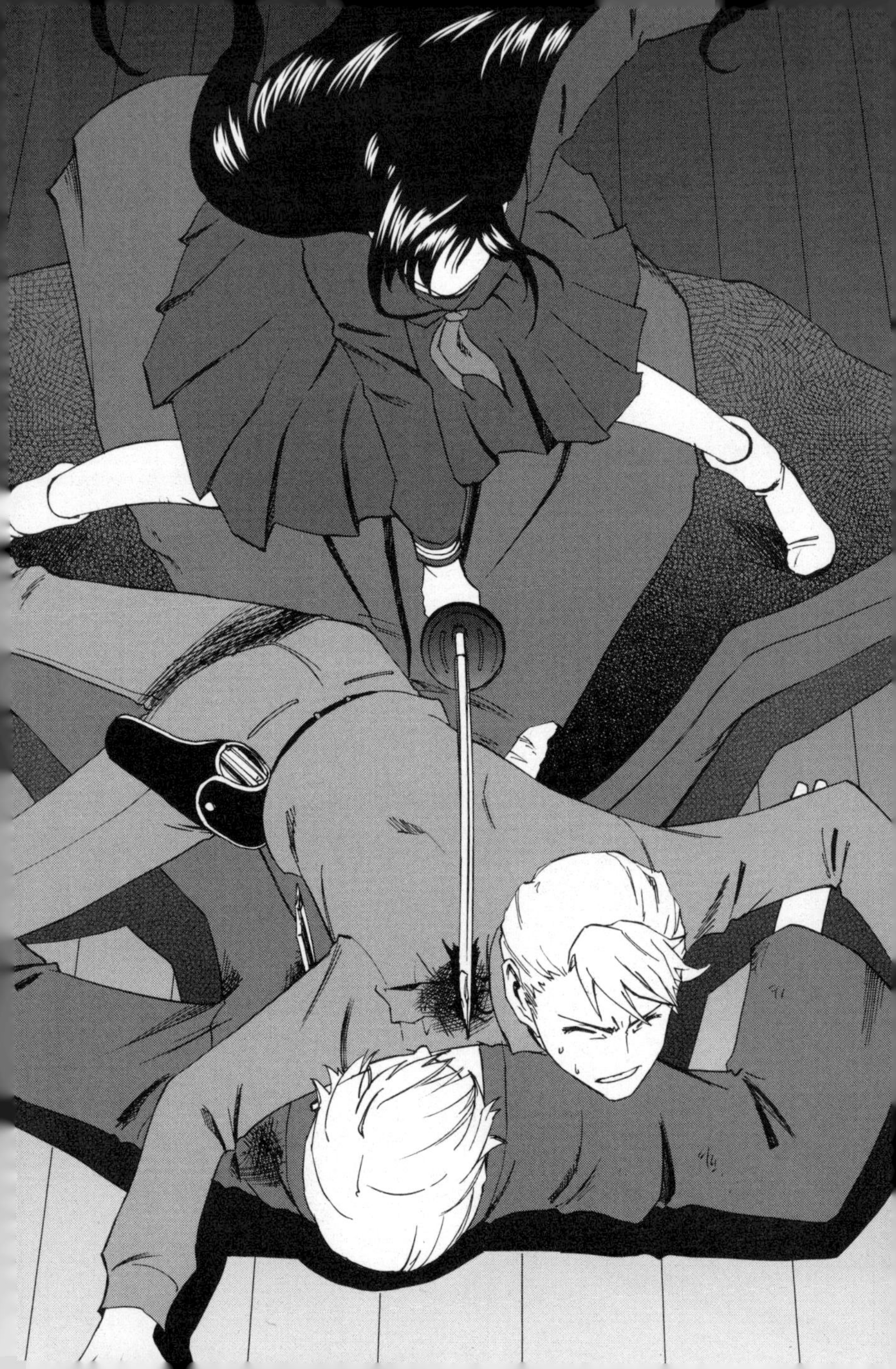

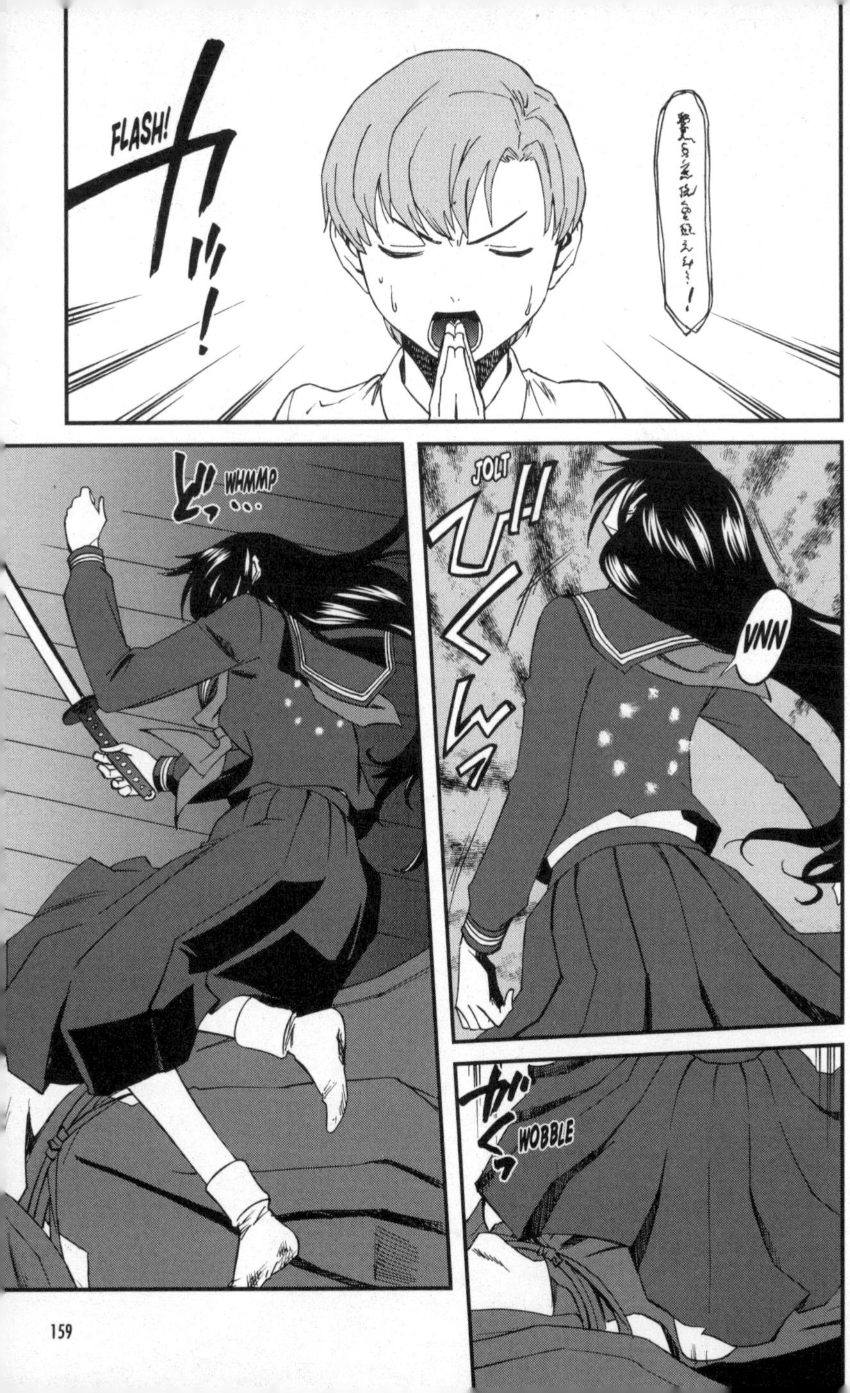
FLASH!
JOLT
VNN
WOBBLE
WHMMP...

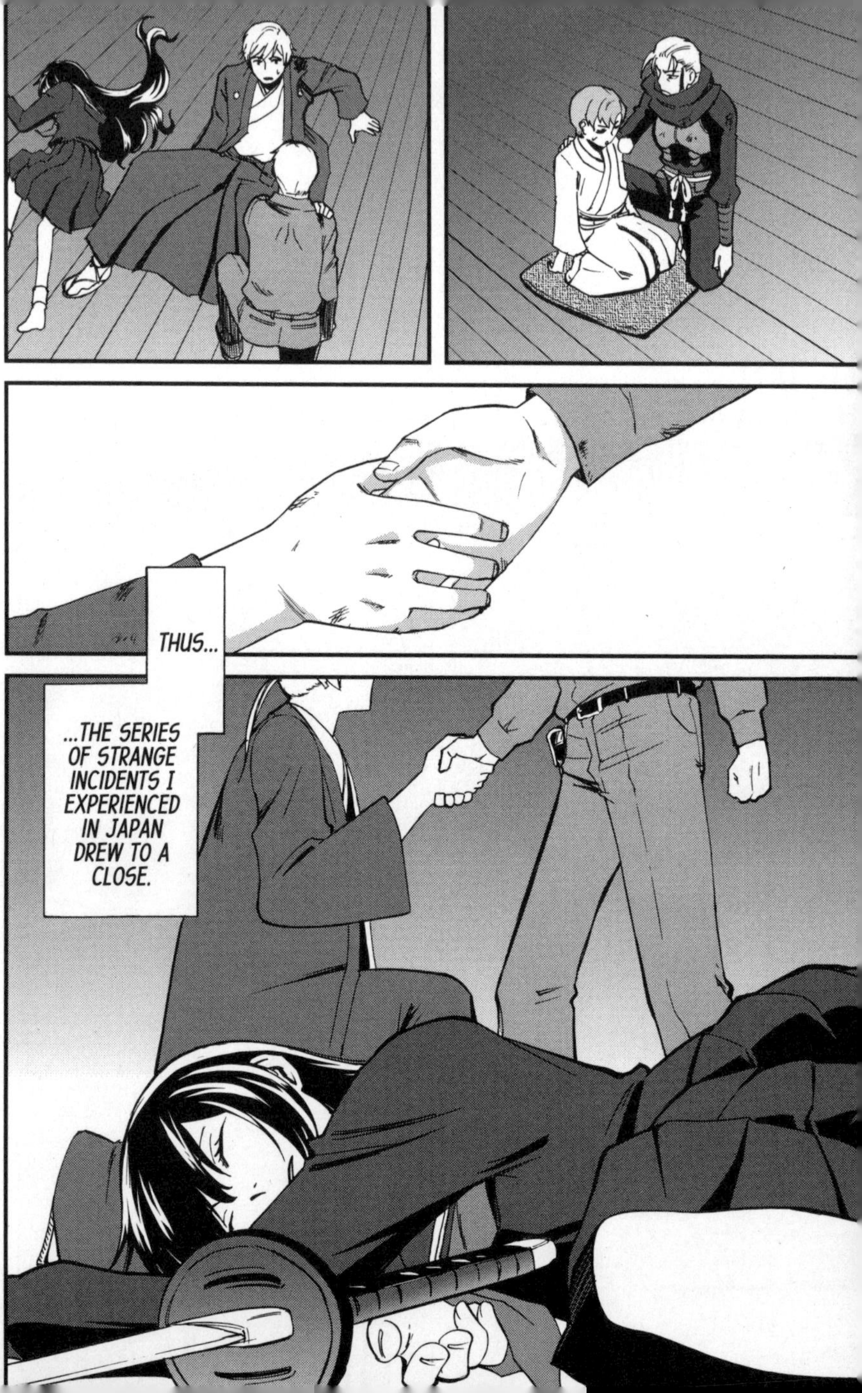
THUS...
...THE SERIES OF STRANGE INCIDENTS I EXPERIENCED IN JAPAN DREW TO A CLOSE.

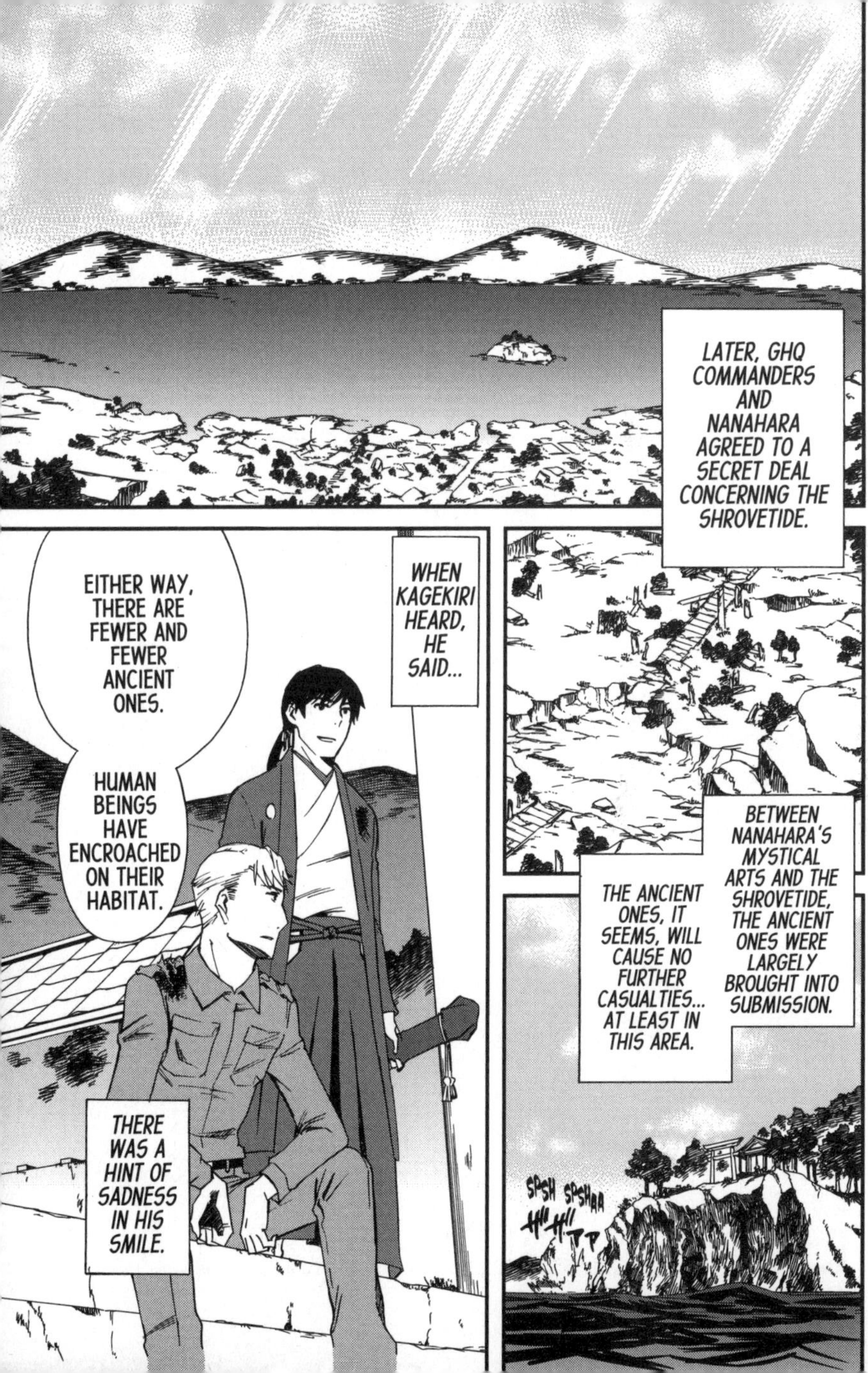
LATER, GHQ COMMANDERS AND NANAHARA AGREED TO A SECRET DEAL CONCERNING THE SHROVETIDE.
BETWEEN NANAHARA'S MYSTICAL ARTS AND THE SHROVETIDE, THE ANCIENT ONES WERE LARGELY BROUGHT INTO SUBMISSION.
THE ANCIENT ONES, IT SEEMS, WILL CAUSE NO FURTHER CASUALTIES... AT LEAST IN THIS AREA.
SPSH SPSHAA
WHEN KAGEKIRI HEARD, HE SAID...
EITHER WAY, THERE ARE FEWER AND FEWER ANCIENT ONES.
HUMAN BEINGS HAVE ENCROACHED ON THEIR HABITAT.
THERE WAS A HINT OF SADNESS IN HIS SMILE.

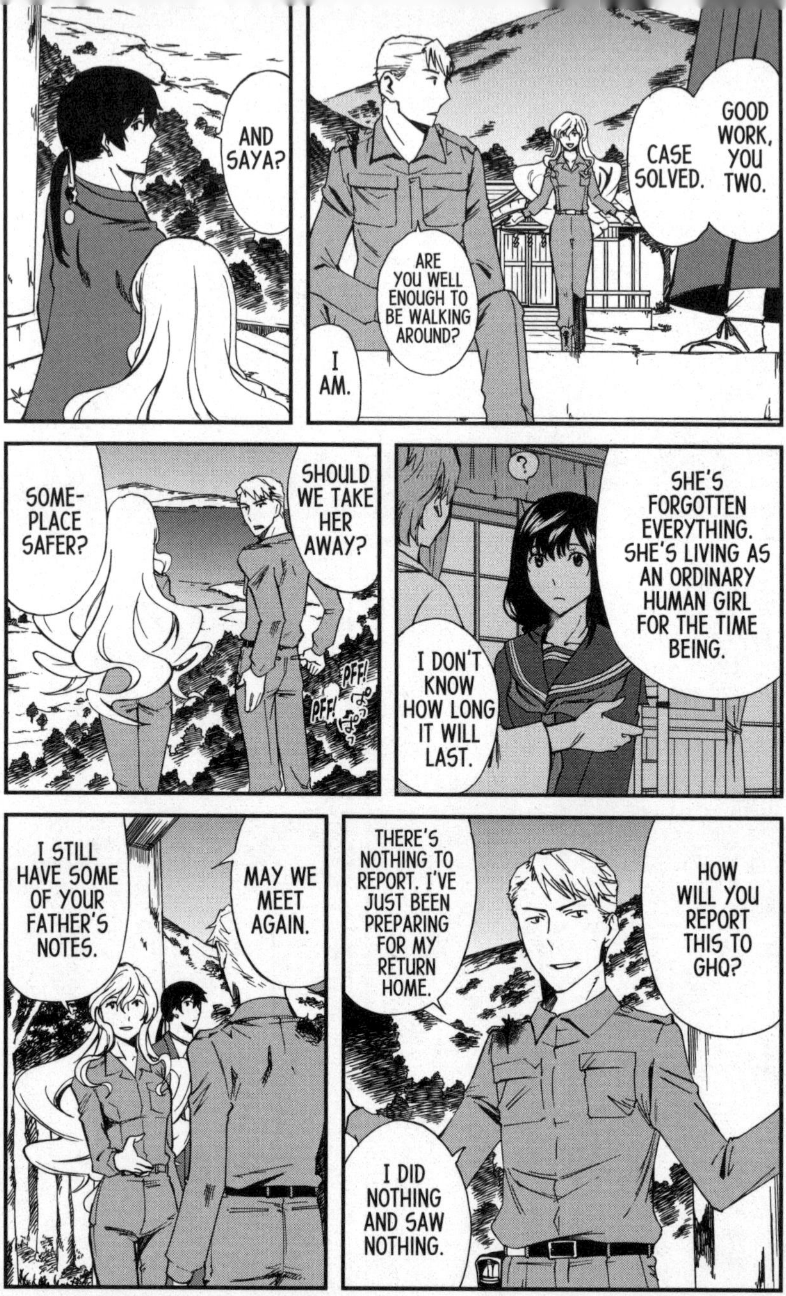
GOOD WORK, YOU TWO.
CASE SOLVED.
ARE YOU WELL ENOUGH TO BE WALKING AROUND?
I AM.
AND SAYA?
?
SHE'S FORGOTTEN EVERYTHING. SHE'S LIVING AS AN ORDINARY HUMAN GIRL FOR THE TIME BEING.
I DON'T KNOW HOW LONG IT WILL LAST.
SHOULD WE TAKE HER AWAY?
SOME-PLACE SAFER?
PFF!
PFF!
HOW WILL YOU REPORT THIS TO GHQ?
THERE'S NOTHING TO REPORT. I'VE JUST BEEN PREPARING FOR MY RETURN HOME.
I DID NOTHING AND SAW NOTHING.
MAY WE MEET AGAIN.
I STILL HAVE SOME OF YOUR FATHER'S NOTES.

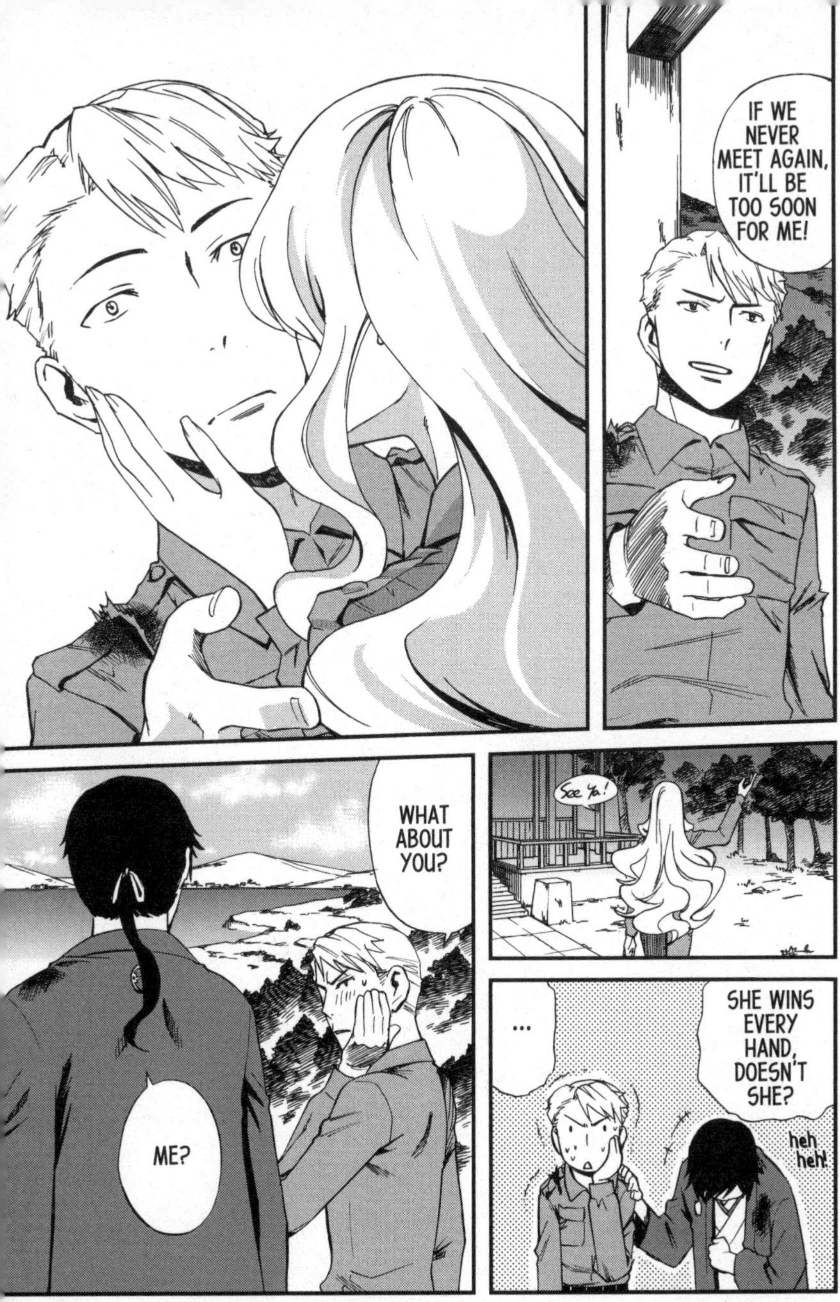
IF WE NEVER MEET AGAIN, IT'LL BE TOO SOON FOR ME!
See ya!
SHE WINS EVERY HAND, DOESN'T SHE?
...
heh heh!
WHAT ABOUT YOU?
ME?

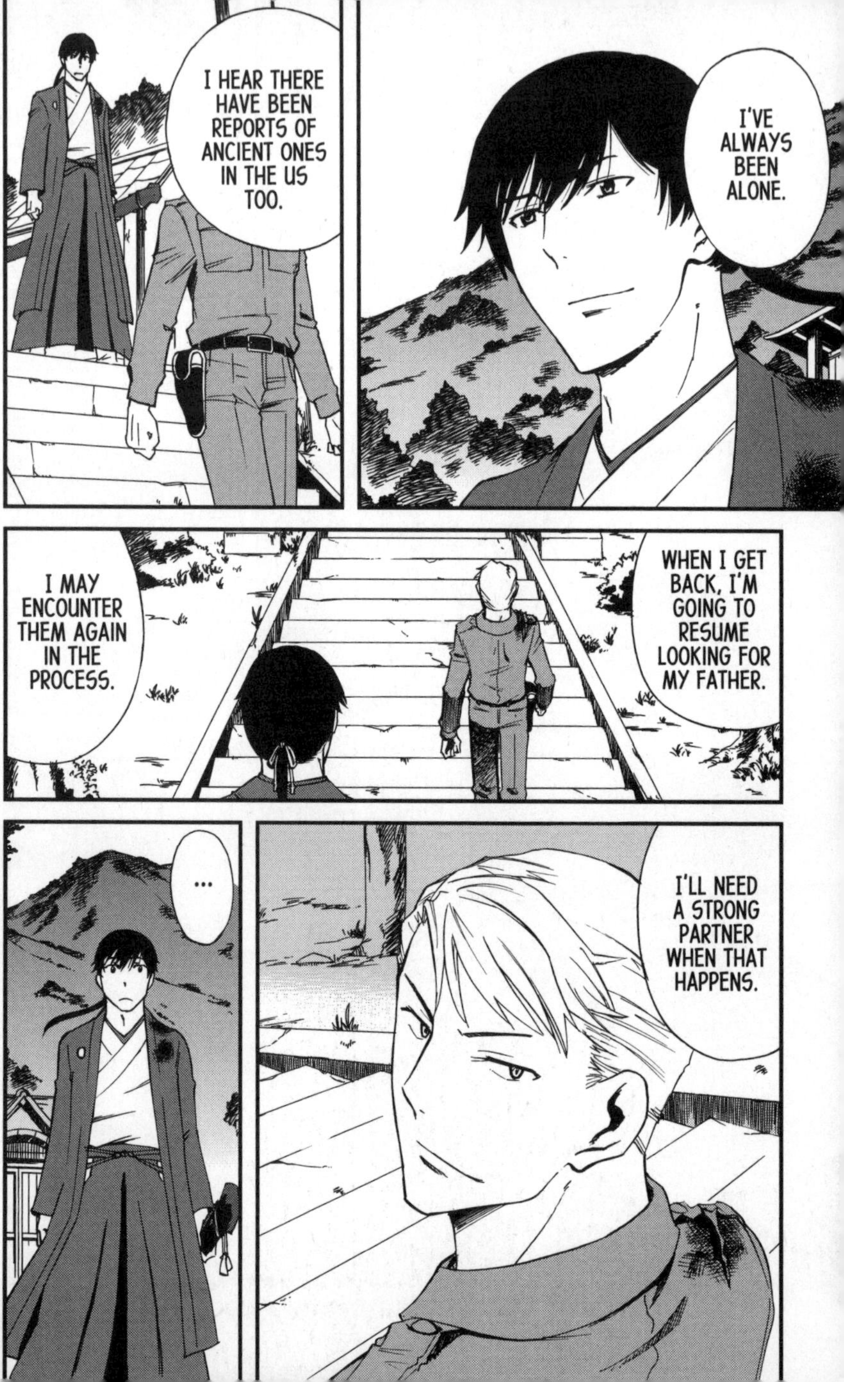
I'VE ALWAYS BEEN ALONE.
I HEAR THERE HAVE BEEN REPORTS OF ANCIENT ONES IN THE US TOO.
WHEN I GET BACK, I'M GOING TO RESUME LOOKING FOR MY FATHER.
I MAY ENCOUNTER THEM AGAIN IN THE PROCESS.
I'LL NEED A STRONG PARTNER WHEN THAT HAPPENS.
...

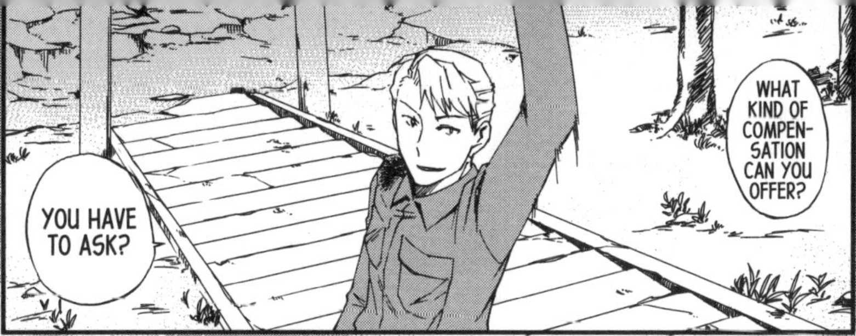
WHAT KIND OF COMPEN-SATION CAN YOU OFFER?
YOU HAVE TO ASK?

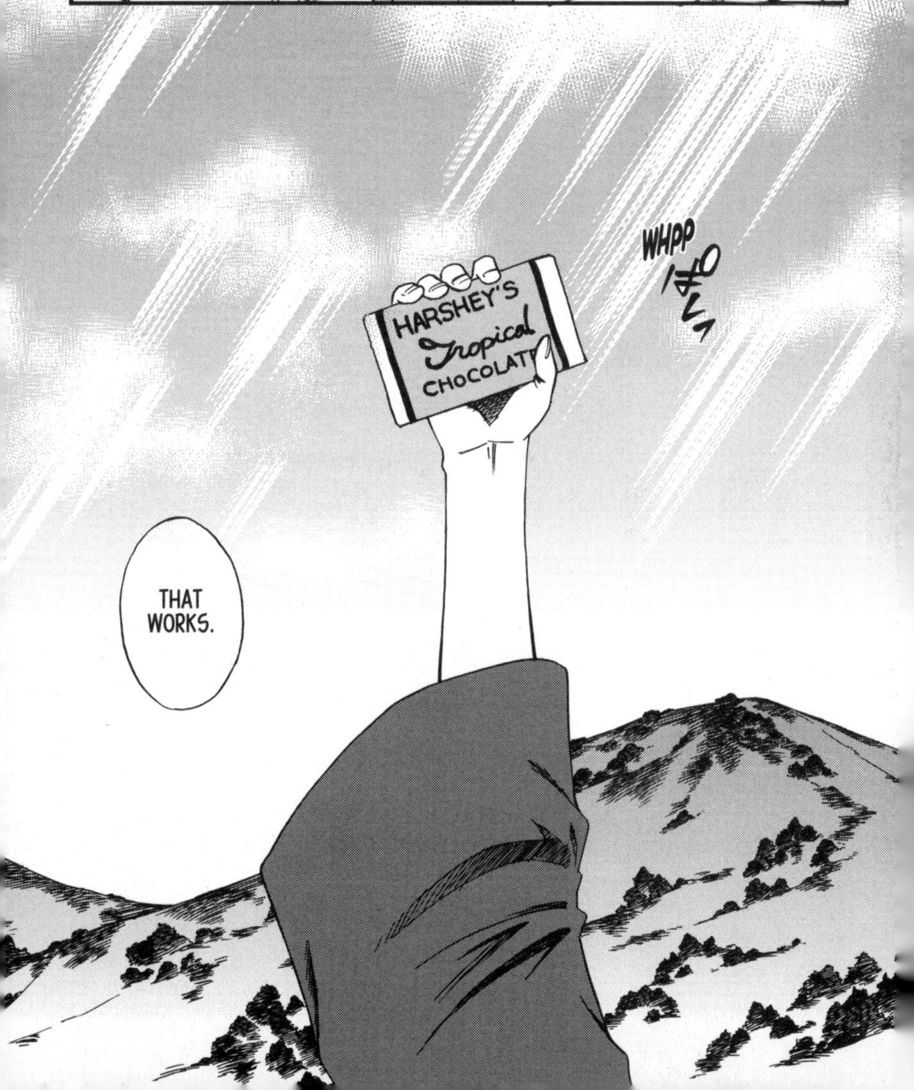
WHPP
HARSHEY'S Tropical CHOCOLAT
THAT WORKS.

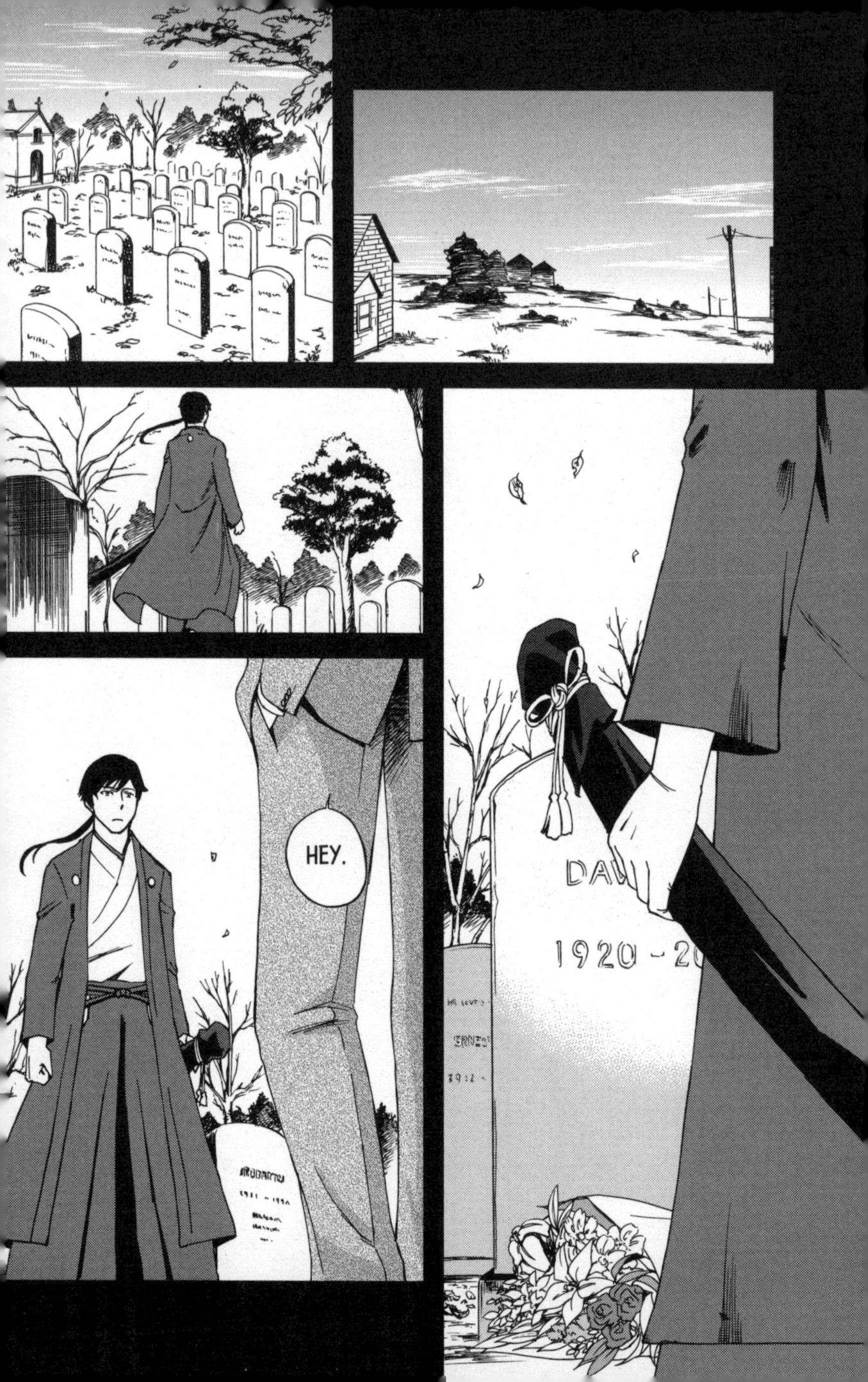
DAV
1920 - 20
HEY.

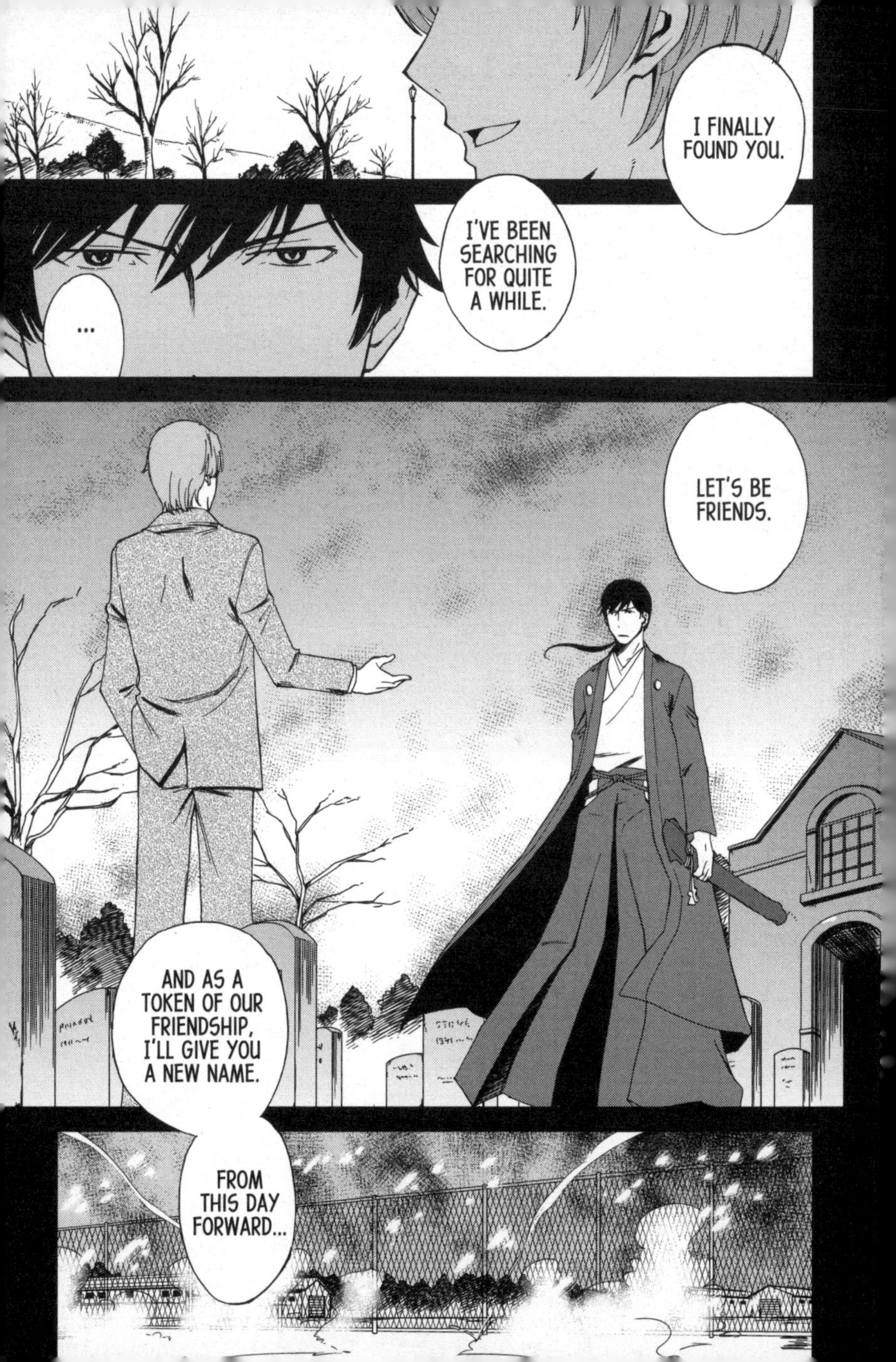
I FINALLY FOUND YOU.
I'VE BEEN SEARCHING FOR QUITE A WHILE.
...
LET'S BE FRIENDS.
AND AS A TOKEN OF OUR FRIENDSHIP, I'LL GIVE YOU A NEW NAME.
FROM THIS DAY FORWARD...

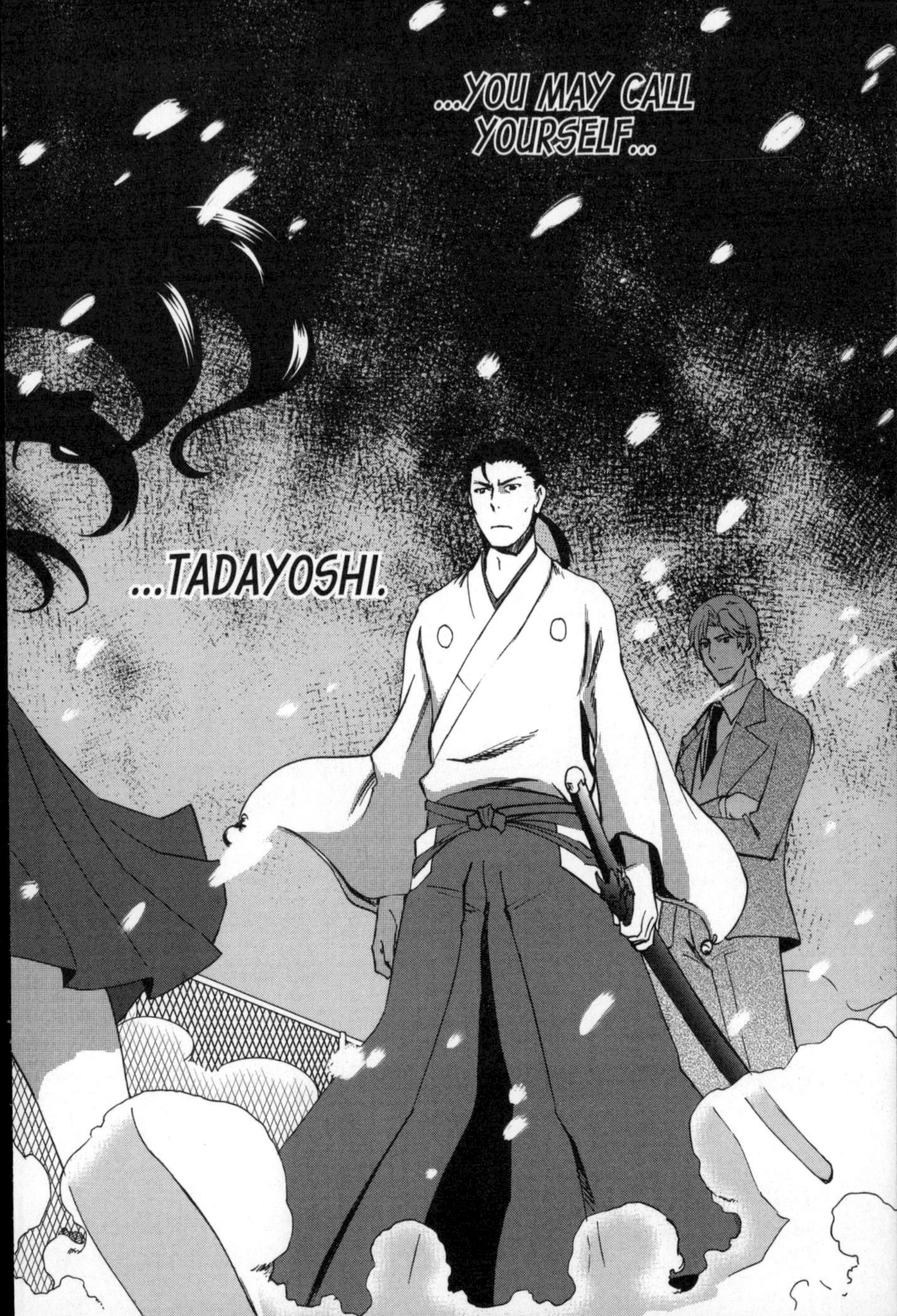
...YOU MAY CALL YOURSELF...
...TADAYOSHI.

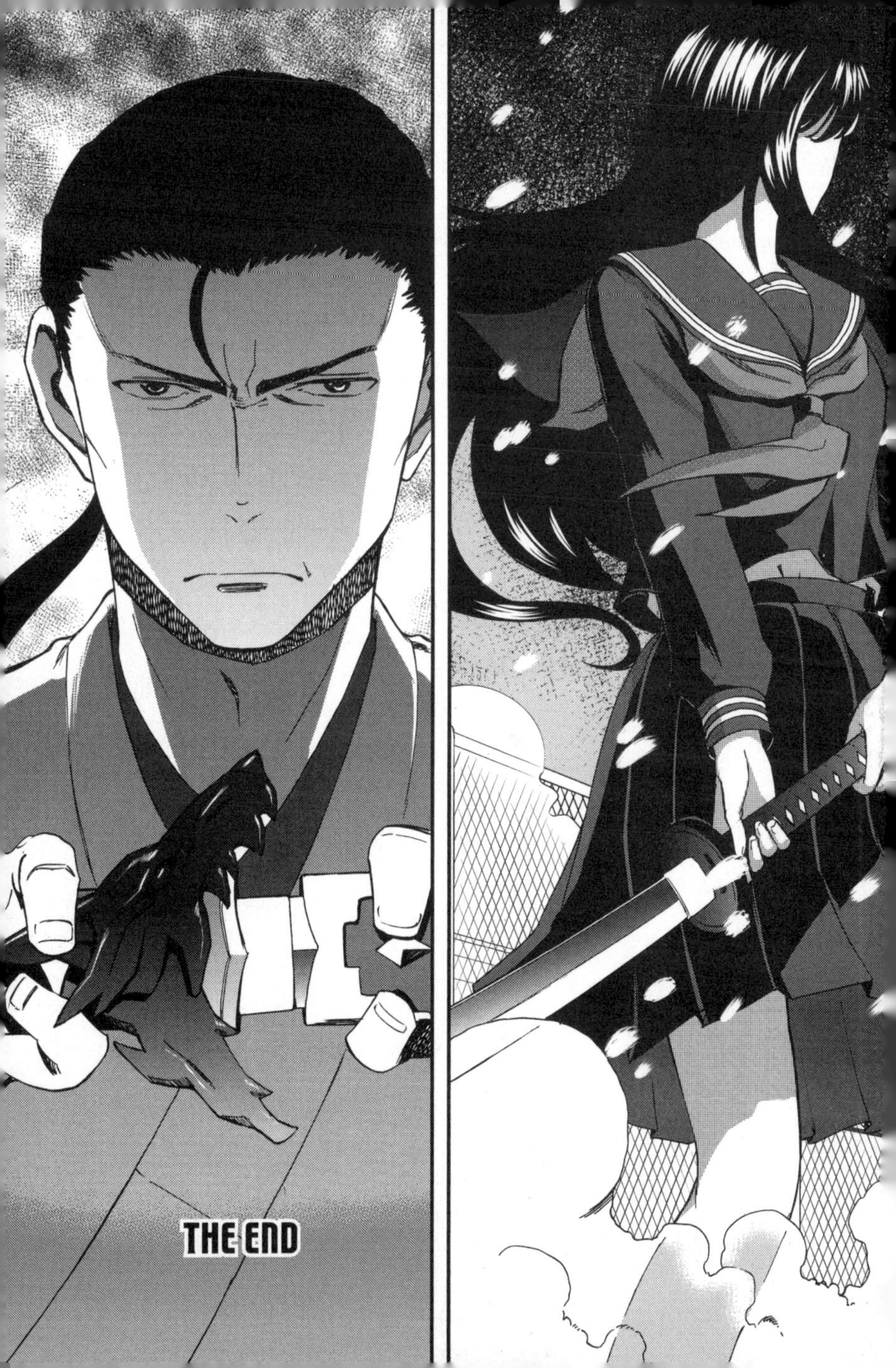
THE END

Hello, readers! This is Ryo Haduki.

Thank you for reading the final volume of *Demonic Moonlight*! David and Kagekiri's battles in Japan are now over, but they'll probably continue to have adventures together elsewhere.

Perhaps a story line about Mickey Cohen–style Prohibition-era gangsters, with the Ancient Ones causing seemingly unsolvable mysteries . . . ?

My mind is filled with fantasies I hope will come true. I feel like a fan myself!

Anyway . . . Thank you, everyone, for reading this!

—Ryo Haduki, 2012

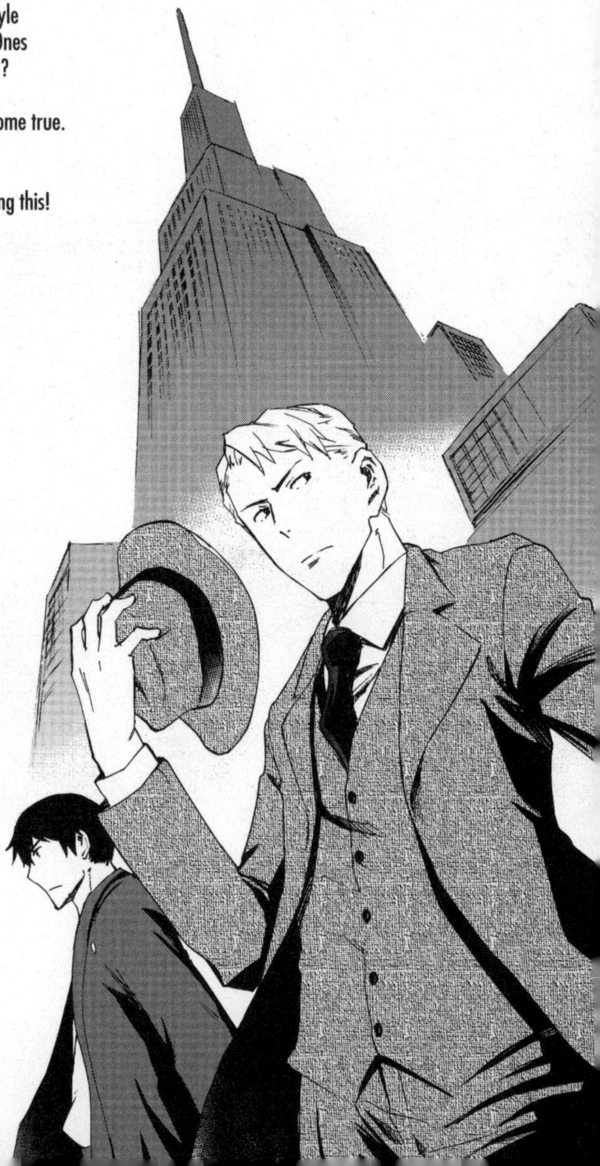

Special thanks for their hard work . . .

Original concept:
Production I.G / CLAMP

Story consultant: Junichi Fujisaki

Assistants: kgr, Puiko, Yami

written by RYO IKEHATA | illustrations by CHIZU HASHII

BLOOD+

Suffering from extreme amnesia, high school student Saya Otonashi can't remember anything from her life beyond the last year. Living with a foster family outside a military base in Okinawa, Japan, Saya's attempts to live a normal life are shattered when a Chiropteran, a horrific vampire-like monster, attacks her. Saved at the last minute by a mysterious man named Hagi, Saya is presented with a sword that awakens in her a warrior's skills and bloodlust, and sets her on a course that will lead her to the answers of her missing memories, and into battle against a race of creatures intent on destroying the world.

The epic adventure that began in the groundbreaking film *Blood: the Last Vampire* and continues through the TV series *Blood+* is brought to life in this all-new series of novels adapting the hit show. Saya's journey of horror, magic, romance, and mystery will stretch across time and around the globe, expanding on the television series with new characters, new adventures, and breathtaking action.

Each novel features all new exclusive illustrations by animated series character designer Chizu Hashii!

VOLUME 1: FIRST KISS
ISBN 978-1-59307-898-0

VOLUME 2: CHEVALIER
ISBN 978-1-59307-931-4

VOLUME 3: BOY MEETS GIRL
ISBN 978-1-59307-932-1

VOLUME 4: NANKURUNAISA
ISBN 978-1-59307-933-8

$8.99 EACH

DARK HORSE BOOKS

BLOOD+ Volumes 1, 2, 3, and 4 © Ryo Ikehata 2009 ©2005 Production I.G • Aniplex • MBS • HAKUHODO. First published in Japan in 2006 by KADOKAWA SHOTEN Publishing Co., Ltd., Tokyo. English translation rights arranged with KADOKAWA SHOTEN Publishing Co., Ltd., Tokyo, through TOHAN CORPORATION, Tokyo. Dark Horse Books® and the Dark Horse logo are registered trademarks of Dark Horse Comics, Inc. (BL 7064)

ASUKA KATSURA

BLOOD+

A companion series to the popular *Blood+* anime hit, Asuka Katsura's official, five-volume manga adaptation delivers moments of jarring violence and nonstop action in a tale that spans several centuries. Kumiko Suekane's two-volume *Blood+ Adagio* manga series explores Saya's struggles at the eve of the Russian Revolution, and Hirotaka Kisaragi's *Blood+ Kowloon Nights* one-shot finds Hagi on a solo adventure in modern-day Hong Kong! These eight manga volumes overflow with mystery, bloodletting, Chiropterans, unique heroes, and tenacious villains! Look for *Blood* and *Blood+* novels—also released by Dark Horse!

MANGA VOLUME 1
ISBN 978-1-59307-880-5
$10.99

MANGA VOLUME 2
ISBN 978-1-59307-935-2
$10.99

MANGA VOLUME 3
ISBN 978-1-59307-936-9
$10.99

MANGA VOLUME 4
ISBN 978-1-59582-194-2
$10.99

MANGA VOLUME 5
ISBN 978-1-59582-241-3
$10.99

BLOOD+ ADAGIO
VOLUME ONE
ISBN 978-1-59582-276-5
$10.99
VOLUME TWO
ISBN 978-1-59582-277-2
$10.99

BLOOD+
KOWLOON NIGHTS
ISBN 978-1-59582-444-8
$9.99

AVAILABLE AT YOUR LOCAL COMICS SHOP OR BOOKSTORE
To find a comics shop in your area, call 1.888.266.4226. For more information or to order direct: •On the web: darkhorse.com •E-mail: mailorder@darkhorse.com •Phone: 1.800.862.0052 Mon.–Fri. 9 AM to 5 PM Pacific Time.

BLOOD+ © Asuka KATSURA © 2005, 2008. BLOOD+ ADAGIO © Kumiko SUEKANE 2006. BLOOD+ KOWLOON NIGHTS © Hirotaka KISARAGI 2006. Production I.G • Aniplex • MBS • HAKUHODO First published in Japan in 2005 by KADOKAWA SHOTEN PUBLISHING Co., Ltd., Tokyo. English Translation rights arranged with KADOKAWA SHOTEN PUBLISHING Co., Ltd., Tokyo through TOHAN CORPORATION, Tokyo. (BL7062)

darkhorse.com

Hiroaki Samura's Eisner Award–winning manga epic

BLADE OF THE IMMORTAL

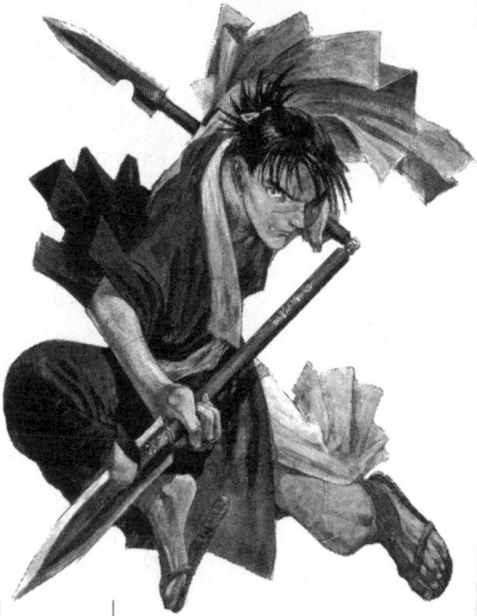

Volume 1: Blood of a Thousand
ISBN 978-1-56971-239-9
$14.99

Volume 2: Cry of the Worm
ISBN 978-1-56971-300-6
$14.99

Volume 3: Dreamsong
ISBN 978-1-56971-357-0
$14.99

Volume 4: On Silent Wings
ISBN 978-1-56971-412-6
$14.99

Volume 5: On Silent Wings II
ISBN 978-1-56971-444-7
$14.99

Volume 6: Dark Shadows
ISBN 978-1-56971-469-0
$14.99

Volume 7: Heart of Darkness
ISBN 978-1-56971-531-4
$16.99

Volume 8: The Gathering
ISBN 978-1-56971-546-8
$15.99

Volume 9: The Gathering II
ISBN 978-1-56971-560-4
$15.99

Volume 10: Secrets
ISBN 978-1-56971-746-2
$16.99

Volume 11: Beasts
ISBN 978-1-56971-741-7
$14.99

Volume 12: Autumn Frost
ISBN 978-1-56971-991-6
$16.99

Volume 13: Mirror of the Soul
ISBN 978-1-59307-218-6
$17.99

Volume 14: Last Blood
ISBN 978-1-59307-321-3
$17.99

Volume 15: Trickster
ISBN 978-1-59307-468-5
$16.99

Volume 16: Shortcut
ISBN 978-1-59307-723-5
$16.99

Volume 17: On the Perfection of Anatomy
ISBN 978-1-59307-782-2
$16.99

Volume 18: The Sparrow Net
ISBN 978-1-59307-871-3
$19.99

Volume 19: Badger Hole
ISBN 978-1-59307-969-7
$17.99

Volume 20: Demon Lair
ISBN 978-1-59582-199-7
$19.99

Volume 21: Demon Lair II
ISBN 978-1-59582-323-6
$19.99

Volume 22: Footsteps
ISBN 978-1-59582-443-1
$19.99

Volume 23: Scarlet Swords
ISBN 978-1-59582-671-8
$19.99

Volume 24: Massacre
ISBN 978-1-59582-751-7
$19.99

Volume 25: Snowfall at Dawn
ISBN 978-1-59582-883-5
$19.99

Volume 26: Blizzard
ISBN 978-1-61655-098-1
$19.99

Volume 27: Mist on the Spider's Web
ISBN 978-1-61655-215-2
$19.99

Volume 28: Raining Chaos
ISBN 978-1-61655-321-0
$19.99

Also by Hiroaki Samura:

Hiroaki Samura's Emerald and Other Stories
ISBN 978-1-61655-065-3
$12.99

Ohikkoshi
ISBN 978-1-59307-622-1
$12.99

The Art of Blade of the Immortal
ISBN 978-1-59582-512-4
$29.99

AVAILABLE AT YOUR LOCAL COMICS SHOP OR BOOKSTORE • To find a comics shop in your area, call 1-888-266-4226
For more information or to order direct visit DarkHorse.com or call 1-800-862-0052 Mon.–Fri. 9 AM to 5 PM Pacific Time.
*Prices and availability subject to change without notice

DARK HORSE MANGA
DarkHorse.com

NEON GENESIS EVANGELION

Dark Horse Manga is proud to present new original series based on the wildly popular *Neon Genesis Evangelion* manga and anime! Continuing the rich story lines and complex characters, these new visions of *Neon Genesis Evangelion* provide extra dimensions for understanding one of the greatest series ever made!

NEON GENESIS EVANGELION Campus Apocalypse

STORY AND ART BY MINGMING

VOLUME 1
ISBN 978-1-59582-530-8 | $10.99

VOLUME 2
ISBN 978-1-59582-661-9 | $10.99

VOLUME 3
ISBN 978-1-59582-680-0 | $10.99

VOLUME 4
ISBN 978-1-59582-689-3 | $10.99

NEON GENESIS EVANGELION COMIC TRIBUTE

STORY AND ART BY VARIOUS CREATORS

ISBN 978-1-61655-114-8 | $10.99

NEON GENESIS EVANGELION The Shinji Ikari Detective Diary

STORY AND ART BY TAKUMI YOSHIMURA

VOLUME 1
ISBN 978-1-61655-225-1 | $9.99

VOLUME 2
ISBN 978-1-61655-418-7 | $9.99

TONY TAKEZAKI'S NEON GENESIS EVANGELION

STORY AND ART BY TONY TAKEZAKI

ISBN 978-1-61655-736-2 | $12.99

NEON GENESIS EVANGELION THE SHINJI IKARI RAISING PROJECT

STORY AND ART BY OSAMU TAKAHASHI

VOLUME 1
ISBN 978-1-59582-321-2 | $9.99

VOLUME 2
ISBN 978-1-59582-377-9 | $9.99

VOLUME 3
ISBN 978-1-59582-447-9 | $9.99

VOLUME 4
ISBN 978-1-59582-454-7 | $9.99

VOLUME 5
ISBN 978-1-59582-520-9 | $9.99

VOLUME 6
ISBN 978-1-59582-580-3 | $9.99

VOLUME 7
ISBN 978-1-59582-595-7 | $9.99

VOLUME 8
ISBN 978-1-59582-694-7 | $9.99

VOLUME 9
ISBN 978-1-59582-800-2 | $9.99

VOLUME 10
ISBN 978-1-59582-879-8 | $9.99

VOLUME 11
ISBN 978-1-59582-932-0 | $9.99

VOLUME 12
ISBN 978-1-61655-033-2 | $9.99

VOLUME 13
ISBN 978-1-61655-315-9 | $9.99

VOLUME 14
ISBN 978-1-61655-432-3 | $9.99

VOLUME 15
ISBN 978-1-61655-607-5 | $9.99

Each volume of *Neon Genesis Evangelion* features bonus color pages, your *Evangelion* fan art and letters, and special reader giveaways!

DARK HORSE MANGA
DarkHorse.com

AVAILABLE AT YOUR LOCAL COMICS SHOP OR BOOKSTORE
To find a comics shop in your area, call 1-888-266-4226 • For more information or to order direct: • On the web: darkhorse.com
E-mail: mailorder@darkhorse.com • Phone: 1-800-862-0052 Mon.–Fri. 9 AM to 5 PM Pacific Time.

PRESIDENT & PUBLISHER
MIKE RICHARDSON

EDITOR
PHILIP R. SIMON

COLLECTION DESIGNER
JACK THOMAS

DIGITAL ART TECHNICIAN
CHRIS HORN

Special thanks to
Michael Gombos, Annie Gullion, and Carl Gustav Horn

BLOOD-C: DEMONIC MOONLIGHT VOLUME 2
© Ryo HADUKI 2012
© 2011 Production I.G, CLAMP/Project BLOOD-C TV/MBS
First published in Japan in 2012 by KADOKAWA CORPORATION, Tokyo. English translation rights arranged with KADOKAWA CORPORATION, Tokyo, through TOHAN CORPORATION, Tokyo. This English-language edition © 2016 by Dark Horse Comics, Inc. Dark Horse Manga™ is a trademark of Dark Horse Comics, Inc. Dark Horse Comics® and the Dark Horse logo are trademarks of Dark Horse Comics, Inc., registered in various categories and countries. All rights reserved. No portion of this publication may be reproduced or transmitted, in any form or by any means, without the express written permission of the copyright holders. Names, characters, places, and incidents featured in this publication either are the product of the author's imagination or are used fictitiously. Any resemblance to actual persons (living or dead), events, institutions, or locales, without satiric intent, is coincidental.

Dark Horse Manga, a division of Dark Horse Comics, Inc.
10956 SE Main Street, Milwaukie, OR 97222
DarkHorse.com

To find a comics shop in your area, call the Comic Shop Locator Service toll-free at 1-888-266-4226.

First edition: August 2016
ISBN 978-1-61655-975-5

1 3 5 7 9 10 8 6 4 2

Printed in the United States of America

executive vice president **Neil Hankerson** • chief financial officer **Tom Weddle** • vice president of publishing **Randy Stradley** • vice president of book trade sales **Michael Martens** • vice president of marketing **Matt Parkinson** • vice president of product development **David Scroggy** • vice president of information technology **Dale LaFountain** • vice president of production and scheduling **Cara Niece** • vice president of media licensing **Nick McWhorter** • general counsel **Ken Lizzi** • editor in chief **Dave Marshall** • editorial director **Davey Estrada** • executive senior editor **Scott Allie** • senior books editor **Chris Warner** • director of print and development **Cary Grazzini** • art director **Lia Ribacchi** • director of digital publishing **Mark Bernardi** • director of international publishing and licensing **Michael Gombos**